Dignity for the Voiceless

DIGNITY FOR THE VOICELESS

Willem Assies's Anthropological Work in Context

Edited by

Ton Salman, Salvador Martí i Puig,
and Gemma van der Haar

berghahn
NEW YORK · OXFORD
www.berghahnbooks.com

Published in 2014 by
Berghahn Books
www.berghahnbooks.com

Library of Congress Cataloging-in-Publication Data

Assies, Willem.
    [Works. Selections]
    Dignity for the voiceless : Willem Assies' anthropological work in context /
edited by Ton Salman, Salvador Martí i Puig, and Gemma van der Haar.
    pages cm. — (CEDLA Latin America Studies ; volume 103)
    Includes bibliographical references and index.
    ISBN 978-1-78238-292-8 (hardback : alk. paper) — ISBN 978-1-78238-
293-5 (ebook)
    1. Social movements—Latin America. 2. Social structure—Latin America. 3.
Indians of South America—Politics and government. 4. Latin America—Social
conditions—1982- 5. Latin America—Politics and government—1980- I.
Salman, Ton, editor of compilation. II. Martí i Puig, Salvador, editor of compilation. III. Haar, Gemma van der, 1968- , editor of compilation. IV. Title.
    HN110.5.A8A67 2014
    306.098—dc23
                                                                    2013041916

British Library Cataloguing in Publication Data
A catalogue record for this book is available from the British Library

Printed on acid-free paper

ISBN: 978-1-78238-292-8 hardback
ISBN: 978-1-78238-293-5 ebook

To Laura Willemijn, loved and cherished

Contents

Part III. Indigenous (Land) Rights

Part IV. Ethnicity and Citizenship

Part V. Political Developments in Bolivia

Foreword

Geert Banck

It was a fateful day in May 2010. Willem had returned home for the weekend of Pentecost from Hannover, where he was a guest researcher at the Leibniz University. At dinner he choked on a piece of meat and fell into a coma, dying days later on May 22. His family, especially his partner Gemma and their young daughter Laura, were left in despair, his many friends in shock. How was this possible? Of course, this is a normal reaction when confronted by such a swift stroke of fate, and words like *fate* and *fateful* could be just a conventional way of expressing in words what was felt by family, friends, and colleagues about this brutally sudden, unacceptable death at the age of 55.

But with Willem Assies these words also express something quintessential, I think, about his personality, the person he was. Let me explain what I mean. In 1987 I met Willem for the first time at Cedla. The occasion was an interview for a PhD research job on urban social movements in Brazil. He had good qualifications, a cum laude MA in anthropology and an article in the prestigious *Journal of Peasant Studies*. Of course, such a job interview is not comfortable for most applicants, but Willem was exceptionally tense, and he stubbornly went through the ritual, mumbling vaguely. For some people it might have been just that, a vague, though theoretically informed, mumbling of phrases. Yet I had the strong feeling that before me was someone with a fascinating intelligence who, nevertheless, was inclined to choose a form of understating his own case. He got the job anyway, which, after going to the Andean highlands, eventually brought him into the coastal lowlands of the "amphibious" city of Recife.[1]

At Cedla he proved to be an outstanding researcher and writer, yet this manner of oral expression remained haphazard and unpredictable during his whole career. This contradiction was always evident, and almost from that first interview in 1987, I compared him with the *poètes maudits*. Those poets were in some way or another defying fate, or struggling with it, often almost inevitably stumbling into fateful situations in the dark corners of daily life. Their tenseness and ineptitude in living their day-to-day lives were closely linked with their creativity in writing. Of course, I am not suggesting that Willem was a "poet damned," but comparable to them he had a problem in daily life with communication, and he also had the knack of getting himself into awkward, if not outright dangerous, situations. I think anyone who knew him well has some anecdote to tell. I remember one about a visit to a landowner somewhere in the Brazilian Amazon region. Willem was sitting with the much older man and his young wife on the veranda drinking a beer. The woman was very proud of having a rose bush in bloom in the garden, which is no small wonder in the Amazon. It reminded her of her paternal home in southern Brazil. Willem left open what happened exactly, save that the young wife and he got on very well. The story ends with the husband taking his revolver out, pointing it at the rose bush and shooting the rose blossoms one by one. Wild West story or pure magic realism, it is a situation that only Willem could have stumbled into.

How are we to understand Willem's creativity as a committed researcher and prolific writer? It goes without saying that he was highly intelligent, but he was also an astute researcher. He had a keen eye for the many contradictions he observed during his fieldwork. He was very good at compiling and dissecting a theoretical debate, always on guard as to the role of the intellectuals in these debates. In the theoretical chapter on social movements, reproduced in this volume, he warns that intellectuals "can never pledge innocence" (original, p. 72); and I think that in this essay he took some satisfaction in concluding that "an authoritarian obsession with the "moment of taking power" had faded" (original, p. 90). He was very distrustful of all forms of power, and this brings me to what I consider the driving force behind all of his research, from Brazilian urban social movements, via Brazil nut exploitation in the Amazon, to indigenous movements in Mexico, and especially toward Bolivia: a deeply felt, intellectually consistent commitment with what Fanon has coined "the damned of the earth," the slum dwellers, the *indígenas*, and all those others at the bottom of society. He was not romantically naive; he had a keen eye for the incongruities of daily life, prejudices and hatreds, petty jealousies, and so on. But deep down in his sometimes difficult but fascinating and deeply compassionate personality, he was consistently moved by the wish to understand the people without a voice. We usually argue that research and theoretical debate on social movements of the "underprivileged" are geared to help "give" them a voice. I think that Willem, to quote his most well-known understatement, would have preferred to say he was just doing his "little bit of fumbling," working alongside them, not over them, so that they themselves could discover and win their own voice. He would probably also admit that it would never be a *unisono* voice. This is what I consider to be Willem's legacy: no human being can live without respect and dignity in their often chaotic everyday life with all its inconsistencies, irrationalities, passions; they must have hope, a sense of beauty, solidarity and, above all, a dose of fascinating common sense.

Notes

1. *To Get Out of the Mud: Neighborhood Associativism in Recife, 1964–1988.* Amsterdam, 1992. Citation on p. 56.

Acknowledgments

The selection of Willem Assies's writings has been published before in peer-reviewed journals and books. We kindly thank all publishers, book editors, and journal editorial boards for their permission to republish. We also thank the many colleagues and friends who so willingly helped us find data, sort out matters, aid in obtaining republication permissions, write introductions, and stimulate us to finish this project. It has been of inestimable value!

Introduction

Gemma van der Haar, Salvador Martí i Puig,
and Ton Salman

Soon after Willem Assies's untimely death it became clear how intensively Assies had been involved in a broad range of lively correspondence with colleagues and students about his work, his ideas, his analyses, and his many publications. From one day to the next, all this came to a halt, leaving his many contacts not only in mourning but also bereft of cherished communications on all the themes Assies had worked and published about. Among these thematic fields—all focused on Latin America—were social movements, agrarian issues, indigenous (land) rights, ethnicity and citizenship, and political developments in Bolivia. To be sure, Assies also published on other fields: on sustainable rainforest extraction, urban grassroots organizations, the theoretical dimensions of land legalization, reforms of constitutions, migration, multiculturalism, decentralization and other state reforms, ethno-politics, democratization, and many other subjects. Reviewing his immense production, however, we believe that social movements, agrarian issues, indigenous (land) rights, ethnicity and citizenship, and political developments in Bolivia are the five thematic fields he dedicated most of his work to.

Another realization was that Assies, as a broadly oriented and prolific researcher and writer, never had the opportunity to bring his work together, or at least compile a selection of his work, to present an overview of his scholarship. His work is widely dispersed over a broad range of books and journals from different publishers, in several languages, concerning various countries in Latin America. Plausibly, many readers of a specific article or thematic compilation might not know about all his *other* work. It made us decide that—not only as a tribute to a cherished husband and an inspiring and loyal friend and colleague, but also as a service to those who have enjoyed and admired some of his work, not realizing the scope, productivity, and astonishingly broad scale—it might be a good idea to assemble at least *part* of his work, on five central thematic fields, in a single publication. It would acquaint readers with the extensive range of his scholarship.

There were certainly many ways this book could have been organized: in chronological order, or according to theoretical approaches, or simply with thematic fields other than the five that were eventually chosen, given that Assies worked on a wide range of issues. In the end, we opted for the following: we chose the five thematic fields mentioned above, and picked—with great difficulty—two publications in each of those fields as a sample of Assies's work. We asked the friends and colleagues who he had worked most closely with him on these fields to help us make a selection and to write a short introduction to situate and contextualize them. Assies's PhD supervisor, Geert Banck, wrote the foreword, and as "editorial compilers," we wrote this introduction.

Obviously, a completely different selection representing Assies's body of work could also have been possible. General and transversal themes like "defending the land," "the struggle for dignity," or "the right to be different" could also have been core themes of this volume, as they are invariably present in his texts, even if the approaches differ according to the community, the country and his theoretical ambition. In the final selection, the five thematic fields of social movements, agrarian issues, indigenous (land) rights, ethnicity and citizenship, and political developments in Bolivia were chosen to acquaint not only the many scholars familiar with only one or two of these thematic fields with the range and diversity of his work, but to inspire a new readership as well.

Assies's contributions were important and timely in the five fields we have selected, and most notably have maintained their relevance to this day. His analyses seriously engaged with the different versions and approaches of an issue or controversy and carefully addressed the arguments brought forward by the opposing parties. He eventually unequivocally took a stand, but phrased it in a cautious, evenhanded manner, and, more importantly, he took the livelihoods, anxieties and dangers of the people actually living or suffering from an experience as his point of departure without, to reiterate, pretending to speak on their behalf or unconditionally taking their side. This resulted in accounts that tried to avoid simple, dichotomous portrayals and instead attempted to do justice to the differences and frictions within the different population sectors and factions. Romanticizing an issue is not characteristic of Assies. He was an iconoclast and this quality—so scarce even in the world of critical thought—often resulted in finding new, complex realities that went beyond well-trodden approaches.

From yet a different angle, it is important to state that even though his articles and writings had a solid anchoring, Assies never seemed to be concerned about laying out the theoretical or methodological framework at the outset. His analyses reveal an actor-oriented approach, whereby the actor is often collective and multilayered. Actors could be social movements, indigenous communities, peasants, or shanty-town dwellers. They would never be omnipotent or morally superior agents or act in an unequivocal, solely rational way. Instead, the actors (whether peasants, indigenous, *pobladores*, or revolutionaries) would be presented as immersed in a multifaceted context and dealing with the constraints that the social environment had imposed upon them.

To recapitulate, Assies gave central stage to the collective and multilayered actor, but always within their context of restrictions, pressures, conditioning factors, and contradictions; consequently, the actor was not polarized as "good or bad." His analyses were never trapped in the school of thought or logic that was prevalent in academic circles at the time. This is why his writings brought new elements to debates that had stagnated or were caught up in stereotypical thinking. Thus, even when addressing such classic themes as dignity or identity, the question of access to land and housing, or scrimmages over the exploitation of resources, Assies's work was innovative and alternative to enduring debates. Even today this quality of freshness gives originality to all the thematic fields addressed in this collection.

In the first thematic field of (urban) social movements under consideration, his work testifies to the process of maturation and moderation that characterized the development of this area of scholarship in the 1980s and 1990s. Research on such social movements that had initially been inspired by neo-Marxist thinking and other, more improbable ideas about creating pacifist, emancipating, and democratizing politico-cultural revolutions had to come to terms with more prosaic realities. For example, it became apparent that changes were slow; new, bottom-up cultures of local autonomies and participative democracy were sometimes tainted by corruption and microdespotism; dependency on the state and party politics also persisted. Assies was one of the first to study and write about these sobering discoveries, as both contributions in this book illustrate. The argument he developed is that better and more sophisticated theories are needed to explain the many "mediations" between concrete conditions and the emergence—or not—of specific types of movements. Among them Assies suggested the notion of political opportunity structure that had traditionally been discarded in the new social movement theory. Assies demonstrated how it could help to reconstruct the complex and multilayered genesis of urban movements, nearly always relating it to specific ways in which political openings were occurring in Brazil. He also pointed to the close links such movements and organizations (in spite of their declarations of autonomy) had with institutions, and he emphasized the importance of finding ways to get their demands translated into institutionalized areas such as municipal edifices and laws and regulations. In this manner, Assies contributed substantially to the "coming of age" of (urban) social movement theorizing. He took a bottom-up approach instead of propagating a grand and pedantic vision foretelling a future of emancipation. Assies had an excellent command of social movement theorizing; his texts explicitly address the political opportunity approaches, the new social movement theories, models of collective action repertoires, and many other conceptual and theoretical traditions.

Equally important in the field of research on agrarian issues was his critical focus on models to restructure production logics and construct sustainable forest extractivism, and on the complexities of emerging peasant or indigenous peasant movements. Any analysis that would isolate one specific element, for example, the quest for sustainability or the emergence of social movements, would not be able to understand or embrace the nature, prospects, and limitations of such initiatives to improve rural life. Assies stressed how different features would be interconnected. As Cristóbal Kay underlines in his short introduction to Part II, Assies's keen eye for the links among economic models, property relations, transnational pressures, and ethnicity turned him at times into a prescient student of agrarian issues.

It is important to emphasize Assies's persistent focus on agrarian and rural issues, because agrarian issues, once considered outmoded and dated, have again become crucially important, in particular from the ecological perspective of sustainability. It is paradoxical that so many years and so many struggles had to take place before awareness about issues such as land possession, water and air quality, and modes and scales of agriculture would again be of vital significance.

Political ecology and sustainable economy have once again taken central stage, and peasants and indigenous peoples with their multiple identities and internal diversities have once again become protagonists in big global controversies. Assies seems to have foreseen this: he was aware that the key resources of the twenty-first century would not be assets such as digital communication facilities, high-tech services, or the urban comfort zone, but the natural resources such as water, minerals, natural gas, biodiversity, and fertile soil that are found in the countryside. His work bridges the emphasis on peasant studies of the 1960s and 1970s and contemporary work on ecology today.

His many publications on indigenous (land) rights are among the most quoted. His ability to combine an obvious sympathy with the struggles of ethnic minorities to have their rights respected along with a critical, conceptually sophisticated analysis of the many loopholes to "arrange" these rights definitely plays a major role here. Assies knew that collective land possession was no panacea for land reforms, and he knew that granting ethnic minorities the right to administer justice according to their own "uses and customs" was a thorny matter that triggered an enormous debate on the scope of human rights, due process, and the nature of sanctions. Perhaps more importantly, Assies realized that indigenous people's demands and contemporary practices were not "millenarian," but the outcome of intense interaction with the surrounding society. Notably, he did not see that as a problem but as the groundwork for promising ways out of the fruitless tugs of war on autonomies and "unsupervised," independent self-governance or segregation-like territorial sovereignty. The demands, he demonstrated, were often partially phrased in terms that betrayed the dialogue with and adoption of "Western" notions and (state) philosophies. Moreover, he observed that "[t]hus the recognition of indigenous jurisdiction may well imply that indigenous authorities are held increasingly accountable for their actions, both by outsiders and inside their jurisdictions" (chapter 6). Seeing such developments as boding well for future prospects on the relationship between multiple ways to administer justice characterizes Assies's imaginative and constructive theorizing.

In the fourth section on ethnicity and citizenship, Assies shows himself to be one of the pioneers in turning down the optimism that had accompanied the constitutional reforms that acknowledged the multicultural makeup of the continent's nation-states. Analyzing various cases, Assies described the serious problems in implementing the promises made in the reformed constitutions as caused by an unwillingness to put them into practice as well as having fundamental conceptual and practical obstacles. Additionally, he built on the idea of the *indio permitido* of Charles Hale, and he illustrated how the neoliberal economic reforms that had seemingly aided the cause of autonomies and cultural rights had in actual fact restricted the opportunities for a more equitable access to resources and power, making ineffective whatever promises about self-determination had been made.

For years Assies has been acknowledged as one of the key experts on ethnicity and citizenship in Bolivia. His accounts of the political turbulence that characterized the country from the 1990s were well received because they combined an in-depth knowledge of facts, figures, actors, developments, and events with imaginative theorizing. Assies's analytical skill is illustrated by his examination of the Water War in Cochabamba in 2000 and the birth of a coalition that seemed to take over the role previously assumed by peasant and workers unions as defenders of the poor, the workers, and those dependent on state public services; it became a required reference for others in their subsequent publications on the demise of Bolivia's old party and political structure.

Assies was a scholar whose contributions to various fields of study more than adequately represented the state of affairs in such debates. The question therefore emerges: what did Assies's work bring to those doing research in the social sciences? We believe three important qualities should be mentioned.

The first is a style of working that begins by deciphering the small to arrive at a more macro level, to collect and connect the elements of the bigger puzzle piece by piece. This strategy goes against what many scholars do, navigating the universe of the big processes, the big comparisons, the encompassing tendencies, often ending up generating cacophony and perpetuating echoes.

The second is a loyalty to a style in which theory is not so much exhibited or demonstrated with endless quotes, but rather emerges in a subtle way to sustain and interpret what is described and conveyed in the text. For this reason, Assies's writing is not enigmatic or compound or dependent on following the latest trends and concepts, or self-important. He avoided inventing terms or concepts that might become new clichés or empty new bottles. Assies, instead, was interdisciplinary, used solid analysis, and worked on the basis of concrete realities.

Finally, there is his sensitive, committed and unprejudiced look at complexities that originated in day-to-day life—a look that took into account humble and inarticulate people and their communities—and led him to reflect on fundamental themes of the social sciences such as freedom, justice, and dignity.

This volume is in essence a sample of his best work; it is extensive, complex, varied, and full of life. It is not schematic or constrained by any sacred theory, nor does it offer a foregone conclusion. In a way, it is more of a patchwork, a kaleidoscope, the result of passions, vital impulses, chances, and serious thought. It is a sample of his work, but in a sense it also reflects his life, full of vitality and wonder.

Introduction

Geert Banck

In the post-1968 intellectual turmoil, debates raged about which strategies were best for a plethora of emancipatory mobilizations such as the peace and liberalization movements, feminist struggles, peasant and indigenous mobilizations, and, last but not least, urban movements. These calls for action were almost wholly grounded in Marxist theoretical debates, be it often mixed with an ever shifting bricolage of Gandhian nonviolent action, Lacanian psychology, Foulcaultian philosophy, and the Beatles' song "Lucy in the Sky with Diamonds" metaphor for drugs-related inspiring insights.

In the spirit of 1968 there was not much room for Komintern orthodoxy, for Leninist central democracy in the name of the dictatorship of the proletariat, or for rather mechanical models of class struggle with the traditional labor movements.

In Western Europe especially, the latter was considered to be outdated. This time it was to be about *new* social movements. As urban squatter movements such as the famous Amsterdam *krakers* movement demonstrated, the struggle was in their specific case primarily about the use of urban space. By occupying empty buildings and houses, often destined to be torn down for speculative urban renewal projects, the squatters fought their battles, of course, against the project developers and realtors. But essentially it was an often violent battle with the *state* as the guardian of private property. The police force was considered to be its repressive apparatus, maintained to protect the capitalist legal order. Though confrontations were sometimes violent, strategies were often couched in playful terms, defying state power with irony and innocuous actions, demonstrating the possibility of a more just, more democratic, more humane use of urban space. As to the Marxist theoretical debate behind all this, the emphasis shifted not only to the role of the state and its repressive apparatus, but also to a more humane and more cultural interpretation of Marx's legacy as expressed in, for instance, the Frankfurt School and Gramsci.

In a long 1990 essay "Of Structured Moves and Moving Structures: An Overview of Theoretical Perspectives on Social Movements," Willem Assies probes this debate, asking himself at a certain moment, with his usual knack for puns, *Is there life on Marx?* His answer is a qualified yes. He then turns his attention to Latin America, which is the part of the essay presented here in the first chapter of this section.

Assies wrote the essay during his PhD research on squatter settlement movements in the Brazilian city of Recife. Of course, these squatters were completely different from the Amsterdam squatters. They were slum dwellers, extremely poor, living in unhealthy shacks on illegally occupied land that often flooded, as reflected in the title of his published thesis "To Get Out of the Mud." The Latin American situation was very different from the European one. Furthermore, in the late 1970s and 1980s, military dictatorships were disappearing, and most of the fierce guerrilla wars were being settled in one way or another. Another difference with Europe was the influence of liberation theology with its "option for the poor," and its use of Paulo Freire's pedagogy of the oppressed. This gave a special ring to the local theoretical debate. Assies presents a concise and fascinating picture of this Latin American view on new social movements, even if it was somewhat dominated by the Brazilian debate. It is one of the best overviews available of that intense theoretical debate, geared to the struggles for more democratic and just societies in Latin America. His insights continue to be relevant for today's Latin American societies.

The second chapter, originally published in 1997, is a detailed analysis of the history of urban protest in Brazil during the long period of what was called the process of redemocratization (mid-1970s to 1992). With a special focus on neighborhood associations, it demonstrates how elections, party politics, and the changing role of the Catholic Church influenced the urban social movements.

1 Of Structured Moves and Moving Structures

An Overview of Theoretical Perspectives on Social Movements

In the preceding part of the essay, not reproduced here, Willem Assies basically explored the developments in (neo)Marxist thinking on (urban) social movements and their significance for "the revolution," in class consciousness and the analysis of the development of capitalism. In the excerpt below, he turns his attention to developments in Latin America.

Latin America: Beyond Marginality and Populism?

When in the 1960s the term "marginality" was coined in Christian Democratic circles in Chile it was meant to refer to those who somehow remained "marginal" to the process of "modernization." Marginality was becoming visible in the rapid growth of shanty towns around the major cities. According to the early theory the inhabitants failed to adapt themselves to the modern way of life. Apathy, anomy, and feeble participation in social, economic, and political processes were thought to be the main characteristics of the slum dwellers. In particular, marginality to the political process was disturbing to the contemporary observers of that time. As far as participation went, they thought, the marginals could easily be manipulated and therefore they might be recruited for "totalitarian" adventures. In the Cold War context of the time "totalitarianism" was, of course, just another word for communism. The situation, according to these theorists, could be remedied in particular through education, which was regarded as the main factor in upward social mobility.

In reaction to this elitist view and in the context of the development of Marxism-inspired varieties of dependency theory, the concept of marginality received a new content. Rather than attributing it to a lack of adaptation of rural/urban migrants, the causes of the phenomena described as marginality were sought in the exclusionary character of dependent capitalism. As a result of the application of labor-saving technologies, it was argued, dependent capitalism was unable to provide sufficient employment in the productive sector. In later versions of this approach more emphasis would be given to the functionality of the marginals, or the informal sector, for capitalist accumulation. Marginality was not simply a result of exclusion, but rather of overexploitation of the labor force. The informal sector, it was argued, is functional in cheapening the reproduction of the labor force. This argument, in turn, could be linked to the theory of articulation of modes of production, resulting in studies of the subsumption of petty commodity producers to capitalist enterprises and of the links between "formal" and "informal" employment. Through these reformulations a distance was taken from the initial views on political marginality, as well as from the Marxist theory of the *lumpenproletariat*. Some even came to see the "excluded" as the revolutionary subject *par excellence*, a sort of mirror-image of the early version of the marginality approach with its fear of "totalitarianism" (cf. Roberts 1978: 136–177).

In the early 1970s the events in Chile drew the attention to the role of squatter-organizations in the political process. By that time the writings of Castells, Lojkine, and Borja started to be read providing a new theoretical framework and coining the term *urban social movements*. Analyses would now be cast in terms of urban contradictions, problems of collective consumption and reproduction of the labor force, and the relation to the state and state power. Meanwhile many of the Latin American countries had come to be ruled by a new type of military dictatorship, however, and urban protest became less visible under the repressive climate. The Peruvian military government, which attempted to co-opt the squatter population, was an exception in this respect.

The rise of the new dictatorships belied the predictions of the modernization theorists who foresaw that economic growth would provide the basis for a more democratic form of politics, the population assimilating Western values and increasingly participating in modern institutions. The Brazilian regime, installed in 1964, became the model for theories of "dependent associated development" and the role therein of the "bureaucratic authoritarian state." In the initial formulations of these theories, the rise of authoritarianism and the increasing exclusion of a major part of the population from political participation were seen as related to the exhaustion of the post-war model of import-substituting industrialization. The shift toward the production of durable consumer goods and the internationalization of the Latin American economies now required, it was argued, an "exclusionary" model after the earlier "inclusionary" model of expansion of the internal market for basic consumer goods and the related populist politics. Authoritarianism was required to break down the defense mechanisms of the population and to increase the concentration of income so as to create an internal market for the products in this phase of industrialization, low wages for the majority of the population at the same time being instrumental to the new forms of integration in the international circuits of capital.

In subsequent discussions a more differentiated view was developed. The "bureaucratic-authoritarianism" model rested on a simple stage model of oligarchic-populist-bureaucratic authoritarian rule, linked directly to export-led development, import-substituting industrialization and internationalization of capital. F. Cardoso and Faletto's earlier work on dependency, which takes into account the particular class structure of the different countries and their particular insertion into the capitalist world economy, provided the groundwork for a more differentiated approach to the relations between regime types and economic development. Instead of the somewhat functionalist understanding of the relation between "stages" of dependent development and regime types the internal class structure of the different countries would be given more weight (F. Cardoso 1973; F. Cardoso and Faletto 1976; Carnoy 1984: 172–207; Collier 1979; O'Brien and Cammack 1985; O'Donnell 1973).

In the course of the 1970s this model of development entered into crisis. If the effects of the first petroleum crisis could be attenuated by an inflow of petro-dollars at low interest rates, the second crisis and the financial policies adopted by the United States to manage its trade deficit triggered the debt crisis and the consequent adjustment-programs with their nefarious effects on the living conditions of the Latin American population. By the end of the 1970s and early 1980s the military started to retreat, unable to manage the cracks in the power blocs that had supported them initially, and the pressure of those groups that had been excluded from those power blocs and the protests of those parts of the population whose participation in whatever power bloc had been out of the question in any case.

New Movements and New Issues

It was in this context that urban movements became increasingly visible again. Simultaneously the number of urban movement studies, initially strongly influenced by the work of Castells, started to grow rapidly. In these studies the distinctive features of the movements arising in the aftermath of military rule were strongly emphasized. They were regarded as new in the sense of being independent from political intervention, be it by populist politicians, as had been the case with so many of the movements of the 1950s and 1960s, or by self-proclaimed revolutionary vanguards. The autonomy of the movements with respect to the political system was regarded as a distinctive feature, justifying their characterization as "new social movements."

Urban movements were perhaps the most prominent and most widespread, but they were not the only "new social movements" in Latin America. Mainwaring and Viola (1984; cf. Mainwaring 1987) have listed a series of movements that they regard as new in the Latin American context, being: the ecclesiastical base communities of the Catholic Church, the women's movement, ecological associations, human rights' organizations, and neighborhood associations. For this listing they take inclination toward affective concerns, expressive relations, group orientation, and horizontal organization as criteria of novelty. "Old" movements are characterized, by contrast, by an inclination toward material concerns, instrumental relations, orientation toward the state, and vertical organization. They also indicate that the base communities and the neighborhood associations are the most popular. The neighborhood associations, Mainwaring and Viola argue, mostly are furthest from the ideal type of the new social movements. Since concern with post-materialistic values and non-state orientedness are criteria for discriminating between "old" and "new" movements the neighborhood associations score low in this respect. Nevertheless, these movements can be regarded as new in that they present a challenge to the political culture of elitism, populism and corporatism. According to Mainwaring and Viola, who focus their attention on Brazil and Argentina, the values and emergence of these new movements can to some extent be explained by four conditions: the adverse political consequences of the military regimes under which they emerged, the crisis of the traditional left, the questioning of the populist style politics that preceded the military regimes, and the development of new social movements in the North, especially Europe and the United States.

Slater (1985), after reviewing various listings of Latin American "new social movements," provides a further insight in the novelty of these movements by specifying the differences and similarities between the new movements of the center and those of the periphery. Tendencies like commodification, bureaucratization, and massification have taken different forms in the peripheral capitalist countries. Fordism and Keynesianism are not particularly relevant in this context, but on the other hand the excessive centralization of decision-making power, the state's incapacity to provide adequate services and the eroding legitimacy of the state, coupled to a skepticism toward the established political parties may provide alternative factors in the explanation of the shape taken by new social movements in Latin America. The first two points make out the specificity of the Latin American movements, whereas the recourse to extra-institutional action and the concern with basis-democracy and independence from the established political parties would be the aspect that various new movements have in common.

If we look at the debate on the new urban movements in Latin America, we see that their relation to the state and the political system is a central issue indeed. In the early studies the self-proclaimed autonomy of the movements in relation to the state was often acclaimed and hardly received critical attention. The processes of "democratic transition" prompted a reconsideration of the issue, however (cf. R. Cardoso 1983). In the period leading up to the so-called transitions popular movements manifested themselves in a variety of ways. The transitions themselves, however, proved to be long, drawn-out processes of negotiated transfers of power to a civilian power bloc, which tended to feel rather at ease with some military presence in the background, since this permitted the civilians in power to warn against extremist experiments. The anti-military unity crumbled rapidly in such situations, which proved how little influence the base-movements actually had on the political process.

This prompted further thinking about and research into the actual relations between the movements and political institutions. The relation to the state turned out to be more complicated than the opposition between social movement and institutional system suggested. The anti-statist discourse of the movements had too easily been taken at face value and too easily been fitted into a theoretical framework that rested on an opposition between social movement and institutional system. In part this model was inspired by Castells's (1977) definition of urban social movements. Secondly, it was inspired by the wish to distinguish the new movements from the manipulated movements of the populist period (e.g., Moisés 1982). Finally, the stress on the extra-institutional character and the autonomy of the new movements got a new impetus from part of the literature on new social movements that emphasized their countercultural character, their role in questioning domination at a micro-level and which opposed strategy and identity (e.g., Evers 1985; Kärner 1987).

The emphasis on autonomy and extra-institutionality, which derived from these various sources, became increasingly problematic in the course of the democratic transitions. Not only had the assumption of a radical antithesis between the movements and the state diverted attention from the fact that the movements also were engaged in negotiations with the state, it also made it difficult to think about practical issues, such as how to advance the process of democratization (cf. R. Cardoso 1983; Espinoza 1984; Silva and Ribeiro n.d.). Thus the issue of if and how the movements can play a role in reshaping the political and institutional system rather than remaining marginal to it, without losing their identity, has come to play a prominent role in the current debate. As Ruth Cardoso (1983) has pointed out, social scientists have played a role in establishing the centrality of the concept of autonomy and they should also play a role in reformulating the concept. They contribute to the self-understanding and self-rationalization of the movements. It is not uncommon that a president of a neighborhood association in Latin America nowadays thinks of himself as "president of a social movement" even if he actually engaged in awfully clientelist and hardly emancipatory political schemes. That only to remind ourselves that intellectuals do not "float freely," even if they are not "anchored in the party." They never can plead innocence.

Apart from the issue of the relationship between movements, the institutional system and democracy a second feature of the current debates and studies of urban movements should be signaled. By the end of the 1970s, when the number of studies of Latin American urban movements started to increase rapidly, one can observe an increasing dissatisfaction with the then rather dominant structuralist Marxist paradigm. It was related to the aversion to regarding individuals as supports of structures and the growing awareness that urban contradictions by themselves do not explain the emergence of collective action. An increasing number of studies now focused on processes of mobilization and the constitution of collective identities, whereas the concern with macroanalysis visibly decreased. In the proliferation of case studies the structuralist paradigm was not replaced by anything equally dominant. The tendency rather was toward conceptual eclecticism. In the more recent studies one finds references to the work of Touraine (e.g., Reyes Posada 1986), Offe (e.g., Jacobi 1989), and related authors as well as some references to resource mobilization and "collective action theories" (e.g., Boschi and Valladares 1983; Boschi 1987), whereas the debate on post-structuralism and post-modernism is raging. Thus, if we consider the debate on urban movements in Latin America we can see that after the studies that were strongly inspired by (structuralist) Marxism, attention shifted to culture and the constitution of identity. Subsequently it shifted increasingly toward the issue of the relationship between movements and the institutional system.

The Paradigm of the 1970s

As was pointed out, the writings of Castells, Lojkine, and Borja had an important impact in recasting the discussion of the urban question in Latin America that until then had been approached within the framework of marginality-theory and the relations of production. Collective consumption and the relations of *reproduction* now became the central concepts in the analysis of what rather indiscriminately came to be called "urban social movements." In the course of time one can observe the emergence of what later has been called "the paradigm of the 1970s." It consisted of a blend of Castells, Lojkine, and Borja with the theory of late dependent industrialization, or peripheral capitalism, starting with a phase of import substitution and the theory of populism as an accompanying phenomenon of this type of industrialization.

The next phase was that of bureaucratic authoritarianism, repressing the populist movements "run wild." When, after a period of savage repression, urban movements became visible again they were regarded as definitely different from those of the populist period. This time they were autonomous and presented a potential challenge to the capitalist state, it was argued. We will briefly examine two contributions that stressed the radical potential of urban movements and nurtured the expectations about the movements that arose in the aftermath of bureaucratic authoritarianism.

One example of the use of the notion of collective consumption in the specific historical context of Brazilian capitalism is provided by the pioneering work of Moisés (1982) on the development of the *Sociedades de Amigos de Bairro* (neighborhood associations) in São Paulo between 1945 and 1970. He sets the development of these associations against the background of the Brazilian process of post-war industrialization and the accompanying populist policies. The basic line of argument is that in the circumstances of accumulation on a "poor basis" the new demands for urban infrastructure, public transport, education and sociocultural facilities, concomitant to the rapid metropolization of the period, were neglected. The state was concerned with improving the conditions of production, above all investing in the infrastructure for industrialization. Collective consumption lagged way behind. At the same time the electoral importance of the urban masses was increasing. In the context of the recomposition of the power bloc in this period, politicians would occasionally appeal to the masses to strengthen their position. This had ambiguous effects. Some of the demands of the masses were incorporated and legitimized and the ideology that the state was there "for all" was propagated, legitimizing the state as a target for demand making. At the same time, however, the state was incapable of meeting these demands and this contributed to a delegitimation of public power and a questioning of its representativity. In the case of the São Paulo *Sociedades* the relation with the state therefore tended to become one of antagonism and confrontation.

This account provides the basis for comparison with the "classical" model of capitalist development meant to question those analyses that, pointing to their heterogeneous class composition, disqualify the Brazilian urban movements for not meeting the standards of the "classical" model of social movements. Latin American reality has its own dynamics, Moisés argues, drawing inspiration from Wefforts's (1986) study of populism.[1] The Brazilian urban movements should be understood as a specific product of the so-called "situation of dependency." He sees two important differences from the "classical" model. The first is that a situation of "dependent" capitalism does not give rise to the development of a working class characterized by homogeneity deriving from their situation on the labor market. Instead it gives rise to the development of "popular classes," whose characteristic is heterogeneity. Secondly, instead of the development of unity deriving from solidarity at the enterprise level, in Latin America solidarity develops on the basis of certain rights that were won in the context of populist politics. Rather than a working-class identity a popular identity is developed. The popular sectors find their unity on a directly political level in confrontation with the state. The *Sociedades* developed particularly at moments when a crisis of hegemony provided the political space for movements at the basis. Although they have been called into being by populist politicians attempting to strengthen their position for a recomposition of the power bloc, the neighborhood associations had a dynamic of their own and were not simply dependent on the state. Basically, therefore, they are an expression of the wish for democratic participation of the popular classes. The *Sociedades* had started to play an increasingly independent role in the early 1960s, but this role was reduced to insignificance in the context of the policies of repression and cooptation following the 1964 coup.[2]

The issue of the relationship between neighborhood organizations and class politics was a central one in the discussion on urban movements in the 1970s. The theme also was discussed in a rather influential article by Evers, Müller-Plantenberg, and Spessart (1979) where they asked themselves if struggles in the reproduction sphere could give rise to the development of a revolutionary political consciousness. Like Moisés their aim is to question the orthodox view that disqualifies neighborhood associations pointing to their heterogeneous class composition and arguing that such organizations can only effect minor changes in the sphere of distribution. They would not be able to develop a revolutionary class consciousness; that is to elaborate an alternative societal project or be a subject of societal transformation. Against this view the authors argue that on a theoretical level there is a close interrelationship between production and reproduction and that social interests cannot be simply related to one or the other. On an empirical level, they argue, one can observe that in the Latin American conjuncture of the time the struggle for the conditions of production and the struggle on the level of reproduction actually fuse.

The importance of struggles in the sphere of reproduction, the authors argue, is related to the phase of "associated industrialization" that followed the phase of import substitution. It is accompanied by a drastic decline in the standards of living and the rise of authoritarian regimes. The most visible aspect is the massive impoverishment in the slums, inhabited by a wide range of groups whose income is insufficient to provide for "decent" housing. Turning to the issue of the relationship between production and reproduction the authors point to the overexploitation of the labor force against the background of the presence of an immense reserve army of labor and argue that the struggle in the sphere of reproduction is an extension of the trade union struggle—also closely related to reproduction—with other means. These forms of struggle become necessary in a situation where trade unions are repressed and where work situations do not provide a basis for organization for the majority of the population. The struggle in the reproduction sphere usually takes shape in a neighborhood organization since it is in their living situation that people become most easily aware of their problems and because living together in a neighborhood provides the conditions for organization. The heterogeneity of class positions can be overcome through the shared experience of struggle. This can be a basis for recognition of the cause of their common problems. A shared objective interest exists since the ultimate cause of impoverishment is the class relations in society. The nonpossessing masses have a strategic interest in societal transformation. It must be recognized that the situation of emergency in which they often live requires direct solutions and that this may give rise to a counterposition of individual and common interests. Individualism, however, can easily turn into its opposite when problems become extreme or when there is an opportunity for collective action.

How then to evaluate the "external" activities of neighborhood associations? The "orthodox" view is that capitalism creates the conditions for organization in the sphere of production, whereas the sphere of reproduction is one of individualization. This however, it is argued, is only partly true. Urban segregation, for example, takes place in the sphere of reproduction but it can be a cause of resistance. Neighborhood associations often develop as a result of a temporary exacerbation of a problem, such as the organization of water supply, the occupation of a terrain or the defense of existing housing conditions. Organization also may develop in the face of state intervention or as a result of the activities of a political party. Although in the last analysis the demands confront capital as a relation of social domination, they are aimed at the state since it is the state that takes care of the aspect of collective consumption and, moreover, through wage regulation, of individual consumption. Consciousness of this all-embracing role of the state in the conditions of reproduction only develops slowly, however. The organizations learn that the effectiveness of contacts through clientelist systems is small and that decisions ultimately are political. Through experience they learn that the state must be the aim of their demands, but this also may give rise to a "state illusion." In view of their situation and of the restrictions on democracy "extra-institutional" action often is the only recourse open to neighborhood organizations. The reaction of the state may either be repression or an attempt at integration. The latter, however, is bound to result in disillusionment and thus the organizations learn not to count on the state. Thus, whereas the potential for resistance increases, it also increasingly is met with repression justified by the ideology of national security.

Finally, turning to the "internal" functioning of the associations, the authors observe that part of the associations may have developed from autonomous initiatives; but that in many cases the situation of the 1950s and 1960s, when organization was promoted from above through clientelist systems, has served as a practice ground for later development. The actual participation of neighborhood inhabitants is influenced by many factors, such as the phases of development of the neighborhood, the nature of the problems, processes of differentiation within the neighborhood, the attitude of the state and the leadership of the organization.

An important feature is that women often play a crucial role in the neighborhood mobilizations. Their position in the reproduction process and the fact that they spend most of their time in the neighborhood provide the experience and the conditions to make them a mainstay for local associationalism. In spite of their crucial role they tend, however, to be underrepresented at the leadership level.

The conclusion is, then, that the struggle of neighborhood associations may provide insights into social reality and can give rise to revolutionary political consciousness, although a petty bourgeois consciousness may also be the outcome. In any case the traditional distinction between struggle in the sphere of production and struggle in the sphere of reproduction cannot be upheld. The struggles of the inhabitants of neighborhoods are not external to the class struggle.

In these two examples one can observe how a critique and an adaption of the "classical model" to the Latin American circumstances were operated in the late 1970s. In the absence of a "genuine" working class, struggles in the sphere of consumption and reproduction were revaluated. In this way neighborhood associations could be substituted for the organizations of the "classical" working class. The specific development of capitalism in Latin America does not result in the constitution of a homogeneous working class and tends to dislocate struggles toward the reproductive sphere. In this sense, the struggles of the urban population can only be "pluriclassist." The meaning of the notion of "pluriclassism," therefore, is often quite different from its European connotations, and some have linked it to notions like "incomplete proletarianization." Rather than a capitalist class, the state becomes the target of the actions of neighborhood associations. Moisés argues that this means that the identity of the actors is "constituted on a political level," rather than deriving from the relations of production. Since the relations with the capitalist state are bound to become antagonistic there are chances for an anti-capitalist political consciousness to develop. Moisés and Evers, Müller-Plantenberg, and Spessart both point to the ambiguous outcomes of the period of populist mobilization. It also served as a practice ground for more autonomous action. Thus, through the notions of "collective consumption" and "pluriclassism" the Latin American urban movements were integrated into the scheme of revolutionary social change to provide a local variant for a "privileged point of rupture" and a "privileged subject," substitutes for a genuine working class. As we saw in our discussion of Laclau and Mouffe such notions have been thoroughly scrutinized in recent years. Rather than assuming that there is a predestined subject for social change the awareness that such a subject must be constructed through political practice out of dispersed elements has gained terrain. Nevertheless, the specificities of the industrialization and urbanization process are important historical and macrostructural features that help to understand why urban movements could come to play such a prominent role in Latin America. They show that "the social" is not pure contingency.

Populism and Autonomy

The contributions by Moisés and Evers, Müller-Plantenberg, and Spessart point to the potential of the movements for autonomous action. On this point they contrast with the studies that stress the vulnerability of the movements to populist manipulation. Whereas the studies just reviewed tend to regard populism as a *phase* in the history of Latin American countries and point to the ambiguity and possible exhaustion of populist tactics in preventing more autonomous action, others rather tend to regard populism as a *structural* feature. The issue of populism plays a central role in Castells's (1983) assessment of urban movements in Latin America, which, as we pointed out, is strongly influenced by the work of Touraine.[3] Rather than pointing to the possibilities for autonomous action, Castells draws the attention to the vulnerability of the urban movements in relation to the political system. Castells's (1983) analysis of urban movements in Latin America starts from the observation that contrary to the expectations of those who believed in the "myth of marginality" and the fears of the world's establishment, social organization seems to be stronger than social deviance in these communities and that political conformism seems to outweigh the tendencies toward popular upheaval. His hypothesis is that these trends can be explained by the same crucial social phenomenon: the local self-organization of squatter settlements and its particular connection to the state and the political system at large in the shape of *urban populism.*

The nation-states of the developing countries, Castells argues, are caught between the political pressures from the traditional oligarchies and the new international economic powers at a time when the popular masses increasingly forward political claims at broader participation. Many states try to adapt by using the leverage of a subordinated popular mobilization to overcome the resistance of the traditional groups and to renegotiate the current patterns of economic dependence within the world capitalist system. In this context the "myth of marginality" persists since it is functional for the political strategy of the state in dependent societies (cf. Perlman 1979: 248–250). In contrast to what the myth would make us believe, urban marginality and the occupational marginality of "informal" employment do not coincide. Occupational marginality is not the source of urban marginality. The latter concept refers to the inability of the market economy, or of state policies, to provide adequate shelter and urban services to an increasing proportion of city dwellers, including the majority of the regularly employed salaried workers, as well as all the people making their living in the so-called "informal sector." The world of marginality is in fact socially constructed by the state in a process of social integration and political mobilization in exchange for goods and services that only it can provide. Thus, the relation between the state and the people is organized around the institutional distribution of urban services coupled with the institutional mechanisms of political control.

The urban population and its movements become dependent on the political system as a result of their vulnerability. This thesis is illustrated with case studies from Peru, Chile, and Mexico. Applying the structural formula for urban social movements shows that the major weakness of the Latin American urban mobilizations is their subordination to the state or a political party. The squatters, the state, and the informal economy, intimately linked to the "formal" sector, are all parts of the same dependent system. The dependent city results from the residents' lack of social control over urban development because of their forced submission to the good will of the state or powerful political agents and to the changing flows of foreign capital. The dependent city, as Castells puts it, is a city without citizens (Castells 1983: 175–212).

This assessment of the role of urban movements in Latin America draws heavily on the work of Janice Perlman (1979), who argued that the urban poor are neither "marginal" nor present a radical challenge to the dominant system. Their precarious position makes them vulnerable to clientelist politics and populist manipulation. This keeps them from playing an autonomous role in the political arena. "They can in no sense be regarded as the agents of their own destinies," Perlman (1979: 261) wrote. This view of things contains a critique of the more optimistic views about the potential of urban movements that were expressed in the studies, which regarded the "marginals" as either a social basis for "totalitarian adventures" or a revolutionary subject *par excellence*. Perlman, however, collected her data in the 1960s. Do her conclusions still apply in the 1970s when urban movements reemerged after the period of authoritarianism that followed the breakdown of the populist tactics of manipulation and containment of the urban population? The studies on the "new urban movements," of which the work of Moisés (1982) and Evers, Müller-Plantenberg, and Spessart (1979) may be regarded as precursors, suggested that populism might rather be a *phase* than a *structural* feature and that one of the movements that emerged in the late 1970s consisted exactly in their autonomy and resistance to political manipulation.

Democratization and the "Common Sense" of the 1970s

In the context of the processes of "democratic transition" the issue of autonomy and the relationship to institutional politics became a central one. Autonomy had become a "common sense" notion. Its meaning partly derived from Castells's (1977) opposition between social movement and institutional action, which is embedded in a dual power perspective. But it also derived meaning from the strategy/identity dilemma that had come into focus with the "culturalist" studies that followed the eclipse of the structuralist-Marxist paradigm. The "common sense" notion of autonomy became increasingly problematic, however. The relation to institutions pushed itself on the agenda in the course of the "democratic transitions." Not only did the focus on autonomy deflect attention away from some of the actual relations between movements and the institutional system, it also was not very helpful in thinking about the practical issue of how to change a political paradigm. In the final analysis democratization has to do with the institutionalization of new channels of institutionalized "participation" and the reform of existing ones.

Some of the pertinent questions in this respect were posed by Ruth Cardoso (1983; 1987; cf. Cruz 1987; Jacobi 1987; Silva and Ribeiro 1985; Telles 1987) in her reviews of the research on Brazilian and Latin American urban movements. Most analysts, she argues, have stressed the novelty of the urban movements that arose in the latter phases of Brazilian authoritarianism, as compared to those of the populist period. The characteristic of autonomy was highly valued and emphasized in most studies. But, she argues, in this way the anti-governmental character of popular manifestations was often taken for a radical opposition to the capitalist state rather than a struggle for a change of political regime. Moreover, a spontaneous character was attributed to the movements to emphasize their autonomy from the "ideological apparatuses of the state," such as the existing parties and trade unions. Thus neighborhood associations tended to be regarded as the more authentic representatives of the popular masses. The state was assumed to be the authoritarian enemy and the target of the mobilizations of civil society but, in contrast to the European studies, little attention was paid to the actual functioning of the state. It was neglected that the process of centralizing authoritarianism was accompanied by a process of administrative reform and a certain amelioration of public services and that modern administrators and efficient planners dialogue with their target populations. The state is not simply the adversary of the movements, but it also is their interlocutor. Hence the relationship between movements and state tends to be much more ambiguous than the one-sided emphasis on "autonomy" suggests. Such considerations led her to question some of the assumptions characterizing the studies of the late 1970s.

The first assumption is that the new urban movements direct themselves against the authoritarian state and oblige it to democratize. Although many studies end by reaffirming the transformative potential of the movements, the actual case studies fail to show the effectiveness of the movements on this point. It may be true that some mobilizations obtain responses from public organisms. This shows an increased flexibility in responding to mobilizations. The actual relation with the state is much more ambiguous than simple confrontation. The impact on the overall activities of the state remains very limited, however, and the control over those activities totally escapes the radius of action of the movements. Secondly, if it is true that the movements obliged society and the state to recognize the presence of the oppressed and their capacity for autonomous action, one must also observe that for the state it seems easier to recognize the leadership of a neighborhood than the popular parties that challenge the functioning of the state as a whole. This leads R. Cardoso to question the notion that the movements are more authentic or representative than the parties, for example. The ideology of autonomy and authentic representation of the interests of "the community" frequently has its corollary in isolation and fragmentation of the struggles. At the same time the state not only functions as a unifier of struggles. Demand making and negotiation with state agencies often has competitive aspects leading to the segregation and separation of struggles. Finally, R. Cardoso questions the thesis that the movements, being new political actors, have an effect of renovation on the existing parties and trade-unions. On this point too she observes actual ambiguity in the relations between movements and parties. Mostly their interaction is of little advantage to the movements and the effects on party structures remains limited. At the same time, however, the skepticism toward political parties and "politics," and the emphasis on autonomy, community, and authenticity has impeded the movements to generalize their experience and limited their effectiveness in the reshaping of politics.

In his article on urban movements in Brazil, Mainwaring (1987) elaborates on the question of why the original expectations of many analysts about the transformative capacity of these movements have not been born out. In the second half of the 1970s urban popular movements burgeoned, but in the course of time it became apparent that their impact remained small. Mainwaring argues that, firstly, rather than a unity of diverse movements the tendency has been toward an extraordinary fragmentation, with few effective linkages between these movements and political institutions. Unity of social movements, except for specific demands and short-term situations, is the exception rather than the rule.

Secondly, the process of formation of a political identity is more complex than most analysts of social movements in Brazil (and many leading European theoreticians) had suggested. He refers specifically to some of the notions of the "1970s paradigm," such as the notion of urban contradictions and argues that the reading of the relationship between these contradictions and social movements has been excessively economistic, ignoring the mediating factors that should be taken into account. Developing a political identity that leads to participation in social movements is the exception rather than the rule. Only a small minority of the people is involved in such movements. Finally, the democratization process, rather than enhancing their unity, has exacerbated the competition among movements. The state became more concerned with those movements and devised populist or clientelist strategies for coopting them. Mainwaring stresses that in a sense this redefinition of the political strategy of the regime represented a victory for the urban movements, but it was not the kind of victory the most optimistic analysts had hoped for. In addition, the sphere of partisan politics became more important in the course of redemocratization, often exacerbating tensions and conflicts within the movements. In spite of these problems the movements have, however, also contributed to redefining the political arena in some important ways. There is an increased sensitivity to popular demands that suggest a partial erosion of the elitism of Brazilian politics. At the same time, Mainwaring observes, the very existence of these traditions tends to limit the capacity of the movements to change them since they play a major role in the shaping of political identities and attitudes toward politics. Nevertheless, the movements have helped the popular classes conquer a sense of identity and citizenship. This may help in strengthening civil society and challenge the elitist and statist traditions, thus contributing to a reshaping of "political culture." The changes have not been dramatic, but they are there (Mainwaring 1987; cf. Mainwaring and Viola 1984).[4]

Both R. Cardoso (1983) and Mainwaring and Viola thus point out that the construction of effective linkages to political institutions, especially parties, would be of crucial importance if social movements are to become a more salient political factor. Vigevani (1989) argues that the movements have remained pre-political and concords with Cardoso that the urban movements have been unable to generalize their experience or to elaborate something like a project. It is the absence of a project, coupled to an anti-political discourse that gave a permanent character to the sectoralization and the localism of their actions. It also contributed to a crisis of the movements in São Paulo when they came to face a totally unresponsive municipal administration between 1986 and 1988. Although the new movements may be the carriers of a new conception of citizenship, Vigevani argues, in the absence of a project it runs the risk of remaining a constricted kind of citizenship that easily drifts toward corporatism, particularism, or utopianism.

The segmentation and absence of a totalizing horizon cannot simply be attributed to a willful and spontaneous turn toward new and punctual orientations of action, as some of the "new social movements" theorists have suggested. Calderón and Jelin (1987: 82) point to the brutal transnationalization of the Latin American economies and the concomitant changes in the social structure, the effects of a period of repression and the discredit of the old populist and classist parties as contributing to this segmentation. Others have pointed to the dispersion imposed by the state, resulting in the exhaustion of urban protests within the different state apparatuses, or to the effects of the economic crisis. Only by articulating a more "totalizing" conception can such problems be overcome. It is in this context that the ideological aspects of the "common sense" notion of autonomy have come under scrutiny. For students of urban movements it became problematical since it deflected attention from the actual relations between movements and the state. For the movements themselves the gap between their autonomist discourse and their—unacknowledged—relations with the political system also became problematic. The discourse of autonomy may serve to strengthen a movement at an initial stage, but it also may become counterproductive when it results in self-marginalization. This point became all the more relevant in the context of the "democratic transitions" that prompted a reorientation of the movements involving a rethinking of the disjunctions between "participation" and "autonomy," "system" and "movement." Hence the search for something like "creative autonomy."

A Practice-Ground for Democracy?

Whereas the expectations about the role of urban movements in reshaping the political arena have been sobered to give way for more realistic assessments, some analysts (e.g., Evers 1985; Kärner 1987) have argued that the real significance of the movements lies in the potential for sociocultural change, rather than political transformation. Evers (1985), for instance, argues that the centrality of the concept of power in the study of social movements has been limiting our understanding of the significance of the contemporary movements. For Evers the concepts of identity and alienation come to play a central role. This significance lies in their quest for an autonomous identity and an attempt at reappropriating civil society from the state. The important thing is autonomy from the tutelage with regard to social movements that characterizes traditional Latin American politics. Such tutelage ranges from conservative paternalism to populist manipulation and left wing instrumentalism. Evers argues that a movement's increased potential for political power can carry with it a decrease in its long-term sociocultural potential. More power almost invariably means less identity, more alienation. Thus the movements are faced with the dilemma of yielding to the weight of reality and becoming an established opposition within the framework of dominant society or to try and uphold an identity of their own, at the price of remaining weak, inefficient and plagued by contradictions. In reality, their only chance of existence lies in a precarious combination of both alternatives (Evers 1985). Notions like "identity," "autonomy," "authenticity," "spontaneity," and "community" have become important ingredients in the discourse of Latin American neighborhood movements as well as in theoretical approaches. It was on the basis of such discourse that many observers at an early stage came to believe in the new movements as a still uncontaminated force. Such views have come under increasing scrutiny, however. The notion of "community," strongly promoted by the Catholic Church and its base communities as well as by urban planners, tends to obscure the fact that "community" or "collective identity" actually is a construct, which does not eliminate the heterogeneity of the participants in terms of status, class, political preferences, or ethical choices (R. Cardoso 1987: 85). Actually, such differences may tend to be obscured and delegitimized for the sake of "community." Rather than challenging relations of subordination at a local level such relations tend to be made invisible. As Durham (1984) has observed the movements often present a "double face." In public they present an image of unity, equality, and consensus, which also pervades their meetings. At the same time, however, the divergences crop up in the slander, personal accusations, and the conscious and unconscious manipulations known to any observer familiar with those movements. This also points to the problems of the democratic experience within these movements. The direct democracy model is practiced in small groups that often are incapable of developing mechanisms for recognizing or negotiating divergent positions. This results in interminable and inconclusive discussions, covert mechanisms of decision making and back-stage politics and frequent splits. Thus, whereas such movements do provide a space to "speak out" and practice certain forms of democracy it cannot be assumed that they are "uncontaminated" or do not present authoritarian practices. It is probably the feminist movement that most clearly has recognized these problems and the evasion of the issue of power, perhaps because a number of myths also played such a prominent role in the emergence and consolidation of the movement. At the VI Latin American and Caribbean Feminist Encounter a series of myths was discussed, namely: that feminists do not want power; that they do politics in a different way; that all women are equal; that women have a natural unity because of being women; that feminism is the politics of women by women; that the small group is the movement; that women's spaces are in themselves guarantee of a positive process; that because a woman feels it, anything is valid; that the personal is automatically political and that consensus is democracy (cf. Vargas 1989: 144). If one substitutes the word "poor" for "women" one can easily see that similar myths also quite often inform the discourse of urban movements and can also be encountered in the studies of these movements (cf. Boran 1989: 85). The feminists who discussed these myths concluded, among other things, that power is needed to change society; that they aspire to do politics in "another way" but that in practice their politics are often backward, arbitrary, victimized, and manipulative, reproducing traditional behavior patterns; that consensus is not the same thing as unanimity and can be a very authoritarian practice since it may conceal differences and because it gives veto power to one person. These problems discussed by the women's movement are in many ways similar to those discussed by Ruth Cardoso (1983), Durham (1984), and Vigevani (1989) and others in relation to urban movements. This has helped to overcome the ingenuous glorification of the movements, characteristic of an uncritical "basism," which in some cases also characterizes studies of the movements. Such features, however, are no immutable givens. The self-critical assessment of the feminist movement shows how movements are capable of confronting their reality with their ideals. They are capable of self-rationalization, and this is how they may advance, albeit sometimes stumbling, toward new social practices (cf. Krishke 1987; Scherer-Warren 1987).

Autonomy and the Outsider

Another aspect of the valuation of autonomy, authenticity, and spontaneity and self-organization is that the role of "external agents" has been obscured. Clientelism is denounced, to be sure, but the role of external agents more sympathetic to the movements is minimized in the discourse of the movements themselves as well as in many studies of the movements (cf. R. Cardoso 1983; Durham 1984; Jacobi 1987; 1988). Nevertheless the clergy, left-wing parties, students, social workers, nongovernmental organizations and lawyers, architects, teachers, and doctors in many cases play a crucial role, the latter often through their professional organizations. Their activities are referred to in many studies, but the emphasis is on the spontaneous self-organization of the popular masses. At best such groups appear as "resources" that have been mobilized and in some instances reference is made to their "pedagogical" activities. More systematic account should be taken of the activities of such "supports." Often they play an important role in turning discontent into collective action and they are crucial in providing the basic infrastructure for continued activity. Moreover, their role in strengthening the position of organizations in negotiation processes should not be underestimated. The role of these agents, in particular the clergy and NGOs, is one of giving advice on organizational, technical, and juridical matters, introducing themes for discussion and reflection on modes of internal functioning of the organizations as well as on the effects of their operation on the political structure, in short, what have been called "pedagogical" contributions. NGOs and the church also often provide some of the basic infrastructure and finance for the operation of associations, and they play a role in establishing contacts with other organizations and the integration in wider articulations. One might even suggest that the "autonomy" from party politics and politicians in many cases depends on the contributions of such organizations. Professional organizations, such as those of lawyers, architects, and social workers also play a crucial role in giving technical advice and helping associations in the course of negotiations. On the other hand we should draw the attention to the role of the executive technobureaucracy. In many cases their role is much more ambiguous than that of simple executors of policies that have been developed at higher levels of the hierarchy. Borja (1975: 115–116) already drew attention to this type of technicians whose role becomes increasingly prominent with the increase of state interventionism in the context of contemporary capitalism. Their ideology of "rationality and neutrality," he argues, runs up against the actual impossibility of real urban planning under capitalist conditions, and this may produce a radicalization of these professionals. Eventually they may come to contribute to the legitimation and the broadening of the actions of urban movements. In a similar way other groups of professionals, such as social assistants (Sposati 1988), clergy, or teachers, may contribute to the mobilization of the population. This implies that such groups cannot simply be thought of as "resources" but that their relation to the movements rather is a negotiated one in which both parties pursue common as well as proper goals. "Outsiders" play an important role in the shaping and criticizing of the "common sense" of the movements and the way "nonmaterial goals" are perceived. Particularly in the case of the church one can observe the differences, ranging from assistentialism, through a-political communalism to a more political stance. The latter nowadays is under increasing pressure from the more conservative parts of the hierarchy, which results in a closing down of part of the support structure of the church. This, in turn, may lead to the emergence of foreign financed alternative structures. To a certain extent such differences can also be observed in the case of nongovernmental organizations (cf. Garcia 1987). Most of them have a left-wing orientation, but one cannot assume that such is always the case. One should not forget that neighborhood associations are a stake in struggles for hegemony and that some "support" groups are interested in promoting a certain type of "a-politicism." Nevertheless, the politicization of neighborhood associations is an ongoing process. Rather than bemoaning it and pointing to the problems it often gives rise to, attention should also be paid to the positive aspects in the sense that politicization is a way of overcoming localism and segmentation.

New Definitions?

"Post-materialistic" value orientations and non-state orientedness are, as we saw, sometimes regarded as the distinctive features of new social movements and these criteria also have been applied to Latin American movements. It draws attention to the fact that there is more in the world than money and administrative power. But it should not obscure the fact that we live in a world that is structured to an important degree by exchange value and state power that elude democratic control. Disqualifying movements that are engaged in material issues as somewhat anachronistic is a mistake. Distributive justice, as opposed to the injustices generated by a system based on exchange value, remains one of the major challenges, and it is certainly not contrary to sociocultural change or democratic culture. Such an assessment takes a welfare state arrangement for granted, instead of recognizing its precarious character, and it is based on a restrictive understanding of culture that may contribute to an irrational *Weltfremd* counterculturalism. Similarly, state orientedness implies a challenge to the present functioning of the capitalist state. Framing the issue in terms of a strategy/identity dilemma results in dodging the question of developing alternative institutional arrangements. That may be no problem as long as "cultural" issues are involved,[5] but it is if one starts thinking about alternative democratic arrangements of production and distribution. Even in post-industrial societies people do not live by symbolic goods alone. Moreover, in Latin

America the relations between civil society and the state are marked by periods of authoritarian rule. In the context of the "democratic transitions" the question is not simply one of "reappropriating civil society from the state" but partly of institutionalizing civil society and citizenship itself. During the periods of authoritarianism the boundaries of "the private" have been violated and the "public sphere," as a sphere of free exchange of opinions, has been invaded by brutal power so that the free exchange of opinions was confined to the "private sphere." And even the boundaries of "the private" were not respected. Democratization involves a redefinition and institutionalization of such "boundaries" and enforcing their respect. It also means giving content to citizenship, not only in the form of the right to participate in elections but also in the form of decent living conditions.

Democracy is the preferable means to these ends and, as we saw, the commitment to democracy is one aspect of the current prominence of the issue of institutions and institutionalization. In Latin America the issue is addressed in specific ways. One of the arguments against the "paradigm of the 1970s" has been that, with its oppositions of social movement and institutional system, autonomy and cooptation, it screened out the notion of political process (Silva and Ribeiro 1985). The old opposition suggests that institutionalization is the negation of movement or that at the moment a movement starts negotiations or starts creating a new order, the movement is finished. Espinoza (1984) proposes the notion of conquest[6] as a way out of the deadlocks of conceptualizing movements in terms of dual power—the movement in the margin of and against the state—or as "micro-experiences"—the movement reduced to a multiplicity of isolated disputes. These questions must be understood against the backdrop of the commitment to democracy and the realities of the actual "transitions through transaction." The institutional spaces being opened constitute far from "ideal speech situations," and in a recent study Jacobi (1989) employs the notion of "structural selectivity," that is the way in which the state filters demands according to compatibility with the accumulation process, to discuss the interaction between urban movements and state apparatuses in São Paulo.

These issues derive their relevance from the experiments in local democratization and the new ways of the state in dealing with urban issues through dialogue rather than repression. Establishing local councils, in which neighborhood associations are invited to participate, surely is an advance over individualizing clientelist ways of dealing with problems. In some way it contributes to turning favors into rights. But what exactly are the competences of such councils? The line between window dressing and an "instrumentalization" of the movements and real decision making power often is a thin one. The "democratic transitions" are not achieved, but have only started. They confront the urban movements with new problems. Although among many students of the movements one can observe a certain deception about the actual influence of the movements on the political process, it also should be noted that the number of neighborhood associations often increases rapidly in the course of "democratic transitions." The outcomes of these processes of reorientation and quantitative growth remain to be seen.

Small wonder that in the course of the debates the question whether the Latin American neighborhood movements constitute a *social movement* sometimes has emerged. John Friedmann (1984) has answered the question affirmatively. He argues that Touraine—and that also applies to many aspects of Castells's (1983; cf. Lowe 1986: 177, 193) evaluation—is wrong in regarding the popular sector as simply "dependent," "having a purely passive voice in politics and as comprising a virtual 'underclass'" (Friedmann 1984: 502). The corollaries of this perception, he argues, are that the underclass cannot become a historically relevant actor; it cannot speak for itself; others must speak for it. Its actions are limited to concrete demands for external assistance. It can easily be co-opted and colonized by the state. Social change cannot come from below. It either must come from a powerful state (and the classes which support it) or from a vanguard that speaks on behalf of those without a voice. In the end, further study of the underclass is useless, because nothing of significance can be expected from that quarter.

Friedmann sees things in a different way. He defines a social movement as "a self-mobilized segment of civil society (or collective actor) engaged in a social and political praxis that leads, when informed by an emancipated [*sic*] interest and when successful, to individual and collective self-empowerment, new social identities, and the self-production of life." After a discussion of the issue Friedmann (1984: 508) concludes that "despite some inherent weaknesses of organization, *barrio* mobilization appears to satisfy virtually all of the formal criteria we have identified for social movements."

Others have taken a different approach to the issue and have argued for a redefinition of social movements, to bring the concept closer to "reality."[7] An example of this tendency toward "redefining social movements" is provided by Nascimento (1987), who proposes to define them as "social practices that constitute social subjects with reference to urban contradictions." In this way he wants to reject the "finalism" of Castells's definition in which the transformative character of social movements played a central role. Such a definition, he argues, has the inconvenience that it is not confirmed by observations and studies in Brazil, and one can even observe the emergence of social movements of a conservative character in the Brazilian metropolises, particularly in relation to the problem of urban violence. Moreover, he argues that the criterion of a popular social basis should be discarded, since it impedes the study of "social movements of the dominant classes." Finally, he rejects the definitions that take formal or organizational characteristics, such as spontaneity/organization, formal/informal, classist/pluriclassist, bureaucratic/democratic, as criteria. In short, he wants a broad and neutral definition that covers just about anything that moves with reference to broadly defined urban contradictions and that does not relate such movements to social change (Nascimento 1987).

In a similar vein, Schuurman has argued that definitions in which the structural change or reform of the society plays a central role alienate themselves from the daily practice of existing urban territorial organizations in the Third World. The criterion of societal transformation reflects a leftist/radical political philosophy, he argues, whereby "at the same time the number of urban social movements answering to the description is decreasing." As an alternative he proposes "a social organization with a territorial based identity, which strives for emancipation by way of collective action."[8] Such a definition broadens the potential field of what may be called social movements and discards the criterion of "reversal of the power structure" of the "wishful" definitions (Schuurman 1989).

Do we really win anything by such redefinitions? Should the criterion of transformative capacity be discarded because at a precise historical moment in Brazil organizations aiming at such a transformation seem to be absent? Are survival strategies the same thing as social movements and has the emancipatory character of survival strategies been underestimated, as Schuurman (1989: 22) suggests? Is the question if such movements will lead to a transformation in the power structure a speculative and not very burning one if at the same time emancipation is defined as "liberation from hierarchical dependency relations" and if it is acknowledged that societal reform is in many instances the only way to ensure true emancipation (Schuurman and Van Naerssen 1989: 3)? Are the urban poor a "marginalized and forgotten group"? Broadening the concept of social movement in the ways proposed seems to be a form of conceptual inflation. There may be other forms of collective action, but social movements are those that have to do something with emancipation and change of institutionalized norms, roles and rules (cf. Melucci 1980). As we saw, Touraine (1978) and Castells (1977; 1983) have suggested other differentiations between social movements and other forms of collective mobilization. It seems useful to retain such differentiations, rather than to screen out aspects like emancipation and progressive change in a seemingly neutral, noncommitted, definition. This implies that not just any mobilization around urban issues can be characterized as an urban social movement. Rather than characterizing any mobilization as a social movement it should be argued in each case why something might be characterized as a social movement, part of a social movement, or as a potential social movement.

On the other hand, the idea that each "societal type" is characterized by a single social movement seems to be untenable. It requires some imagination to bring women's movements and regional movements under the same denominator of anti-technocratic movements, for instance. Such an approach suggests that each society is characterized by a single dominant structuring principle from which all forms of domination, exploitation, and subjection derive. Denying the possibility of such reductionism does not imply denying the possibility that a specific type of movement may play a particularly prominent role due to the specific structuring of a society and the tensions it generates. The particularly prominent role of the working class movement in the industrializing Western European societies was not only related to workplace organization, but rather to the particular imbrication between workplace organization and the living situation characteristic of the industrialization process. It is this imbrication that may provide important insights into the strength of the European working class movement of the late nineteenth and early twentieth century. It may also provide an insight into the development of social struggles in the ABC area in São Paulo, for instance (cf. Kowarick 1985; Vink 1985). The Latin American urban movements may not be "the" subject for societal change in the sense of providing a substitute for a "disciplined forward marching proletariat taking charge of the whole of society." However, their role can hardly be overlooked, and they have not just been invented by leftists in search of a new subject to carry the "red lantern of social change." The increase in numbers of urban associations over the past twenty years can easily be documented, and it hardly comes as a surprise that urban issues have provided one of the main bases for contestation in the context of the transformation process that Latin American societies have undergone during this period. These associations may be vulnerable, but it goes much too far to characterize them as simply "dependent" and subjected to "external manipulation." In this respect there certainly is a difference between the associations of the 1950s and the more recent ones. The latter are able to entertain a more diversified network of articulations which enables them to play a more autonomous role.

As we saw, the assessment of such associations has ranged from optimism to pessimism, often depending on the particular case and conjuncture studied. Looking at the often contradictory and ambiguous amalgam of practices that goes by the name of "urban movements," they seem to be more than just "survival strategies." They surely are motivated by survival, but they cannot be reduced to just that. They also play a critical role that supersedes survival. Rather than being a marginalized and forgotten group the urban poor have, through collective action, been capable of making themselves heard. Turning favors into rights they contribute to giving content to the notion of citizenship. It is not the notion of "change," as such, which is problematic but rather, as we saw in our review of the ongoing debate, the relationship between the notions of "change" and "autonomy." In these debates the old antithesis between reform and revolution, as expressed in the thesis that "reform only serves to strengthen the system" and its implication that "change" can only be accomplished "outside and against the system" has come under scrutiny. Such views have, historically, been disastrous and such a juxtaposition of "reform" and "revolution" is unnecessary. Thus, the image of change may be said to have changed. The idea of a big switch that can be pulled by a conscious vanguard, resulting overnight in a new society, has been abandoned. There may be "overdetermined" moments and points of rupture, but the authoritarian obsession with the "moment of taking power" has faded. Societal change simply is more complex than that but, as Galileo said: "Eppur si muove."

Notes

Originally published in Willem Assies, Gerrit Burgwal, and Ton Salman. 1990. *Structures of Power, Movements of Resistance: An Introduction to the Theories of Urban Movements in Latin America*. Amsterdam: CEDLA, 9–98. The republished text is a part of the original essay, basically the last twenty pages, adapted and shortened. We thank CEDLA for their permission to republish.

1. Weffort situates populism in the context of a crisis of the oligarchic power bloc resulting from industrialization, the emergence of a new middle class, and the transition to mass politics involving the urban popular masses.

2. One might say that this analysis shows how populist politics relied on a multiplication of political spaces—clientelism—in the context of a reconstitution of the power bloc. When an overflow of meaning tended to break through the parameters of the system, transforming handouts into rights, as was the case in Brazil in the early 1960s, this created the situation that ultimately led to the 1964 intervention. The turn to authoritarianism was not simply the reflection of a transition to a next predetermined phase of industrialization, but was intimately related to specific development in the different countries, as was extensively shown in the discussions on bureaucratic authoritarianism (cf. Collier 1979; O'Brien and Cammack 1985).

3. Touraine, as we saw, distinguishes social movements from historical struggles. The latter result from the modification of social movements resulting from a mode of state intervention in the context of a mode of development, that is the transition from one mode of production (industrial and informational modes, in Touraine's terminology) to another. He distinguishes three modes of development: the liberal, the contractual, and the voluntarist. The first corresponds to the situation of the central capitalist countries where the transition from one mode of production to another was performed without much interference of the state. The last corresponds to the socialist countries where the role of the state was decisive. The contractual mode of development is situated in between the two and corresponds to situations in which national-populist states struggle against a situation of dependency. In such situations social

movement cannot constitute themselves as genuine social movements since they inevitable become tied up with a mode of state intervention and therefore with politics and consequently lose their identity (Touraine 1973: 489–512; 1988: 240–258). This scheme, which can be extended and rendered more complex through a game of transmutation (Touraine 1976: 9–47, 232–250; 1978: 133–177; 1988), provides the basic framework for Castells's (1983) recent comparative study of urban movements, although the unacknowledged terminological "slippage" between Castells and Touraine should be noted.

4. A curious feature of their contribution is that Mainwaring and Viola (1984) adopt the criteria of non-state orientedness and post-materialistic values as discriminating between "old" and "new" movements, since at the same time they attempt to evaluate the contribution of these movements to the process of democratic transition, that is a change of political regime. Their definition of novelty seems to be a rather unreflected adoption of a view most clearly expressed by Evers (1985), which, as we saw, is rather problematic in its aversion to institutionalization (the strategy/identity issue) as well as the conceptualization of "material" demands as something that cannot go together with sociocultural change or, more specifically, the development of a "democratic culture."

5. Though, as Soper (1989: 97) comments, "such sentimentalism for the 'Symbolic' will not recommend itself to those women who have yearned for a bit more 'systemic' encroachment into their cherishing preserve in the form of proper public child care, not to mention wages for housework."

6. Rather than the "process" inspired by more "pluralist" collective action theories.

7. Reflecting upon the discussion on definition and the "transformative potential" of urban movements Gohn (1988: 332) has expressed her surprise about the self-critical—one would nearly say repentant—attitude that many Brazilian authors have taken lately. In trying to understand the fact that the movements have not lived up to the expectations one of the arguments has been that this is because the theoretical approach of the 1970s was tinged with utopianism. Gohn goes on to argue that it was the movements that did not advance sufficiently to effect substantial transformations, not simply because analysts have been utopianist or ingenuous, but because the movements did not succeed in making anything out of the crisis of hegemony of the late 1970s.

8. One inconvenience of this definition is that it does not contain any reference to "the urban" and might as well apply to an ethnic movement far from any city.

References

Althusser, Louis. 1976 [1974]. "Ideologie et appareils ideologiques d'etat." In *Positions 1964–1975*. Paris: Éditions Sociales.

———. 1986 [1965]. *Pour Marx*. Paris: La Découverte.

Althusser, Louis., and Ëtienne Balibar. 1978 [1968]. *Lire le capital I*. Paris: Maspero.

———. 1975 [1968]. *Lire le capital II*. Paris: Maspero.

Arato, Andrew. 1973/74. "The Second International: A Reexamination." *Telos* 18 (Winter): 2–52.

Arnason, Johann. 1986. "Culture, Historicity and Power: Reflections on Some Themes in the Work of Alain Touraine." *Theory, Culture & Society* 3, no. 3: 137–152.

Aronowitz, Stanley. 1988. "The Production of Scientific Knowledge: Science, Ideology, and Marxism." In *Marxism and the Interpretation of Culture*, eds. C. Nelson and L. Grossberg. Urbana and Chicago: University of Illinois Press.

Bakunin, Michael. 1972. *Staatlichkeit und Anarchie und andere Schriften*. Frankfurt, Berlin, Vienna: Ullstein.

Barros, Robert. 1986. "The Left and Democracy: Recent Debates in Latin America." *Telos* 68 (Summer): 49–70.

Bell, Daniel. 1973. *The Coming of Post-Industrial Society.* New York: Basic Books.

Bobbio, Norberto. 1981 [1969]. "Gramsci en de opvatting van de burgerlijke maatschappij." *Te Elfder Ure 28/Marxistiese Staatstheorie 2: Gramsci* 25, no. 2: 367–396

———. 1978a. "Is There a Marxist Theory of the State?" *Telos* 35 (Spring): 5–16.

———. 1978b. "Are There Alternatives to Representative Democracy?" *Telos* 35 (Spring): 17–30.

———. 1978c. "Why Democracy?" *Telos* 36 (Summer): 43–54.

Boran, Anne. 1989. "Popular Movements in Brazil: A Case Study of the Movement for the Defence of the *Favelados* in Sao Paulo." *Bulletin of Latin American Research* 8, no. 1: 83–110.

Borja, Jordi. 1975. *Movimientos sociales urbanos.* Buenos Aires: Ediciones Siap-Planteos.

Boschi, Raúl R. 1987. "Social Movements and the New Political Order in Brazil." In *State and Society in Brazil: Continuity and Change*, ed. J. D. Wirth, E. de Oliveira Nunes, and T. E. Bogenschild. Boulder and London: Westview Press.

Boschi, Raúl R., and Lícia. do Prado Valladares. 1983. "Problemas teóricos na análise de movimentos sociais: comunidade, ação coletiva e o papel do estado." *Espaço e Debates* 3, no. 8: 64–77.

Boswell, Terry E., Edgar. V. Kiser, and Kathryn. A. Baker. 1986. "Recent Developments in Marxist Theories of Ideology." *The Insurgent Sociologist* 13, no. 4: 5–22.

Braverman, Harry. 1974. *Labor and Monopoly Capital.* New York and London: Monthly Review Press.

Brinton, Maurice. 1970. *The Bolsheviks and Workers' Control 1917 to 1921, the State and Counter Revolution.* London: Solidarity.

Bruhat, Jean. 1975. "Der franzosische Sozialismus von 1848 bis 1871." In *Geschichte des Sozialimus III*, ed. J. Droz. Frankfurt, Berlin, Vienna: Ullstein.

Buci-Glucksmann, Christine. 1980 [1975]. *Gramsci and the State.* London: Lawrence & Wishart.

Calderón Gutierrez, Fernando. 1987. "Os movimentos sociais frente a crise." In *Uma revolução no cotidiano? Os novos movimentos sociais na América do Sul*, ed. I. Scherer-Warren and P. Krischke. São Paulo: Editora Brasiliense.

Calderón, Fernando and Elizabeth Jelin. 1987. "Classes sociais e movimentos sociais na América Latina." *Revista Brasileira de Ciências Sociais* 2, no. 5: 67–85.

Camacho, Daniel. 1987. "Movimentos sociais: algumas discussões conceituais." In *Uma revolução no cotidiano? Os novas movimentos sociais na América do Sul*, ed. I. Scherer-Warren and P. Krischke. São Paulo: Editora Brasiliense.

Cardoso, Fernando H. 1973. "Associated Dependent Development: Theoretical and Political Implications." In *Authoritarian Brazil: Origins, Politics and Future*, ed. A. Stepan. New Haven, CT and London: Yale University Press.

———. 1981. "Regime Politico e mudança social." *Revista de Cultura e Política* 3: 7–25.

Cardoso, Fernando H., and Enzo Faletto. 1976 [1969]. *Abhängigkeit und Entwicklung in Lateinamerika.* Frankfurt: Suhrkamp Verlag.

Cardoso, Ruth C. L. 1983. "Movimentos sociais urbanos: balance crítico." In *Sociedade e política no Brasil pós 64*, ed. B. Sorj and M. H. T. de Almeida. São Paulo: Editora Brasiliense.

———. 1987. "Movimentos sociais na América Latina." *Revista Brasileira de Ciências Sociais* 1, no. 3: 27–37.

———. 1988. "Os movimentos populares no contexto da consolidação da democracia." In *A democracia no Brasil: dilemas e perspectiva*, org. F. Wanderley Reis and G. O'Donnell. São Paulo: Vértice.

Carlo, Antonio. 1973. "Lenin on the Party." *Telos* 17 (Fall): 2–40.

Carnoy, Martin. 1984. *The State and Political Theory*. Princeton, NJ: Princeton University Press.

Castells, Manuel. 1974 [1973]. *Movimientos sociales urbanos*. Mexico City: Siglo XXI.

———. 1977 [1972]. *The Urban Question*. London: Edward Arnold Publishers.

———. 1983. *The City and the Grassroots*. London: Edward Arnold Publishers.

Clark, John. 1979/80. "Marx, Bakunin and the Problem of Social Transformation." *Telos* 42 (Winter): 80–97.

Clegg, Stewart. R. 1989. *Frameworks of Power*. London, Newbury Park, New Delhi: SAGE Publications.

Cohen, Jean. L. 1982. "Between Crisis Management and Social Movements: The Place of Institutional Reform." *Telos* 52 (Summer): 21–40.

———. 1985. "Strategy or Identity: New Theoretical Paradigms and Contemporary Social Movements." *Social Research* 52, no. 4: 663–716.

Collier, David. ed. 1979. *The New Authoritarianism in Latin America*. Princeton, NJ: Princeton University Press.

Connell, Raewyn W. 1979. "A Critique of the Althusserian Approach to Class." *Theory and Society* 8 no. 3: 303–345.

Coraggio, José L. 1985. "Social Movements and Revolution: The Case of Nicaragua." In *New Social Movements and the State in Latin America*, ed. D. Slater. Amsterdam: CEDLA.

Corten, Monique, and Annemiek Onstenk 1981. "Sterft, gij oude vormen en gedachten; een feministische kritiek op leninistische organisatieprincipes." *Socialisties-Feministiese Teksten* 6: 81–110.

Cruz, Rafael de la. 1987. "Os novos movimentoss: encontros e desencontros com a democracia." In *Uma revolugao no cotidiano? Os novos movirnentos sociais na América do Sul*, ed. I. Scherer-Warren and P. Krischke. São Paulo: Editora Brasiliense.

Durham, Eunice R. 1984. "Movimentos sociais: a construção da cidadania." *Novos Estudos Cebrab* 10: 24–30.

Eder, Klaus. 1982. "A New Social Movement?" *Telos* 52 (Summer): 5–20.

———. 1985. "The 'New Social Movements': Moral Crusades, Political Pressure Groups, or Social Movements?" *Social Research* 52, no. 4: 869–890.

Espinoza, Vicente. 1984. "Movimiento popular urbano y procesos de institucionalización politica." *Proposiciones* 11: 57–65.

Evers, Tilman. 1985. "Identity: The Hidden Side of New Social Movements in Latin America." In *New Social Movements and the State in Latin America*, ed. D. Slater. Amsterdam: CEDLA.

Evers, Tilman, Clarissa Müller-Plantenberg, and Stefanie Spessart. 1979. "Stadtteilbewegung und Staat: Kämpfe im Reproduktionsbereich in Lateinamerika." In *Lateinamerika: analysen und berichte 3*, ed. V. Bennholdt-Thomsen, T. Evers, and K. Meschkat. Berlin: Olle und Wolter.

Fals Borda, Orlando. 1988. "El nuevo despertar de los movimientos sociales." In *Participacion comunitaria y cambio social en Colombia*, O. Fals Borda et al. Bogotá: DNP, CINEP, ACS, UNICEF.

Featherstone, Mike. 1988. "In Pursuit of the Postmodern: An Introduction." *Theory, Culture & Society* 5, no. 2–3: 195–217.

Forman, Shepard. 1971. "Disunity and Discontent: A Study of Peasant Political Movements in Brazil." *Latin American Studies* 3: 14–16.

Foucault, Michel. 1966. *Les mots et les choses*. Paris: Gallimard.

Fraser, Nancy and Linda Nicholson. 1988. "Social Criticism without Philosophy: An Encounter between Feminism and Postmodernism." *Theory, Culture & Society* 5, no. 2–3: 83–104.

Friedmann, John. 1984. "The Latin American *Barrio* Movement as a Social Movement: Contribution to a Debate." *Journal of Urban and Regional Research* 13, no. 3: 501–510.

Garcia, Francisco G. 1987. "Las Organizaciones No Gubernamentales de Desarrollo y los Procesos de Democratización en America Latina." *Socialismo y Participación* 40.

Geras, Norman. 1987. "Post Marxism?" *New Left Review* 163: 40–82.

Gerratana, Valentino. 1981 [1969]. "Gramsci en het begrip van de burgerlijke maatschappij." *Te Elfder Ure 28/Marxistiese Staatstheorie 2: Gramsci* 25, no. 2: 397–402

Giddens, Anthony. 1986 [1984]. *The Constitution of Society.* Cambridge, U.K.: Polity Press.

Gohn, María da Glória M. 1988. "Luta pela moradia popular em São Paulo: movimentos de moradia 1975/85." In *ANPOCS: ciências sociais hoje.* São Paulo: Vértice/ANPOCS.

Gramsci, Antonio. 1986 [1971]. *Selections from the Prison Notebooks.* London: Lawrence & Wishart.

Habermas, Jürgen. 1981a. "Toward a Reconstruction of Historical Materialism." In *Advances in Social Theory and Methodology: Toward an Integration of Micro- and Macro-Sociologies,* ed. K. Knorr-Cetina and A. V. Cicourel. Boston, London, Henley: Routledge & Kegan Paul.

———. 1981b. "New Social Movements." *Telos* 49 (Fall): 33–37.

Hobsbawm, Eric. 1978 [1959]. *Primitive Rebels.* Manchester: Manchester University Press.

———. 1980. "Movimentos pre-politicos em areas perifericas." In *O estado autoritario e movimentos populares,* coord. P. S. Pinheiro. São Paulo: Paz e Terra.

———. 1987. *The Age of Empire 1875–1914.* London: Weidenfeld & Nicolson.

Honneth, Axel., Eberhard Knödler-Bunte, and Arno Widmann. 1981. "The Dialectics of Rationalization: An Interview with Jurgen Habermas." *Telos* 49 (Fall): 5–31.

Jacobi, Pedro R. 1987. "Movimentos sociais: teoria e pratica em questão." In *Uma revolução no cotidiano? Os novos movimentos sociais na América do Sul,* ed. I. Scherer-Warren and P. Krischke. São Paulo: Editora Brasiliense.

———. 1988. "Movimentos sociais e estado: efeitos politico-institucionais da ação coletiva." In *ANPOCS: ciências sociais hoje.* São Paulo: Vertice/ANPOCS.

———. 1989. *Movimentos sociais e politicos públicas.* São Paulo: Cortez.

Jameson, Fredric. 1989. "Marxism and Postmodernism." *New Left Review* 176: 31–46.

Jessop, Bob. 1984 [1982]. *The Capitalist State.* Oxford, U.K.: Basil Blackwell.

Kärner, Hartmut. 1987. "Movimentos sociais: revolucão cotidiano." In *Uma revolução no cotidiano? Os novos movimentos socials na América do Sul,* ed. I. Scherer-Warren and P. Krischke. São Paulo: Editora Brasiliense.

Kollontaj, Alexandra. 1983 [1921]. *De Arbeidersoppositie.* Amsterdam: IPSO.

Kowarick, Lucio. 1985. "The Pathways to Encounter: Reflections on the Social Struggle in São Paulo." In *New Social Movements and the State in Latin America,* ed. D. Slater. Amsterdam: CEDLA.

Kriegel, Annie. 1975. "Die Internationale Arbeiterassoziation." In *Geschichte des Sozialismus III,* ed. J. Droz. Frankfurt, Berlin, Vienna: Ullstein.

Krischke, Paulo J. 1987. "Movimentos sociais na transição politica: contribuções da democracia de base." In *Uma revolução no cotidiano? Os novos movimentos socials na América do Sul,* ed. I. Scherer-Warren and P. Krischke. São Paulo: Editora Brasiliense.

Kunneman, Harrie. 1986. *De Waarheidstrechter.* Meppel: Boom Publishers.

Laclau, Ernesto. 1977. *Politics and Ideology in Marxist Theory.* London: New Left Books.

———. 1981. "Teorias Marxistas del estado: debates y perspectivas." In *Estado y politica en América Latina,* ed. N. Lechner. Mexico City: Siglo XXI.

———. 1984. "Transformations of Advanced Industrial Societies and the Theory of the Subject." In *Rethinking Ideology: A Marxist Debate,* ed. S. Hänninen and L. Paldán. Berlin: Argument Verlag.

———. 1985. "New Social Movements and the Plurality of the Social." In *New Social Movements and the State in Latin America,* ed. D. Slater. Amsterdam: CEDLA.

———. 1988. "Metaphor and Social Antagonisms." In *Marxism and the Interpretation of Culture*, ed. C. Nelson and L. Grossberg. Urbana and Chicago: University of Illinois Press.

Laclau, Ernesto, and Chantal Mouffe. 1985. *Hegemony and Socialist Strategy*. London: Verso Books.

———. 1987. "Post Marxism without Apologies." *New Left Review* 166: 110–112.

Lechner, Norbert. 1986. *La democratización en el contexto de una cultura postmoderna*. Working Paper no. 292, April. Santiago: FLASCO,

Lenin, Wladimir Iljitsj. 1971. *Ausgewählte Werke*. Moscow: Progress.

———. 1976 [1921]. *Wat te doen?* Amsterdam: Pegasus.

Levi-Strauss, Claude. 1962. *La pensée sauvage*. Paris: Plon.

Livesay, Jeff. 1989. "Structuration Theory and the Unacknowledged Conditions of Action." *Theory, Culture and Society* 6, no. 3: 263–292.

Lojkine, Jean. 1980 [1977]. *O estado capitalista e a questão urbana*. São Paulo: Martins Fontes.

Lowe, Stuart. 1986. *Urban Social Movements: The City after Castells*. Houndmills: Macmillan.

Lukács, Georg. 1988 [1923]. *Geschichte und Klassenbewusstsein*. Darmstadt: Luchterhand.

Luxemburg, Rosa. 1974. *Schriften zur Theorie de Spontaneität*. Reinbek: Rowohlt.

Lyotard, Jean-François. 1979. *La condition postmoderne*. Paris: Minuit.

Macdonell, Diane. 1987 [1961]. *Theories of Discourse*. Oxford, U.K.: Basil Blackwell.

Mainwaring, Scott. 1987. "Urban Popular Movements, Identity, and Democratization in Brazil." *Comparative Political Studies* 20, no. 2: 131–159.

Mainwaring, Scott, and Eduardo Viola. 1984. "New Social Movements, Political Culture, and Democracy: Brazil and Argentina in the 1980s." *Telos* 61 (Fall): 17–52.

Marx, Karl. 1974. *Oekonomisch-philosophische Manuskripte*. Leipzig: Reclam.

———. 1984. *Pre-Capitalist Economic Formations, with an Introduction by E. J. Hobsbawm*. New York: International Publishers.

Marx, Karl, and Frederic Engels. 1970. *Selected Works*. Moscow: Progress.

———. 1974. *Staatstheorie, Materialien zur Rekonstruktion der marxistischen Staatstheorie*. Frankfurt, Berlin, Vienna: Ullstein.

Melucci, Alberto. 1980. "The New Social Movements: A Theoretical Approach." *Social Science Information* 9, no. 2:199–226 .

———. 1985. "The Symbolic Challenge of Contemporary Movements." *Social Research* 52, no. 4: 789–816.

Meschkat, Klaus. 1971. *Die Pariser Kommune von 1871*. Cologne: Infodruck.

Moisés, José A. 1982 [1979]. "O estado, as contradiçõesu e os movimentos sociais." In *Cidade, povo e poder*, J. A. Moisés et al. Rio de Janeiro: Paz e Terra.

Monteiro, Hamilton de Mattos. 1980. *Crise agrária e luta de classes: o nordeste brasileiro entre 1850 e 1889*. Brasília: Horizonte.

Moore, Barrington, Jr. 1977 [1966]. *Social Origins of Dictatorship and Democracy*. Harmondsworth: Penguin Books.

Mouffe, Chantal. 1984. "The Sex/Gender System and the Discursive Construction of Women's Subordination." In *Rethinking Ideology: A Marxist Debate*, ed. S. Hänninen and L. Paldán. Berlin: Argument.

———. 1988. "Hegemony and New Political Subjects: Toward a New Concept of Democracy." In *Marxism and the Interpretation of Culture*, ed. C. Nelson and L. Grossberg. Urbana and Chicago: University of Illinois Press.

Mouzelis, Nicos. 1978. "Ideology and Class Politics: A Critique of Ernesto Laclau." *New Left Review* 112: 45–61.

Nascimento, Eduardo P. do. 1987. "Notas sobre o conceito de movimentos sociais urbanos." *Revista de Desenvolvimento Urbano e Regional* 2, no. 1: 41–57.

Nunes, Edison. 1989. "Carências urbanas, reivindicações sociais e valores democráticos." *Lua Nova* 17: 67–91.

O'Brien, Philip, and Paul Cammack, eds. 1985. *Generals in Retreat: The Crisis of Military Rule in Latin America*. Manchester: Manchester University Press.

O'Donnell, Guillermo. 1973. *Modernization and Bureaucratic-Authoritarianism*. Berkeley: University of California.

Offe, Claus. 1985. "New Social Movements: Challenging the Boundaries of Institutional Politics." *Social Research* 52, no. 4: 817–868.

———. 1988. *Partidos políticos y nuevos movimientos sociales*. Madrid: Editorial Sistema.

Ortner, Sherry B. 1984. "Theory in Anthropology since the Sixties." *Comparative Studies in Society and History* 26, no. 1: 126–166.

Paramio, Ludolfo. 1987. "Del radicalismo reivindicativo al pluralismo radical." In *Cultura política y democratización*, comp. N. Lechner. Buenos Aires: CLASCO, FLASCO, ICI.

———. 1989 [1987]. "Após o Dilúvio: Introduçao ao Pós-Marxismo." *Lua Nova* 16.

Perlman, Janice. 1979 [1970]. *The Myth of Marginality*. Berkeley, Los Angeles, London: University of California Press.

Poulantzas, Nicos. 1974 [1970]. *Fascisme et Dictature*. Paris: Seuil, Maspero.

———. 1975 [1974]. *Klassen im Kapitalismus Heute*. West Berlin: VSA.

———. 1980a [1968]. *Pouvoir politique et classes sociales I*. Paris: Maspero.

———. 1980b [1968]. *Pouvoir politique et classes sociales I*. Paris: Maspero.

———. 1983 [1979]. "O estado, os movimentos sociais, o partido (Ultima entrevista com nicos poulantzas)." *Espaco e Debates* 3, no. 9: 70–79.

Quijano, Anibal. 1979. *Problema agraria y movimientos carnpesinos*. Lima: Mosca Azul Editores.

Reis, Fabio Wanderley. 1988. "Identidade, politica e teoria da escolha racional." *Revista Brasileira de Ciências Sociais* 3, no. 6: 26–38.

Reyes Posada, Alejandro. 1986. "La participación en la acción colectiva y la autoproducción de la sociedad." In *Participación comunitaria y cambio social en colombia*, O. Fals Borda et al. Bogotá: DNP, CINEP, ACS, UNICEF.

Roberts, Brian. R. 1978. *Cities of Peasants: The Political Economy of Urbanization in the Third World*. London: Edward Arnold Publishers.

Rudé, George. 1980. *The Crowd in History*. London: Lawrence & Wishart.

———. 1981. *Ideology and Popular Protes*. London: Lawrence & Wishart.

Scherer-Warren, Ilse. 1987. "O caráter dos novos movimentos sociais." In *Uma revolução no cotidiano? Os novos movimentos sociais na América do Sul*, ed. I. Scherer-Warren and P. Krischke. São Paulo: Editora Brasiliense.

Schneider, Dieter M., ed. 1971. *Pariser kommune 1871 II, texte von Marx, Engels, Lenin und Trotzki*. Reinbek: Rowohlt.

Schuurman, Frans J. 1989. "Urban Social Movements: Between Regressive Utopia and Socialist Panacea." In *Urban Social Movements in the Third World*, ed. F. J. Schuurman and T. van Naerssen. London and New York: Routledge.

Schuurman, Frans J., and Ton van Naerssen, eds. 1989. *Urban Social Movements in the Third World*. London: Routledge.

Silva, Luis A. Machado da, and Ana C. T. Ribeiro. n.d. "Paradigma e movimento social: por onde andam nossas idéias?" In *ANPOCS: ciências sociais hoje*. São Paulo: Cortez.

Skocpol, Theda. 1984 [1979]. *States and Social Revolutions: A Comparative Analysis of France, Russia and China*. New York: Cambridge University Press.

Slater, David. 1985. "Social Movements and a Recasting of the Political." In *New Social Movements and the State in Latin America*, ed. D. Slater. Amsterdam: CEDLA.

Smart, B. 1982. "Foucault, Sociology, and the Problem of Human Agency." *Theory and Society* 11, no. 2: 121–141.

———. 1987 [1986]. "The Politics of Truth and the Problem of Hegemony." In *Foucault: A Critical Reader*, ed. D. C. Hoy. Oxford, U.K. and New York: Basil Blackwell.

Soper, Kate. 1989. "Feminism as Critique." *New Left Review* 176: 91–112.

Souza-Martins, José de. 1985. "Los campesinos y la politica en el Brasil." In *História politica de los campesinos Latinoamericanos, Vol. IV*, coord. P. Gonzales Casanova. Mexico City: Siglo XXI.

Sposati, Aldaíza. 1988. *Vida urbana e gestão da pobreza*. São Paulo: Cortez.

Stuurman, Siep. 1985. *De Labyrintische Staat*. Amsterdam: SUA.

Telles, Vera da Silva. 1987. "Movimentos sociais: reflexões sobre a experiência dos anos 70." In *Uma revolução no cotidiano? Os novas movimentos sociais na América do Sul*, ed. I. Scherer-Warren and P. Krischke. São Paulo: Editora Brasiliense.

Therborn, Goran. 1980. *The Ideology of Power and the Power of Ideolog*. London: Verso.

Tilly, Charles, Louise Tilly, and Richard Tilly. 1975. *The Rebellious Century*. Cambridge, MA: Harvard University Press.

Touraine, Alain. 1973. *Production de la societé*. Paris: Seuil.

———1976. *Les Sociétés Dependantes*. Bruxelles: Duculot.

———1978. *La voix et le regard*. Paris: Seuil.

———1988. *Politique et société en Amérique latine*. Paris: Odile Jacob

Vargas, Virginia. 1989. *El aporte de la rebeldía de las mujeres*. Lima: Flora Tistán.

Vigevani, Tullo. 1989. "Movimentos Sociais na Transicao Brasileira: A Dificuldade de Elaboracao do Projeto." *Lua Nova* 17: 93–109.

Vink, Nico. 1985. " Base communities and urban social movements." In: *New Social Movements and the State in Latin America*, ed. D. Slater. Amsterdam: CEDLA, 95–125.

Weffort, Francisco. 1986. *O populismo na Política Brasileira*. 3ª ed. Rio de Janeiro: Paz e Terra.

2 Urban Social Movements, Democratization, and Democracy in Brazil

Introduction

When Brazil entered its drawn-out process of democratic transition in the mid-1970s, one of the striking phenomena was the proliferation and vitality of neighborhood-based organizations and activism among the urban poor. Had not a kind of consensus been reached by then among social scientists about the latter's relative conservatism and lack of revolutionary aspirations? That consensus had partly developed in response to versions of marginality theory that either feared or cherished a revolutionary propensity among the urban poor. Their social discontent, it was now argued, was limited, since they had turned out not to be so marginal after all, but they were vulnerable and therefore would hardly be prepared to take risks (see Kleinpenning 1978: 217). Nevertheless, the poor were politically active. The Cost of Living Movement, which originated in the Mother Clubs and Ecclesiastical Base Communities of São Paulo's outskirts in 1972, six years later presented a petition with 1.3 million signatures to the federal authorities in Brasilia. It caught widespread attention as a prominent example of the new activism of the urban poor. Through this movement slum-dwellers played a leading role in "the fight to win back the streets as an arena for political expression" (Kucinski 1982: 64).

The new activism was accompanied by a proliferation of studies of what soon came to be called the "new urban social movements." The tone was set in the opening chapter of a pioneering anthology of studies on popular movements which stated that, if previous studies of the urban popular classes in Brazil had largely been dedicated to explaining their absence from the political scene, the time had come to deal with their presence (Singer and Brant 1980). Such statements also suggest the connections between the Brazilian debate and the ongoing process of political transition. Questions of political strategy were always on the horizon and, following a national agenda, the debate was linked to current global debate about the future of democracy and socialist strategy.

The first studies were often inspired by a structuralist Marxist framework. By the early 1980s more culturalist and actor-oriented viewpoints became predominant and, somewhat later, "institutionalist" interpretations made an appearance and drew attention to the interface between movements and the institutional system/state apparatuses. In this way, the Brazilian debate reflected international trends in social movement research, where traditions rooted in different continents gradually entered into an increasingly rich and fruitful exchange. This is manifest in the calls for a synthesis between identity-centered theories and strategy-oriented perspectives. The former approach was linked to the body of new social movement theory that emerged in Europe from the 1970s and also tended to predominate in Latin America. The latter drew inspiration from the North American resource mobilization and political process tradition.

Curiously, the once so prominent Marxist tradition in Brazil, which inspired the "paradigm of the 1970s" (Assies 1990: 73), seems to have fallen victim to a sort of amnesia, or perhaps a patricidal denial of the roots of much of the debate. Nevertheless, despite the ossified structuralist scholastics that it had sometimes turned into before being abruptly relegated to oblivion, such a macro-level approach does go some way toward explaining the prominence of urban conflict in Brazil. If it falls short in answering the questions of the "when?" and the "how?" of movement emergence, it may have something to say about the "why?"

The various strands of social movement theory have their strong and weak points. Thus while the culturalist and identity-oriented tradition often tends to disregard both conditioning factors and the strategic features of movement activity, the "resource mobilization and political process approaches have tended to reduce movement activity to mere strategy without paying much attention to normative features or motivations beyond utilitarian cost-benefit calculation" (Salman 1990). Communication among the different traditions has increased in recent years, together with a mutual recognition that something can be learned from dialogue.

The new activism of the urban poor, of which the Cost of Living Movement was one of the more visible manifestations, was among the phenomena that marked the beginning of a protest cycle. The cycle ran its course between about 1975 and 1990. It reached its peak around 1984, the year of the campaign for direct presidential elections—*Diretas-Já*—which mobilized millions of Brazilians. Using notions from different theoretical perspectives, I shall examine the issues of the why, when, and how of urban social movements in Brazil. I shall then sketch their trajectory through the protest cycle and finally discuss the outcomes of their activities in terms of their contribution to democratization and democracy.

Why?

A question most directly themalized in the paradigm of the 1970s concerned the conditions of emergence of urban protest. The basic texts of this theoretical elaboration can be found in two collections published in 1977 and 1981 (Moisés 1977; 1981). It drew on the new Marxist theories of urban social movements developed by Castells (1972), Borja (1975), and Lojkine (1977). Their insights were related and adapted to the Brazilian situation by linking them to theories of late dependent industrialization and the political regimes that accompanied the process, namely, populism and the new authoritarianism that had been imposed in 1964.

The notion of urban contradictions was central to these theories. It refers to the contradiction between the increasing need for collective consumer goods for the reproduction of labor power as a result of capitalist development and the logic of public and private investment that tends to privilege services and infrastructure in support of the accumulation process. If this contradiction exists in the "classic" capitalist countries, it was argued, it is exacerbated under the conditions of capitalist accumulation on a "poor basis" in the peripheral countries. In these countries, the labor force tends to be overexploited while, at the same time, access to land, housing, and basic goods and services vital to the subsistence of workers is precarious or nonexistent.

A second feature of the paradigm was that it absorbed some ideas from the theories of populism, notably concerning the structural heterogeneity of the Brazilian subaltern classes, which was contrasted with the relative homogeneity of the working class of the "classic" capitalist countries. In such a context of structural heterogeneity, it was argued, neighborhood (rather than shop floor) references and issues of collective consumption (rather than wages) would play a key role in the formation of a popular (rather than a class) consciousness. And the state—as the agent of redistribution—(rather than the employer) became the target, an aspect that also related to the experience of populism, which had legitimized the state as an addressee for demand making.

On the basis of such theoretical elaborations, the orthodox Marxist view of urban struggles as only secondary to the class struggle was rejected for its Eurocentrism. Latin America has its own specific dynamics, it was argued and, in a situation of peripheral capitalism, urban movements were to play a particularly prominent role in the anti-capitalist struggle. These elaborations contributed to outlining the conditions of emergence of the new urban movements. They fell short, however, as far as activism and "consciousness" among the urban poor was concerned. Despite some references to historical experience, activism and consciousness tended to be viewed as arising spontaneously from the contradictions experienced by the urban poor. Structural conditions, however, only provide the backdrop, the raw material that potentially nourishes social struggles, but "between concrete conditions of existence and social struggles, there are many mediations" (Kowarick 1986: 16). That brings us to the questions of when and how.

When?

If the raw material for social struggles is there, why do they only erupt at certain moments? The concept of political opportunity structure, developed in the resource mobilization and political process literature, is a useful tool in approaching this question. It refers to the dimensions of the political environment that provide incentives for people to undertake collective action by affecting their expectations for success or failure. The features most commonly included are the relative openness or enclosure of the institutionalized political system, the stability or instability of ruling alignments and cleavages within and among elites, the availability of influential allies, and the state's capacity and propensity for repression (Foweraker 1995: 71; Tarrow 1994: 86). Shifts in the opportunity structure may precipitate a protest cycle that, in turn, affects the structure of opportunity.

I have already mentioned in passing the historical experience of populism in Brazil and the incorporation of theories of populism into the new theorizing about urban movements in the 1970s. Populism was related to the unstable alignments of the "compromise state" that had come into being with Vargas's takeover in 1930. The underlying dynamic of the populist political regime and its compromise politics consisted of playing off the masses' desire for mobility against the oligarchy's fear of revolution. In moments of elite cleavage, politicians might appeal to the urban masses for support in exchange for some concessions or handouts. This form of legitimation relies on a tradeoff between social and political rights and tends to reduce the urban population to a "mass for maneuver" in the political game. On the other hand, such concessions were perceived as rights and contributed to a sense of citizenship and demands for increased participation. The fear of increasingly autonomous and radical mobilization of the popular masses contributed to the military clamp-down in 1964.

The installation and gradual hardening of the authoritarian regime foreclosed the prospects for enhanced popular participation and integration. It also belied the predictions of modernization theorists who held that economic development on the periphery would bring with it political stability and democracy. Some analyses of the rise of the new authoritarian regimes in Latin America tended to stand this thesis on its head and to assert that economic development on the periphery leads to authoritarian rule. And, if that were the case, the only way out would be a structural transformation of society that is socialism. If, moreover, the ambiguity of the populist game had allowed for a perception of the capitalist state as an addressee for demand making, the mask of ambiguity had been dropped in 1964. Therefore, it was argued, rather than addressing and petitioning the state, the new movements moved "against the state" (Oliveira 1977: 75). In suggesting spontaneous mass resistance to the authoritarian capitalist state, such views were appealing and certainly played a motivating role in the expansion of urban movements. A closer look at events with the help of the concept of political opportunity structure reveals a more complex picture, however.

The 1964 coup, carried out by a coalition of different groups of the military establishment, had enjoyed the backing of a broad, but heterogeneous, array of social sectors united in their fear of chaos and revolution. It included diverse fractions of the dominant classes, as well as important sectors of the petit bourgeoisie, the liberal professions and the new bureaucratic middle classes. The Catholic Church had also expressed its support. By the mid-1970s, fissures in this alignment became increasingly visible. Once the attempted guerrilla movements of 1967–1971 had been crushed, the terrorist hard-liners among the military gradually lost influence. In 1974 a new military president announced "distension," a relaxation of authoritarianism aiming at the institutionalization of a military civil authoritarian regime. In the same year, however, the Brazilian miracle economy underwent the effects of the oil shock. Industrialists started a campaign against state intervention in the economy, which they feared would protect the state sector from the effects of the oil crisis and leave the private sector exposed. Meanwhile, middle-class groups had gradually become disaffected and the church had moved into clear opposition to the regime. By the end of the year, elections for federal deputies unexpectedly turned into a plebiscite against the regime. What is known as the "reawakening of civil society" had begun, first exploring the limits of "distension" and then expanding them and forcing the announcement of a "democratic opening"—a negotiated transition to civilian rule—in 1979.

After ten years of authoritarian rule, which had been particularly repressive between 1968 and 1974, the political opportunity structure was therefore changing. Opportunities alone, however, do not account for the emergence of social movements. They must be seized. They constitute an external resource for groups prepared to make use of them, shape and expand them. This directs attention to the how of movements.

How?

Neighborhood organizations had existed before in Brazil. The Associations of Friends of the Neighborhood (SABs) that emerged in São Paulo in the

1950s with strong links to populist politician Jânio Quadros' political machine are the most often quoted example of the "old" movements. One feature of the new urban movements that has been stressed to underscore their newness was that their ideology would be completely different from that which inspired the movements of the previous decade. Instead of attributing their problems to negligence by the authorities, which might be overcome by drawing their attention sufficiently, privation was now attributed to the very social organization inherent in capitalism. Moreover, clientelist politics—the exchange of votes for favors—were rejected as immoral at best, and the new movements set a high value on active participation, a guarantee to their being the "authentic" expressions of the popular neighborhood movement (Singer 1980: 91). Such features distinguished the new movements from those of the populist period and also set them off from the left-wing tradition of manipulative vanguardism.

Movements do not simply and spontaneously spring from urban contradictions, however, and many interventions were indeed involved. Outlining the historical roots of Brazil's "new popular movement," Eder Sader (1988: 144) refers to three institutions that had entered into an existential crisis and therefore opened up for innovation. The Catholic Church was losing ground among the population and launched the strategy of base communities. The Left had been defeated and disarticulated and sought new forms of "integration with the workers." And the trade-union structure, emptied of any meaningful content or function, motivated the emergence of a new trade unionism, of which future presidential candidate Lula da Silva was a main exponent. These three institutions "in crisis" made up micromobilization contexts—social networks that underpin "identity" (Foweraker 1995: 20)—from which the new popular movement emerged.

The Catholic Church, which in 1968 had endorsed liberation theology and the strategy of ecclesial base communities (CEBs), was crucial in the new urban movements (Lehmann 1990: 88–147). The "popular church"—semi-independent from the official church—engendered a maze of interlocking social networks, ranging from the local to the national level. At the most basic level, the CEBs constituted micromobilization contexts and spaces for discursive and symbolic elaboration inspired by the "methodology" of seeing, judging, and acting:

> We began the meeting reading a passage from the Gospel, you see? On the journey of the People, how the people developed, the Old Testament etc. And we commented a little, you see? . . . Through the work in the communities (we found out) that God is the father of everybody, you see? That he is not stepfather to one and father to the other. He is everybody's father. So

if I am suffering? Why? Because somebody makes me suffer. So we should find out who makes us suffer (Interview, Recife, November 10, 1988).

In such gatherings would-be squatters might, for example, prepare for taking the "promised land." Wider networks could be mobilized, and mass might be read to legitimize a squat and avoid bloody confrontations with the police. Resources for drawing up petitions or pamphlets, meeting spaces, legal assistance, and funding for small neighborhood projects could be obtained.

Beside pastoral workers, other agents involved in the social construction of the popular movement were militants from various left-wing groups, sectors of the new middle class such as welfare workers, urban planners, and academics and sympathizers from the liberal professions, such as lawyers. Through pedagogical efforts and by offering their professional knowledge, these "external actors" sought to contribute to the growth of the movement. Some of them found employment in a growing sector of NGOs "at the service of the popular movement" (Landim 1988). The church, left-wing parties, NGOs, and universities provided the institutional framework for a support network in civil society and points of intersection and articulation between middle class and popular activism (Assies 1994). Beyond the local level, grassroots activists participated in all sorts of courses, conferences, and citywide, regional, and national meetings, where they "exchanged experiences" and discussed future activities. This web of interlocking social and institutional networks, for which the church was a central support, accounted for discursive alignment and purposefulness. It constituted an ethico-political field self-identified as "the popular movement" (Doimo 1995).

The Protest Cycle

The Cost of Living Movement emerged from the base communities and Mother Clubs of São Paulo's peripheries to become a campaign of national impact. Other such movements were the Movement for Housing, a Movement of Struggle against Unemployment, a Health Movement, and a Movement for Collective Transport. They were among the multifarious manifestations of the popular movement and arose as components of the protest cycle of the 1975–1990 period.

Once a protest cycle has taken off, it generates its own dynamic. It is not a simple matter of "what goes up must come down," but a play of moves, alliances, and countermoves, the outcomes of which cannot be established beforehand. After the "early risers" have set an example and exposed the vulnerability of the authorities, others join the fray and adversaries, allies, and authorities react (Tarrow 1994: 155). In the course of the cycle, new issues emerge and impact the agenda and the opportunity structure is shaped and reshaped. With hindsight, one can distinguish several phases in the cycle.

1975–1979

This was the period of reawakening of civil society and the emergence of the "authentic" movements. Beside the growth of neighborhood activism, the metal workers' strikes in the São Paulo region marked the emergence of a new trade-unionism. New branches for pastoral work were created, such as the *Pastoral das Favelas*, and NGO activity also expanded. As urban movement activism proliferated and the electoral process became more important, the state was forced to develop a strategy to respond to them. Repression gave way to trivialization and clientelist practices became more widespread.

1979–1985

The PROMORAR housing program was a hallmark of this shift to flexible response. It was launched in 1979 and would resolutely be tuned down after the 1982 elections—crucial to the engineering of the transition process— when the government felt safe enough to take austerity measures. It was announced that the program was to benefit the lowest-income sectors, an intention that had been heard before. More importantly, it replaced the policy of favela removal with a policy of on-site improvement and, above all, the new program would be "participatory." Through this program and others promoting "communitarian action" funding became available to be applied in clientelist responses and the creation of parallel neighborhood organizations, meant to shore up support for the party of the regime, the *Partido Democratico Social* (PDS) (Assies 1992: 154–160).

The dynamics of party organization among the opposition also impacted on neighborhood organizations. The *Partido dos Trabalhadores* (PT), claiming to be the authentic political representation of the popular movement, emerged alongside the *Partido do Movimento Democratico Brasileiro* (PMDB), the somewhat left-of-center broad front opposition party involved in the negotiations over the transition. This development was reflected in the creation of rival national level umbrella organizations for the popular movement, the *Articulação Nacional dos Movimentos Populares e Sindicais* (ANAMPOS) and the *Confederação Nacional das Associações de Moradores* (CONAM). Such dynamics promoted an increase in the number of neighborhood organizations, as well as rifts between the self-proclaimed "authentic" organizations and other new organizations, some of them true rivals and others just relatively innocent newcomers exploring the opportunities opened up by the early risers.

During this period the church gradually started looking after its institutional interests, became more restrictive and conservative and disengaged itself from the popular movements. The movements were "emancipated." This development was paralleled by the loosening of ties between the church and the NGOs. Their typical trajectory was one from organizations associated with the church toward secularization and from assistentialist work to a more political outlook (Fernandes 1988: 9). The Workers' Party (PT) became the main referent in the ethico-political field of the "popular movement."

This was the period of ascendance in the protest cycle, of febrile petitioning and pressuring at the local level and of more general campaigning and articulation. The *Diretas-Já* campaign in 1984 was the most massive manifestation in the cycle. That cause was lost, however. An electoral college elected Tancredo Neves, who never assumed office, however, as he was overtaken by a fatal illness. In the event, presidential power was transferred to Jose Sarney, who had only recently been the leader of the pro-military party.

1985–1988

One of the first things allowed after the return to civilian rule were direct elections for mayorship in the state capitals and other cities that, until then, had fallen under national security regulations. Left-wing parties or coalitions won the elections in various cities. Experiments with alternative forms of more democratic and participative local government spread (Assies 1993). In Fortaleza, capital of Ceara, a Workers' Party administration attempted "popular government." At a national level, the agenda was set by the preparations for a new constitution. Its elaboration was accompanied by intense lobbying and mobilization around popular amendments presented by the National Movement of Struggle for Urban Reform, an articulation of movements, NGOs, and professional associations. Some of its suggestions would be included in somewhat watered-down versions in the 1988 constitution, which, for the first time, contained a chapter on urban policies.

The constitution was decentralizing and municipalist, a tendency that found support throughout the political spectrum. It increased the share of total Brazilian tax revenues going to municipalities. It broadened the scope of municipal policies, strengthened the role of the legislature, enhanced opportunities for popular participation and introduced some new instruments for urban policy. The translation of these principles into practice depended on their elaboration in state and municipal legislation. At the municipal level, this involved the formulation of Municipal Organic Laws and the elaboration of Master Plans for cities with over twenty thousand inhabitants.

1988–1992

In the 1988 municipal elections the Workers' Party won in some thirty municipalities, including São Paulo. Before 1988, experiments with "popular administration" and government through "popular councils" had already taken place in various municipalities. These experiments had made clear that governing effectively at a local level was a quite complicated matter, but little systematic thought had been given to the issue. That changed now. New experiments in which popular participation and efficient local government were to be combined got under way. While the 1988–1992 Workers' Party administration in São Paulo had not been an undivided success, in other cities, innovative participatory policies fared better.

Meanwhile, however, the protest cycle came to a close. Mobilizations and protests did occur in the early 1990s, but they took a different form, as in the Movement for Ethics in Politics that accompanied the impeachment process against President Collor. As an offshoot of the Ethics in Politics Movement, the Movement of Action for Citizenship, against Hunger and for Life emerged in 1993. It was a broad-based campaign, rather than a movement, with extensive media coverage. Different social sectors, including the private sector and public enterprises participated in the collection of food and clothes for the poor as a manifestation of social solidarity.

This is, of course, an extremely sketchy outline of some of the main features of the protest cycle and the trajectory of urban movements and movement organizations in the Brazilian democratic transition. In the late 1970s, the movements helped force the authoritarian regime to redefine its political strategy. By the first half of the 1980s, aside from their local pursuits, local level groups, activists, and networks were involved in loosely coordinated, mainly decentralized, nationwide thematic movements around issues like housing, public transport, and health care. During the elaboration of the 1988 constitution, an effort was made to capitalize such activism through the presentation of popular amendments; this marked what was called the shift from confrontation to "propositional action," a development that was further accentuated after the 1988 municipal elections. The gains of the new constitution were to be worked out at a local level in the confection and formalization of new local opportunity structures through the municipal Organic Laws and Master Plans. At the same time, a series of new experiments with innovative local government was under way. If neighborhood activism became less visible and more of a routine by the end of the protest cycle, this did not mean that it disappeared or did not leave a trace. It underwent transformations and contributed to institutionalizing "rituals for democracy." Let us take a closer look at the outcomes.

Outcomes

A new generation of neighborhood associations has emerged since the 1970s. Many have some roots in the meetings of reflection on the life of the poor in the light of the Gospel promoted by pastoral agents. In "solving the problems of the community" they at first often had recourse to self-help. Many local problems, however, can be resolved only through the intervention of municipal agencies. Task groups would be set up to tackle problems of water supply, sanitation, landslides, a school, or a nursery. To pressure the administration, delegations would be sent to make demands. "To get things done," a local leader argued, "you go there and smudge the man's carpet."

In the course of time, such groups underwent a transformation. An informal communitarian model initially predominated, but, by the early 1980s, this tended to be replaced by the more formal model of organization of Residents' Associations with an elected directory. Soon the organization would try to get a headquarters of its own, with the help of NGOs, the church or friendly politicians. NGOs and pastoral agents were often concerned about this development. It tended to be viewed as a result of imposition by the state, which asked for "official representatives," or as a sort of contagion of the communitarian model by its environment, engendering repetition of the relations of power and knowledge characteristic of Brazilian society.

Such a view of institutionalization, however, is somewhat limited. The formal model may have been promoted through interaction with the state, but it is also part of the popular cultural patrimony. Neighborhood residents might be rather proud of having gained the right to organize according to their own wishes. Moreover, the communitarian model should not be romanticized. It often fails to develop mechanisms to deal with internal divergences. Authoritarian mechanisms may crop up to maintain cohesion. Power can very well operate informally and practices of participation and grassroots democracy can turn into empty rhetoric and ritualized procedure. The formalization of organizations was often related to an expansion of their scope of action and efforts to broaden their local base. It can contribute to accountability and transparency of responsibilities and organizational positions. It is no guarantee for democratic functioning, but neither can it be regarded as a priori less democratic.

By the mid-1980s, the initial wave of optimism about the new urban movements gave way to skepticism about their political potential. One reason behind such disappointment was that, in the early analyses, in the name of a critical social science, a social science was produced that was engaged but rather uncritical (Cardoso 1983: 84). The number of people actually involved in grassroots activism was rather small. Moreover, the great attention paid to the expressive aspects often obscured the more pragmatic and installment side of neighborhood activism. Furthermore, the impact on the state tended to be overestimated. Mobilizations obtain responses from public agencies, but in part this merely shows the increased flexibility of such agencies in coping with client groups. The overall activities of the state, however, escape the radius of action of the movements. Nevertheless, as we have noted, the urban movements and their support groups had some impact on the 1988 constitution. In an environment of democratization and greater openness to the pressure of neighborhood movements, decentralization and municipalization seem to have contributed to what Ribeiro (1995: 140) calls "the paradox of the lost decade": while labor market conditions deteriorated and the relative decline in the numbers of the poor stagnated, investment at the municipal level was redirected to the needier areas and social policy performance improved, thus contributing to an improvement in social conditions.

On the other hand, the effective participation of grassroots activists in the elaboration of municipal Organic Laws and Master Plans remained limited. It was mostly NGOs and professional associations that participated, and some mobilization might occur around specific issues. The incorporation of provisions in the Master Plans about the "social function" of urban land and the introduction of measures to facilitate regularization of "illegal settlements" is an advance in which grassroots mobilization certainly played some role. Many municipalities also introduced decentralizing measures and new possibilities for participation through a variety of councils, as well as through possibilities for direct democracy, such as referenda and the right of popular initiative to submit legislative proposals. Formally, this opens up new opportunities, but the effectiveness of such mechanisms is as yet unclear and will partly depend on developments in local opportunity structures that promote or discourage participation. The more radical attempts at local democratization and popular participation are instructive in this respect. They developed from the early proposals for "popular administration" and "government through popular councils." Such proposals were principally supported by the Workers' Party, but actually were little more than slogans and vague ideas about setting up a direct democracy system of popular councils parallel to and in confrontation with the bourgeois state to prepare for a revolutionary rupture, as was the case of Fortaleza between 1985 and 1988. As in other cases, such proposals resulted in disastrous conflicts among the executive, the city council, and the local party organization. Friction between the executive and the local party frequently led to splits between mayors and the party, while lack of flexibility in dealing with the municipal legislature added further conflict. In such a situation, popular councils would be rapidly reduced to mere pawns in the game. On the other hand, the attempts at creating such councils made it increasingly obvious that "the urban social movement" was far less homogenous than had sometimes been thought and that its dynamic is often rather parochialist. It proved to be rather difficult to reconcile the logic of direct action of neighborhood organizations with the logic of representation through popular councils (Assies 1993; Doimo 1995). The victory in thirty-two towns, including São Paulo, in the 1988 municipal elections took the party by surprise. It had hardly reflected upon the dilemmas thrown up by its advocacy of popular councils and tended to think of elections as a means of building profile and membership, rather than as a path to state power. After 1988, however, the issue started to be addressed in internal party debate. The party had to come to terms with the fact of being "in government." This resulted in the replacement of the model of "government through popular councils" by a model that stressed the "negotiation of conflicts and interests." It reaffirmed the authority of the executive based in an electoral mandate and substituted the idea of "popular government" with that of "governing for everyone" to the benefit of the majority of the population. In São Paulo, the Workers' Party administration had some success in inverting the priorities of investment and introducing progressive tax schemes, but much less in promoting the participation it had intended.

In other cities, however, and notably Porto Alegre, experiments with participative budgeting have been more successful. Through rounds of meetings in the administrative districts into which the city has been divided and subsequent city-level meetings of delegates, the population participates in the definition of investment priorities. The process was given wide publicity, placing emphasis on its importance for "the Porto Alegre which is not on the map." According to estimates, no fewer than one hundred thousand persons participate in the process, which was initiated in 1989 and will run for at least another four years after the third consecutive Workers' Party victory in the 1996 municipal elections. Such policies of promoting public debate on the allocation of municipal budget resources have a manifest pedagogic intent. They attempt the institutionalization of public spaces for the confrontation and negotiation of diverging interests in the city. In relation to neighborhood organizations, they seek to break through the corporatism of local level organizations and to undercut clientelism, the counterpart of corporatism. If such efforts run the risk of turning into mere "plebiscitarian populism" dominated by the executive and its supporters (Frey 1996), they also may implicate a profound reconceptualization of the idea of "social transformation." As Lehmann (1990: 147) and Foweraker (1995: 98) have observed, the assumption of earlier radicalisms that there could be no democracy or citizenship without a total "transformation of society has been eclipsed and the theme of citizenship is placed at the forefront of popular movements. This was by no means evident from the outset, however. The present language of rights emerged only gradually, accompanying the shift from confrontation to "propositional action" and the redefinition of the relationship with the institutional sphere (Doimo 1995: 128, 213).

This surely involves what Foweraker (1995: 75) calls a strategic self-transformation. But perhaps it entailed more than a shift from a more expressive identity orientation toward an instrumental approach to the state and the adoption of a different action repertoire, as if these were "phases" inherent in the logic of collective action. It also signifies the adoption of democracy and citizenship as strategic values, not just as a new "action repertoire" convenient for the situation of the moment—that is instrumental—but as ends in themselves, objectives to be constructed. The old distinction between formal and real democracy, while still instructive, has lost its discriminating edge. Democracy and citizenship are viewed as incremental and mutually reinforcing strategies. While they do not imply a rupture with established institutionality, they nevertheless imply its transformation.

Notes

Originally published in 1997 as "Urban Social Movements, Democratization and Democracy in Brazil" in ed. T. van Naerssen, M. Rutten, and A. Zoomers, *The Diversity of Development, Essays in Honour of Jan Kleinpenning*, Assen: Van Gorcum, 302–313. We are grateful to the editors and Van Gorcum Publishers for their permission to republish.

References

Assies, W. 1990. "Of Structured Moves and Moving Structures." In *Structures of Power, Movements of Resistance: An Introduction to the Theories of Urban Movements in Latin America*, W. Assies with T. Salman and G. Burgwal. Amsterdam: CEDLA, 9–98.

———. 1992. *To Get Out of the Mud: Neighborhood Associativism in Recife, 1964–1988*. Amsterdam: CEDLA.

———. 1993. "Urban Social Movement S and Local Democracy in Brazil." *European Review of Latin American and Caribbean Studies* 55: 39–58.

———. 1994. "Urban Social Movements in Brazil: A Debate and its Dynamics." *Latin American Perspectives* 21, no. 2: 81–105.

Borja, J. 1975. *Movimientos sociales urbanos*. Buenos Aires: Ediciones Siap-Planteos.

Cardoso, R. C. L. 1983. "Movimentos sociais urbanos: balanco critic." In *Sociedade e politica no Brasil pós 64*, ed. B. Sorj and M. H. T. de Almeida. São Paulo: Editora Brasiliense.

Castells, M. 1972. *La question urbaine*. Paris: Maspéro.

Cohen, J. L. 1985. "Strategy or Identity: New Theoretical Paradigms and Contemporary Social Movements." *Social Research* 52, no. 4: 663–716.

Doimo, A. M. 1995. *A vez e a voz do Popular: movimentos sociais e participação politica no Brasil pós-70*. Rio de Janeiro: ANPOCS and Relume-Dumará.

Fernandes, R. C. 1988 Sem fins lucrativos. In *Sem fins lucrativos: as organizações naõ-governementais no Brasil*, ed. L. Landim. pp. 8–23. ISER, Rio de Janeiro.

Foweraker, J. 1995. *Theorizing Social Movements*. London and Boulder, CO: Pluto Press.

Frey, K. 1996. "Crise do estado e estilos de gestao municipal." *Lua Nova* 37: 107–138.

Kleinpenning, J. M. G. 1978. *Profiel van de Derde Wereld: Een Inleiding tot de Geografie van de Onderontwikheling*. Assen: Van Gorcum.

Kowarick, L. 1986. "Urban Movements in Contemporary Brazil: An Analysis of the Literature." Paper presented at the 11th World Congress of Sociology, New Delhi, August 18–23.

Kucinski, B. 1982. Brazil: *State and Struggle*. London: Latin America Bureau.

Landim, L., ed. 1988. *Sem fins lucrativos: as organizações não-governemetais no Brasil*. Rio de Janeiro: Instituto de Estudos da Religião.

Lehmann, D. 1990. *Democracy and Development in Latin America: Economics, Politics and Religion in the Post-War Period*. Cambridge, U.K.: Polity Press.

Lojkine, J. 1977. Le *Marxisme, l'Etat et la question urbaine*. Paris. Presses Universitaires de France.

Moisés, J. A., et al. 1977. *Contradições urbanas e movimentos sociais*. Rio de Janeiro: Paz e Terra and Centro de Estudos de Cultura Contemporânea.

Moisés, J. A., et al. 1981. *Cidade, povo e poder*. Rio de Janeiro: Paz e Terra and Centro de Estudos de Cultura Contemporânea.

Oliveira, F. de. 1977. "Acumulação monopolista, estado e urbanização." In *Contradições urbanase movimentos sociais*, J. A. Moisés et al. Rio de Janeiro: Paz e Terra and Centro de Estudos de Cultura Contemporânea.

Ribeiro, L. C. de Queiros 1995. "A (in)governabilidade da cidade? Avancos e desafios da reforma urbana." In *Governabilidade e pobreza no Brasil*, org. L. P. Valladares and M. P. Coelho. Rio de Janeiro: Civilização Brasileira.

Sader, E. 1988. *Quando novos personagens entraram em cena*. Rio de Janeiro: Paz e Terra.

Salman, T. 1990. "Between Orthodoxy and Euphoria: Research Strategies on Social Movements, A comparative Perspective." In *Structures of Power, Movements of Resistance: An Introduction to the Theories of Urban Movements* in *Latin America*, W. Assies with T. Salman and G. Burgwal. Amsterdam: CEDLA.

Singer, P. 1980. "Movimento de Bairro." In *São Paulo: O povo em movimento*, ed. P. Singer and V. C. Brant. Petrópolis: Livraria Vozes: 83–107.

Singer, P., and V. C. Brant, eds. 1980. *São Paulo: O povo em movimento*. Petrópolis: Vozes.

Tarrow, S. 1994. *Power in Movement: Social Movements, Collective Action* and *Politics*. Cambridge, U.K. and New York: Cambridge University Press.

Part II

Agrarian Issues

Introduction

Cristóbal Kay

Willem Assies published about nine essays on specifically agrarian issues. Besides the two essays selected for this section, his other agrarian essays are Assies 1997, 2000, 2005, 2006, 2008, 2009a, and 2009b. Twenty-five years separate the publication of the two selected articles. The first article discusses the 1969 agrarian reform in Peru, while the second article deals with some aspects of the 1996 so-called "Ley INRA" in Bolivia, or *Ley del Instituto Nacional de Reforma Agraria* to gives it its full title. This essay on Peru is his first publication and it is based on his MA thesis in anthropology for the University of Amsterdam where he graduated cum laude in 1985. This essay was to remain his sole publication on Peru. His other publications on agrarian issues are on Brazil and Mexico or deal more generally with Latin America. But his early experience in Peru opened his eyes to the plight of the indigenous peoples, which was to become one of his major research interests in neighboring Bolivia as well as in Mexico and other Latin American countries. Both selected essays were originally published in *The Journal of Peasant Studies*, which was privileged to publish six of his articles, more than any other journal.

In his first published article Assies evaluates the Peruvian agrarian reform (1968–1980) within the Marxist debate on the various paths of transition to capitalism. He critiques Alain De Janvry's (1981) thesis that the agrarian reform is an attempt to create a socially articulated pattern of accumulation and development. According to De Janvry this would be achieved by stimulating the rise of an industrial national bourgeoisie and by shifting from the Junker-road (or landlord-road) to the farmer road of capitalist development in agriculture. While this may have been the aim of the military governments' agrarian reform, Assies doubts whether such a national bourgeoisie would emerge despite the subjection of the agrarian sector to the interests of industrial accumulation. He critiques De Janvry for arguing that the 1969 Peruvian agrarian reform is leading to a farmer-road of capitalist development and for underestimating the potential of the associative agrarian reform sector and in particular of the coastal cooperatives (CAPs). He also critiques those authors who argued that a state-capitalist road to agrarian capitalism was emerging. While he acknowledges the influence of the state on the CAPs he characterized them as a collective form of simple commodity production. In developing his characterization of the CAPs Assies follows the analysis of Rosa Luxemburg who "characterized co-operatives as 'hybrids': the socialization of production on a small scale in the context of capitalist exchange relations." While he acknowledges that the disintegration of the CAPs may lead to peasantization he still expressed the hope that the cooperatives could be converted into "peasant communities in which forms of collective and individual production can be combined."

In the mid-1990s Assies carried out research on the sustainable development of tropical forest resources in which he discusses the social, economic, and political aspects of Brazil nut (which he refers to more appropriately as "Amazon nuts") exploitation in the Amazon regions of Bolivia and Brazil. Among the outcomes of this project is an article in which Assies (1997) uses a political economy approach to critique market-based strategies of forest conservation, i.e., the belief that through commercial extraction of non-timber forest products, like Brazil nuts and rubber, it is possible to achieve simultaneously the goals of forest conservation and the economic development of the rural population involved in those activities. He introduces into his analysis of the dynamics of the extractive economy "the notion of an agro-extractive cycle which includes rubber tapping, Amazon nut gathering and agriculture" (Assies 1997: 46). Another outcome of this project is the second selected essay in which Assies focuses on the rubber tappers and the development of rubber production since the 1880s in the Bolivian Amazon. He places his analysis of the rise and decline of the rubber trade and the transformation of labor relations within the Marxist debate on modes of production. He critiques those authors who assume that unfree labor is always a pre-capitalist relation. Instead, returning to a thesis he already expounded in his first essay he finds it more helpful to use the Marxist concept of simple commodity production to comprehend the relations between the rubber tappers and their employers. Furthermore, this labor system was "accompanied by a 'moral economy' of its own, and was wrapped up in a discourse about paternalist ties of patronage and *compadrazgo*. But paternalism and its doctrine of reciprocal obligations . . . develop as a way of mediating irreconcilable class and racial conflicts."

Assies also refers in this selected essay on the increasing conflicts over land and forest resources in the Bolivian tropical lowlands and how this led to major mobilizations of peasants and indigenous peoples such as the long march in 2000 for "Land, Territories and Natural Resources." In his view the 1996 Ley INRA only inflamed the situation as this neoliberal land legislation and market-led agrarian reform failed to meet the demands of the peasantry. Assies's analysis was most prescient as this march and many others that followed spawned by shortcomings of the 1996 Ley INRA would eventually lead to the election to the presidency of Evo Morales in 2005 and to a new constitution some years later with the aim of addressing Bolivia's historical problems. It is to the credit of Assies that in this essay he highlighted early on the importance of Bolivia's unresolved "agrarian and land question" and stressing its close link to the "indigenous question."

Notes

This introduction is partly extracted from my article "A Tribute to Willem Assies (1954–2010): Reflections on His Contribution to Peasant and Indigenous Studies," *Journal of Peasant Studies* 38, no. 2 (2011): 459–477.

References

Assies, W. 1997. "The Extraction of Non-timber Forest Products as a Conservation Strategy in Amazonia." *European Review of Latin American and Caribbean Studies* 62: 33–53.

———. 2000. "Lands, Territories and Indigenous Peoples' Rights." In *Current Land Policy in Latin America*, eds. A. Zoomers and G. van der Haar. Amsterdam: KIT Publishers and Frankfurt: Vervuert Verlag, 93–109.

———. 2005. "The Challenge of Diversity in Rural Latin America: A Rejoinder to Jean-Pierre Reed (and Others)." *Journal of Peasant Studies* 32, no. 2: 261–371.

———. 2006. "Land Tenure Legislation in a Pluri-cultural and Multi-ethnic Society: The Case of Bolivia." *Journal of Peasant Studies* 33, no. 4: 569–611.

———. 2008. "Land Tenure and Tenure Regimes in Mexico: An Overview." *Journal of Agrarian Change* 8, no. 1: 33–63.

———. 2009a. Land Tenure, Land Law and Development: Some Thoughts on Recent Debates." *Journal of Peasant Studies* 36, no. 3: 573–589.

———. 2009b. "Legal Empowerment of the Poor: With a Little Help from Their Friends?" *Journal of Peasant Studies* 36, no. 4: 909–924.

De Janvry, A. 1981. *The Agrarian Question and Reformism in Latin America*. Baltimore, MD: The Johns Hopkins University Press.

3

The Agrarian Question in Peru

Some Observations on the Roads of Capital

Under the military governments of Velasco (1968–1975) and Morales Bermúdez (1975–1980) one of the most important agrarian reforms of South American history took place in Peru. According to Alain de Janvry (1981) this reform involved a shift from a Junker-road to a farmer-road toward the development of capitalism in Peruvian agriculture. In the first part of this study de Janvry's approach to the "agrarian question" and his evaluation of the Peruvian reform will be discussed. It will be argued that he overestimates the importance of farmer-type capitalism and pays too little attention to the cooperatives established during the reform. Focusing the discussion on the cooperatives in the coastal region it will be argued that these enterprises can be understood, to an important extent, as a form of simple commodity production. In the final part of the article a case study of the cotton producing cooperatives in the province of Ica will be presented.

Introduction

The Peruvian agrarian reform, which started in 1969, stood out for its relatively swift execution, its focus on the most modern enterprises, in contrast to reforms only touching marginal or traditional enterprises, and for its non-redistributive character emphasizing the formation of production cooperatives. The reform was part of an ambitious project of industrialization under military guidance, which was meant to set in motion a process of permanent and self-sustained industrial development. In his work on the agrarian question and reformism in Latin America Alain de Janvry suggests that Peruvian military reformism should be interpreted as an attempt to establish what he calls *a socially articulated pattern of accumulation*. The agrarian reform involved, in his view, a shift from the Junker-road to the farmer-road toward the development of capitalism in agriculture (de Janvry 1981).

In this article I will discuss this evaluation of Peruvian military reformism and the agrarian reform. To begin with, I shall examine de Janvry's general approach to the development of capitalism and the agrarian question, focusing on this theory of social articulation and the connected theory of functional dualism. Then I will turn to his evaluation of Peruvian reformism and point out that it was not so much the outcome of a struggle between an export-orientated socially disarticulated alliance on the one hand and a socially articulated alliance centered on a national bourgeoisie interested in the development of a home market on the other, in spite of the rhetoric of the Peruvian Revolution. Much more important was the subjection of the agrarian sector to the interests of industrial accumulation. Cheap food policies, one of the main causes of stagnation in the agrarian sector and of the lack of capitalist development in food production, which de Janvry expects to be overcome by the establishment of a socially articulated alliance (de Janvry 1981: 151, 162–169, 220–221), were continued.

The removal from power of the landed elite in 1968, rather than promoting a farmer-type development in Peruvian agriculture, opened the way to state intervention in the agrarian sector on a scale that had been inconceivable before. Food prices had, before 1968, been the main object of state intervention. Such intervention was intensified and broadened and came to include traditional export products such as sugar and cotton, of which an ever larger share had become destined for the internal market. The objective of these policies was to promote industrial growth.

At the same time, the formation of cooperative enterprises provided an opportunity to push prices below what would have been acceptable to capitalist agriculture. The establishment of an *associative sector* has been one of the main achievements of the Peruvian agrarian reform. This sector consists of various forms of cooperative enterprise. The most important forms are the *Cooperativas Agrarias de Producción* (Agrarian Production Cooperatives) (CAP) and the *Sociedades Agrícolas de Interés Social* (Agricultural Societies of Social Interest) (SAIS). The SAIS-model was designed for the stockbreeding areas of the *sierra*. In a SAIS, of which about sixty were established, the former hacienda-lands are farmed by a service cooperation consisting of the permanent workers and tenants of the estates. The surrounding peasant communities with claims to the hacienda lands also became members of the SAIS, but they did not receive any land. Instead they were to receive a share of the profits of the enterprise, technical assistance and services. For the communities this was not a very viable solution and many SAIS have now been invaded by their member communities.

In this article our attention will be focused on the CAP-type cooperatives. Including the twelve agro-industrial sugar complexes, which were expropriated on the first day of the reform, about six hundred enterprises of this type have been established. The CAP-model was designed for the modem haciendas of the coastal region, turning the permanent laborers of these enterprises into *socios* (members of the cooperative). Theoretically these were meant to be "pure" production cooperatives: indivisible production units, collectively owned and self-managed by the *socios*.[1] De Janvry's classification of reforms, according to the distinction between a Junker-road and a farmer-road toward the development of capitalism in agriculture, blinds him to the importance of the cooperative sector in Peru. These enterprises should not be neglected, however, and Kay (1982: 166) has even argued that the Peruvian reform represents a state-capitalist road to agrarian capitalism. In his view the cooperatives are essentially state enterprises. Such a characterization, based above all on the twelve sugar-producing CAPs, is much too limited, however, and Caballero (1977: 152; 1980: 89) emphasizes that besides the state capitalist dimension of the CAPs the cooperative self-management dimension should not be neglected. Cooperativization was imposed by the state and the cooperatives have been subjected to extensive regulation and other forms of state intervention, but within the CAPs there is no direct representative of capital. The situation of the person coming closest to this position, the *gerente* (administrator), is very ambivalent since within certain limits set by the state he can be hired and fired by the *socios*. And this happens quite often. In this article it will be argued that in their self-management dimension, these enterprises can be understood as a form of simple commodity production in which labor is only formally subsumed under capital. The capitalist social formation in which the CAPs operate and the interventions of the state are part of the *conditioning situation* (Dos Santos 1976: 76–77) in which a *cooperative rationality* (Matos Mar and Mejía 1980: 221) develops. In the second part of the article I will discuss the development of labor relations in the cotton-producing CAPs of the province of Ica in this context and I will explore the ways in which these CAPs have reacted to something quite similar to what Bernstein has described as the *simple reproduction squeeze*.[2]

The Theory of Social Articulation

De Janvry's assessment of the Peruvian reform should be seen against the background of his views on the development of capitalism. The framework is provided by Amin's models of autocentric vs. extraverted economies, the former characterized by sectoral articulation, the latter by disarticulation.[3]

This model is then complemented by a theory of social articulation in the central economies vs. social disarticulation in the periphery. According to de Janvry, following Sweezy and Amin, the dialectic between production and circulation, or between the capacity to produce and the capacity to consume of the system, is the essence of the crises of capitalism: structural crises due to social disproportionality (de Janvry 1981: 24, 28). In an *autocentric economy*, however, an objectively necessary relation is supposed to exist between "the derived demand for capital goods and the final demand for wage goods" since the ultimate end of the production process is "to produce commodities for human consumption." In this case wages are not only a "loss" but also a "gain" for capital. Social articulation, the increase of wages in proportion to productivity, is "the condition for reproduction of capital on an expanded scale without crises."

Social articulation is mediated by the rise of social democratic political regimes using the enhanced planning capacity of the state to create the conditions for dynamic equilibrium by neutralizing the tendency toward underconsumption, without questioning the system as such (de Janvry and Garraman 1977; de Janvry 1981: 16, 26–32; Amin 1976: 72–75).

Whereas social articulation serves as an internal solution to the problems of central capital this model of accumulation is at the same time sustained through relations with the periphery. The peripheral economies are kept from adopting a socially articulated pattern of accumulation by the center through an alliance of international capital, dependent bourgeoisie, and landed elites. Their logic is one of disarticulated accumulation based on cheap labor and cheap food that ultimately serves to sustain the central model by improving the rate of profit and absorbing financial surpluses. In these *extroverted economies* wages are only a "loss" to capital and growth is dissociated from the needs of the masses (de Janvry and Garraman 1977; de Janvry 1981: 20–26, 32). In the long run, however, capitalist growth through import-substitution will, in de Janvry's view, also bring about the conditions for the establishment of a socially articulated alliance. Eventually, growth will give rise to a *national bourgeoisie*, which is defined as "the producers and traders of wage goods" (de Janvry 1981: 41). Together with the agrarian bourgeoisie (those fundamentally involved in the production of wage foods), the peasantry and the proletariat, the national bourgeoisie can form an alliance creating the logic for a socially articulated pattern of accumulation in which cheap labor and cheap food are no longer functional to the accumulation process (de Janvry 1981: 41, 220–221). The Peruvian experiment, along with the populist regimes of Vargas in Brazil, Perón in Argentina, and Betancourt in Venezuela, is cited as an example of the attempts to establish the hegemony of such an articulated alliance (de Janvry 1981: 40–45). In this way de Janvry takes issue with the "development of underdevelopment" school and seeks to reestablish the theory of the progressive role of capitalism in which unequal development and peripheral *capitalism* are but *phases* in the "normal process of social change" (de Janvry 1981: 18–25).

This view of things is open to criticism on several points. To begin with, the analysis in terms of the contradiction between production-capacity and consumption-capacity has been characterized by Anthony Brewer as being "both right and, crucially, wrong" (Brewer 1980: 252). The relation between sectors (or departments of production) is indeed essential, but consumption is not more fundamental than investment (Brewer 1980: 33–34, 133–135, 256). De Janvry, as Amin, heavily emphasizes the tendencies toward underconsumption, but neglects the reality that consumer demand in a capitalist framework is not an independent factor but derives from the spending of capitalists directed to making profits. Therefore the analysis in terms of the contradiction between the capacity to produce and the capacity to consume does not provide the key to the explanation of wage levels. There is no mechanism whereby a divergence of wages from the required level can be corrected. If they are too high there is a crisis, and if they are too low there is a crisis. In either case wages will be forced down, so that there is no remedy if wages are too low (Brewer 1980: 256). Capitalism is just not that concerned with the needs of the masses.

The problem becomes quite clear when de Janvry points out that the national bourgeoisie, who should objectively be interested in raising wages, often vigorously opposes wage increases, thus contradicting its "class interest in the sphere of circulation" (de Janvry 1981: 44). The explanation of wage levels, then, should not be sought in social articulation, capitalism, as it were, "discovering" a new market in the working classes as a solution to the realization problem, but rather in class struggle. The expansion of the market for consumer goods in Western Europe was the result of wage increases extracted through class struggle in a context of diminishing labor reserves, technological change, and the transition to imperialism and monopoly capitalism. In spite of rising productivity there was, until the 1880s, nothing like a proportional increase in wages but rather a stagnation of real wages and a rising rate of surplus value. The world market was an extremely important outlet, but this was not "because real wages in the center did not increase sufficiently" (Amin 1976: 76). Capitalism, even in the center, is not necessarily socially articulated. Capitalist growth in the center, however, has been sectorally articulated from the beginning. At the same time the industrial revolution and the development in transport made sectorally disarticulated accumulation elsewhere a possibility and a tempting one at that, since the terms of trade moved in favor of exporters of primary goods at least until 1880. Sectoral disarticulation became an important feature of, for example, the Peruvian economy, a feature that has proved quite difficult, if not impossible, to overcome within a capitalist framework (FitzGerald 1979: 77, 266–267; Iguíñiz 1979: 72; Thorp and Bertram 1978: 269–274, 321–327).

Moreover, writing at the end of the conjuncture of the 1970s, when Third World industry seemed to grow independently, at least in some countries, de Janvry seems to nurse quite high expectations about the rise of national capitalisms in the periphery, whereas the center is in decline. By now it has become clear that the changes in the international division of labor are more complicated than that, and it may be asked if the bourgeoisie of the periphery is particularly interested in the development of the home market as such. The Peruvian bourgeoisie is notorious for its lack of enthusiasm for national economic development (FitzGerald 1979: 49, 119, 36; Thorp and Bertram 1978: 322–323). We may therefore ask if de Janvry is not throwing out the baby with the bathwater in his criticism of the dependency approach. Rather than affirming the primacy of class structure over surplus extraction attention should be paid to their interrelations (de Janvry 1981: 22; Goodman and Redclift 1981: 43).

We come to the conclusion that there is no objective need for, or immanent tendency in, capital to raise wage levels as a means of solving the problem of the realization of surplus value. The schemes of reproduction are not the framework for the solution of the contradictions of capitalism but rather the framework within which these contradictions can be analyzed. They should not be taken for reality itself (Hickel 1972; Rosdolsky 1972). De Janvry's refutation of the "development of underdevelopment" approach, equalizing growth with development in a somewhat old-fashioned way and emphasizing the role of a national bourgeoisie, is not convincing.

The Theory of Functional Dualism and the Concept of Simple Commodity Production

Another aspect of de Janvry's approach is his theory of functional dualism, which, in the context of his criticism of the "development of underdevelopment" school, can clearly be read as a criticism of marginalization theories. Whereas marginalization has been described as the outcome of capitalist growth, dualism, by contrast, rather is to be understood as a transitional phenomenon of the dissolution of pre-capitalist modes of production that will eventually be overcome in the course of capitalist development (Bennholdt-Thomsen 1979: 47; Roberts 1981: 110, 160–170). Dualism, according to de Janvry, is functional in a context of disarticulated accumulation. Full proletarianization of the labor force does not occur because there is no need to create a home market out of rising wages. On the contrary, the "traditional" sector, providing cheap labor and cheap food, permits wages paid to be far below the price of subsistence. The main manifestations of this dualism are subsistence production and simple commodity production. Peasant commodity production is seen as a phase in the transition from communal and semifeudal modes of production to the capitalist mode. Eventually, full proletarianization of the peasantry and unimodality will occur even if it is only by the back door, the peasantry being outcompeted for access to land. This, however, does not bring about the end of functional dualism, which is said to be *recreated* in the informal urban sector, which becomes a new source of subsidies for the maintenance and reproduction of labor power. Eventually, dualism will be overcome as a result of the development of a socially articulated pattern of accumulation in which it will not be functional any more (de Janvry 1981: 37–39, 84, 261).

This account is problematical on the one hand, for the way in which the concept of simply commodity production is used and, on the other hand, for its functionalist explanation of the existence of the peasantry and the "informal sector." As to the first point, de Janvry's reasoning is based on a failure to distinguish between the formal concept of simple commodity production and its historical manifestations of which peasant production is only one (de Janvry 1981: 96–106; Friedmann 1978, 1980; Chevalier 1983: 181). In my view, the concept of simple commodity production does not have much to do with dualism and there is nothing essentially precapitalist about it. It is a form of production that is a normal feature of capitalist social formations, that is, social formations characterized by generalized commodity production in which reproduction outside the commodity economy has become impossible (Bennholdt-Thomsen 1979: 71, 74; Chevalier 1983: 164, 174; Friedmann 1980: 163).[4]

The discussion of the formal aspects of simple commodity production and the more or less complete subsumption of labor under capital need not be tied to the empirical case of agriculture (Friedmann 1980: 161) or restricted to "subsistence activities" (Bennholdt-Thomsen 1982; de Janvry and Garraman 1977; de Janvry 1981: 39). Separating the discussion from these empirical cases allows us to see that the model applies to "a wide range of practices which can be understood without resorting to a mechanical application of structural articulation theory" (Chevalier 1983: 177) or its dualist variant (de Janvry 1981: 94–110). In formula simple commodity production can be represented as Commodity-Money-Commodity (C-M-C), to sell in order to buy. Sweezy (1968: 139) has pointed out that, for example, the production of labor power by the households of the working class under capitalism takes the form of simple commodity production.[5] But the concept may also be applied to self-employment and its more or less incomplete subsumption under capital in the so-called "informal sector," which has been arbitrarily restricted to urban areas (Breman 1976), or to the new forms of incompletely subsumed labor made possible by the introduction of the individual sewing-machine and, more recently, the personal computer. [6] Applying the concept to production cooperatives Gutelman (1979: 160) has characterized these enterprises as "collective simple commodity producers." Rather than speaking of dualism we may say that in a context of generalized commodity production, C-M-C and M-C-M (Money-Commodity-more Money; capitalism) are two sides of the same coin, the latter representing the mode of existence of those who can live off other peoples' labor, the former the mode of existence of those who cannot.[7] If, on the one hand, there is nothing essentially pre-capitalist about the concept of simple commodity production, on the other hand the contemporary peasantry and the "informal sector" can be seen as products of capitalist growth; in the Peruvian case the Junker-development in agriculture in a sectorally disarticulated economy. In his theory of the industrial reserve army of labor Marx related the development of a relative surplus population to the process of capital accumulation, thus criticizing Malthus and Ricardo, who thought population growth to be connected with wage levels. It should be noted, though, that Marx assumed capitalist growth to be sectorally articulated on a national level. This is clear from his discussion of the surplus population in its latent form, which is located in the countryside. In contrast to industrial capitalism, the development of capitalism in agriculture is accompanied by an absolute decline in the demand for labor power since land, unlike capital, cannot be produced. Whereas in industry the movement of the labor reserve is cyclical, in agriculture it is not (Marx Capital I: chap. 23). We could say then, that the development of capitalism in agriculture brings about the growth of an "absolute" population surplus. It is the growth of capitalist industry that turns this absolute surplus into a relative one. Disarticulated capitalist growth thus can contribute to the growth of an enormous latent reserve army of labor.

The characterization of the peasantry and the "informal sector" as *traditional* can only be accepted if we share de Janvry's expectations of capitalist development. Moreover, rather than explaining the existence of this "traditional sector" out of its functionality for capital accumulation in the center we should ask why capitalism is not developing much faster under such favorable circumstances (Brewer 1980: 227, 248). De Janvry seems to assume that full employment, conveniently (Laclau and Mouffe 1985: 75–88) splitting society into its essential categories of wage labor and capital and creating an urban proletarian vanguard through rapid industrialization, is the normal outcome of capitalism (de Janvry 1981: 226–228). Marginality, in this view, is only the result of what is euphemistically called "premature proletarianization" (de Janvry 1981: 262), eventually to be overcome by the need for market creation.

There are, however, many reasons to question such an "optimistic" view of capitalism fulfilling its historical mission in the periphery (Lipielz 1982). The "dualization" of the economy has resulted from capitalist growth, which is, as has been argued, neither very nationalistic nor particularly concerned with the needs of the masses. The problem is that the population surplus, as far as it cannot be functionalized in profitable activity, is marginalized and, as far as capital is concerned, left to pauperization. The criticism of the marginalization concept, based on the "Brazilian Miracle" has not been altogether convincing since the performance of the miracle in reducing marginality has not been that spectacular (Bennholdt-Thomsen 1979: 50–55). In any case, the number of miracle countries seems to be quite limited and Peru rather belongs to the group of newly deindustrializing countries. Even if Peruvian capitalism had been more autonomous this would probably have changed little for the majority of the population (FitzGerald 1979: 20–23, 89–99; Thorp and Bertram 1978: 326).

Marginality is not simply the result of labor-saving technology turning the quantity of the labor reserve into a new quality and thus justifying the use of the concept of marginalization instead of proletarianization (Bennholdt-Thomsen 1979: 75). It is also related to the history of sectorally disarticulated growth in the periphery and to the monopoly structure of present day capitalism, which has made the emergence of a "grassroots" capitalism, through differentiation among simple commodity producers, quite difficult since the possibilities for independent accumulation are severely restricted (Caballero 1984: 18, 21; García-Sayán 1980: 43–48; Goodman and Redclift 1981: 109). For the specific case of the marginalized peasant commodity producers of the Peruvian sierra Caballero (1984: 28–29) argues that they reproduce themselves, not because they are functional to capitalism as suppliers of cheap food or cheap labor, in which their role is rather restricted, but because capitalism is incapable of absorbing them.

Industrialization and Agrarian Reform: The Case of Peru

We will now briefly review how the agrarian question came to be posed in Peru and how this resulted in the agrarian reform of 1969. Then we will turn to a discussion of de Janvry's evaluation of this reform and the role of production cooperatives. From the late 1940s to the mid-1960s the Peruvian economy was "swept forward on a wave of expanding export production" (Thorp and Bertram 1978: 253) in which fishmeal and mining products replaced cotton and sugar as the major exports. In this context a process of import substitution had started in the course of the 1950s, largely as a result

of US investment in assembly plants for durable consumer goods and stimu-
lated by the very liberal industrial promotion policies of the Peruvian governments. In the 1960s industry surpassed agriculture in its contribution to the
national product. The industrialization process, however, remained heavily
dependent on the performance of the export sector since many inputs and
capital goods had to be imported. By the early 1960s the limits of growth in
the export sector were being touched on, resulting in a steadily deteriorat-
ing balance of payments (FitzGerald 1979: 80–87; Iguiñiz 1979; Throp and
Bertram 1978: 252–256, 261–274).

It was against this background that the relative stagnation of the agrarian
sector attracted attention (Hopkins 1981; Thorp and Bertram 1978: 276–
278). The sector failed to keep pace with the growth of industry and popula
tion. Its contribution to export earnings declined as a result of falling world
market prices after the mid-1950s and the overvaluation of the sol (Hopkins
1981: 89). Food production for the urban market and production destined
to the agro-industries[8] rose, mainly as a result of the switch from cotton to
food production in the coastal region due to declining cotton prices (Thorp
and Bertram 1978: 276), but failed to keep pace with the growth of demand.
Rather than stimulating local production in the traditional food-producing
areas of the sierra a choice was made for the much easier import of wage
foods, cheapened by the US export promotion policies of P.L. 480, which
were processed and handled by a few multinational enterprises. Thus, the
supply of several basic urban food products came to be controlled by a few
oligopolistic agro-industries heavily dependent on imports. These policies
and the price regulations, to which several food products for direct urban
consumption were subjected, are reflected in a steady decline of food prices
relative to the general price index in the course of the 1950s. An ever greater
share of export earnings had to be earmarked for food imports (Hopkins
1981; Samaniego 1980: 204–207; Samaniego 1984: 222–231; Thorp and
Bertram 1978: 274–278).

When, by the early 1960s, the export boom came to an end the relative
stagnation of the agrarian sector, its consequences for the balance of payments and its inflationary potential became ever more problematic. At the
same time the old oligarchy, consisting of the financial bourgeoisie, the agro-
exporting bourgeoisie, and the *gamonales* (traditional highland landowners)
was losing its hegemonic position in Peruvian society. On the one hand, the
position of the *gamonales* fraction was undermined by large-scale peasant
unrest starting in the second part of the 1950s in reaction to the Junker-
development taking place in the *sierra*. On the other hand, the dominance
of the oligarchy came to be perceived as a major obstacle to further industrialization (Caballero 1980: 72; FitzGerald 1979: 57; Paige 1978: 165, 190;

Samaniego 1980: 203; Thorp and Bertram 1978: 294). This does not mean, however, that the project of industrialization was one of a national industrial bourgeoisie, which was virtually nonexistent (FitzGerald 1979: 49, 278; Thorp and Bertram 1978: 273). Radier, in the course of the 1950s it was the so-called *sectores medios*, of which the National Society of Engineers and the "newly professionalized" military are examples, that, under the influence of ECLA theories of development, had started advocating land and tax reforms and a more active role of the state in furthering the process of import-substituting industrialization (FitzGerald 1979: 47–57; Iguíñiz 1979: 13; Stepan 1978: 127–136; Valderrama 1976: 14–23, 43–46). It was out of concern for the problems of national security and of industrialization, which were seen as interrelated, that the armed forces staged their first institutional coup in 1962. Thereby they impeded the oligarchy, at the time in coalition with the APRA, from remaining in power, and they started the first land reform programs in areas of major peasant unrest. In the elections of 1963 Belaunde Terry, promising land and tax reforms that at the time were also advocated by the Alliance for Progress (Feder 1971: 171–258), was duly elected president. When he failed to implement the reforms and ran into difficulties for other reasons, the armed forces, under the leadership of Velasco and influenced by the radical critics of early ECLA theory, once more took power to try and complete the import substitution process (Stepan 1978: 254). The 1969 agrarian reform was conceived as a precondition for further industrialization. Its main goals were reactivating agrarian production, integrating the rural population into the national economy, and implementing an agrarian policy tuned to the needs of industrial development (Alvarez 1983: 106; Mejía 1980: 21; Valderrama 1976: 49, 495–496). It was essentially a nonredistributive reform, and first of all it was aimed at the most modern enterprises, not only because such a move would break the power of the oligarchy, but also since these enterprises were expected to be most capable of providing funds for industrial accumulation.

The subordination of the reform to industrialization was obvious in the mode of land transfer involving a process of state supervised sale and purchase. The former owners were partly paid in agrarian debt bonds, convertible into cash when used for investment in new industrial plant, a possibility that was hardly made use of, however (Caballero and Alvarez 1980: 54–73; Matos Mar and Mejía 1980: 121, 294; Gutelman 1979: 190). The new owners of the land, mostly organized in some sort of cooperative, had to pay off an agrarian debt to the state, thus covering the issue of the bonds. This debt provided the overall pretext for direct state intervention in the new enterprises, which was particularly extensive in the sugar CAPs (Stepan 1978: 190–230; Zaldivar 1974: 30–39). It goes too far, however, to call the cooperative just state capitalist enterprises (Kay 1982), if only because the state would have been quite incapable of fully assuming the managerial role of the former land-owning class (García-Sayán 1980: 70, 91; H. Martínez 1980: 137–140, 146). In 1977 a great number of enterprises did not even have a *gerente* (administrator) (Mejía 1980: 17). The remaining part of the agrarian debt was written off in 1979. Although the total sum involved was not very significant in macroeconomic terms it has been a heavy burden on many cooperatives (Caballero and Alvarez 1980: 72). Far more important than this, however, was that the exclusion from power of the landed class, as such, made possible manipulation of intersectoral-exchanges on a much larger scale than before (Matos Mar and Mejía 1980: 296). State enterprises came to play an important role in the trade in several products. The list of locally produced foods for direct urban consumption subjected to price controls was extended, whereas the prices of products destined to the agro-industries were kept low through competition from imports. When, after 1973, the prices of these imports started to rise they began to be subsidized by the state in order to keep urban food prices low, to the detriment of local producers. As before, the peasantry remained at the margin of this oligopoly-dominated model of urban food supply (Alvarez 1983: 116–164; Figueroa 1980; Lajo Lazo 1980; Samaniego 1980). Cotton was, as we will see, another product subjected to price controls meant to favor industrial development. Whereas the prices of agricultural products were thus kept low, the prices of industrial inputs for agriculture rose, especially after 1973 (Alvarez 1983: 146, 324; D. Martínez and Tealdo 1982: 96–97; Matos Mar and Mejía 1980: 272).

In the "second phase" of the Peruvian experiment a major shift occurred in economic policy. The "first phase" policies had run into serious trouble. The military government failed to raise sufficient internal resources for the realization of its ambitious plans. International capital was holding back, and domestic capital became particularly hostile to the military innovations. Market expansion was achieved through participation in the Andean market rather than through a significant change in income distribution as a result of the reforms (FitzGerald 1979: 128–136, 270). At the same time the Velasco government was unwilling to mobilize the population in its support. Instead, it increasingly relied on loans of international banks, abundantly available after the 1973 oil crisis, in the vain hope that Peru would soon become an oil exporter too. Export revenues rather stagnated, however, and by 1976 this led to a balance of payments crisis, followed by orthodox stabilization policies: freezing wages, cutting food subsidies,[9] reducing public spending, and devaluing the currency. This marked the shift from a policy of import substitution to a policy of export substitution.

From that moment on, the export orientation of the economy has been reinforced by a policy of promotion of nontraditional exports and the application of IMF recipes from 1977 onwards (FitzGerald 1979: 178, 232, 292). The economic policies of the second Belaúnde regime (1980–1985) have further enforced this model of export-led growth. This did not resolve the balance of payments problems, and for the population the consequences have been disastrous, but it has contributed to the consolidation of new financial-industrial power groups, playing their part in the international division of labor (Latín America Bureau 1985: 81–105).

Evaluating the Reform: The Farmer Road?

According to de Janvry the Peruvian experiment has been an attempt at the establishment of a socially articulated pattern of accumulation, while the agrarian reform involved a shift from a Junker-road to a farmer-road toward the development of capitalism in agriculture (de Janvry 1981: 43, 136–140). As to the first point, we may doubt that the required socially articulated alliance was present in Peru. The "experiment" rather resulted from the weakness than from the strength of a national bourgeoisie (FitzGerald 1979: 56; Kay 1982: 165; Valderrama 1976: 14–23). It was in this context that the military reformers, linking the concept of national security with industrialization, could play their relatively autonomous role. Domestic capital, however, proved quite hostile to the military innovations. The agrarian bourgeoisie was excluded altogether whereas, on the other hand, popular support for the "revolution" met with increasing repression (FitzGerald 1979: 287; Latín America Bureau 1985: 42–80; Thorp and Bertram 1978: 309, 318–323). As has been suggested by Stepan (1978: 123), inclusionary policies, or populist rhetoric at least, may be linked only to the first phase of the industrialization process. Once this "easy phase" (FitzGerald 1979: 265) is over, the power of the oligarchy broken and industrial hegemony established, policies may become increasingly exclusionary again (FitzGerald 1979: 178, 289–292). Rather than being a first step in the development toward the "interior," import substitution may be a phase in the transition from a primary goods exporting economy to an economy geared to the export of "nontraditional goods" that is a new form of articulation to the world market. How about the agrarian reform then? In de Janvry's view wage labor relations will eventually be established in agricultural production along either of the two basic roads indicated by Lenin: the farmer-road or the Junker-road. Following this lead de Janvry constructs an empirical characterization of class differentiation, indicating that the peasantry grows but simultaneously loses its status as commodity producer, and a typology of land reforms (de Janvry 1981: 121, 203).[10]

Applying this scheme to the Peruvian reform it is classified as involving a shift from the Junker-road to the farmer-road to the development of capitalism in agriculture. Concluding his characterization of class differentiation in the Peruvian countryside de Janvry writes that the development of capitalism in Peruvian agriculture, which was established before 1969 on the Junker-road, accelerated rapidly in the 1970s through large-scale state intervention in agricultural production. The process of land reform not only destroyed the power of the landed elites on the coastal plantations, but it also provoked the appearance of a large number of middle-sized commercial farms that were formed by the subdivision of haciendas (de Janvry 1981: 139). In support of this conclusion, he points out that the largest increase in the number of farms and in the percentage of farmland took place in farms of 20–100 hectares. This increase is indicated by a rate of change of 140 percent, between 1960 and 1970, in the number and a rate of change of 129 percent in area over the same period. At the same time there has been an increase in farms of 5–20 hectares, which is also taken to indicate the formation of a capitalist class in agriculture which develops along the farmer-road. It should be noted, though, that the starting point was one of extreme polarization. The rate of change does not give an indication of the weight of a sector. The number of enterprises of 20–100 hectares grew, it is true, but only from 3 percent to 5 percent of the total, whereas the percentage of farmland increased from 5 percent to 9 percent (de Janvry 1981: 139). Moreover, the size of an enterprise does not say much about its nature.[11]

Blinded by his classificatory scheme of farmers vs. Junkers, de Janvry only sees the indirect effects of the reform and has very little to say about its most important direct achievement: the formation of an associative sector.[12] The associative sector, CAPs and SAIS together, received about two-thirds of the land transferred in the reform process (Caballero and Alvarez 1980: 26), and by 1980 these enterprises owned about one-fourth of agricultural land in Peru while about 8.5 percent of the economically active rural population belonged to them, if we do not count the *comuneros* who only nominally benefited from their incorporation in the SAIS (Matos Mar and Mejía 1980: 190). In 1977 the associative enterprises accounted for about 22 percent of the value of the agricultural product. They produced half of the products destined for the agro-industries and export and 10 percent of the products for direct urban consumption (Caballero and Alvarez 1980: 79–83; Samaniego 1984: 236; Zegarra 1983: 72). In these figures, no difference is made between SAIS-type and CAP-type enterprises, but it should be clear that the

CAPs and among them especially those in the coastal region, play an important role.

The CAP-type enterprises received, in terms of standardized irrigated hectares, half of the land transferred in the reform process (Caballero and Alvarez 1980: 26). Of the total value of assets transferred by the reform, the coastal CAPs received 75 percent, the twelve sugar CAPs accounting for 38 percent and the other 312 CAPs in this region for 37 percent (Caballero and Alvarez 1980: 63; H. Martínez 1980: 160–118). During the 1970s these CAPs absorbed more than 40 percent of the credit available for the agrarian sector. Most of the credit supplied by the Banco Agrario was destined for the production of cotton, rice, potatoes, and maize for agro-industrial use, all crops in which the coastal cooperatives play an important role (Alvarez 1983: 214–228; D. Martínez and Tealdo 1982: 93–114).

We may conclude then that de Janvry overestimates the impact of the 1969 reform on farmer-type capitalist development. At the same time he underestimates the role of the associative sector and in particular that of the coastal CAPs. Rather than involving a shift from a Junker- to a farmer-road the Peruvian reform intensified the subjection of the agrarian sector to the interests of industrial accumulation. In the context of the industrialization process and the state policies aimed at promoting this process agricultural production became a relatively unprofitable business (Alvarez 1983: 57, 290–300; Matos Mar and Mejía 1980: 355; Vergopoulos 1980: 163, 266–267; Zegarra 1983: 73). Prices for urban wage foods were kept at a low level, whereas the costs of production rose sharply after 1973, resulting in a squeeze on the enterprises using industrial inputs, such as cooperatives and farmers. After some fluctuation in the early 1970s the terms of trade further deteriorated in the latter part of the 1970s, when subsidies on fertilizers were cut and, moreover, credit and tax policies tightened (Alvarez 1983: 129–145, 164, 296–299; Billone, Carbonetto, and D. Martínez 1982; Matos Mar and Mejía 1980: 271–274).

It is not surprising then that the agrarian reform failed to reactivate the sector (Matos Mar and Mejía 1980: 254–258, 338–343) and that in the course of the 1970s many cooperatives ran into trouble (D. Martínez and Tealdo 1982: 62; Mejía 1980: 17, 21). There certainly is some truth in the argument of D. Martínez and Tealdo (1982: 171) that these problems were rather due to the price system than to the form of land-ownership—individual or collective—as was argued by the second Belaúnde government with its doctrinaire faith in private enterprise. In spite of the squeeze to which they were subjected and in spite of the post-1980 agrarian policies that strongly encouraged the disintegration of the enterprises, many cooperatives survived until a movement toward restructuring gained momentum in 1982, a year of disaster for Peruvian agriculture. The ways in which the cooperatives reacted to the conditioning situation described can to an important degree be understood in terms of what Matos Mar and Mejía (1980: 221) have called a cooperativerationality. They argue that, as a result of the mystification of legal cooperative property, the enterprises do not require an average rate of profit to survive. Although maximum returns are pursued, just as a capitalist enterprise would do, a cooperative remains in business if this is not attained. In this respect the cooperatives follow a pattern comparable to that of the peasant economy (Matos Mar and Mejía 1980: 295).

Gutelman (1979: 160) makes a similar point describing cooperatives as "collective simple commodity producers." In these enterprises the worker-members are also the collective owners of the means of production, and therefore Gutelman characterizes the production relations in the cooperatives as being formally socialist.[13] The participation of cooperatives in a capitalist market economy, however, requires that the member-workers subject themselves to a capitalist labor discipline, which is as much as saying that these self-employed workers (Caballero 1978: 59) are formally subsumed under capital. Against this background I would like to discuss the development of labor relations and the incomplete subsumption of labor under capitalism the cotton-producing CAPs in the province of Ica, to return to the more general discussion at the end of the article.

Socios and *Eventuales*: The Problem of "Group Egoism"

When, in 1982, I started my field research in Ica I was especially interested in the ways in which cooperatives used the labor power of nonmembers. This had been an important issue during the reform. After the establishment of the first cooperatives, in particular the sugar-producing CAPs on the north coast, it became clear that the number of *socios* (members) of these CAPs tended to decrease while, at the same time, the number of nonmember wage workers or *eventuales*[14] tended to increase. The recruitment of *eventuales* was not only related to seasonal labor requirements but seemed to be a structural feature of the CAPs (Caballero 1978: 57–58). The income differences between *socios* and *eventuales* grew. The latter were badly paid and often cheated. Mostly they had to do the harder jobs and their work would be closely supervised. They were excluded from most of the cooperative services. In this way they contributed to the economic results of the enterprises without sharing in the benefits distributed among, the members. Thus a new exploitative and often conflictive relationship arose between *socios* and *eventuales*, a thorn in the flesh of the reformers who hoped to establish a new solidary society and who, moreover, saw their plans of expanding stable employment in the agrarian sector at a rate of 4.3 percent yearly thwarted (Matos Mar and Mejía 1980: 155, 249; McClintock 1981: 271–217; Stepan 1978: 218).

The reformers reacted by trying to press the CAPs into increasing their membership.[15] In these attempts the creation of the government sponsored *Confederación Nacional Agraria* (CNA), which was meant to represent the interests of the agrarian sector within the corporative framework the military rulers had in mind, played an important role (Stepan 1978: 225; McClintock 1981: 263–269). On the one hand, the new organization was meant to organize those not directly benefiting by the reform, especially *eventuales, comuneros,* and *minifundistas,* in order to supervise them and to keep these dangerous classes from falling under the influence of class organizations critical of the regime such as the *Confederación Campesina del Perú* (CCP) (CENCIRA 1976: 45). On the other hand, the CNA was meant to provide the political leverage for the inclusion of the cooperatives into a sector of "Social Property" so as to make them contribute more to regional and national development and the creation of new jobs, among other things (Matos Mar and Mejía 1980: 210–216). The cooperative members vigorously resisted such plans, which in their eyes would amount to a sharing of poverty. The reformers, in turn, accused the "labor aristocracy" of the better-off cooperatives of *group egoism,* impeding the attainment of the "collective goal" of establishing a new society (Caballero 1978: 74; McClintock 1981: 38, 84, 320; Stepan 1978: 216–226; Valderrama 1976: 473–476). Other observers, more critical of the utopian rhetoric of the regime, spoke of the *class schizophrenia* or the *double consciousness* of the *socios* who, according to them, were acting on the one hand as proletarians in state capitalist enterprises and, on the other hand, as owners of capital in the exploitation of other proletarians (Caballero 1980: 94; García-Sayán 1980: 89; Rubín de Cells 1978: 11).

However, this situation of "cooperative capitalism" in which the *socios,* through their wages and their share in returns, received part of the surplus value extracted from the *eventuales* (Caballero 1978) was only an accident on the roads of capitalism. A new labor discipline arose in the cooperatives, not as a result of direct state intervention but rather as a result of the squeeze which, in the context of the absence of alternative employment, had forced the *socios* into a certain identification with their enterprises.

In the following we will see how the breakdown of the power relations of the old hacienda system, as a result of the reform, caused labor discipline to be a major problem for the Iquenean CAPs. This gave rise to a sort of cooperative capitalism, the hiring of nonmember wage labor on a large scale, thus shifting the burden of discipline. In the longer run, however, a new discipline emerged as a result of the squeeze to which the CAPs were subjected. The *socios*, and their families, were increasingly subsumed under capital again, albeit only formally, whereas the *eventuales* have increasingly been marginalized.

The Province of Ica

The province of Ica is situated on the Peruvian coast about 300 kilometers south of Lima. In the colonial period the region became one of the major wine-producing areas of South America exporting its product to the cities and the mining centers. The labor force consisted mainly of African slaves.

This changed in the course of the nineteenth century as a result of the expansion of the world market for cotton and the abolition of slavery in 1854. By the end of the century, cotton was actually replacing grapes as the major cash crop. Whereas on the northern sugar plantations wage labor relations were established, new forms of *yanaconaje* (sharecropping) were introduced in Iquenean cotton production. In the harvest season this labor force would be augmented by seasonal migrants, brought down from the *sierra* by *enganchadores* (labor recruiters), thus starting the migratory movement that would soon become self-perpetuating (Eguren, Fernández, and Tume 1981: 46–49; Hammel 1969: 16–24; Paige 1978: 151).[16] Concentration of landownership increased with the rise of cotton production, *hacendados* pushing out smallholders and sharecroppers in various ways. Their resistance, organized in one of the most important early peasant federations in Peru, was broken in the notorious *Masacre de Parcona* of 1924 (Oré 1983; 1984).

In the following decades technical change made a greater centralization of the production process feasible and desirable. Mechanization made the maintenance of a permanent labor pool on the haciendas superfluous. Especially in the late 1940s and early 1950s this, among other things such as political pressure, resulted in the rapid elimination of sharecropping (Eguren, Fernández, and Tume 1981: 49–54; Hammel 1969: 23; Paige 1978: 152). One of the consequences was a process of rapid urbanization through the growth of the Iquenean *barriadas* (shanty towns) (CEDINC 1979; Hammel 1969: 11, 61). After the 1940s cotton production once more expanded rapidly until an all-time high point was reached in the early 1960s when cotton covered about 90 percent of all agricultural land in the province (Hammel 1969: 20; Eguren, Fernandez, and Tume 1981: 65; Thorp and Bertram 1978: 173–179, 236–238). The modernized haciendas kept a small permanent labor force, supplemented in peak seasons with the labor of seasonal migrants, local *minifundistas* and inhabitants of the *barriadas*. By that time seven families owned about half of the agricultural land in the province.

In 1970 the agrarian reform started in Ica and five years later the province counted twenty-one *Cooperativas Agrarias de Producción* (CAPs). These take up about 40 percent of the agricultural land in the Ica Valley, and about 35 percent of the economically active male rural population became member of a cooperative. In most cases these are the former permanent laborers of the haciendas.

The concentration of landownership increased during the reform, as a result of the reformers' predilection for the formation of large enterprises of which they expected better returns as a result of economies of scale. Thus, one of the Iquenean CAPs was composed of forty formerly independent production units or *fundos*, totaling 1,000 hectares. Other CAPs consist of, for example, three former *fundos* totaling 947 hectares, or ten *fundos* totaling 836 hectares, or one *fundo* of 577 hectares. In this way the number of very large enterprises, of more than 500 hectares, increased. At the same time the number of middle-sized enterprises was about halved, whereas the number of farms smaller than five hectares increased (CORDEICA 1980; CEDINCA 1982).

The Iquenean Cooperatives and Their Problems

Cotton has remained the principal product of the Iquenean CAPs. At its lowest point in 1977, it still took up to 50 percent of the harvested area. On the one hand the decline was due to the fall in cotton prices, on the other hand to the attempts of the reformers to promote food production by decree (Matos Mar and Mejía 1980: 261). In many cases such a shift proved difficult or unprofitable (CENCIRA 1975: 44) and land was reverted to cotton again. The difficulties which the CAPs have met in the course of the 1970s can be, to an important extent, attributed to the system of commercialization established by the military regime and the price policies it pursued.

The trade in cotton was monopolized by the state in 1974 (FitzGerald 1979: 183), first through the *Empresa Pública de Comercialización de Harina y Aceite de Pescado* (EPCHAP), which also handled fishery products, and four years later through the *Empresa Nacional de Comercialización de Insumos* (ENCI). State policies were aimed at the promotion of local industry, and this implied that the state monopolies would provide the textile industries with cheap raw material. Thus in 1975 the internal cotton price was set at 92 percent of the, then depressed, world market price, and four years later it was down to 53 percent (Eguren, Fernández, and Tume 1981: 118, 174, 261, 264). Meanwhile, the costs of production rose. If, in 1970, 549 kg of product sufficed to cover the basic costs of production (seed, fertilizers, plague control, water, tractor hours, and labor) of one metric ton of raw cotton, in 1980 these costs took 749 kg out of every ton (Billone, Carbonato, and D. Martínez 1982: 59). The prices paid by the state monopolies thus increasingly failed to cover the real costs of production. Moreover, the payments made by EPCHAP and ENCI were made with great delay, thus undermining the financial liquidity of the CAPs and increasing their dependence on credits. Already, in 1975, the CCP mounted a campaign against this form of state monopoly. Whereas EPCHAP proved profitable, taking 15 percent of the turnover to cover costs, it did not pay "just prices" to the producers as was one of its stated goals (Valderrama 1976: 400, 593). After 1979 the difference between the internal price and the world market price was reduced but not eliminated, although this was not of much help to the producers any more (Eguren, Fernández, and Tume 1981: 261).

Until 1975 the internal market had been an important outlet for the textile industries, but for the most dynamic of them the external market had become increasingly important. For one thing, they profited from the price rise for synthetic fibers as a result of the 1973 oil crisis. This export orientation was reinforced by the economic policies of the "second phase" and the consequent reduction of purchasing power of the population, real wages being about halved in five years. Moreover, it was promoted by the CERTEX subsidy system for nontraditional exports, the provision of cheap raw materials by ENCI, a policy of devaluation-inflation, and, last but not least, cheap labor power, automatic wage adjustments in the textile sector being abolished in 1975 (Eguren, Fernández, and Tume 1981: 179, 278–281). In this way, the part taken by textiles in nontraditional exports rose from 7 percent in 1970 to about 29 percent in 1978 and 37 percent in 1982 (Eguren, Fernández, and Tume 1981: 264).Thus, the industrialization policy and the policy of export diversification have been at the expense of the direct producers of cotton, amongst them the Iquenean CAPs (Alvarez 1983: 242–249). Most of the other crops of the Iquenean CAPs are sold *en chacra* (on field) to a *mayorista de chacra*, who sometimes also takes care of the harvest and transports the product to a *gran mayorista* (large wholesaler). Lima and Arequipa are important outlets. Prices paid are generally low. The producers lack storage and first transformation capacity which most often has not been included in the reform program (CENCIRA 1975: 44–51). The establishment of a *Central de Cooperativas,* meant to assist the CAPs in the sale of their products and the purchase of inputs, has been of little help since it became a pool of corruption and ended in bankruptcy by the end of the 1970s. As a result of the delay in payments by ENCI and low cotton prices, among other things, the CAPs have increasingly become indebted to the *Banco Agrario.* Together with the rising interest rate this expressed itself in rising "costs of administration" (CEDINCA 1982: 6). The credit policies of this bank, its bureaucracy, its inflexibility, the insufficient credit coverage, and the delays in credit supply are a long standing and general (Alvarez 1983: 214–227; D. Martínez and Tealdo 1982: 98–114) source of complaints on the part of the CAPs and their *gerentes*. Through its credit policy, which in large part determines the choice of crops, and through more or less direct supervision of the indebted CAPs, the bank is an important agent in the formal subsumption of cooperative labor. We could go on enumerating the greater and small problems coming to the CAPs from the outside like taxes, state meddling, the agrarian debt, the problem of land titles, and the drought that has affected the region since 1978, causing huge losses and leading to an emergency situation for the whole of Iquenean agriculture in the early 1980s. The main problem has been that prices did not keep pace with the rising costs of production. At the same time, the CAPs have had to face numerous internal problems, which are intensified by these external pressures. Partly, the internal problems are related to the imposition from above of the cooperativization program. The CAPs are characterized by a kind of organizational dualism. On the one hand, there is the cooperative self-management organization structure. The General Assembly is the highest organ, choosing an executive Administration Council and a Supervisory Council, which is meant to control the doings of the Administration Council and the *gerente* (administrator). On the other hand, there is the enterprise organization structure headed by the *gerente*. The latter is mostly contracted from outside the cooperative and has to be approved of by the Ministry of Agriculture. The hierarchical organization structure of the enterprises has not changed much since the time of the hacienda, but the power of what the *socios* often—though jestingly—call *nuevos patrones* (new bosses), meaning not only the *gerente* and the white-collar workers but often the members of the councils as well, is not the same any more. The position of the *gerente* is very unstable. Rather than being the all-powerful *patrón* of the old times, or the manager of a state capitalist enterprise, he is in an ambivalent position, which gives rise to conflicts with the *socios* on the one hand and conflicts with state agencies and the bank on the other. Lower down the hierarchy the *jefes de campo* (supervisors) are now chosen by the *socios*. The self-management organization structure mostly functions badly. The majority of the *socios* lacks detailed knowledge of, for example, financial matters at the enterprise level. However, the General Assembly is often consulted before decisions are taken, so as to avoid later conflicts, giving rise to what is called *asambleismo*: consulting the Assembly on too many problems which should be solved more quickly. On the other hand, problems are often treated on an ad hoc basis, and then mostly when it is too late. This is, for example, the case with problems of corruption, embezzlement and "individual appropriation of collective assets." These occur at all levels of the enterprises and are often discussed. The top level, however, provides the best opportunities and is the most difficult to control. These are some of the reasons for the reemergence of syndical organizations within the CAPs, in spite of the propaganda of the reformers, who affirmed that there would be no need for such organizations within a cooperative framework. We will later return to the dynamics of trade-unionism in Ica.

Cooperatives and Labor Force

To discuss labor relations in the cooperatives we can, rather crudely, distinguish three periods between 1972 and 1982, according to the composition of the labor force and the mode of recruitment. This will show how, gradually, the CAPs came to rely more and more on internally recruited labor.

From 1972 to 1976

In this initial period the labor discipline of the old hacienda system broke down. *Socios* often worked no more than three to four hours on their *tarea* (task). To make up for this large numbers of *jornaleros* (day laborers) were recruited, mostly to do the harder jobs such as digging, weeding, or cleaning the irrigation channels. Their work would be closely supervised. The wages of the *jornaleros* are basically determined by the regional minimum wage. The wages of the *socios*, by contrast, start from a basic wage set by the General Assembly, though within limits set by the state. On top of this they receive bonuses, premiums, gratifications, and a share in the economic results of the enterprise, which partly are profits resulting from the employment of non-member wage labor.[17] For the *socios* this was a period of *bonanza* (Matos Mar and Mejía 1980: 221). The wage difference between *socios* and *eventuales* increased. At the outset, the daily wage of a *socio* was about 135 percent of that paid to the *eventuales*; later it would rise to about 200 percent. Differences in total income must even have been larger. A second group of laborers, recruited basically from outside the CAPs in this period, are the *destajeros* (piece-workers) or cotton pickers who are paid according to the amount of cotton picked in a day. Sometimes they are assisted by *ayudantes* (helpers), mostly their children. Some are individually contracted, but the CAPs also made use of the services of the despised *enganchadores* or *contratistas*. The cotton harvest used to be the occasion for large seasonal migrations from the *sierra*, but nowadays probably the majority of the *destajeros* is recruited in the urbanized areas surrounding the city of Ica. Both groups, *jornaleros* as well as *destajeros*, have been the victims of many dishonesties. Bonuses and premiums to which they were entitled were often only partly paid, if at all.

From 1976 to 1980

The low cotton prices of 1975 and the rising price of inputs led to the first negative results of the Iquenean CAPs since their foundation. They more or less recovered from the blow, but after 1978 the situation steadily worsened. In this period the *socios* started losing out in the race with inflation. To cut labor costs the employment of *jornaleros* was reduced, whereas the *socios* increased their labor input.[18] The duration of employment of *jornaleros* was shortened and their numbers decreased, first slowly, later through mass dismissals. Some of them appealed to the Ministry of Labor, pointing out that after several years of work they considered themselves to be *eventuales permanentes* having a right to stable employment. In some cases this resulted in a settlement *ex pacto laboral* in which the CAPs mostly denied the *eventuales* the status of *permanente*, but promised them priority in case the CAP contracted outside labor. In any case, the number *of jornaleros* was reduced to a minimum. The president of one of the CAPs explained to me that "before there would always be something to do after the harvest, like digging and that kind of work, but now the *socios* do it," and according to another president this could be attributed to a "better *concientización* of the *socios*." One of the *eventuales* was talking about the same thing when he informed me that "before we could find work for nine months a year, but now we can only work as *destajeros, ya no hay nada* (there is nothing anymore)." In the meantime a new group rose within the CAPs, the so-called *remplazantes* (replacements). Over the years, the number of *socios* had slowly decreased as a result of retirement, death, migration, etc. Eventually their places might be taken by new *socios*. Especially the *eventuales* with a *pacto laboral* hoped to gain access to the CAPs in this way. Their aspirations were thwarted, however, when around 1978 retiring *socios* started to appoint their own *remplazantes* by means of a notarial act, a procedure ratified by the General Assembles, thereby making cooperative membership inheritable.

After 1980

Around 1980 most of the CAPs entered into a state of acute crisis. Periodically they are not even able to pay the *socios* for lack of liquid funds. To "pull through their enterprises" the *socios* have occasionally worked on Sundays for no wages but this was not very successful, inter alia because it gave rise to conflicts between the field laborers and the white-collar workers who also worked, albeit in their office. Consequently the work on Sundays for the good of the enterprise has mostly been abandoned but, on the other hand, the white-collar workers and *nuevos patrones* were criticized for their attitude and in times of need they also have to give a hand in the fields. More important, it was decided that the cotton harvest would be done by the CAPs themselves, relying basically on their internal labor reserve. Now it was the turn for the *destajeros* to be drastically reduced in number. Moreover, the lucky ones remaining are now employed under a new form of the *ayudantes* system. This means that they are employed, at best, as helpers of the cotton-picking *socios*. The recruitment of *ayudantes* (assistants) is, to be sure, formally restricted to the close relatives of the *socios*, but some former *destajeros* have also been employed under this system. The amount of cotton picked by the *ayudante* is added to the amount of the *socio* who gets paid accordingly and can redistribute part of his pay to his helpers. Thus only the *socio* is formally employed and general labor costs are reduced. The Iquenean CAPs thus came to rely basically on the labor power supplied by the *socios*, the *remplazantes*, and their families. Recruitment of outside labor has become incidental, and in the early 1980s many CAPs introduced a clause in their statutes formally restricting labor recruitment and access to membership to close relatives of the *socios*. This is in contrast to the criteria of the early reform period: being a head of a family, over eighteen years old, able to work but lacking sufficient land. This development has not been a mere result of demography, such as children of *socios* growing up. The pace of the process was set, to an important degree, by the impact of outside forces, particularly the squeeze to which the CAPs have been subjected. To maintain their family income the *socios* have had to increase their efforts and eventually have had to set their families to work. School absenteeism among the children of *socios* seems to be rising, for example. The days of "cooperative capitalism," exploiting outside labor, are over. Thereafter there has been a return to the *explotación familiar* (the exploitation of family members), as an adviser of the CNA somewhat bitterly remarked.

Trade Union Fever

The developments outlined above have had their repercussions on trade union activity in the Ica region. The *Federación Provincial de Campesinosde Ica* (FEPCI), affiliated to the CCP, has been directing its attention largely to the organization of *eventuales* and landless peasants. The organization reached the height of its influence in 1978 but then quickly crumbled. The reform process had come to a standstill and could not be influenced any more. Attempts to do so met with increasing repression. Moreover, the crisis affecting the region and the reduction in the employment of *eventuales* made their organization increasingly difficult after the initial resistance of which the labor pacts were a result. Last, but not least, political rivalries among the FEPCI leadership have contributed to the disintegration of the organization. The *Liga Agraria Juan Velasco Alvarado* is affiliated to the CNA. The *Liga* consists of representatives of the cooperatives, mostly appointed by the Administrative Council. Although the *Liga* is capable of mobilizing the *socios* in defense of the CAPs it has not succeeded in really taking root among them, mainly as a result of its ambivalence toward real trade union activity. Financial disorder, partly caused by the sharp reduction in government sponsoring after 1978 (Matos Mar and Mejía 1980: 329; McClintock 1981: 268), and internal quarrels have further weakened the organization. The organizational vacuum now starts to be filled, however. New organizations emerge and unions that had become inactive as a result of the anti-trade union rhetoric of the reform period are given a new breath of life. Seeing what was supposed to be the basis of his organization crumble away, the president of the *Liga Agraria* spoke of *a fiebra syndical* (trade union fever). The new trade unionism revolves around two main poles. The first is the problem of badly functioning cooperative democracy. Trade unions serve as a means to check the actions of the *nuevos patrones*. In this way the *socios* seek to increase control over their enterprises. Simultaneously, a second tendency is at work. The emerging organizations, and particularly the revitalized ones, are often rooted in the different *fundos* that have been incorporated into the CAPs. As such they play an important role in the discussions about restructuring the CAPs. This issue came to the foreground when the Agrarian Promotion and Development Law of 1980 allowed the cooperatives to "parcelize" their land by dividing it into individually owned plots. Parcelization, however, is generally not proposed as a solution to the problems of the Iquenean CAPs. The first CAP in the province to be restructured came close to this alternative, but this was the enterprise that had been composed out of 40 former *fundos*. For the other CAPs this is not a very viable option, since it would involve an extensive breakup of the production structure. Rather sectorization is being proposed. The former *fundos* would then to a large extent become administratively independent, allowing much more self-management by the workers. This might result in the establishment of a number of smaller cooperative enterprises relying on their internal labor supply and combining collective production with production on small plots in private use. Instead of total disintegration we thus witness an adaptation of cooperative agriculture to the squeeze to which it has been subjected.

Conclusion

The effects of the 1969 reform on the development of farmer-type capitalism in Peruvian agriculture may have been much less important than has been suggested by de Janvry. The most direct achievement of the reform, the establishment of an associative sector, cannot be bypassed, and Kay (1982) has even argued that the reform should be characterized as an attempt at a state capitalist road. In this article attention has focused on the CAP-type enterprises in the coastal region. Slightly more than half of the six hundred CAPs that were established as a result of the reform are located in the coastal region. Of the latter the agro-industrial sugar complexes are, in many ways, a special case.[19] Many of the other CAPs belong to the group of most modernized and market-integrated enterprises, and they play an important role in the supply of several key products of the region, such as cotton, rice, maize, and sorghum for agro-industrial use in the poultry industry and potatoes. Although the role of the state, in establishing and supervising the CAPs and through its influence on the price and credit system has been great, their cooperative self-management dimension (Caballero 1977: 154; 1980: 89) or their dimension as a collective form of simple commodity production (Gutelman 1979: 160) should be taken into account in the discussion of these enterprises. Rosa Luxemburg provides a useful framework for the discussion of this dimension (Caballero 1977: 154; 1980: 89; Gutelman 1979: 160). She characterized cooperatives as "hybrids": the socialization of production on a small scale in the context of capitalist exchange relations. Since production is dominated by exchange the workers of such an enterprise, to remain competitive, have to subject themselves to the discipline of capital. They have to play the role of their own capitalist. It is this contradictory situation that accounts for the problems of labor discipline in cooperative enterprises. If the contradiction between the mode of production and the mode of exchange is not superseded such enterprises will tend either revert to capitalist enterprises or to dissolve (Luxemburg 1974: 44). Let us briefly review the case of the Iquenean CAPs against this background. In the first years the *socios* had the opportunity to reject the labor discipline of the hacienda period. Since the state was unable to restore discipline the CAPs came to rely heavily on outside wage labor. The state as well as the *socios*, whose income partly derived from the surplus value extracted from the *eventuales*, profited from this situation of not-so-pure cooperativism. This is the situation described by Caballero (1978) in his article on *eventuales* in the coastal CAPs, and of which Kay (1982: 156) writes that in this way the *socios* "might degenerate into State-associated quasi-capitalist employers of cheap and unorganized labor." This situation of "cooperative capitalism" did not last long, however. In his analytical model of this situation Caballero (1978: 66–67, 75) assumes product prices and costs of production to be fixed. If, however, prices fall and/or production costs rise the income of the *socios* will fall unless they increase their efforts and reduce the employment of *eventuales*. Thus the *socios* increasingly became subsumed under the discipline of capital again. Another possibility would have been to reduce the number of *socios* and replace them with hired labor. Thus the CAPs would revert to capitalist enterprises. Obviously, for the great majority of the *socios* this is not a realistic solution and such tendencies are resisted, for example, by making CAP-membership inheritable through the appointment of *remplazantes* by the *socios*. How then about the other possibility by Rosa Luxemburg, the dissolution of the CAPs? This seems to fit better the development of the coastal CAPs in the latter part of the 1970s. Already in the late 1970s larger or smaller plots in private use existed illegally in many CAPs and it has been argued that it was only state intervention that kept the enterprises from completely falling apart (Caballero 1977: 155; 1978: 60; 1980: 91; Kay 1982: 157). Let us see what happened after 1980. The second Belaúnde regime attributed the continuing stagnation in the agrarian sector in large part to the property relations established in the 1970s. Parcelization of the CAPs was strongly encouraged by the government, which thus opted for a sort of redistributive counterreform. This happened in the context of very orthodox free market policies. Price controls were abolished for most producers but this benefited middlemen and agribusiness rather than the direct producers. Moreover, Peruvian agriculture was expected to become internationally competitive, meaning that it had to face uncontrolled imports which quite often were subsidized by the exporting countries. Climatic disturbances further aggravated these problems, leading to a general agrarian crisis in 1983 (Latín America Bureau 1985: 100–102). It was in this context of crisis and government policies that clearly aimed at the destruction of cooperative agriculture (Méndez 1982) that the movement toward parcelization of the coastal CAPs gained momentum in recent years. In 1984 more than one-third of these CAPs were being in some way restructured, while by now the proportion may have risen to two-thirds. According to a survey by the Ministry of Agriculture, by the end of 1986 exactly half of the 618 CAPs established during the agrarian reform were changing or had changed their enterprise model (*Resúmen Semanal* 1986). Quite often the decision to parcelize was not so much made out of petty bourgeois enthusiasm for private proprietorship on the part of the *socios* (de Janvry 1981: 218, 264–248) but rather because they had little choice in the face of the desperate financial situation of the enterprises. Full parcelization would mean that, on the average, assuming equal distribution, each *socio* would receive about 4 hectares. An important part of coastal agriculture would thus be peasantized. Disadvantages of parcelization exist not only at the technical level but also because of the few services the CAPs provide and their function as defense mechanisms. It is not surprising, then, that many *socios* seem to have second thoughts about the connections between private property and wealth as depicted by the Belaúnde regime (Arévalo and Revesz 1984; Kay 1982: 157; Méndez 1982). In Ica the process of parcelization started relatively late and, as we saw, alternatives to complete parcelization were sought. For the coastal region as a whole there seems to be a whole gamut of modes of restructuring, depending on factors such as productive infrastructure, trade union activity (Bolhuis and van der Ploeg 1985: 523–595), cooperative performance, etc. Quite often parcelization is only partial and cooperative structures are not only fully abandoned. The dynamics of the parcelization process have only recently started to be studied (Arévalo and Revesz 1984; Gonzales and Torre 1985; Portugal 1985).[20] It is clear, however, that this complicated process can hardly be understood in terms of an abstract opposition between "individualism" and "collectivism" (de Janvry 1981: 218). Rather, there seems to be a great variety of combinations of individual and collective strategies.

The post-1980 policies did not dynamite Peruvian agriculture since the reasons for its stagnation lay not so much in an absolute "inefficiency" of cooperative agriculture as in the forms of articulation of the agrarian sector with the rest of the economy. The disintegration of the CAPs may, for the moment, lead to the peasantization of an important part of coastal agriculture (Arévalo and Revest 1984; Gonzales and Torre 1985). At the same time the signs of capitalist development in agricultural production are still quite scarce or, as one Peruvian observer remarks: when, today, we try to find the process of reconcentration of land, the return of the *gamonales* or the consolidation of middle size owners, we find that there is no generalized phenomenon of this kind. Only embryonic manifestations. It would be a fatal error not to understand the general dynamics of what is happening in the countryside nowadays. The present phase has not yet culminated in the destruction of agrarian cooperativism and the affirmation of the smallholders. The counterreform advances only slowly and with many contradictions. What is lacking are proposals about how to stop it (Wiener 1985: 167; my translation). As we have seen, neither the military governments nor the Belaúnde regime did much to relax the most important "material determinants of the agrarian crisis" (de Janvry 1981: 151). Not only did the prices of wage foods remain subject to strong downward pressures, but traditional exports such as cotton were also subjected to price controls in the context of the shift toward a new model of accumulation, which remained sectorally disarticulated, sustained this time by the production of nontraditional exports. Any agrarian policy aimed at reactivating production will at least have to do something about the problem of costs and prices, whatever road is chosen for further development. It was only after the disaster year 1983 that the Belaúnde government loosened the tax and credit squeeze on agriculture somewhat, tried to reduce production costs and established some very modest price stabilization schemes. These policies have been extended by the new APRA government which, in this respect, seems to give more content to the "priority for agriculture" than its predecessor. However, in spite of the fact that during its electoral campaign the APRA affirmed that priority would be given to the associative sector the policies of the new government on this point have, until now, been far from clear and lack any coherence. The most important proposals as to how to stop the counterreform come from the peasant organizations CCP and CNA. The CNA has always been a staunch defender of cooperativism and of the agrarian reform implemented by the Velasco government, which it wants to deepen and extend. In the latter part of the 1970s the organization was rapidly radicalized and came to coordinate activities with its one time rival, the CCP.

The CCP is less tied to the cooperative models, as they were established by the reformers, but rather than leaving the restructuring of the cooperatives to the forces of the market the organization proposes to overcome the problems of the cooperatives through a process of democratic restructuring. One of the possibilities suggested by the CCP is the conversion of cooperatives into peasant communities in which forms of collective and individual production can be combined. At the same time the organization has moved beyond its old program, centered on the "struggle for land," which has been extended to include a "struggle for production centered on alternative credit, distribution and land-use proposals aimed at really serving the needs of the masses" (CCP 1981). Thus the CCP seeks to unify smallholders and members of cooperatives in a struggle aimed at overcoming the contradictions between several forms of simple commodity production and the mode of exchange or, as Dos Santos (1976: 77) wrote: faced by a conditioning situation people may either choose among various alternatives internal to that situation or they may seek to change the conditioning situation itself.

Notes

Originally published in 1987 as "The Agrarian Question in Peru: Some Observations on the Roads of Capital," in *The Journal of Peasant Studies* 14, no. 4, 500–532. We thank the *Journal of Peasant Studies* and Taylor & Francis for kindly giving us permission to republish this article.

1. For a discussion of these models and their development in the course of the reform process, see: Matos Mar and Mejía (1980: 191–222, 130–141), Valderrama (1976), and Zaldivar (1974).

2. "The objective of the simple reproduction 'squeeze' then is to act as one of the mechanisms of intensifying the labor of the household to maintain or increase the supply of commodities without capital incurring any cost of management and supervision of the production process" (Bernstein 1977: 65).

3. This model is derived from Marx's reproduction schemes developed in *Capital II*. Note, however, how de Janvry shifts from a model in which the departments of production, or sectors, producing means of production and consumer goods, are pivotal, to a model opposing a modern to a traditional sector thus coming close to the dualist models of modernization theory.

4. That the "demarcation point" of generalized commodity production (McEachern 1976: 452) has been reached in Peru is beyond doubt. Monetary income, derived from wage labor and self-employment accounts for about 60 percent to 70 percent of total income of Peruvian rural families (Caballero 1984: 18–20). García-Sayán (1980: 35) estimates that subsistence production contributes 16 percent at most (in the *sierra*). Many peasants sell their crop in order to buy wage foods, such as noodles and bread, for which the ingredients are in large part imported.

5. See also Meillassoux's discussion of the (re)production of labor power and the transformation of the domestic community into the patriarchal family, which is not (yet?) really subsumed under capital (Meillassoux 1975: 10, 150–154, 213–218).

6. On one of the occasions where Marx (*Capital III*, chap. 14) discusses the problem of subsumption under advanced capitalism rather than in relation to "the early forms in which capital appears" (Chevalier 1983: 171), he relates the more or less incomplete subsumption of labor under capital to the *size of the surplus population*, on the one hand, and to the *nature of the labor process* in certain branches of production, on the other. To account for the existence of simple commodity production in agriculture Friedmann (1978: 88, 95) emphasizes technical aspects, whereas Goodman and Redclift (1981: 12–15) list several factors such as risk, production time and technology but also unequal exchange mechanisms due to the dominance of industrial capital, the availability of land, population growth, labor absorption in industry and the strength of the various rural social classes.

7. That is to say that their means of production do not function as capital, production not being based in wage labor. This implies that the concept of profit does not apply to simple commodity producers since they do not appropriate surplus value (Friedmann 1978: 79; Chevalier 1983: 178). Therefore de Janvry's discussion of the "nonprofit motivation" of peasants and other simple commodity producers is beside the point. A profit-making simple commodity producer is just as absurd as a profit-making proletarian, although some simple commodity producers may succeed in converting their assets into capital investments if and when the opportunity offers (Chevalier 1983: 177). On the other hand, the concept of opportunity wage (Friedmann 1978: 96; 1980: 174; Chevalier 1983: 160) may be useful in avoiding an all too mechanical interpretation of "total dispossession" as the sole criterion for real proletarianization.

8. For a more precise analysis of the "relative stagnation" of the sector Alvarez (1983: 36–39) and Hopkins (1981: 69) distinguish four categories of products exhibiting different tendencies of growth and stagnation:

    (1) products for direct urban consumption (including rice, beans, beef, pork, some poultry, part of the milk production, and potatoes produced in the coastal region). This group of products increased its share in the total value of agricultural production from 23 percent in 1948–1952 to 47 percent in 1976;

    (2) products for the "restricted market," destined basically to local consumption in rural areas (maize for human consumption, wheat, barley, potatoes produced in the *sierra*, yuca, mutton, wool) 49 percent in 1948–1952 and 27 percent in 1976;

(3) agro-industrial inputs (cotton, sugar, coffee, the major part of milk produced, fodder maize, and barley for beer production); 6 percent in 1948–1952, and 18 percent in 1976; and

(4) export products (cotton, sugar, coffee, wool, according to the quantities exported); 23 percent in 1948–1952, and 8 percent in 1976.

9. For the producers this was not of much help since at the same time demand decreased sharply as a result of the impoverishment of the population (Alvarez 1983: 164). Moreover, only part of eventual price increases reaches the direct producers (Hopkins 1981: 84–87; Figueroa 1980).

10. This typology contains three major types: (1) "reforms that imply some redistribution of land but that do not challenge the *precapitalist* estates" domination of agriculture; (2) reforms that promote the *transition* to capitalism in agriculture toward either the Junker- or the farmer-road of development; and (3) reforms within *capitalist* agriculture, either to induce a shift from Junker-road to farmer-road or to redistribute the land within either. To each type of reform that implies either a transition or a shift of road there also corresponds the possibility of counter reform" (de Janvry 1981: 205).

11. The diversity among private enterprises larger than 5 hectares is very great, and the number of farmer type enterprises should not be overestimated. Besides really modem capitalist enterprises, which are mostly located in the coastal region and concentrated in quite specific branches of production, many other enterprises larger than 20 hectares should rather be classified as belonging to the "semifeudal" or Junker type, left more or less untouched by the Teform, but not very promising in terms of capitalist development (García-Sayán 1980: 75–77; Matos Mar and Mejía 1980: 188–189). On the other hand the peasantry may be much more important than suggested by de Janvry. Caballero (1977: 150) even suggests that *campesinos*, of which in this case he does not give a clear definition, control more than half the agricultural land. Alvarez (1983: 107–108) points out that in the case of the *sierra* the large haciendas of more than 50 hectares controlled only 20 percent of the land in terms of standardized irrigated hectares, whereas the peasantry, those who own less than 5 hectares, controlled 37 percent In these terms the role of the peasantry in landownership is much more important than the 6.5 percent mentioned by de Janvry. For other comments on the data used by de Janvry see: García Sayán (1980: 32–33) and D. Martínez and Tealdo (1982: 28–30).

12. It should not be forgotten that the emphasis on the formation of cooperatives partly resulted from the lack of enthusiasm of the rural bourgeoisie for its newly assigned role. Moreover, one of the first modifications of the reform law, in November 1969, was meant to check the process of private parcelization in response to worker protests against its consequences for employment (Matos Mar and Mejía 1980: 163–165; Valderrama 1976: 71, 83; Zaldivar 1974: 39–44).

13. As the same time Gutelman (1979: 156) describes the relations of production in the cooperatives as "pre-capitalist." Whereas the simple commodity aspect thus makes cooperatives pre-capitalist, the collective aspect makes them post-capitalist. Thus we would have the case of an articulation between three modes of production. On the one hand this points to the limitations of dualist and articulationist theories (FitzGerald 1979: 127). On the other hand we may ask if dualist theories, labeling everything "abnormal" as pre-capitalist, are not somewhat backward looking. The idea that cooperatives might represent a step forward in the democratic control over the means of production stems from Marx (*Capital III*, chap. 27) and in the *Civil War in France*, the starting point for the discussions on proletarian dictatorship, he even showed quite some enthusiasm (Marx and Engels 1970: 291). Lenin, much more concerned with state control than with forms of direct worker control over production, was much less enthusiastic (Lenin 1971: 761–766), whereas Rosa Luxemburg discussed cooperativism in the context of her attack on reformism (Luxemburg 1974: 44).

14. *Eventual* is here used in contrast to *estable*, that is, someone having stable employment. According to the Labor Stability Law, in vigor from 1970 to 1978, anyone having worked for more than three months without interruption would have a right to labor stability. If we speak of *eventuales permanentes* we mean people who are employed as *eventuales* for long periods, sometimes year after year, but who in spite of this are denied the right to employment security. The word *eventual* is often confusing. On the one hand it is used to designate people who occasionally work as wage laborers, spending most of the time on their own land, for example seasonal migrants. In this case it points to the occasional character of the *supply* of labor power. This may have been the original sense of the word. On the other hand, the word indicates the instability of employment and we use it in this sense, which reflects the occasional character of *demand* and suits the present situation better.

15. It was argued that instead of adopting capitalist criteria of profit maximization the new enterprises should adopt criteria of "social interest." Rather than letting the number of member workers be determined by the point where marginal product equals remuneration, the enterprises should extend the number of *socios* beyond this point and remunerate them on the basis of average productivity "like in a peasant economy" (Caballero 1978: 79; CENCIRA 1976: 75; Stepan 1978: 218). Mostly such proposals were resisted by the CAPs. However, as we will see, the CAPs may over time tend toward a similar situation as a result of the squeeze to which they were subjected and their inability to lay off member labor. Bolhuis and van der Ploeg (1985: 323–394) discuss the case of a CAP that explicitly pursued a policy of increasing employment.

16. Usually the role of *enganchadores* in forcing people into wage labor is emphasized. Although this may have been important we should bear in mind that nowadays their power derives from their control of employment opportunities

17. Caballero (1978: 67, 70) calls this *ingress no ganado* (unearned income), but it is nothing but a share in the profits of "cooperative capitalism." For an overview of the state-prescribed redistribution of enterprise results between the state, enterprise accumulation and the *socios*, see Matos Mar and Mejía (1980: 137), McClintock (1981: 221–226), and Zaldívar (1974: 37).

18. In one of the Iquenean CAPs they worked 5.3 days per week in 1974; 5.2 days in 1978; 5.7 days in 1980; and 5.9 days in 1982. At the same time labor was intensified.

19. The sugar CAPs were subjected to extensive state intervention from the beginning (Matos Mar and Mejía 1980: 191–197; Stepan 1978: 190–229; Zaldívar 1974: 30–39), reaching a high point in 1977 (Kay 1982: 157). Sustained by high export prices these CAPs did quite well until 1975, in spite of very low internal prices, heavy taxation and rising costs of production (Alvarez 1983: 181–184, 254–258). With the fall of world market prices the sugar CAPs entered into an acute crisis, aggravated by droughts. The Belaúnde government had plans for restructuring and reprivatization of these enterprises but until now nothing much has happened.

20. Gonzales and Torre (1985) contains a number of very interesting studies of the parcelization process in the coastal region. Unfortunately I only lately received a copy and was not able to use it in this study.

References

Alvarez, Elena. 1983. *Política económica y agricultura en el Perú, 1969–1979*. Lima: Instituto de Estudios Peruanos.

Amin, Samir. 1976. *Accumulation on a World Scale*. New York and London: Monthly Review Press.

Amin, Samir, and Kostas Vergopoulos. 1980. *La question paysanne et le capitalisme*. Paris: Editions Anthropos.

Arévelo, Jorge, and Bruno Revesz. 1984. *Piura: las parcelaciones un asunto candente*. Cuzco: CIPA and Centro de Estudios Rurales Andinos "Bartolomé de Las Casas."

Assies, Willem. 1985. "Landhervorming in Peru; kooperaties en arbeidsreserve, het geval Ica." Internal document, Amsterdam.

Bennholdt-Thomsen, Veronica. 1979. "Marginalität in Lateinamerika: eine Theoriekritik." In *Lateinamerika: analysen und berichte V*, ed. V. Bennholdt-Thomsen, T. Evers, and K. Meschkat. Berlin: Olle und Wolter.

————. 1982. "Subsistence Production and Extended Reproduction. A Contribution to the Discussion about Modes of Production." *Journal of Peasant Studies* 9, no. 4: 241–254

Bernstein, Henry. 1977. "Notes on Capital and the Peasantry." *Review of African Political Economy* 10: 60–73.

Billone, Jorge, Daniel Carbonetto, and Daniel Martínez. 1982. *Términos de intercambio ciudad-campo 1970–1980*. Lima: CEDEP.

Bolhuis, Eppo, and Jan Douwe van der Ploeg. 1985. *Boerenarbeid en stijlen van landbouwbeoefening*. Leiden: Leiden Development Studies.

Breman, Jan, 1976. *Een dualistisch arbeidsbestel? Een kritische beschouwing van het begrip "de informele sector."* Rotterdam: Van Gennep.

Brewer, Anthony. 1980. *Marxist Theories of Imperialism*. London: Routledge and Kegan Paul.

Caballero, José María, 1977. "Sobre el caracter de la reforma agraria peruana." *Latin American Perspectives* 4, no. 3: 146–159.

————. 1978. "Los eventuales en las cooperativas costeñas peruanas: un modelo analítico." *Economía* 1, no. 2: 57–80.

————. 1980. "El fracaso del modelo agrario militar." In *Realidad en el campo peruano después de la reforma agraria*, ed. C. Amat y León. Lima: Centro de Investigación y Capacitación (CIC).

————. 1984. "Agricultura peruana y campesinado: Balance de la investigaciónreciente y patrón de evolución." *Apuntes* 14: 3–38.

Caballero, José María, and Elena. Alvarez. 1980. *Aspectos cuantitativos de la reforma agraria*. Lima: Instituto de Estudios Peruanos.

CCP. 1981. *2° Consejo nacional CCP, informes y resoluciones*. Lima: CCP.

CEDINCA. 1979. *Tate*. Work document.

————. 1982. *Instalación de una planta de hilados de algodón*. Ica: CEDINCA.

CENCIRA. 1975. *Comercialización de productos agrícolas: caso: central de cooperativas José Carlos Mariátegui, Ica*. Lima: CENCIRA.

————. 1976. *Los eventuales y los mercados de trabajo en la agricultura: Valles Jequetepe y Zaña*. Lima: CENCIRA.

Chevalier, Jaques 1983. "There is Nothing Simple about Simple Commodity Production." *Journal of Peasant Studies* 10, no. 4: 153–186.

CORDEICA. 1980. *Anuario estadístico*. Ica: CORDEICA.

de Janvry, Alain. 1981. *The Agrarian Question in Latin America*. Baltimore and London: John Hopkins.

de Janvry, Alain. and Carlos Garramón. 1977. "The Dynamics of Rural Poverty in Latin America." *Journal of Peasant Studies* 4, no. 2: 206–215.

Dos Santos, Theotonio. 1976. "The Crisis of Development Theory and the Problem of Dependence in Latin America." In *Underdevelopment and Development*, ed. H. Bernstein. Harmondsworth: Penguin Books.

Eguren, Fernando, Jorge Fernández, and Fabian Tume. 1981. *Producción algodonera e industria textil en el Perú*. Lima: DESCO.

Feder, Ernest. 1971. *The Rape of the Peasantry.* New York: Anchor Books.

Figueroa, Adolfo. 1980. "Política de precios agropecuarios e ingresos rurales en el Perú." In *Realidad en el campo peruano después de la reforma agraria,* ed. C. Amat y León. Lima: CIC.

FitzGerald, Edmund Valpy Knox. 1979. *The Political Economy of Peru 1956–1978.* Cambridge, U.K.: Cambridge University Press.

Friedmann, Harriet. 1978. "Simple Commodity Production and Wage Labour in the American Plains." *Journal of Peasant Studies* 6, no. 1: 71–100.

———. 1980. "Household Production and the National Economy: Concepts for the Analysis of Agrarian Formations." *Journals of Peasant Studies* 7, no. 2: 158–184.

García-Sayán, Diego. 1980. "La cuestion agraria y las clases sociales en debate." In *Agro: clases, campesinado y revolución,* ed. F. and D. Eguren García-Sayán. Lima: DESCO.

Gonzales, Alberto, and German Torre, eds. 1985. *Las parcelaciones de las cooperativas agrarias del Perú.* Chiclayo: Solidaridad.

Goodman, David, and Michael Redclift. 1981. *From Peasant to Proletarian.* Oxford, U.K.: Basil Blackwell.

Gutelman, Michel. 1979. *Structures et reformes agraires.* Paris: Maspero.

Hammel, Eugene A. 1969. *Power in Ica.* Boston: Little, Brown.

Hickel, Rudolf. 1972. "Lieseanleitung zu den Marxschen Reproduktionsschemata." In *Das Kapital II.* , K. Marx. Frankfurt, Berlin, Vienna: Ullstein.

Hopkins, Raúl. 1981. *Desarrollo desigual y crisis en la agricultura peruana 1944–1969.* Lima: Instituto de Estudios Peruanos.

Iguíñiz, Javier. 1979. "Interpretaciones de la evolución de la economía peruana." In *La investigación en ciencias sociales en el Perú,* ed. J. Iguilñiz. Lima: Tarea.

Kay, Cris. 1982. "Achievements and Contradictions of the Peruvian Agrarian Reform." *Journal of Development Studies* 18, no. 2: 141–170.

Laclau, Ernesto, and Chantal Mouffe. 1985. *Hegemony and Socialist Strategy.* London: Verso Books.

Lajo Lazo, Manuel. 1980. "La crisis de la alimentación y el papel de la agroindustria." In *Promoción agraria ¿Para quién?,* ed. J. M. Mejía Lima: Tiempo Presente.

Latín America Bureau. 1985. *Peru Paths to Poverty.* London: LAB.

Lenin, Wladimir Iljitsj. 1971. "Über das Genossenschaftswesen." In *Ausgewählte Werke.* Moscow: Progress Verlag.

Lipietz, Alain. 1982. "Marx or Rostow?" *New Left Review* 132: 48–58.

Luxemburg, Rosa. 1974. "Sozialreform oder Revolution?" In *Schriften zur Theorie der Spontaneität.* Reinbek: Rowohlt Verlag.

Martínez, Daniel, and Armando Tealdo. 1982. *El agro peruano 1970–1980.* Lima: CEDEP.

Martínez, Héctor. 1980. "Las empresas asociativas agrícolas peruanas." In *Realidad en el campo peruano después de la reforma agraria,* ed. C. Amat y León. Lima: CIC.

Marx, Karl. *Das Kapital I–III.* Frankfurt, Berlin, Vienna: Ullstein.

Marx, Karl, and Friedrich Engels. 1970. *Selected Works.* Moscow: Progress.

Matos Mar, José, and José Manuel Mejía. 1980. *La reforma agraria en el Perú.* Lima: Instituto de Estudios Peruanos.

McClintock, Cynthia. 1981. *Peasant Cooperatives and Political Change in Peru.* Princeton: Princeton University Press.

McEachern, Doug. 1976. "The Mode of Production in India." *Journal of Contemporary Asia* 6: 444–457.

Meillassoux, Claude. 1975. *Femmes greniers et capitaux.* Paris: Maspero.

Mejía, José Manuel. 1980. "De la reforma agraria a la promocióna. Un análisis crítico de la nueva política agrarian." In *Promoción agraria ¿Para quién?* ed. J. M. Mejía. Lima: Tiempo Presente.

Méndez, Manuela J. 1982. "Las cooperativas agrarias de producción y las parcelaciones: situación actual y perspectivas." In *Situación actual y perspectivas del problema agrario en el Perú*, ed. F. Eguren. Lima: DESCO.

Oré, María Teresa. 1983. *Memorias de un viejo luchador campesino: Juan H. Pévez.* Lima: ILLA/TAREA.

———. 1984. "Pasado y presente en la conciencia popular: la memoria colectiva del campesinado iqueño." *Análisis* 12: 72–88.

Paige, Jeffrey M. 1978. *Agrarian Revolution.* New York: The Free Press.

Portugal Vizcarra, José A. 1985. *Parcelaciones de las empresas asociativas: nueva estructura agraria en el Perú.* Lima: Consultaría de Proyectos Agro-Industriales.

Resúmen Semanal. 1986. Año IX: No. 395. Lima: DESCO.

Roberts, Brian. 1981. *Cities of Peasants.* London: Edward Arnold Publishers.

Rosdolsky, Roman. 1972. "Der Streit um die Marxschen Produktionsschemata." In *Das Kapital II.*, K. Marx. Frankfurt, Berlin, Vienna: Ullstein.

Rubín de Celis, Emma. 1978. *¿Que piensa el campesino de la reforma agraria?* Piura: CIPCA.

Samaniego, Carlos. 1980. "Perspectivas de la agricultura campesina en el Perú." In *Realidad en el campo peruano después de la reforma agraria*, ed. C. Amat y León. Lima: CIC.

———. 1984. "Estado, acumulación y agricultura en el Perú." *Estudios Rurales Latinoamericanos* 7, no. 3: 199–262.

Stepan, Alfred. 1978. *The State and Society: Peru in Comparative Perspective.* Princeton: Princeton University Press.

Sweezy, Paul Marlor. 1968. *The Theory of Capitalist Development.* New York and London: Monthly Review Press.

Thorp, Rosemary, and Geoffrey Bertram. 1978. *Peru 1890–1977: Growth and Policy in an Open Economy.* London and Basingstoke: Macmillan.

Valderrama, Mariano. 1976. *7 Años de reforma agraria peruana.* Lima: Pontificia Universidad Católica.

Vergopoulos, Kostas. 1980. "Capitalisme difforme." In *La question paysanne et le capitalisme*, ed. S. Amin and K. Vergopoulos. Paris: Editions Anthropos.

Wiener, Raúl. 1985. "La situación de la reforma agraria y parcelación privada." In *Las parcelaciones de las cooperativas agrarias del Perú*, ed. A. Gonzales and G. Torre. Chiclayo: Solidaridad.

Zaldívar, Ramón. 1974. "Agrarian Reform and Military Reformism in Peru." In *Agrarian Reform and Agrarian Reformism*, ed. D. Lehman. London: Faber and Faber.

Zegarra, Walter. 1983. "Las cooperativas agrarias peruanas: situación y perspectivas." *Socialismo y Participación* 22: 67–77.

From Rubber Estate to Simple Commodity Production

Agrarian Struggles in the
Northern Bolivian Amazon

Facts are simple and facts are straight
Facts are lazy and facts are late
Facts all come with points of view
Facts don't do what I want them to
Facts just twist the truth around
Facts are living turned inside out

—Talking Heads, *Crosseyed and Painless*, 1980

Introduction

In October 2001 the Bolivian government convoked an "Earth Summit" (*Cumbre de la Tierra*) to be held a month later. The previous years had seen an escalation of peasant unrest. In the Andean highlands the peasantry had turned increasingly to militant action with strong ethnic overtones. In the eastern tropical lowlands a colonists' movement had gathered strength, and in the year 2000 a movement of landless peasants had erupted, eliciting a violent response from large landowners who, in turn, pressured the government with their own claims. By the end of June that same year indigenous people of the tropical lowlands had initiated their "Third March" under the banner of "Land, Territories, and Natural Resources" and were joined by peasants from the region.[1] The "Earth Summit" ended in failure. Conditions were hardly propitious as in early November a clash between landless peasants and alleged paramilitaries had claimed seven lives, and peasant organizations were suspicious about the intentions of a government that had recently signed an agreement with the *Camara Agropecuaria del Oriente* (CAO), representing the large landowners and cattle-raisers of the Santa Cruz region, which ran quite counter to peasant interests. In the course of November the "Summit" was renamed "Encounter," reflecting reduced expectations, and when it took place by the end of the month some of the principal peasant organizations made a show of absence and announced that they would organize a summit of their own.

What the surge of peasant and indigenous people's movements made clear was that the agrarian and forestry legislation introduced in 1996 had failed to resolve the problems it was meant to address. The extremely slow, patchy, and often landlord-biased implementation of the 1996 *Ley del Servicio Nacional de Reforma Agraria*, also known as *Ley INRA*, generated frustration. Moreover, this law failed to address the problems that had accumulated in the Andean highlands since the 1953 Revolutionary land reform, and it is hard to apply in other specific regional contexts.

The *Ley Forestal* generated its own set of conflicts. Forestry concessions that had been granted overlapped with territorial claims by indigenous peoples, and in 1999 the Banzer government had issued a decree allowing the conversion of rubber estates in the northern Amazon region into concessions under the 1996 Forestry Law, opening the way to a consolidation of a neo-latifundist tenure structure to the detriment of the local peasantry. This was one of the direct motives for the indigenous-peasant "March for Land Territories and Natural Resources," which successfully pressured the government to repeal the decree and to modify the regulations for the implementation of the *Ley INRA*. In this article I will focus on the specific constellation in the northern Bolivian Amazon region that provided a major incentive for the "Third March," and I will seek to relate the issues at stake in the region to the broader debate on agrarian and forestry legislation. The history of the region has been marked by the rubber economy that arose in the final quarter of the nineteenth century. By 1985, however, rubber extraction entered into a final crisis. This heralded the beginning of a process of economic reconversion marked by changes in labor relations and forms of resource use.

In the first section of this article I will outline the rise and demise of the rubber economy and show how, with the decline of the rubber estate system independent peasant-extractivist communities emerged, while at the same time control over and access to resources, rather than control over people on which the estate system was based, became increasingly important. In the next section I will sketch the rise of a new regional economic constellation after 1985, when the production of Brazil nuts became a major economic activity in the region. The third section of the article offers a further analysis and discussion of the regional transformations in the labor regime, in patterns of landholding, and access to resources. This analysis delineates the latent tension between "owners" of *barracas* (former rubber estates) and the emerging *comunidades libres* (free communities). This conflict of interests became manifest when the 1996 land and forestry legislation started to be implemented in the region. Section four discusses this new legislation, shows how it triggered the "Third March," and examines the outcomes of this peasant-indigenous mobilization. The concluding section sums up the argument and looks at the future prospects for the region.

The Rise and Decline of the Rubber Trade

This section provides a brief introduction to the region and describes how, alongside the rubber estates, a sector of free communities has come into existence and competes for resources with the established local agrarian elite. For convenience the century in which rubber production dominated from around 1880 until 1985 is divided into three periods. The first covers the rise of the rubber economy and the consolidation of the "Suárez Empire," which came to dominate the region until it disintegrated after 1940. The period from 1940 to 1985 is characterized by the emergence of a much more fragmented system of *patron*-run estates, while in the interstices of this system the first free communities emerged. This constellation changed drastically as a result of the final collapse of the rubber trade after 1985. The new Brazil nut-centered economy would be built from the rubble left after the collapse of the rubber economy.[2]

The Rise of the Rubber Trade and the Consolidation of the Casa Suárez (1880–1940)

Until well into the nineteenth century what nowadays is the northern Bolivian Amazon region was still designated as "land to be discovered." The national border with Brazil was ill defined. The 1867 Ayacucho Treaty mentioned a line running from the confluence of the Beni River and the Mamoré, which then forms the River Madeira, to the unknown headwaters of the Javari River. This rainforest region was inhabited by various indigenous peoples such as the Araona, Cavineño, Tacana, Ese Ejja, Chácobo Pacahuara, and Yaminahua, descendants of whom can still be found in the region. Other groups have been decimated or displaced (Lema Garret 1998; Stoian 2000a: 82, 123; Weber 1994). To the south the rainforest gives way to the Moxos plains, a swampy savannah region interspersed with patches of forest. This had been a region of Jesuit missionary effort that resulted in the establishment of some twenty-five mission towns. After the expulsion of the Jesuits in 1767, *mestizo* cattle ranchers became the dominant class in the region. Only a few missionaries and some explorers in search of El Dorado ventured into the rainforest to the north and often lost their lives there.

In the course of the nineteenth century, however, the rainforest region was incorporated into the world economy. The extraction of forest products, particularly cinchona bark (for quinine), brought new incursions, but all this paled beside the rubber boom. The perfection, in 1839, of the vulcanization process opened the way for new applications, resulting in growing demand for this commodity from the industrializing countries. In 1888 Dunlop invented the pneumatic tire, first used for bicycles. It was the emergence of the automobile industry at the end of the century, however, that triggered the rubber boom between 1900 and 1913. Rubber extraction swept through the Amazon region following the river systems. From the north, Brazilians made their way upstream along the Juruá, Purus, and Madeira Rivers, and from the south Bolivians went downstream along the Beni River.[3] When Brazilian and Bolivian rubber exploiters met, boundary conflict ensued and resulted in war. In 1903 Bolivia saw itself forced to sign the Treaty of Petrópolis, by which it ceded the territory of Acre to Brazil. A new national border was thus established, which delimited the northern Bolivian Amazon. The town of Riberalta, founded in the late nineteenth century, became the most important regional center. The present-day province of Vaca Díez in the Department of Beni and the five provinces in the Department of Pando constitute the bulk of the Bolivian Amazon region, and it is on this area that this article will focus.

By the late nineteenth century Bolivian explorers entered the northern rainforest region to engage in the rubber trade. One of them was Antonio Vaca Díez, the "Bolivian Cecil Rhodes," who in 1897 would drown together with the notorious Peruvian rubber baron Fitzcarraldo, whom he visited on returning from a business trip to Europe. In 1880 Vaca Díez had sponsored an expedition by Edwin Heath, who found that the Beni River effectively flowed into the Madeira, a discovery that greatly increased the feasibility of rubber production in the region since it provided a route toward the Amazon and thereby to the Atlantic trade. These pioneers explored the rivers and staked out the areas they took possession of by marking some trees on the riverside and claiming all that was behind as part of their estates or *barracas*. Then workers would be recruited and shipped to the rubber region. They were the last link in a chain of *habilitos* in which goods were advanced in return for the future delivery of rubber. This system, which will be discussed in more detail below, reached down from the large trade houses in Belém and Manaus, through the patrons of the rubber estates, to the rubber tappers.[4]

The *barracas* consisted basically of a main-house on the riverside, where administration, storage facilities, and the *pulpería* (company store) were concentrated, and a number of *centros*, settlements of a few huts in the forest from which the rubber trails would start. Each worker would be assigned a number of trails to work: in the morning he made incisions in the trees on which were affixed small pots to collect the rubber; in the afternoon he returned to collect the produce and then coagulate it above the smoke of wood chips to form balls of wild rubber. These would then be delivered to the main-house every fortnight or so in exchange for a new supply of basic necessities such as rice, sugar, manioc, and other essentials.

Rubber production in northern Bolivia eventually came to be dominated by the Casa Suárez (the House of Suárez). In 1882 the Suárez brothers, who were engaged in river trade, established their headquarters in Cachuela Esperanza, a strategic location on the Beni River, as it was the only place where navigation was completely interrupted by rapids that had to be bypassed by a short detour along the river bank. Until the late nineteenth century the Casa Suárez was hardly involved in rubber production. It advanced goods against future delivery of rubber and many a *barraquero* (estate owner) became indebted to the Casa Suárez. From 1895 onward, however, the Casa Suárez started taking over *barracas* from their indebted owners, and by 1916 the Suárez empire was consolidated. The Casa Suárez became a highly integrated enterprise, which at the height of its power laid claim to about 75 percent of the Bolivian Amazon region and handled some 60 percent of Bolivian rubber production. The company had offices in London and a number of other cities. Its headquarters in Cachuela Esperanza came to include a radio-telegraph station, residential blocks, a hotel, a restaurant, a cinema, a hospital under Swiss direction, and a number of large machine shops. Including its holdings in Beni dedicated to cattle raising to supply the rubber estates to the north, the enterprise extended for about 180,000 square kilometers. Patriarch Don Nicolas Suárez became known as the "Rockefeller of the rubber trade" (Fifer 1970; Pacheco 1992; Roca 2001: 241–255; Sanabria Fernández 1988).

As we shall see in more detail below, the 1913 crash in rubber prices, due to competition from plantation-produced rubber from the British and Dutch colonies, triggered important changes in the organization of production. In the first place, as imports became more difficult, local agriculture became more important. In the second place, Brazil nut production emerged as a complementary activity. Brazil nuts are harvested between December and March, the rainy season when rubber tapping is not possible. However, in contrast to the tendency toward fragmentation into smaller estates that could be observed in other rubber producing regions (Costa 1992: 59; Martinello 1988: 47–61), the Suárez empire remained largely intact during the interwar period.

The Fragmentation of an "Empire" and the Rise of the First Free Communities (1940–1985)

Rubber production in the Amazon region saw a brief upsurge during the Second World War, but then resumed its secular decline in the face of competition from plantation produce and synthetic rubber. Brazilian exports dropped by about 40 percent from 1945 to 1946 (Martinello 1988: 293). Production of native rubber in the region was saved from total collapse by price support policies implemented by the Brazilian government, both in response to pressures by estate owners and rubber traders and also for strategic reasons. Domestic consumer prices in Brazil might be up to three times the world market rate (Pinto 1984). Bolivian producers also benefited from these schemes, and this was formalized in the 1958 Roboré Treaty (Pacheco 1992: 255–256). The 1970s saw another brief upsurge in rubber prices in the context of the oil crisis, but thereafter the Brazilian price support scheme again became its main prop until the system was abandoned in the mid-1980s.

Meanwhile, however, Nicolas Suárez, the patriarch of the Casa Suárez, had died in 1940, and this set the stage for the disintegration and fragmentation of the Suárez empire (Roca 2001: 255–264). Its estates were sold off or simply taken over by the administrators. The entrepreneurial organization of Casa Suárez gave way to what Pacheco (1992) calls *barracas patronales* of various sizes. Where before Nicolás Suárez had been "the patron" whose *barracas* were managed by "administrators," the number of smaller *patrons* now proliferated. The emergence of the *barraca patronal* basically meant a simplification and, according to Pacheco, often a harshening of labor relations. Borrowing the imagery evoked by Aramburu (1994: 85), we might say that the "golden age" of the "big patrons" was over. At the time of the Casa Suárez the labor force had been relatively diversified. Some sectors received cash salaries, and there was even something resembling a social policy. With the decline of the rubber trade, and the demise of this entrepreneurial mode of organization, relations were simplified to those between the *patrones* and *trabajadores empatronados* (Pacheco 1992). The infrastructure of earlier times fell into disuse and gradually decayed. Abandoned and overgrown machinery and dilapidated barracks can still be seen in Cachuela Esperanza. The Riberalta-based Seiler Company, earlier the Braillard Company and by the late 1960s taken over by the Hecker family, remained as a more or less "entrepreneur type" venture.

Alongside the *barracas patronales* a sector of *comunidades libres* started to expand, either as a result of the abandonment of *barracas* by their patrons or through the settlement by rubber tappers in areas not controlled by patrons.[5] The households in these communities relied on rubber tapping, small-scale agriculture, and Brazil nut gathering; the complementary set of activities of a year-round agro-extractive cycle (Assies 1997a: 8–10). At the same time the disintegration of the Suárez empire opened the way for the emergence of a system of independent river-traders who came to play an important role in a complex web of *habilitos*, centered in the town of Riberalta and linked to Brazilian trade circuits. This trade web tied together the various components of a much more fragmented system. Using data from the 1984 Agrarian Census, held just before the final collapse of the rubber trade, Ormachea and Fernández (1989: 30) calculate that there were 5,523 agricultural establishments in the region, covering 3,120,833 hectares out of a total of 8,626,100 hectares for the whole region. The average size of the holdings was 565 hectares, but distribution was rather skewed, with 88 percent of the holdings smaller than 500 hectares and occupying 9 percent of the land, and 4 percent of the holdings larger than 2,500 hectares occupying 79 percent.[6] Of the 5,523 establishments, about 3,200 were dedicated mainly to rubber and Brazil nut extraction. Data from a smaller sample suggest that about half of them were smallholdings, possessing up to 499 rubber trees and relying on family labor. The other half were *barracas*, relying on "outside," but mainly resident, labor and accounting for 78 percent of the rubber trails. Among the *barracas*, 95 percent were classified as small, possessing between 500 and 4,999 rubber trees (Pacheco 1990; 1992: 177).

The Collapse of the Rubber Trade after 1985

After 1985, the Sarney government in Brazil started dismantling the state agency regulating the rubber trade, and some years later the Collor government virtually abandoned all price support schemes. Rubber prices dropped to a historical low, and the rubber trade came to a virtual standstill. This had a dramatic impact on the emerging constellation described in the foregoing section.

The collapse of the rubber trade was accompanied by an accelerated spatial relocation of the population. Since rubber production disappeared as the mainstay of year-round economic activity, the *barraca* system ceased to be the main mode of socio-spatial organization. The *barraca* "was doomed as an institution; it only remained as a geographic space," as one *barraca* owner put it. The more remote *barracas* in particular saw a decline in their population, which tended to move to or establish *comunidades libres*, or to migrate to the urban areas. The collapse of the rubber trade also implied a contraction of the itinerant trader networks, since there was little to trade any more for most of the year. This further contributed to a modification of rural settlement patterns, since the *comunidades libres* tended to establish themselves at strategic and more accessible sites alongside the rivers, and at a later stage along the roads that began to be improved by the late 1980s.[7] While rubber production had sustained a dispersed settlement pattern, its decline prompted a clustering of the population, and, whereas rubber extraction had been the cornerstone of the agro-extractive cycle, agriculture now became the central element with Brazil nut gathering as an important source of cash income. Agriculture would be primarily subsistence-oriented, although depending on the location and the distance from markets, it might be articulated in a complex fashion with market exchanges (Assies 1997a: 59–64).[8] Alongside the peasantry, particularly in the vicinity of the urban centers, one finds medium-sized farms (*granjas*), often dedicated to fattening of cattle or the production of some commercial crop. It is estimated that the cultivated area in the region expanded from 21,000 hectares in the early 1980s to around 48,000 hectares in the early 1990s (Henkemans 2001: 52).

Another, no less important, consequence was massive rural urban migration. Census data from 1976 and 1992 indicate a decline of the rural population in all the provinces of the Department of Pando, while the urban population in the Province of Nicolas Suárez, that is the town of Cobija, grew at a rate of 5.8 percent annually. The urban population of the Province of Vaca Díez in the Beni Department, that is, the towns of Riberalta and Guayaramerín, also increased at a rate of 5.1 percent per year. The Vaca Díez province was the only province where the rural population increased, at a rate of 0.5 percent per year. This reflects a clustering of the *comunidades libres* around the towns (Assies 1997a: 45–46). While these national-level census data indicate the transformations in the region, some authors (Henkemans 2001: 65; Pacheco and Ávila 2000: 60; Stoian 2000a: 193) include local data referring to 1985. Such data suggest that the latter year was a turning point, after which migration greatly accelerated. The collapse of the rubber trade thus may be assumed to have been a major push factor in the migration process. The main point is that the urban population in the region grew from 33,508 in 1976 to 81,161 in 1992 and, according to preliminary census data, to 117,559 in 2001, respectively making up 44, 66, and 71 percent of the total regional population.[9]

The Rise of the Brazil Nut Trade

It was from the debris of the rubber economy that a new regional economy arose, this time centered largely on Brazil nut production. As we have seen, Brazil nut production started from the 1920s onward, and by the 1950s it had become an important economic activity in northern Bolivia, with a total value often equaling and sometimes surpassing that of rubber exports (Stoian 2000b: 281). Some *beneficiadoras* (processing plants where nuts are shelled) had been established from the 1930s onward, by the Casa Suárez among others. Processing capacity went through some ups and downs during the following decades, but around the mid-1980s all *beneficiadoras* had closed due to the difficult economic and political situation in the country and the decline of the regional economy (Assies 1997a: 46; Bojanic Helbingen 2001: 60 63; Coesmans and Medina 1997: 149–150; Stoian 2000b: 280–285).

The panorama changed radically during the second half of the 1980s. Various factors contributed to this development. By the mid-1980s some US importers had "discovered" northern Bolivia as a source of Brazil nuts that could be purchased at a price between 30 percent and 40 percent below Brazilian export prices. In 1987 a British firm began importing Bolivian nuts on a massive scale (Holt 1992).[10] The expansion of the new trade was also facilitated by the structural adjustment policies implemented by the Paz Estensorro government in 1985.

Improvement of road connections to the Pacific also contributed to Bolivian exports, as did the reputation of Brazil nuts as a forest-friendly product (Assies 1997a; 1997b). By the end of the 1990s some twenty *beneficiadoras* were operating in northern Bolivia, the great majority in Riberalta, and about five more outside the region.[11] Total export volumes soared from 10,000 metric tons in 1986 to over 30,000 metric tons by the late 1990s. More importantly, whereas in 1986, when all *beneficiadoras* were closed, the nuts were exported in-shell, by the late 1990s virtually the total volume of exports consisted of shelled nuts. The total value of exports had risen from about US\$9 million in the late 1980s to about US\$30 million ten years later. Bolivia had overtaken Brazil as the world market supplier of Brazil nuts, which should arguably have been renamed "Amazon nuts" (Assies 1997a: 1). Brazil nut production became the driving economic activity in northern Bolivia.

Two other economic activities also became important in the region. One is palm heart production, which surged from 1992 onward. By the late 1990s it contributed some US\$7 million to the regional income but then disappeared, even before depletion of the stock, due to international competition and the drying up of the Brazilian market after some Brazilians allegedly died after consuming the Bolivian product. The other activity is timber production. The value of timber exports from the region increased from about US\$1 million in the mid-1980s to about US\$20 million by 1997 (Stoian 2000b: 291).[12]

A small group of *beneficiadora* owners have become the key players in the new regional economy, displacing the *barraquero* sector. *Beneficiadora* owners largely finance the Brazil nut harvest through a revamped *habilito* system, and some of them are also involved in the timber or palm heart industry. Some *beneficiadoras* have been set up with local capital, others are owned by large Bolivian corporations, which may also be involved in other ventures such as soya production. By the early 1990s the *beneficiadora* owners set up an organization of their own, the *Asociación de Beneficiadoras del Nordeste* (ABAN), which later fused with the *Camara de Exportadores del Norte* (CADEXNOR). These organizations partly replaced the *Asociación de Productores de Goma y Almendra* (ASPROGOAL), which had been founded in 1973 to represent the then locally dominant *barraqueros*. ASPROGOAL membership declined from some 160 members to about 40 around 1995. Occasionally, however, ASPROGOAL rises from the ashes, as we will see in the following section.

The *beneficiadoras* process the Brazil nuts and finance a good part of the harvest. Processing is done with the help of small manually operated cracking devices.[13] Initially the units of production often were no more than sheds, but quality concerns have brought improvements, also to some labor conditions. For processing the Riberalta *beneficiadoras* employ some four thousand to six thousand individuals, mainly women, for about seven to eight months of the year (Coesmans and Medina 1997). Shelling nuts has become the main source of urban employment in Riberalta. By the time of the harvest season the *beneficiadoras* have often processed and marketed their stock of nuts, and lay off their workforce, many of whom join their husbands during the nut harvest.

Raw material for the *beneficiadoras* basically comes from two sources. *Barracas* contribute an estimated 60 to 65 percent and *comunidades libres* the remainder. An outstanding feature that should be borne in mind in discussing the configuration that emerged after 1985 is the change in urban rural relations. As noted, the collapse of the rubber trade brought the demise of the *barraca* as the dominant mode of socio-spatial organization and triggered an unprecedented process of demographic relocation. The rapid shift of population to the urban centers meant that an urban labor pool, or reserve army of workers, became available and has come to play a significant role in the emerging Brazil nut economy. The permanent population of the *barracas* has declined dramatically, and sometimes only a caretaker is left. Urban-based labor gangs have come to play a key role in the Brazil nut harvest in the *barracas*, as well as in the exploitation of other forest products. Each year, in December, between five thousand and six thousand people leave Riberalta's peripheral neighborhoods for the Brazil nut harvest.

The section below outlines the changes in labor relations in the course of the process of economic transformation outlined above, and at the competition over access to land and resources between *barraca* owners and the *comunidades libres.*

Land, Labor, and the Agrarian Structure

Labor Relations during the Rubber Era

The workforce during the early rubber era was mainly recruited outside the region. The local indigenous population was hostile and mostly unwilling to work on the *barracas* carved out on their territories. In a recent letter the heir to one of the enterprises that arose alongside the Casa Suárez affirms:

> For in case you do not know, Monsignor, nearly all the people that worked for the Braillard Enterprise, later Seiler and then Hecker, were people that we brought from Apolo, Ixiamas, Tumupasa, Reyes, Rurrenabaque and from various communities along the Beni river up to Puerto Linares. You can recognize them by their way of dressing and because it was they who introduced the custom of the "tipoy" and they were organized under the command of a Captain, who they elected from among themselves, and every fortnight in their traditional ceremonies on Thursday they would use the drug "hallahuasca," a custom that still survives in some places. All the men that we brought from Caupilan had the right to a paid return once they had paid off their advances. Very few returned. I am talking in the plural because I do not conceal what my father and grandfather did; I acknowledge and accept it. . . . With the exception of the indigenous peoples that the priests managed to evangelize, among them those of Puerto Cavinas on the Beni river, all other "savages" that lived on the navigable rivers were exterminated once the repetition rifle became available, because thanks to this tremendous weapon the "white man" gained supremacy and thanks to it he could practically exterminate all tribes. Before this invention the savage had the advantage. . . . A hundred years ago genocide was committed in our region, a killing without mercy in the search for rubber lands where the only obstacle to their exploitation was the savage man, who had to be killed by all possible means.[14]

Once the first *barracas* had been staked out workers would be recruited, mainly in the Santa Cruz region and among the indigenous population of the Beni plains, often by deceit if not by force (Sanabria Fernández 1988: 95–96). After being transported to the *barraca*, the worker would be supplied with the basic tools for work and survival, and an account was opened to keep track of the debt thus incurred, as well as for the future purchases at the *pulpería* in exchange for the "black gold."

At the height of the rubber boom a large part of the goods sold to the rubber tapper was imported. Thus Sanabria Fernández (1988: 131) asserts that Bolivians imported Chinese rice, Cuban sugar, and Brazilian coffee and *cachaça* (cane alcohol), which totally displaced similar products earlier imported from Santa Cruz. In order not to divert the workforce from the main activity, and to enforce relations of dependency, subsistence farming by rubber tappers was, often effectively, discouraged on the estates though patrons might supervise the centralized production of some staples on a *chaco patronal* (plot cultivated under patron supervision) during the offseason. On the other hand, in times of high rubber prices the tappers may have preferred to buy imported luxury food (Romanoff 1992: 131; Stoian 2000a: 77).

An issue that requires attention here is the controversial question of the relations of production and the role of the *habilito* system. A question that often emerges in the literature on the Amazonian rubber economy is why it was not "rationalized," and why it did not give rise to fully capitalist relations of production and a plantation system. Labor relations in the context of rubber production have often been described as a coercive and harsh system of debt peonage. Weinstein (1993), however, reconsidered this view and attributed the persistence of "pre-capitalist" relations and the system of debt peonage to an alliance between rubber tappers and traders based on mutual self-interest. Due to various circumstances such as the dispersion of material resources, the mentality of the rural population, the initial scarcity of capital, and the enormous distances to be overcome, she argues, an economic system emerged in which production largely remained under control of the direct producer and surplus extraction occurred at the level of exchange. Patrons and traders were unable to establish direct control over the labor force, and for its part the labor force resisted such direct control. Weinstein's view, in turn, has been challenged by Barham and Coomes (1994a; 1996), who adopt a neo-institutional economic perspective, and argue that the debt system, or debt-merchandise contract as they call it, was relatively efficient in terms of transaction costs and risk reduction. Wage labor, they argue, would be inefficient in the context of the rubber boom since it would involve high transaction costs in monitoring the efforts of a highly scattered workforce to ensure the full delivery of the produce, because rubber tappers might be tempted to sell it to itinerant traders. On the other hand, the markup on supplies and the discounts on rubber were justified by risks such as product loss in transport or the loss of labor time of the tappers due to illness, desertion, and tapper mortality rates of 25–30 percent (and occasionally as high as 50 percent). The clients, in return, would be assured of the delivery of needed goods and insurance (or leniency, I would say) in times of illness or other mishaps.[15]

Recently, Bojanic Helbingen (2001) and Stoian (2000a), in their studies of the northern Bolivian region, have taken up this lead in order to challenge the usual view of the *habilito* system as "brutal, unfair, exploitative and thus as an undesirable bondage system" (Bojanic Helbingen 2001: 93). Their work invites further scrutiny of the forms of labor recruitment, labor relations, and their transformation in the region. I will first focus on the early rubber era and then on the transformation and current forms of the *habilito* system.

One of the most surprising features of Stoian's (2000a) argument is his assertion that Bolivian rubber tappers chiefly received fixed monthly wages in the early rubber era and that therefore they should be considered proletarians in a context of "primitive capitalism." Only at a later stage were these fixed wages replaced by piecework rates. According to Stoian, the payment of fixed wages in northern Bolivia deserves special attention, since it suggests that labor relations in this region were less exploitative than is "often assumed in a general way" about conditions during the rubber boom. This view, he argues, is rooted in the idea that rubber tappers received piece rates, an arrangement that transfers "the risks of illness and adverse weather to tappers, who reputedly received only nominal prices for the rubber delivered." The payment of fixed wages, moreover, would be remarkable in view of Barham and Coomes' argument about transactions costs, and it refutes Weinstein's view that relations of production during the rubber boom were pre-capitalist and resembled a feudal mode of production. Conditions in northern Bolivia during the early rubber era were less exploitative than might have been the case elsewhere, and fully, though "primitive," capitalist labor relations predominated (Stoian 2000a: 62–63, 123–126).

Stoian, however, overstates his case, both for "primitive capitalism" and the extent of "proletarianization" of the labor force. On the basis of a contract reproduced in Pacheco (1992: 237–238), for example, he argues that eight indigenous laborers hired from their apparent owner, a Mr. C. M. Barbery, by the Casa Suárez, "were granted sick leave of up to one month without losing their wage," but fails to note that it was Mr. Barbery himself who received these wages (Stoian 2000a: 63).[16] In fact, the contract suggests conditions of indigenous slavery. Most of the contracts cited by Stoian refer to activities other than rubber tapping, for example a muleteer's contract; and the one that *does* refer to rubber tapping stipulates a piece rate for rubber production and a fixed wage for off-season activities. On the other hand, he is right in pointing to stipulations regarding medical assistance, though here one may raise the question as to whether this was anything more than legal formality (see below). And, despite often citing Sanabria Fernández, he fails to note that this author precisely sets apart the rubber tappers when stating that among the overall workforce these "were not salaried in the strict sense of the term" (Sanabria Fernández 1988: 129).[17]

Stoian's (2000a: 77) objection to the "prevailing image" of rigid forms labor control as a "subtle form of slavery" is not that convincing. Let us look at some of the features of the early rubber era. As noted, the local indigenous population was mostly antagonistic to recruitment into rubber tapping, and in a report on his expedition to the region in the late 1890s General Pando recommended their extermination, though finally some uneasy balance of mutual tolerance was achieved (Fifer 1970; Roca 2001: 229; Stoian 2000a: 80–83). The labor force came from elsewhere and was recruited in various ways. During the early rubber era, when the pioneers established their estates, there was something like a "rubber rush." People, including shop owners, professionals, public servants, and craftsmen, left the impoverished Santa Cruz region for the "rubber fields" on their own account and often found work there in the administrative sector of the *barracas* or as overseers or subcontractors, etc.; and they were salaried (Sanabria Fernández 1988: 93–94, 99). Recruiting rubber tappers and boatmen required for transport, however, was another matter. A number of them were recruited, often forcibly, from among the indigenous population of the Moxos plains that had been subject to missionary efforts. Others were recruited in and around the urban area of Santa Cruz under the *enganche* regime: that is, literally, by being "hooked up." Let us look at those two groups, which came to constitute the bulk of the workforce, and who were not "salaried in the strict sense of the term."

The indigenous peoples of the Moxos plains had been converted to Christianity by the Jesuits from the end of the seventeenth century. After the expulsion of the Order in 1767, *mestizo* farmers and ranchers took control and set the population to work, as cattle ranching expanded in these savannah lands. Some had become involved in the cinchona trade but the situation changed dramatically after 1860, when the rubber trade took off and boatmen and rubber tappers were needed. When forcible recruitment became widespread, many fled southeastward to the Securé forests. By 1887, Andrés Guayocho, a local shaman, started to call on the indigenous population to leave the town of Trinidad and establish itself in the nearby townships of San Lorenzo and San Francisco. A messianic movement emerged that took off on a search for the *Loma Santa* ("the sacred hill"), a place without evil where they could reestablish contact with their saints and would be free from suffering and exploitation. In the view of the dominant class the following gradual but uninterrupted exodus from Trinidad was nothing less than the beginning of an insurrection. They formed a "War Committee," led by, among others, Nicolás Suárez, usually depicted as the empire builder and benevolent patron who brought progress to these remote lands. An armed column marched on San Francisco in order to force the Indians to mend their ways. They met with resistance, however, and twenty-one were killed, after which a punitive expedition of 150 men was sent out from Trinidad. This time, the indigenous population chose to flee into nearby forest areas where they were cruelly persecuted. Andrés Guayocho was captured and brutally whipped to death. Meanwhile in the Securé region, rumor had it that the Indians were preparing a rebellion. They were surprised while attending mass and the men received between five hundred and six hundred lashes a piece, while the women received between two hundred and three hundred. Nine men and one woman died as a consequence. Many of those who could escape capture, or worse, fled toward the Chimane forest in search for the Loma Santa. Forced recruitment soon resumed (Jones 1995; Lema Garret 1998: 11; Roca 2001: 119–133).

In Santa Cruz labor recruitment took place through the *casas de enganche*. By various means people were lured into signing a contract, after which they would receive an advance payment, but would also be locked up until they could be shipped to the rubber fields. Once sufficient recruits had been contracted for a shipment, they would be walked out of town under armed surveillance through Beni Street "from where people go, never to return." Outside the town they were chained together and then marched for five or six days to the harbor of Cuatro Ojos from where they were shipped up north (Sanabria Fernández 1988: 96). While General Pando, after his expeditions to the North, recommended the extermination of local indigenous peoples, he was moved by the conditions of those who had been "hooked" in this manner and initiated legislation to protect those recruited on *enganches*, which was adopted in 1896. The *Ley de Enganches* stipulated that rubber tappers should receive a monthly or annual salary, their trip to the rubber fields should be paid for by the employer, they should receive free medical assistance, be provided with a register of their current account, receive a return ticket, could not be transferred to another employer without their consent, and a limit put on the payment advanced. A register of "hooked" recruits was to be established by the Security Police, preference was to be given to contracts extending to workers conditions such as the freedom of labor, and "hooking" indigenous people was prohibited.[18] The law pinpointed many of the abuses in contracting rubber tappers (Roca 2001: 117), and it was to be honored in the breach (Sanabria Fernández 1988: 97). Roca (2001: 110) reports that, according to the norms of the contemporary Civil Code on the freedom of contract, a clause could be inserted by which the contracted party explicitly foregoes "any benefit" in his favor and quotes several contracts in which the benefits of the 1896 law are annulled. Furthermore, the rubber barons filed recourse with the Supreme Court, which declared the law anti-constitutional since it applied only "north of the fourteenth parallel" and not nationwide.

Forced labor recruitment continued. During one of his visits to Riberalta in the early twentieth century, P. H. Fawcett, a British colonel and member of the Royal Geographical Society who worked on the Peru Bolivian boundary survey, witnessed the arrival of one such "cattle" transport and learned that the workers concerned were not sold through public auction, like Indians, but by way of private transactions for the value of their debt (Paz 1999: 156–158).[19] The Prefect of the Beni Department was involved in the trade and connived at the forcible recruitment of workers, peasants, and Indians, who were dressed like soldiers to be illegally shipped to the "rubber fields." In response to such abuses an organization, the "Social Defense," was created in 1906 in Santa Cruz. It denounced these forms of recruitment and sometimes prevented shipments of workers. By presidential order the organization was denied legal status and declared "seditious." Forced recruitment declined only after the rubber price crash in 1913, and the completion of the Beni Mamoré railway, which reduced the need for boatmen (Roca 2001: 118–119; Sanabria Fernández 1988: 137–143; Souza 1980).

When, after 1909, the British government started to investigate the denunciations against the Peruvian Amazon Company for atrocities committed in the Peruvian Putumayo region, a delegate was also sent to the Bolivian rubber region. Although in London representatives of the Casa Suárez had declared that their *barracas* would be open to inspection by anyone, the delegate Mr. Gosling was received in Cachuela Esperanza and Riberalta for some days but was not allowed to travel to the rubber fields. He denounced the debt peonage in the northern Beni region as a form of undisguised slavery and noted that debts were heritable. The reports on the Bolivian rubber region noted widespread abuse, but surmised that things were not as bad as in the Putumayo, since the high market value and the relative scarcity of labor in Bolivia made it "uneconomical to treat human life lightly" (Fifer 1970: 137 40; Roca 2001: 179).

The picture that emerges shows, in the first place, that some sectors of the workforce, particularly those not engaged in rubber tapping, received fixed wages while at the same time being engaged in debt relations, but contracts do not say how accounts were settled or if and when cash appeared in the process. However, there is no indication that, in contrast to other rubber regions, Bolivian rubber tappers "chiefly received fixed wages in the early rubber era" (Stoian 2000a: 63). In the second place, the account thus far calls into question the rejection of the interpretation of debt bondage as a coercive relation in favor of a view according to which both parties to the relation benefit from the arrangement, as implied by Weinstein (1993), Barham and Coomes (1996), and also by Stoian. The latter asserts that "only if we acknowledge the varied and often contradictory factors that have led to the emergence of such systems entailing advantages and disadvantages for all parties involved we can do justice to the people who, after all, keep these systems alive" and affirms that the survival of such systems, albeit modified, is due to their "functional significance" (Stoian 2000a: 119).

One issue is that the neo-institutional/neo-classical economists argument hinges on the assertion that the rubber trade was competitive rather than monopolistic (Barham and Coomes 1996: 33; Stoian 2000a: 110). In northern Bolivia, by contrast, it was much rather monopolistic.[20] Given the belief in competition for clients, these authors reinterpret the debt bondage relation. Downplaying the indebtness and bondage aspects, therefore, they view the *habilito* as credit that "enables" the rubber tapper to do his job and thus gain an income. It ceases to be a coercive method of extracting surplus labor, and thus a source of acute and continuing struggle between rubber tapper and employer, and becomes instead a noncoercive, tension-free and thus benign form of patron-clientage, a mutually beneficial arrangement freely entered into by all concerned. Occasionally one even finds hints about debt bondage as a source of difficulty, distress, even for the benign employer. The *habilito* system is viewed by such authors as a rational economic response to imperfections in the markets for credit, insurance, information, and factors of production since it reduces transaction costs (Barham and Coomes 1996: 68; Stoian 2000a: 111). It is precisely from such a perspective that Barham and Coomes (1996: 65–68, 109) object to Weinstein's claim that the relations of production were precapitalist and resembled a feudal mode of production. They argue that these relations are *chosen* by "those below," rather than enforced "from above," and are therefore in essence "free." What exists systemically is not an economically inefficient pre-capitalism but rather an economically efficient form of capitalism, based on free labor relations chosen by and to the benefit of all.

Stoian (2000a: 122, 125), on the other hand, criticizes the feudalism thesis, arguing that labor was separated from the land and from the means of production and that it received a fixed wage or a piece rate. I do not think, however, that it is very useful to frame the issue in terms of a feudalism/capitalism debate or to assume that unfree labor is everywhere and always a pre-capitalist relation. It is not the place here to rehearse the debate over capitalism and labor regimes or forms of labor control. I will limit myself to quoting Marx, who, in his essay on pre-capitalist economic formations, affirmed that "[i]f we now not only call the plantation-owners in America capitalists, but (affirm) that they *are* (capitalists), this is because they exist as anomalies within a world market based upon free labor" (Marx 1974: 358).[21]

To understand the relations between rubber tappers and their patrons/employers, and the role of the *habilito* system, I think it is more helpful to turn to the concept of simple commodity production, and in particular Chevalier's (1983) argument that specific forms of simple commodity production can be treated as variations of capitalism, and therefore as subjected to a flexibly defined process of labor's subordination (formal and real) to capital. This view of simple commodity production may be combined with the notion of "captivity," which suggests that patrons created a "virtual" or "captive" market where the exchanges in fact are a barter, but are symbolized in monetary value through the "book of accounts" (Geffray 1995; Lescure, Pinton and Emperaire 1994). To be sure, patrons claimed ownership of the object of production, the forest, although the legal status of such claims was somewhat obscure, and in fact their claims were rooted in "custom." Rubber tappers, on the other hand, "owned" some means of production with which they were provided on arrival, and the cost of which they had to pay off subsequently with their produce rather than their labor power.[22] They maintained a degree of control over the production process in the absence of mechanisms of real subsumption due to the dispersed nature of wild rubber collection. The debt peonage system thus can be viewed as a variety of simple commodity production, formally subsumed under capital, and characterized by the extraction of absolute surplus value through monopolized exchanges. Viewing rubber tappers as a specific "captive" category of "self-employed" laborers also sheds light on their struggle for more autonomy. The *habilito* system was accompanied by a "moral economy" of its own and was wrapped up in a discourse about paternalist ties of patronage and *compadrazgo*. But paternalism and its doctrine of reciprocal obligations, as Genovese (1976) has shown, develop as a way of mediating irreconcilable class and racial conflicts.[23]

Until now the focus has been on production relations as they emerged during the early rubber era and the boom period, and, in passing, it has been noted that at the height of the rubber boom many consumer goods that were previously imported from Santa Cruz were displaced by foreign imports after the 1913 crash. As imports became more difficult, local agriculture tended to expand and the rubber estates sought to diversify their trade by engaging in the production of Brazil nuts, which became significant in northern Bolivia around 1930. Woortman (1996) describes this process as one of "internalization of the conditions of reproduction" and suggests that agriculture and Brazil nut gathering at this conjuncture may have constituted "functional equivalents." While in some cases subsistence agriculture among rubber tappers might be tolerated, in other cases agricultural production would be centralized under the control of the patron/employer while rubber tapper households would be set to gather Brazil nuts and then exchange the latter produce for subsistence goods in much the same way as rubber (Lescure 1993: 15; Lescure, Pinton and Emperaire 1994; Woortman 1996).[24]

Although economically speaking both the patron and the *barraca* organization mostly held their own, the main elements of a year-round agro-extractive cycle of complementary activities that could potentially sustain a rubber tapper's household were now in place.[25] In northern Bolivia rubber tapping was confined to two phases in the dry season (April to December). The first lasted from April to June. During the latter phase, when economic activity in the region was affected by the cold winds from the south, rubber extraction was suspended, only to be taken up once again in October, until the rainy season, which starts in December, made further extraction impossible. From mid-December until March was the season for Brazil nut gathering. The period when rubber tapping was suspended, from July to September, could be dedicated to related agricultural laboring tasks, mainly the preparation of fields by clearing and burning the forest. The onset of the rainy season from the end of November marks the sowing season for dry rice and corn that can be harvested from February to April. Other important staple products would be manioc and bananas (Assies 1997a: 8–10). Hunting and fishing provided proteins.

The mention of households in this context is not fortuitous. A further "sign of the crisis," as Woortman (1996: 14) calls it, was the increasing presence of women on the rubber estates and the emergence of family life among rubber tappers. If during the first period a predominantly male workforce had been recruited, now family life would be encouraged in order to tie the rubber tappers to the estates.[26] While rubber tapping remained a mainly male economic activity, therefore, women and children came to play an important economic role in the emerging subsistence agriculture and/or in complementary activities such as Brazil nut gathering.

By making it necessary for rubber tappers to expand their agricultural operations sometimes controlled by the patron and sometimes under control of the rubber tapper household in order to enable the unit of production (the rubber tapping household) to reproduce itself economically, the decline of the rubber trade brought about what one may call a "peasantization" of the rubber tapper. This tendency gathered momentum with the disintegration of the Suárez empire and the emergence of a new organizational constellation made up of, on the one hand, patron-run estates, and on the other, emerging free communities. The collapse of the rubber trade after 1985 brought a further decline of the estates as a form of social organization and led to the consolidation of the free communities and a rapid increase in urbanization. It was from this situation that the Brazil nut economy emerged.

The Transformation of Labor Relations after 1985

In considering the way in which the production relations in the northern Bolivian Amazon were transformed, it is necessary first to consider changes to the labor regime in the *barracas*. Whereas formerly the latter were populated all year round, now many *barracas* have been virtually abandoned. *Barracas patronales* continue to exist, but with an often strongly reduced number of inhabitants. In her recent study Henkemans (2001) describes one such *barraca* and the way the *habilito* system still works there. Many of its inhabitants have left, and those remaining have ambiguous feelings about the patron who, in their opinion, has evolved into a mere merchant who no longer takes care of his laborers, which forces them to develop new ties of mutual support and social security. The patron, in turn, depends heavily on the presence of cheap laborers:

> He needs to give the laborers incentives to stay on the *barraca* or to prevent them from leaving in another way, for example by causing them to be indebted to him. The habilito system still works well for that purpose, because the remote *barraca* remains almost completely isolated from urban centers, and the patron can largely control the transportation of outgoing extractive products and incoming food products. The whole system is based on making the laborers indebted to him, or making them think they are. As long as this is the case, many workers do not dare to leave. The veterans in the *barraca* have ambiguous feelings about their position. On the one hand, they are proud of the fact that they have become confidants of the patron due to their long service. On the other hand, they regret that they never had the courage or the ability to leave and become independent (Henkemans 2001: 92).

While in this case a group of permanent inhabitants has remained, in other *barracas* only a caretaker is present most of the time. By the time of the Brazil nut harvest, the *zafreros* (Brazil nut harvesters) arrive. Nowadays they are largely contracted in the urban areas, mainly Riberalta, and in this context the *habilito* system has taken new forms.

If the *beneficiadoras* own their *barracas*, they may provide a *habilito* to labor contractors who, in turn, recruit gang labor. Otherwise, the *habilito* may go to a *barraquero*, who may either contract workers himself or do this through a labor contractor. They provide the workers with an advance, the new *habilito*, which is often used for large expenses, such as the purchase of new clothes, new shoes, and school utensils for the children. By mid-December the harvesters, often accompanied by various family members, are shipped to the distant *barracas*, to return two or three months later. Riberalta harbor is bustling with small boats loaded with rice, noodles, cooking oil, toothpaste, soap, and other essentials, the workers themselves sitting on top. Others may travel in trucks. During their stay in the *barracas*, where living conditions generally are dismal (Henkemans 2001: 90–91), harvest laborers will collect nuts and deliver them to the central storehouse or to the payoles, storage facilities located deeper in the forest, where an account will be kept of their deliveries and expenses. These accounts will be settled in the city at the end of the harvest. By the mid-1990s about two-thirds of the Brazil nut harvesters, or some five thousand to six thousand persons, were recruited in urban areas, mainly Riberalta. Employment opportunities are scarce in these towns, especially for male workers, and casual labor is rampant (Verheule 1998).

Thus, in urban contexts the *habilito* still plays a role in the recruitment of labor, and until recently debt obligations continued to be an important aspect of this process, as revealed in surveys carried out in 1994 and 1996, which show that harvesters ran up debts and felt obliged to work them off, either by remaining in the forest longer than planned or by promising to work for the same contractor the next harvest (Assies 1997a: 54; Verheule 1998: 87). However, while the latter sources already point out that the *habilito* system was running into difficulties in urban contexts, Stoian (2000a: 118) and Bojanic Helbingen (2001: 87 106) describe how the rupture of the close patron ties that prevailed in the *barracas* has resulted in an outright crisis of the *habilito* system. Workers may take the advance payment without fulfilling their obligations; contractors may cheat in the post-harvest settling of accounts or not settle them at all. During the harvest, contractors attempt to mislead workers, and vice-versa, over the volume and weight of nuts collected; food consumed may also be overpriced. The climate is one of widespread distrust in which all parties seek ways to deceive the other, setting off a spiral of fraudulent transactions. Nonetheless, Bojanic Helbingen argues, hardly any unskilled jobs will be done if no advance payment is made, which leads him to the conclusion that the *habilito* system will persist in the near future but that it needs to be modernized, along with a formalization of labor relations. Whether that can be done remains problematic. Employers may be interested in disciplining the workforce involved in the Brazil nut harvest, but at the same time informal labor relations in the context of extensive underemployment (Verheule 1998) contribute to the profitability of the Brazil nut industry (Assies 1997a: 56–59).[27]

Communities and Estates: The Latent Conflict

The other source of raw nuts in the northern Bolivian Amazon are the *comunidades libres*, which account for 35 to 40 percent of the harvest. As has been noted, these communities came into being in the context of the disarticulation of the *barraca* system, and they rely on a combination of peasant agriculture and extractivism. The relative economic importance of agriculture in relation to extractivism varies and is a function both of the location of the communities themselves and also of the size of the family holding within communities. The migration and resettlement process triggered by the collapse of the rubber trade resulted in relatively high rural population densities in the Vaca Díez province. Family holdings within the communities in this area range between 20 and 80 hectares in size, and peasant proprietors dedicate themselves mainly to a mix of subsistence and market-oriented slash and burn agriculture.[28] The city of Riberalta is a main outlet for agricultural produce such as rice, bananas, and, more recently, some agro-forestry products promoted by nongovernmental organizations. Brazil nut production takes a subsidiary role, given the relatively small size of the family parcels. After harvesting crops on their own parcel, many families also join the workforce harvesting on the *barracas* in order to obtain a monetary income (Henkemans 2001).

The inhabitants of communities in the less populated Department of Pando have access to significantly larger areas of forest. Here agriculture is mainly subsistence-oriented, due to the distance from urban markets. Brazil nut production is a major source of monetary income for these communities. Nuts may be sold directly to a *beneficiadora* or through an intermediary. Communities have tended to cluster along the Riberalta Cobija road. It is the competition over access to the road and to Brazil nut stands that underlies the potential for conflict between the emerging *comunidades libres* and the *barracas* in this region, a latent antagonism that manifested itself in the Third Indigenous-Peasant March during July 2000. Understanding the nature and dimensions of this conflict requires some further consideration of the dynamics of the regional economy, as well as the role in this of the new land and forestry legislation introduced in 1996.

As noted, the *beneficiadora* owners have become a key group in the regional economy, overshadowing the once dominant *barraqueros* who have become increasingly dependent on the *beneficiadora* owners to finance their operations during the Brazil nut harvest. By the mid-1990s this economic imbalance resulted in the takeover or purchase of *barracas* belonging to indebted *barraca* owners by the owners' *beneficiadoras*. A process of vertical concentration was taking shape through the elimination of the *barraquero* from the production chain. While some of the *beneficiadoras* had been created through investment by *barraqueros*, others had been created through investment from outside the sector. Through vertical integration the *beneficiadoras* sought to control part of their own supply of wild nuts. Most of them acquired *barracas,* where the Brazil nut crop would be harvested by a seasonal labor force recruited from nearby urban areas.

This tendency toward vertical integration casts some doubts on the expectations about a "democratization" of the Brazil nut industry, according to which the role of the *comunidades libres* in supplying its raw material might gradually expand. This in turn would benefit the peasant sector, among other things by raising their monetary income, and at the same time contribute to forest conservation (DHV 1993a). In view of the tendency toward vertical integration, the expectations about a democratization of the industry have been the subject of criticism (Assies 1997a). It was argued that production by the *comunidades libres* would complement that of the *barracas* for two reasons. In communities near the urban centers, parcel sizes tend to be relatively small, and the commercial output of Brazil nuts is therefore less significant than subsistence agriculture. By contrast, the more remote communities face logistical problems in getting their harvest out of the forest.[29] Aside from assuring a steady supply of raw material, in this context vertical integration and harvesting by means of urban-based gang labor might yield a competitive advantage and may become a profitable option.

This argument has raised some controversy. According to Stoian (2000a: 139) it is a "pessimistic outlook." He argues that in the context of a booming Brazil nut economy and growing production, the relative shares of nuts produced by *barracas* and communities remained the same, but that the greater volume produced by the communities implied competition over access to resources. Communities pushed the *barracas* into less accessible areas.[30] Furthermore, he points to the ongoing conversion of *barracas* into communities. Finally, the vertically integrated *barracas* produce no more than one-fifth of the harvest, the remainder coming from peasant communities and *barracas patronales.* The peasantry not only benefited economically from the Brazil nut production boom through higher prices, therefore, but also produced more. It is not at all clear, however, just how this process corresponds to "democratization." What it does underline is the dependence of the profitability of vertical integration on an additional condition: namely, that world market prices for Brazil nuts are high. As we will see below, in 2001 prices plummeted, and local demand for raw nuts contracted. Under such conditions *beneficiadora* owners may desist from or reduce exploitation of their *barracas,* and instead purchase their raw material from peasants whose logic is subsistence- rather than profit-oriented, and for whom Brazil nuts are an important source of cash income. Under such conditions the relative share of the peasantry in the production of raw nuts may increase, but this would be a democratization of poverty.

In contrast to this critical view, Bojanic Helbingen (2001: 101) asserts that vertical integration increases transaction costs, which might lead eventually to a reversal of the vertical integration process itself, with *barracas* being returned to the *barraqueros*. Evidence for such a reversal is hard to find, however. If the process of vertical integration and concentration of landholding halted, it would be for other reasons, such as the uncertainty about future implementation of the agrarian and forestry legislation and the irregularity of tenure rights. By the year 1999, when the issue of conversion of the *barracas* into concessions under the 1996 Forestry Law had become a major issue, the organizations of *barraca* owners presented a list that distinguished between "traditional" and "nontraditional" *barracas*, the latter being those claimed by enterprises involved in the process of vertical integration. According to that list, ten enterprises claimed ownership of 38 *barracas* covering a total of 1,675,781 hectares, whereas 162 smaller *barracas*, the "traditional" ones, claimed a total of 1,719,010 hectares. It was such claims, which according to a letter of the *Superintendencia Agraria* (November 16, 1999) implied that "there would be hardly any land left for the communities," that provoked the "Third March."[31] We now turn to a consideration of the 1996 land and forestry legislation, which, together with Supreme Decree No. 25532, allowed for the conversion of the *barracas* into new concessions and thus triggered the "Third March."

The 1996 Land and Forestry Legislation, the *Barraca* Decree, and the "Third March"

By the 1990s it had become clear that an overhaul of Bolivian land and forestry legislation was in order. The existing legislation was outdated, and its implementation had become thoroughly corrupt. While debate over reform had started in the 1980s, this would eventually be introduced under the Sánchez de Lozada government (1993–1997) as part of a far-reaching package of "second generation" institutional reforms complementing the structural adjustment policies introduced in 1985. The 1996 Bolivian land and forestry legislation reforms, however, stood out among similar changes carried out in Latin America for not simply following the neo-liberal *zeitgeist*. While the World Bank, for example, pressured Latin American governments to adopt only market-oriented reforms, which, it was believed, would not only promote efficiency but also benefit the poor (Deininger and Binswanger 2001), the Bolivian reforms incorporated both market-oriented and social justice elements (Urioste and Pacheco 2000). The 1953 revolutionary land reform had sought to expropriate properties that were either unutilized/

underutilized *latifundia* or operated under precapitalist tenure and labor relations. It effectively eradicated the hacienda system in the Andean highlands of Bolivia, but failed to resolve the demand for land. The redistribution of land in the Bolivian highlands eventually resulted in minifundization, while the occupation of the eastern tropical lowlands, which accelerated in the 1960s, was characterized by the formation of huge landholdings, surrounded by smallholding colonists. Meanwhile, the institutions involved in land policies became seriously corrupt.

The 1953 land reform law had created the *Servicio Nacional de Reforma Agraria* (SNRA), and in 1965, when the redistribution in the highland region was declared complete, an *Instituto Nacional de Colonización* (INC) had been created to promote the occupation and settlement of the eastern lowlands. Both institutions were charged with the distribution of public funds and were supposed to complement each other's activities. Complementarity, however, was absent in practice, and the two institutions dedicated themselves to the distribution of lands through far from transparent procedures. While in the western highlands of Bolivia peasant and community holdings were subject to a process of land fragmentation, in the eastern lowlands by contrast huge land holdings emerged as a result of policies pursued by the authoritarian military governments of René Barrientos (1964–1965 and 1966–1969), Hugo Banzer (1971–1978), and the narco-dictatorship of Luis García Meza. In the eastern lowlands, particularly around Santa Cruz, most land became monopolized by a small group of large landholders and agribusiness enterprises, dedicated to industrial farming (soya and oilseeds) and/or extensive livestock ranching.

By the 1980s it was clear that land distribution had become extremely skewed, though exact data on tenure patterns were not available due to the irregular and corrupt distribution practices. It is estimated that between 30 and 60 percent of the land may be subject to overlapping claims, and that 60 percent of the owners do not have regular titles. The 1984 agrarian census suggests that out of 22.6 million registered hectares, 15 percent was possessed by 308,000 small and medium-sized holdings, against 85 percent occupied by 6,000 large owners (Solón 1995). Other estimates also suggest extreme polarization. (MACPIO 2001: 51–53; Hernaíz and Pacheco 2000: 156–161). In 1992, after yet another case of corruption had been denounced, it was decided to "intervene" the land reform and colonization institutions, and their actions were suspended in order to open the way for a *saneamiento* (clarification) of land rights. This required reform of the 1953 legislation. A further issue that required attention was the demands made by the indigenous peoples of the eastern lowlands who had made themselves "visible" through their "First March" in 1990, which had resulted in the recognition of eight indigenous territories.[32] During their "Second March" in 1996, in the context of the debate on new agrarian legislation, they would present sixteen new territorial demands. This, too, had to be dealt with in new legislation.

It took four years of negotiations among government officials, indigenous peoples, and peasant and landowners representatives before the *Ley del Servicio Nacional de Reforma Agraria* was adopted in 1996 (Assies 2000; Salvatierra 1996; Solón 1995). The outcome of the negotiation process was a "hybrid" law that did not fully satisfy anyone but seemed to be acceptable. It introduces some elements of market-oriented reforms but at the same time retains important elements of the social justice orientation embodied in earlier legislation (Urioste and Pacheco 2000). The law thus recognizes various types of landholding that fulfill a "social function." It is assumed that these lands are used primarily for subsistence production by peasants or indigenous peoples. These lands are either prohibited from being bought and sold, or where such market transfers are permitted subject to specific conditions/restrictions; furthermore, they are not liable to land tax. The *solar campesino* (peasant yard) and the smallholding cannot be divided or mortgaged, but may be sold only insofar as not expressly prohibited by law. Collectively titled community properties and *tierras comunitarias de origen* (TCO), the much larger holdings cannot be sold at all. By contrast, medium-sized properties and property held by agricultural enterprises fall into a category of lands that are supposed to fulfill an "economic-social" function. These holdings may be sold and mortgaged and are subject to a land tax. The law thus seeks to guarantee the tenure rights of middle and large properties on the condition that they fulfill an economic-social function and that they pay taxes. Abandonment would be cause for a reversion of land to the state.[33] This was meant to remedy the concentration of land. Holdings that reverted to the state would fall into the category of public lands (*tierra fiscal*) and as such could then either be granted (*dotación*) at no cost to peasant and indigenous communities or sold off (*adjudicación*) at market value through public auction. Land grants would be given priority over selling off. In its initial clauses, the 1996 law contains stipulations regarding the rapid titling of the eight indigenous territories that had been recognized in the wake of the 1990 indigenous march, and admitted sixteen new claims, which were immobilized pending future regularization within ten months. These territories, with a total surface of nearly 15 million hectares, are to be regularized as *tierras comunitarias de origen* (TCO). The implementation of the new legislation would involve the clarification (*saneamiento*) of tenure rights and subsequent titling. This process should be completed within ten years (i.e., by the year 2006).

The 1996 Forestry Law was also the outcome of a negotiation process (Pavez and Bojanic Helbingen 1998), an attempt both to remedy the flaws of the 1974 forestry legislation and to provide a better fit between land tenure and forest exploitation. As a result of the earlier law, grants made independently of tenure rights and logging concessions overlapped with communal/ indigenous lands and other forms of possession or property. Furthermore, the 1974 law had enabled an enormous concentration of concessions by a small number of enterprises, it had failed to promote sustainable forest use, and its administration was plagued with corruption (Contreras-Hermosilla and Vargas Ríos 2001). The 1996 law foresees a regime of concessions of forty years' duration where state-owned forests (*tierras fiscales*) are concerned. Such concessions can be transferred, are heritable, and can be renewed. Private owners and indigenous peoples can be authorized to exploit forest resources within their property or TCO. Indigenous peoples are granted the exclusive rights over forest resources within their TCOs. Within the Bolivian municipalities, up to 20 percent of the state-owned forests can be set aside for use by locally based social associations.[34]

The new forestry regime made exploitation of resources conditional upon the elaboration of management plans and also introduced a new license system. Whereas the 1974 law linked payment for a license to the volume of forest resources extracted, under the new law the license fee for timber exploitation was set at a minimum of US$1.00 per hectare for concessions of state-owned forests to the timber industries. Private owners can be authorized to exploit forest resources on their land merely by paying the minimum license fee. Since the concessions would be auctioned, the expectation was that in this case the license fee would rise above the US$1.00 level. The law allowed for the conversion of existing concessions into new ones under the present regime, but it was expected that the license fee system would prompt a reduction in the number of concession areas. The remaining areas would revert to the state, which might then allocate them to indigenous communities or auction them off as new concessions. Indigenous peoples would have to pay the same license fee, but only for the area effectively exploited within their TCO. For nontimber forest products, the license fee was set at US$0.30 per hectare.

As will be seen below, these two laws provide the framework for the disputes over land and resources in the northern Bolivian Amazon region. Generally speaking, it can be said that the implementation of the *Ley INRA* has been extremely slow. By November 2001 title clarification had only taken place for 13 percent of the rural lands, while 33 percent were still being processed. Final titling was proceeding even slower. At the same time, very little land has been reverted to the state, so in the event the concentration of landholding has scarcely changed. In the absence of clear stipulations about the social economic function of land, decisions were left to the discretion of INRA officials. In the case of the TCOs clarification has made some progress, due to international support, but at the same time the process of clarification has meant that holdings of third parties were consolidated, resulting in a significant reduction of the area to be granted to indigenous peoples. Similarly, "studies of spatial necessities" often resulted in significant reductions of the area recommended for titling. By the year 2000, only one TCO had been titled, together with part of another. Furthermore, in 1997 the Forestry Superintendency allowed the "voluntary conversion" of logging concessions, part of which overlapped with TCOs, that were in the process of consolidation.[35] Finally, the INRA law brings no solution whatever for the specific problems of the highland peasantry. It is in this context that demands for the modification or, in the case of the radical highland peasant movement, even abrogation of the INRA law have emerged. On the other hand, large landowners have become increasingly militant in the defense of their interests. The disputes that cropped up in northern Bolivia are to be understood in this general context.

Supreme Decree No. 25532

Although the 1996 Forestry Law provided for the possibility of converting existing concessions into new ones under the new forestry regime, *barraqueros* had made little effort to do so. For one thing, they had never really bothered to acquire concessions: their claims were based rather on "custom." Moreover, they argued that the new license fee system was inadequate for Brazil nut production. In the past they had paid a fee per volume extracted (though one may doubt that this system ever really worked). Finally, they argued that the new forestry authorities did not accept their proposals for conversion of their claims. All in all, little had been done to implement the new legislation in the region and *barraqueros* probably would have liked to leave things just like they had been in the past. Emerging pressures for regularizing land tenure and forestry rights under the new laws, however, prompted them, and particularly the larger ones represented in CADEXNOR, to move on this issue and to lobby for their interests. In October 1999 their efforts were rewarded with Supreme Decree No. 25532 of 5 October 1999, also known as the *Decreto de las Barracas*.[36]

The decree mentions that the 1996 Forestry Law establishes that where areas with Brazil nut, rubber, palm heart, and similar resources are concerned concessionary preference will be given to traditional users, peasant communities and local social associations. Although the notion of "traditional" is taken generally to mean either peasant or indigenous users, the decree then argues that the *barracas* are traditional rubber- and Brazil nut–producing establishments that cover extensive forest areas in the north of the country, where they have enjoyed "inveterate and traditional" access to these resources that are the principal socioeconomic mainstay of the region. On the basis of such considerations the decree then stipulates that the *barracas* should be recognized as concessions for the exploitation of nontimber forest products under the new regime, respecting the legally acquired rights of third parties. The Forestry Superintendency should directly convert these areas, through administrative act and without an auctioning process. The decree further mentions a list of requirements and a formula for the calculation of license fees to be paid, and in one of its final dispositions establishes that this process of voluntary conversion will not imply the renunciation of titling procedures initiated or pursued with the competent authority. This opened up the possibility for a further conversion into property under the agrarian legislation.[37]

Chronicle of a Conflict Foretold

Soon after the decree was issued, the Agrarian Superintendency wrote a letter to the Minister of Sustainable Development and the Environment in which it recognized that the decree constituted a positive step toward the recognition of the customary rights of the *barraca* owners, but that it might generate some conflict with peasant communities and other "equally traditional possessors."[38] The decree seeks to be careful in respecting the rights of peasant and indigenous communities, the letter argues, but in fact at the moment it is impossible for such communities to sustain their property rights, since they are no more than simple possessors as long as the process of *saneamiento* has not been concluded. Out of the 6.3 million hectares in the Department of Pando, only 330,000 (5 percent) have been distributed under the agrarian reform legislation, which means that the vast majority of the rural population does not have duly regularized property rights. Moreover, the *saneamiento* process has not even started in the region, and the Pando branch of the *Instituto Nacional de Reforma Agraria* (INRA) has not yet been institutionalized. Under such conditions the decree means that the communities will be deprived of property rights and the use of resources, although they should be considered traditional settlements. The Agrarian Superintendency then calculates that the decree would hand over some 3 million hectares of land (48 percent) to the *barracas*. If one takes into account that in the Department of

Pando an area of 126,000 hectares (2 percent) has been reserved for cattle raising, that timber concessions occupy some 250,000 hectares (4 percent), that natural parks cover a further 14 percent, and if water resources and ecological obligations are also taken into account, the conclusion can only be that hardly any land will be left for the communities.[39] Given the potential for conflict, the Superintendency proposed that the property rights of communities and others should be clarified through the *saneamiento* process before proceeding with any conversion of the *barracas*. Finally, the Superintendency suggests that, given the particularities of the economic activities in the region, the areas to be allocated to the different types of users should be discussed in the context of new regulations for the implementation of the *Ley INRA* instead of leaving the issue to the discretion of the INRA.

With this letter the Superintendency outlined in unambiguous terms the potential for conflict in the region, but its words of warning went unheeded. Instead, the Bolivian government decided in May 2000 to extend the period for applications for conversion of *barracas*, initially set at the end of April 2000, to the last day of July 2000. By then conflict was brewing (Betancur 2000).

A War of Manifestos

Shortly after the Agrarian Superintendency had hoisted its early warning signals, peasant communities and indigenous peoples of the northern Amazon region issued a declaration invoking, among other things, ILO Convention 169, which establishes that indigenous peoples should be consulted over legislation that affects them. Arguing that the decree would result in the expulsion or eviction of peasant and indigenous communities to the benefit of the *barraqueros*, the signatories of the declaration rejected the decree and demanded that titling of community lands should precede any conversion. They also decided to ask for the intervention of the *Defensor del Pueblo* (human rights ombudsman) and announced an intention to undertake action if their demands were ignored or overruled. This declaration was soon followed by an open letter addressed to "public opinion" issued by the indigenous people's organization CIRABO on December 1, 1999. The next day saw a demonstration in Cobija, capital of the Department of Pando, organized by the rural workers' organization; the latter announced that to indicate its rejection of Decree 25532, roadblocks would be set up on December 13, 2000.

The *barraquero* sector did not fail to react. In its own open letter, similarly addressed to public opinion, ASPROGOAL replied to the letter issued by CIRABO, which it accused of having initiated a disinformation campaign. According to ASPROGOAL Decree 25532 aimed at the recognition of the *barraqueros'* historical and legally acquired rights. ASPROGOAL argued that the *barraca* owners historically had undertaken sustainable development and protection of the forest in the region and that their economic activities depended on the extraction of nontimber products, which did no harm to the forest. It claimed recognition of the *barraca* owners' rights "passed down from father to son" through a policy that would grant "juridical security," and would thus legalize their conservation activities and allow for the elaboration of a socioeconomic development strategy for the region. It further questioned some of the assertions and claims made by CIRABO. According to ASPROGOAL, not only were the rights of peasant and indigenous communities fully guaranteed in the decree, but the lands immobilized for future titling as TCOs also stood in no relation to the actual numbers of the indigenous populations involved. It suggested that CIRABO was manipulated by "foreign" interests outside the region, to the detriment of the local entrepreneurs "who at present help some 12,000 families, which work in the collection of the *castaña* and other fruits of the forest, improving the internal product of the Bolivian Northwest."[40] ASPROGOAL announced that it would defend Decree 25532 at "whatever cost" (*hasta las últimas consecuencias*). About the same time the Civic Committee of the Riberalta Region, the "Thought and Muscle of the Bolivian Amazon," issued a public manifesto following a similar line of reasoning, this time reproaching the Agrarian Superintendency for its comment on Decree 25532. The manifesto was signed by several urban organizations that participate in the Civic Committee, such as the Federation of Neighborhood Associations, the President of the Vigilance Committee, the President of the Federation of Rubber and Brazil Nut Workers, and the President of the Federation of Factory Workers. An urban coalition was being forged in support of the claims made by the *barraquero* sector, though in a reply to the ASPROGOAL and Civic Committee statements CIRABO called into question the real degree of support among urban organizations.[41] CIRABO's reply also refers to "conditions of semi-slavery" in the *barracas*, and once again rejects Decree 25532, which, it pointed out, would benefit only those who "claim to be entrepreneurs" (*quienes dicen llamarse empresarios*). In support of their campaigns, both the peasantry and the *barraqueros* invoked the "struggle for poverty reduction," one of the slogans of the Banzer Government. However, whereas the peasant and indigenous organizations pressed for redistribution of land to achieve that goal, the *barraqueros* merely presented themselves as the protagonists in the struggle against poverty.

In the event, the threatened roadblocks announced by peasant organizations for December 13, 1999, did not materialize, since the Department of Pando Prefecture called for a dialogue, which was to take place on 22

December. The meeting was postponed until January 15, 2000, and peasant organizations expected that it would be decisive. The meeting ended in failure. First of all, the Pando Prefecture had "forgotten" to send official invitations to the peasant federation and the civil society organizations supporting it. Furthermore, the composition of the governmental delegation remained unknown until the last moment. When the meeting finally took place, the representatives of national and local peasant and indigenous organizations, and the civil society organizations with whom they worked, found that the governmental delegation consisted of the INRA director and Senator Peter Hecker, one of the principal landowners and *barraqueros* of the region. Since this delegation had no power of decision, and because the choice of Senator Hecker as a principal delegate was considered insulting in view of the Hecker family's history of confrontation with peasant and indigenous organizations, the latter walked out. They later agreed to talk with the INRA Director and the Pando Prefect, but no point of convergence or consensus was found. As allowed for by the INRA law, peasants insisted that *saneamiento* should precede any conversion of *barracas*, and any attempt to implement Decree 25532 would be met with legal, political and other kinds of opposition to prevent this.

Marching for "Land, Territories and Natural Resources"

In April 2000 an eighteen-point manifesto was launched by indigenous peasant organizations, and in June a thirty-one-point platform of demands was issued, to be pressed for with a march for "Land, Territories and Natural Resources." A few days later the *Defensoría del Pueblo* (national human rights ombudsman) demanded that Decree 25532 be declared anti-constitutional, and on June28 some five hundred peasants and indigenous people started their march from the region to participate in the Great National Assembly of Indigenous Peoples (GANPI) that was to take place in the city of Santa Cruz, where they arrived on July 5. The next day both CIRABO and the *Coordinadora de Pueblos Etnicos de Santa Cruz* (CPESC) withdrew from the GANPI, accusing the CIDOB leadership of brokering a deal with the government, and announced that they would continue their march, now heading for the national capital itself, La Paz. An agreement between CIDOB and government delegates who had arrived to negotiate at the GANPI was indeed signed on July 7. According to the dissidents, it postponed solutions and contained empty promises. They resumed their march on July 11 and reached the town of Montero two days later. Negotiations with a government delegation resulted in another agreement in the early hours of July 16.

By then, in an effort to stop the march and keep it from growing, the Council of Ministers had on July 10 annulled Decree 25532, well within the twelve-day term that had been agreed earlier with CIDOB. Important points of the Montero agreement were the cancelling of an internal INRA resolution that made it possible to declare land available for concessions without first duly clarifying the rights of local people, the setting of clear terms for the titling of four TCOs, the creation of a fund with a starting capital of US$10 million for the reactivation of the peasant, indigenous and colonist economy, and a modification of the regulations of the *Ley INRA*. These modifications accepted, among other things, the following two crucial arguments. First, that the minimum surface area to be granted to families in peasant and indigenous communities in the northern Amazon region should be 500 hectares.[42] And second, that clarification of property rights in the northern Amazon region, as well as in the Gran Chaco region of the Tarija Department, should start immediately and be concluded within a year.[43] Furthermore, the procedures for titling in favor of peasants, colonists, and indigenous peoples were simplified, and a series of technical norms were modified, including a clearer definition of the norms regarding the economic-social function of land on farms up to 500 hectares.[44]

The Aftermath of the March and the Crisis of the Brazil Nut Trade

After the march, implementation of the 1996 legislation gradually got underway in the region. In the Department of Pando, the INRA structure finally became more or less institutionalized, though it remained subject to strong political pressures. "Polygons" were defined, that is areas where the demarcation of properties was to start, and in some cases INRA brigades initiated their evaluation of tenure claims, accompanied by peasants who were trained by local NGOs to keep watch over the process, and denounce irregularities such as the creation of "phantom communities" by *barraqueros*, the deforestation of areas to prove the presence of economic activity, or the "lending" of livestock by cattle raisers to one another, so as to provide visiting INRA brigades with the necessary "proof" of economic activity. In the Vaca Díez Province the process proceeded somewhat more rapidly. The density of settlement implied that boundaries between holdings had often already been established, and political pressures from the departmental government were less frequent than in Pando. Regularization of TCOs in favor of indigenous peoples in the region also made some progress. Out of the four demands for TCOs, titles were issued for part of the area demanded in two cases.

Meanwhile, the question of what to do with the *barracas* remained on the agenda. After the abrogation of Decree 25532, the *barraquero* sector had started to lobby for a law that would permit the conversion of the areas they claimed into new concessions under the Forestry Law, or into properties under agrarian legislation. By October 2001 a draft law was circulating and a provisional agreement was brokered among *barraquero* associations and the leadership of the Pando Peasant Federation, which however soon withdrew its support for the proposal. The draft law foresaw the "voluntary conversion" of traditional *barracas* into new concessions and established an upper limit of 25,000 hectares, although *barraquero* organizations continued to pressure for conversion of their *barracas* into property under the agrarian legislation. It will, however, be difficult for them to prove that the *barracas* fulfill an economic social function, since labor relations are informal, debt-peonage relations persist, and production is not mechanized in any way. On the other hand, one large *barraquero*, ADN Senator Peter Hecker, claimed that a huge concession should be granted for the exploitation of *sangre de grado*, a small tree locally used for medicinal purposes. A US firm was interested, and this could be a million-dollar business. The venture would increase regional income and at the same time promote forest conservation, he claimed.

The push and pull over a law on the conversion of *barracas* developed amid a crisis in the Brazil nut trade. After years of low exports, Brazil increased its own production significantly in 2001; Bolivia itself also produced more than in previous years and was finally left with a stock of 157,000 boxes of shelled nuts. With the world market saturated, prices plummeted, and the *beneficiadora* owners announced that in the 2001–2002 harvest they would not be able to pay more than 4 *bolivianos* per crate of raw nuts. They later offered 8 *bolivianos* (about US$1.25), but this was still much less than the 20 *bolivianos* paid in the forest during the 2000–2001 season. Furthermore, they decided that the harvest would be limited, in order to stabilize prices and to allow them to sell the surplus production from the previous season. The obvious consequence would be unemployment for thousands of people in the region. Some four thousand *zafreros* from the urban areas would be left without employment during the harvest season, and employment of some three thousand *quebradoras* and their four thousand "helpers" would be severely cut back.[45] To solve the problem, it was proposed that the Bolivian state should create a special fund to reactivate the regional economy and pay an additional 10 *bolivianos* per crate harvested to the *zafreros*. In the forest, the *zafreros* would receive coupons worth 100 *bolivianos* for every ten crates of Brazil nuts delivered, and after the harvest they could cash their coupons in town. By mid-December, when harvesters are usually shipped to the *barracas*, a government representative visited Riberalta to announce that the scheme had been approved, but that some technical details still had to be worked out.[46] By then, the president of the *zafrero* union was already selling official membership cards to his clients at 10 to 20 *bolivianos* apiece. Peasant organizations, however, vehemently rejected the proposal, since it might be used to demonstrate that the *barracas* did indeed perform an economic social function. The government sought to tie approval of the subsidy scheme to support for a new *barraca* law and, after its failed "Earth Summit," announced that it would organize regional encounters to find solutions for regional problems.

Concluding Comments

Conflicts over land and resources have become increasingly frequent in Bolivia over recent years. This suggests, among other things, that the land and forestry legislation introduced in 1996 has failed to resolve the problems it was meant to address. It generated expectations that were not fulfilled due to a lack of political will. Moreover, it is often hard to apply in particular local situations. This article has discussed the implementation of the new legislation and the issues it brought to light in the specific regional context of the northern Bolivian Amazon.

To do so, it was necessary to outline the historical development of the regional rural economy, tracing the emergence and consolidation of the rubber estate system and its fragmentation after 1940. It has been argued that there is little reason to revise the prevailing view of the rubber economy in the region and its forms of organization, which are usually characterized as rather harsh and exploitative. Labor recruitment during the early period of rubber extraction was often coercive, and the workforce was not treated particularly well, although excesses like those reported from the Peruvian Putumayo region did not occur. Debt-peonage was the prevailing mode of labor recruitment and control, and there is no convincing evidence in support of the oft-heard argument that this was a relatively benign and, under the conditions, "rational" system. The interpretation of Barham and Coomes has been shown not to apply in the region, because it hinges on the idea of generalized competition for clients among patrons and merchants. Such conditions did not obtain in the northern Bolivian Amazon region up to 1940. In a similar vein, the evidence presented by Stoian in support of his argument that fixed-wage relations for rubber tappers prevailed during the early rubber era, and that this would shift most of the risk to the patron, was found to be far from convincing. Some of the contracts he cites actually confirm the presence of indigenous slavery, while others point to piece rates for rubber tapping and fixed wages for off-season activities. The workforce could not be considered to have been "salaried in the strict sense of the term," a point emphasized by Sanabria Fernández.

This, however, does not lead to a disagreement with Stoian's characterization of the early rubber era as one of "primitive capitalism," although a caveat is in order. As noted, even Marx considered North American plantation owners as capitalists, because they exist as "anomalies in a world-market based in free labor." For this reason it does not seem useful to frame the discussion in terms of the feudalism/capitalism debate. Instead, it has been suggested that Chevalier's view of simple commodity production may be combined with the pervasive notion of "captivity," which conveys the element of employer/ patron domination and monopoly, and the virtuality of a "cash economy" in which cash hardly ever materializes. Rubber tappers in the northern Bolivian Amazon region can thus be viewed as simple commodity producers, formally subsumed under capital and subject to the extraction of absolute surplus value through monopolistic domination by a patron who brokers their relation to the market. Their economy, however, was fully "commodified," in the sense that rubber was exchanged for subsistence goods in the penumbra of a captive market operating through the patron's ledger. Establishing "free communities" can be understood as the antithesis of this "captivity," and thus as an emancipatory response on the part of simple commodity producers.

Free communities emerged in the context of a sustained crisis of the rubber economy. It was precisely this crisis that shaped the conditions of emergence of the *comunidades libres*, since it prompted the "internalization of the conditions of reproduction." On the one hand, the crisis opened the way to the emergence of an agro-extractive cycle, which combined rubber tapping, agriculture, and Brazil nut gathering as complementary activities that could potentially sustain what was in effect a peasant household established by the rubber tapper. The development of rubber tapper subsistence production, one might say, entailed a process of decommodification, while rubber tapping and Brazil nut gathering were to become sources of cash income. On the other hand, the crisis promoted the formation of households through a new patron strategy to perpetuate "captivity" by promoting household life, often deciding who was to marry whom and establishing fictive kinship relations with the parents and offspring, for what it was worth. While the internalization of the conditions of reproduction had occurred in the wake of the 1913 crash in rubber prices, after 1940 the process of socioeconomic differentiation between patron-run (instead of "administrator managed") estates and *comunidades libres* gathered momentum.

The final unraveling of the rubber economy after 1985 brought a new dynamic to the region. It accelerated the decline of the estate system and the formation of independent communities. Rural migration modified the pattern of spatial occupation of the region. The location of the independent communities correlates with the size of parcels within the communities and the relative weight of agricultural and extractive activities. At the same time, a process of rural urban migration contributed to the formation of an industrial reserve army of urban labor that lacked employment opportunities. During the Brazil nut season, harvesters are recruited from this labor pool to work in the *barracas*, where the permanent population has been drastically reduced and conditions have deteriorated. Although in remote *barracas* debt peonage still persists, in the urban context the *habilito* system as a form of labor recruitment for the Brazil nut harvest has entered into a crisis with uncertain outcomes. The system may either be extinguished or substantially modified in tandem with a formalization of labor relations.

Decree 25532, which allowed for the conversion of *barracas* into new concessions under the 1996 Forestry Law and left open the possibility for further conversion into property under the INRA Law, brought to light the latent conflict between *barraqueros* on the one hand and the peasantry and indigenous rural population on the other. Whereas the decree allowed for the consolidation of *barracas* first and the subsequent clarification of peasant and indigenous tenure rights, the "Third March" successfully pressured for abrogation of the decree and the implementation of the INRA Law in the region while at the same time modifying the norms and procedures for its implementation. According to the new regulations, the peasant communities should be granted at least 500 hectares per family, which would allow them to generate a reasonable income basically derived from the extraction of forest products.

Whether and how the norm will be applied remains to be seen. In Vaca Díez Province, where rural population is densest, parcels in the peasant communities vary between 20 and 80 hectares, whereas in the Department of Pando they have access to larger areas. There too, however, location is important. *Barraqueros* argue that the peasantry seeks to occupy their lands and installations and that, if peasants want land, they should move to the more remote areas. The *barraquero* sector itself has introduced a distinction between traditional and nontraditional *barracas*. According to the leader of an organization of traditional *barraqueros*, the nontraditional ones could be reduced in size so as to make it possible to grant peasant communities sufficient land, albeit in more remote areas. As the clarification of tenure rights gets under way, both communities and *barraqueros* seek to consolidate their claims. Communities are constructing infrastructure with the help of local NGOs that apply for funding from Bolivian poverty relief schemes. For their part, *barraqueros* have cleared forest areas in order to establish their presence, an important consideration in the light of future property claims.

The outcome of the implementation of a new tenure regime in the region will be politically determined. Neither the peasantry nor the *barraqueros*, despite their entrepreneurial rhetoric, are in favor of a market-led reform process, although there is an element of deception here. Peasants and indigenous people seek tenure according to the INRA regulations for land that fulfills a social function and which, at least at the moment, may not be sold or mortgaged.[47] *Barraqueros* seek conversion of their *barracas*, which they claim fulfill an economic social function, through an administrative procedure. If concessions were ever put up for auction, they argue, they would lose out against transnational capital.[48] And they continue pressuring for the conversion of the *barracas* into regionally defined medium-sized properties under the tenure regime of the INRA law, which would bring them "juridical security." Their discourse of "juridical security" is extremely ambiguous, however. They present it as a "freezing" of their "inalienable rights," rather than as a condition for the operation of market forces, but various interviewees soon got into difficulties when asked how this type of "juridical security" was to be reconciled with their claim to perform an economic social function, which implies that they would fall under the market-oriented regime of the INRA law. They simply want full property rights over their *barracas*, and while some might indeed want to work them, others will surely want to sell them as soon as it becomes opportune and profitable to do so. This outcome would, of course, relaunch the process of vertical integration and concentration of forest-land in the hands of a few agribusiness enterprises.

Market-led reform is not a viable option in the region. Experience shows that land markets are highly segmented.[49] There may be a considerable volume of land transactions within farm-sized groups, but land sales across farm-sized group boundaries are either absent or contribute to further polarization. Simply put, the land market is not a level playing field.[50] In Bolivia, the mechanisms that were meant to correct such tendencies toward concentration have been rather effectively sabotaged as a result of the lobby for the reduction of the taxes and license fees that were to stimulate the market process. Under the questionable premise that such reductions will contribute to economic reactivation, the Bolivian government has been quite willing to grant such reductions.

A further issue that emerges is the question of "poverty reduction." Peasant organizations and sympathizing NGOs maintain that redistribution of tenure rights in favor of the peasantry and indigenous peoples is a precondition for improving their livelihood. *Barraqueros* and *beneficiadora* owners view themselves as the protagonists of poverty alleviation. The by now familiar Hecker brothers regularly come up with grandiose schemes that would require the granting of huge concessions for the exploitation of natural resources in the region, or for conservation and carbon dioxide capturing. The areas to be set aside for such schemes often coincide with indigenous peoples' territorial claims, and it is not very clear how the profits would eventually "trickle down."[51] Neither is there much to be expected from the smaller "traditional" *barraqueros*. They lack capital, and mostly seem keen to rid themselves of the "responsibilities" that went with the moral economy of the *barraca patronal*, while at the same time seeking "juridical security," perpetuating forms of debt-peonage, and claiming the monopoly over the trade in products extracted from their *barraca*. In some cases *barraca* owners have entered local politics and managed to become mayor of the municipalities created under the 1994 Popular Participation Law, while in other cases *barraqueros* have set up a Territorial Base Organization under the same law, thus creating "phantom communities" where they hold sway. For their part, peasant and indigenous communities, with the help of NGOs, are engaged in consolidating their claims, constructing infrastructure to justify these claims, and diversifying their production through agro-forestry schemes. They also seek funding from governmental poverty alleviation programs and the Popular Participation Law.

Meanwhile, preliminary data from the 2001 census suggest that the decline in absolute numbers of the rural population registered between 1976 and 1992 has been reversed. In the period 1992 2001 urbanization continued apace, while the rural population of the region grew by 1.8 percent annually. Although the data are still preliminary, this reversal of the tendency toward absolute decline may be due both to the efforts of NGOs to improve rural living conditions and also to the increased investment in rural areas under the Popular Participation Law. The data also suggest that rural population growth in Vaca Díez Province is higher than in the Pando Department.[52] This points to a continuing concentration of the population in the vicinity of urban centers where people can combine involvement in agricultural or agro-forestry activities with the benefits of urban services, such as education. The demographic dynamics of the region need further research when more detailed and definitive census data become available, for example to assess the growth of the emerging regional subcenters. However, one may safely assume that the bulk of this population growth takes place in the *comunidades libres*, through migration from the *barracas*, natural growth, and perhaps some return migration from the urban areas. What the future will bring will very much depend on the outcome of the current struggle over land and access to resources between agribusiness enterprises and simple commodity producers, itself merely the latest stage in a long history of such conflict in the northern Bolivian Amazon.

Glossary and Acronyms

adjudicación: sale by auction of public lands to private enterprises or farmers who perform an economic-social function

barraca: (rubber and/or Brazil nut) estate

barraca patronal: patron-run *barraca*, in contrast to "adminstrator"-run *barracas* in the context of the more "entrepreneurial" organization model that characterized the House of Suárez

barraquero: owner of a barraca

beneficiadora: processing plant where Brazil nuts are shelled

centro: forest settlement of a few huts in a *barraca* from where rubber trails start

Centro de Desarrollo Forestal: Centre for Forest Development, local executive agency under the 1974 Forestry Law

chaco patronal: field cultivated under supervision of the patron

comunidad libre: free community

Corporación Boliviano de Fomento: Bolivian Development Corporation

Defensor del Pueblo: (human rights) ombudsman

dotación: land grant to peasant or indigenous communities; land that performs a social function

enganche: coercive form of labour recruitment, literally "hooking" a worker

fregues: subcontractor on a rubber estate

granja: medium-sized farm

habilito: advance payment, known in Brazil as *aviamento*

Ley del Servicio Nacional de Reforma Agraria, Ley INRA: Law on the National Service for Agrarian Reform, also known as INRA-Law (1996)

Ley Forestal: Forestry Law (1996)

motosierrista: chain-saw owner

payol: storage place in the forest for Brazil nuts

pulpería: company store

quebradora: worker (usually a woman) who shells Brazil nuts in a *beneficiadora*

saneamiento: clarification of land rights

solar campesino: peasant yard

tierra fiscal: public land

trabajadores empatronados: workers in a barraca patronal

zafrero: Brazil nut harvester

ABAN: *Asociación de Beneficiadoras del Nordeste*, Association of Beneficidoras of the Northeast

ADN: *Acción Democratica Nacionalista*, Nationalist Democratic Action (political party)

ASPROGOAL: *Asociación de Productores de Goma y Almendra*, Association of Producers of Rubber and Brazil nuts (*barraqueros*)

CADEXNOR: *Camara de Exportadores del Norte*, Chamber of Commercial Exporters of the North

CAO: *Camara Agropuecuaria del Oriente*, Chamber of Commercial Agriculturalists of the East

CIDOB: *Confederación Indígena del Oriente, Chaco y Amazonía Boliviana*, Confederation of Indigenous Peoples the Bolivian East, the Chaco and the Amazon
CIRABO: *Central Indígena de la Región Amazónica de Bolivia*, Indigenous Central of the Bolivian Amazon Region
CPESC: *Coordinadora de Pueblos Étnicos de Santa Cruz*, Coordinating Organization of Ethnic Peoples of Santa Cruz
CPIB: *Central de Pueblos Indígenas del Beni*, Central Organization of the Indigenous Peoples of Beni
GANPI: *Gran Asamblea Nacional de Pueblos Indígenas*, Grand National Assembly of Indigenous Peoples
ILO: International Labour Organization
INRA: *Instituto Nacional de Reforma Agraria*, National Agrarian Reform Institute
NGO: Non-Governmental Organization
TCO: *Tierras Comunitarias de Origen*, Original Community Lands (legal figure for the regularization of indigenous territories)

Notes

This chapter was originally published in 2002 as "From Rubber Estate to Simple Commodity Production: Agrarian Struggles in the Northern Bolivian Amazon," *Journal of Peasant Studies* 29, no. 3–4, 83–130. We are grateful to the *Journal of Peasant Studies* and Taylor & Francis for allowing us to reproduce the text here.

1. From the 1970s onward the indigenous peoples of the eastern lowlands had begun to organize with the help of anthropologists and NGOs. This led to the formation of an umbrella organization, the *Confederación Indígena del Oriente, Chaco y Amazonía de Bolivia* (CIDOB), in 1982. In 1990, on the initiative of the *Central de Pueblos Indígenas del Beni* (CPIB), which confronted logging interests in that Department, the peoples of the lowlands undertook a much publicized "March for Dignity and Territory." In response to this march, which suddenly made the lowland indigenous people visible, the then President Paz Zamora signed a series of decrees recognizing indigenous territories, and Bolivia ratified ILO Convention 169 (Concerning Indigenous and Tribal Peoples in Independent Countries). A "Second March," under the banner of "Land and Territory," took place in September 1996 in the context of the debate and negotiations over new agrarian legislation. The *Ley del Servicio Nacional de Reforma Agraria*, which will be discussed below, was adopted in October 1996 (Assies 2000). A glossary and a list of acronyms can be found at the end of this article
2. It should be noted that this periodization departs from the conventional one that takes the collapse of rubber prices in 1913 as a major conjunctural break. Although, as we will see, the 1913 crisis had important effects, the power of the Casa Suárez remained intact.
3. It is estimated that between 250,000 and 500,000 people, mostly males, moved into the Brazilian Amazon region, particularly after a drought hit the northeast in 1877. About one-third of them are estimated to have moved into the Acre region, which soon became the most important rubber producing area in Brazil (Costa 1992: 39; Martinello 1988: 38). Sanabria Fernández (1988: 94) estimates that between 1860 and 1910, some eighty thousand people from the Bolivian side moved northward, particularly from the Santa Cruz region. According to Stoian (2000a: 63) this figure may well be a gross overestimate.
4. In Brazil this system is known as the *aviamento*.

5. Though its effects in northern Bolivia were rather limited, the 1953 agrarian reform law contributed to the consolidation of such communities (Ormachea 1987; Ormachea and Fernández 1989). Officially, according to the 1953 law, rubber tappers would have received two trails to exploit and a small property for agricultural use, totaling up to 500 hectares. The larger properties would be affected according to the norms established for agriculture or cattle raising in the tropical or subtropical regions, and their maximum extension would be 50,000 hectares in the cases involving cattle herds in excess of ten thousand head. The remaining land would revert to the state.

6. It should be stressed that in view of the highly irregular process of land allocation these data refer to claims rather than to properties. Of the smallholders, at best 5 percent ever managed to get hold of a title to their parcels, while titles acquired for large holdings are often questionable and frequently unclear as to the real size and location of the area. On the other hand, concessions for forest product exploitation had been given out ever since 1920, and some were reconfirmed during the 1940s by the *Corporación Boliviano de Fomento*. When this agency was dissolved in 1985, the Regional Development Corporation took over this task, though the 1974 Forestry Law made the *Centros de Desarrollo Forestal* responsible for granting permits. In fact, exploitation was based on traditional claims and a few renewed permits. In the early 1990s registration of such permits was nonexistent (DHV 1993b), and fees due for exploitation of Brazil nuts were hardly ever paid. In 1996 the Riberalta Forestry Development Centre tried to negotiate payment with the owners of Brazil nut processing plants.

7. Based on a survey of 163 rural settlements, Stoian and Henkemans (2000) have elaborated a detailed classification, which distinguishes four types of *barracas* and six types of independent community. Their analysis of demographic trends details the increase in population in the communities and the decline of the population in *barracas*, as well as the influence on this process of location. They point to the emergence of some regional subcenters, often located at river crossings where, in the absence of bridges, cars have to be brought over by boat. The rise of these subcenters was also influenced by the 1994 Popular Participation Law, the aim of which was administrative decentralization and a strengthening of the municipal level. In fact it not only strengthened the few actually existing municipalities but created over 250 new municipalities where they had been virtually nonexistent before (Calla 2000; Nijenhuis 2000).

8. Part of the crop is often sold at harvest time, when prices are low, and staples then have to be bought later in the year when prices are on the rise. This is due partly to the need for cash and partly to the lack of adequate storage facilities. In 1994–1995 the Riberalta municipality promoted a relatively successful food security program in some nearby communities, where as a result storage capacity was installed and marketing was improved, resulting in better prices. In 1996, peasants in the area expressed their satisfaction and stated their intention to expand rice production. In remoter areas subsistence agriculture predominates and agricultural produce is bartered, rather than sold (Assies 1997a: 63).

9. For a discussion of the "urban question" in Riberalta, see van Beijnum (1996) and Verheule (1998).

10. This caused a temporary surge in international prices due to competition among buyers on the Bolivian scene, and a misreading of events by Brazilian exporters, who attributed the reduction in supply to a harvest shortfall in Acre rather than to the newfound market outlets for Bolivian producers who now shipped their produce through the Pacific port of Arica (Holt 1992). Export prices for shelled nuts went from around US$0.90 per pound in the mid-1980s to US$1.70 per pound in 1989, and then dropped again, according to data from the *Instituto Nacional de Promoción de Exportaciones* (INPEX) and LaFleur (1992).

11. Data supplied by the *Asociación de Beneficiadoras del Norte* (ABAN) and also from my own field data for 1994–1997. See also Bojanic Helbingen (2001: 61) and Coesmans and Medina (1997: 150).

12. For a discussion of resources and resource use in the region, see Beekma, Zonta and Keijzer (1996). See also the DHV (1993b) studies, as well as Bojanic Helbingen (2001), Henkemans (2001), and Stoian (2000a).

13. Some processing plants have experimented with mechanical shelling, freezing shells and then projecting them against a hard surface, all with variable success.

14. Letter from Federico G. Hecker H. to Monseñor Luis Morgan Casey, Vicario Apostólico de Pando, Riberalta, March 3, 2000. The letter, written on the occasion of a land dispute, elicited an ironical reply from the local indigenous organization, the *Central Indígena de la Región Amazónica de Bolivia* (CIRABO). The latter first thanks Mr. Hecker for acknowledging the genocide perpetrated by his forebears, then enumerates the surviving indigenous peoples, and finally tells Mr. Hecker to go and claim property in his homeland, Switzerland, instead of telling the Tacana to return to their homelands, from whence they were dragged by his ancestors (CIRABO, "Rechazamos guerra sucia en contra de los derechos de los pueblos indígenas en el Norte amazónico de Bolivia," Riberalta, March 8, 2000).

15. The debate concerns the failure of sustained development in the Amazon region. In contrast to the claim about the draining off of surplus, Weinstein (1993) argues that the failure of Amazon development was due to the persistence of pre-capitalist relations, which she attributes to a tapper trader alliance. Tappers preferred a certain autonomy rather than engaging in wage labor on plantations, which would have allowed for the development of significant internal markets. Barham and Coomes (1994b; 1996; Coomes and Barham 1994), in contrast, argue that the *habilito* system was an efficient institutional arrangement under the circumstances, and that it allowed for significant local surplus retention. They propose a Dutch disease model to explain the failure of Amazon development. As to the possibilities for plantation production, it should be noted that Dean (1989) has argued that efforts to do this failed basically because of an endemic American leaf blight. In other words, whereas Weinstein locates the difficulty at the level of production relations, Dean attributes the same difficulties to the nature of the productive forces.

16. According to the contract Mr. Barbery "authorized" the Casa Suárez to pay the workers 10 *bolivianos* per month, "in merchandise or money," whereas he himself would receive 100 *bolivianos* per worker per month. At the time the nominal exchange rate was 12.5 *bolivianos* for every pound sterling (Sanabria Fernández 1988: 130).

17. Sanabria Fernández (1988: 129) notes that there were cases of upward mobility among this group, but also that many, when receiving payment (in English pounds) at the end of the season, rapidly spent it, and had to reopen an account. The message of such stories is as clear as it is moralizing and apologetic: a dedicated and hardworking rubber tapper, who does not fall ill, despite rampant malaria and snake bites, and who does not squander his credit at the end of the season, could become a subcontractor (*fregues*) and even a patron. No examples are given of rubber tappers becoming patrons at this time, and claims regarding the possibility of upward mobility are consequently problematic.

18. The law is reproduced in Roca (2001: 114–116). See also Sanabria Fernández (1988: 97) and Pacheco (1992: 73–74).

19. Fawcett also reported ill-treatment of rubber tappers to the British Foreign Office (Fifer 1970).

20. When in the 1880s La Paz–based explorers entered the northern Bolivian Amazon to stake out their claims, they met with fierce resistance from the Santa Cruz-based pioneers (Sanabria Fernández 1988: 59, 67; Roca 2001: 209–213). The situation became monopolistic with the consolidation of the Suárez empire. According to one of the heirs of the Riberalta-based Braillard Company, later Seiler and finally Hecker Hnos. (Hecker Brothers), it was not for nothing that its main *barracas* were called *Conquista* (Conquest) and *Fortaleza* (Fortress). This reflected their confrontation with the Suárez monopoly (personal

communication from Peter Hecker in 1996). The imagery of free access and unbridled competition among a variety of entrepreneurs and merchants to win the clients' favor does not hold in this case. Just like a single swallow does not a summer make, so an occasional "interloper" does not make for generalized competition.

21. Note that I do not follow the translation by Jack Cohen in Eric Hobsbawm's edition of the *Formen* (Marx 1965: 119). The translation states: "If we now talk of plantation-owners in America as capitalists, if they *are* capitalists. . . ." The German text, however, is quite clearly affirmative: "sondern daß sie es *sind*. . . ." A more accurate translation might have saved a lot of ink and paper.

22. Although it was invariably a legal fiction, rubber tappers were formally viewed as the owners of their product, which they, contractually, were obliged to sell only to the patron who had "enabled" them to produce it. The patron thus was the "mediator" and the "threshold" between the rubber tapper and the market, and in effect controlled the circulation of goods within his realm, a "virtual market," an arrangement that was the basis of his "paternalist exploitation" (Geffray 1995: 13–36).

23. Patron domination relies on a combination of violence and "favours" that create strong, though ambiguous feelings of dependency and mutual obligation (Geffray 1995). A striking example of such contradictory feelings can be found in a document of the Brazilian *Conselho Nacional de Seringueiros*, the organization of "autonomous rubber tappers" founded by Chico Mendes, when it complains that "[N]ot one government ever made the necessary social investment that could cover the costs previously met by the patrons, the *seringalistas*, with the object of maintaining their domination. The whole weight fell on the rubber tapper, as government evaded its obligations" (CNS 1991). On this point, see also Aramburu (1994).

24. In his famous study of hunger as a man-made phenomenon, Josué de Castro (1963: 106–107) noted that the decline of the rubber trade was accompanied by an improved diet, due to the expansion of subsistence agriculture. The phenomenon is also noted by Romanoff (1992: 131).

25. It was reported that a number of "free communities" came into existence at this time, either as a result of patrons abandoning their *barraca* or by people moving into unoccupied areas (Ormachea 1987).

26. As Costa Sobrinho (1992: 65) notes, women might even be imported by the patrons as one more item among the *aviamento* supplies, the Brazilian equivalent of the *habilito*.

27. It should be noted that since the early 1990s attempts have been made to formalize labor relations obtaining in the Brazil nut harvest and also in the processing plants, but with limited success. Formalizing labor relations during the harvest would require that the real employers, the *beneficiadora* owners and the *barraqueros*, assume direct responsibility as employers, rather than transferring it to the contractors (Assies 1997a: 55 6). As to profitability, *beneficiadora* owners complain a lot, and the Hecker brothers like to tell anyone who wants to hear it that actually they are "socialists of sorts" by virtue of providing employment to the population of a backward region while earning hardly anything themselves. During my research in 1995 and 1996, however, I was shown some feasibility studies for *beneficiadoras*, which showed rather handsome profit expectations, and I made an approximate calculation of the distribution of benefits from the nut trade in Bolivia. This showed that out of the world market price for a kilogram of shelled nuts, 16 percent goes to the *zafrero* (harvester), 11 percent to the *barraquero*, and 8 percent to the *quebradora* (the women who shell the nuts in the *beneficiadoras*). The remaining 64 percent consists of operating costs for the processing plants, transportation costs, intermediary costs, and profits. I concluded that the *beneficiadora* owners had no reason at all to complain (Assies 1997a: 59). According to Stoian (2000a: 144), who does not address the methodological issue of the calculation

involved, my view is an "impressionistic" one which unjustifiably attributes "excessive gains to the entrepreneurial class." Implying that "erroneous but perhaps politically motivated results can be produced," he then argues that "the facts . . . are different," and that "the profit after taxes of a typical processing plant is rather modest." Although he does estimate the share of *beneficiadora* owners, which I did not do, Stoian's (2000a: 146) calculation does not contradict my findings where the other actors are concerned. The harvester's share in the world market price of a pound of nuts could go from 14 percent to 34 percent in an exceptionally good year (1997–1998), the *barraquero* share is 14 percent in that same year, and the *quebradora* share is 8.4 percent. According to this calculation the *beneficiadora* owner's share was 11.3 percent. Bojanic Helbingen (2001: 70) provides some insight into how this translates into incomes from the nut trade. The 25 *beneficiadora* owners earn US$5,000 per month, all year round, which means an annual income of US$60,000. The 5,800 harvesters are employed for three months a year and during this period earn only US$173 per month, or US$520 per year. The 2,500 *quebradoras*, who are formally employed to work nine months per year and themselves earn US$160 per month, or US$1,443 per year, while their 4,000 informally employed "helpers" also work nine months annually, but earn only US$40 per month or US$360 per year. Three hundred and fifty *barraqueros* earn US$500 during six months or US$3,000 per year. According to Bojanic Helbingen (2001: 82) such data not only do "not reflect a high inequality in the distribution of income," but they show that the lower income groups (harvesters and *quebradoras*) get a daily or monthly wage higher than that paid by other forms of employment available to non-skilled labor. He recommends calculating Gini coefficients and Lorenz curves. Elsewhere Bojanic Helbingen (2001: 174) shows that 80 percent of the households in the region live below the US$2 line and 44 percent live below the US$1 line: in other words, they are extremely poor. The 18 percent who are "not poor" account for 36 percent of the regional income and the 4.5 percent in the "higher income" bracket for 15 percent.

28. The average parcel size in the area is about 50 hectares. This is barely sufficient for sustainable slash and burn agriculture, based on the cultivation of about 2 hectares and a regeneration period of about twenty-five years. Soils in the region as a whole are extremely poor and hardly apt for agriculture. One study (DHV 1993b) suggests that the costs of slash and burn agriculture are economically higher than the value it produces. Extraction of forest products would therefore be an alternative, and at the same time would contribute to forest conservation. According to a document prepared by an NGO in Riberalta, in order to earn about US$1,727 per year, a peasant household containing six persons and relying on a combination of agriculture and extractivism would need access to between 300 and 500 hectares of forest land. Similar calculations have been made for the Brazilian extractive reserves, which were created in response to the rubber tappers movement led by Chico Mendes (Allegreti 1990; 1994; Brown and Rosendo 2000; Mendes 1992).

29. Henkemans (2001) discusses the problems of a remote community attempting to become independent from a patron.

30. On the other hand, Stoian points out that vertical integration was accompanied by a tendency toward horizontal integration, which is a diversification of production into palm heart production and logging.

31. In the course of the year 2000, when clarification of land rights had finally started, and after the "Third March," a technical commission made up of interested parties and various civil society organizations identified 167 communities in the Vaca Díez Province and 307 in the Pando Department. The total number of *barracas* may be around 300 to 350.

32. In Bolivia the highland Indian population rejects the term *indígena* and instead insists on being called *originario*, which in their view better indicates that they were there before either the Spanish conquest or the subsequent formation of the Bolivian state. The indigenous

population of the lowlands is estimated at some 220,000 people belonging to thirty different groups. The Quechua, Aymara, and Uru of the highlands would number over 4 million.

33. In practice the paying of tax was taken as proof that land fulfilled its economic social function, a point that was immediately challenged by peasant organizations

34. This is meant basically to provide an area to be used by chainsaw owners (*motosierristas*), who until then had exploited resources in a highly irregular way. They now should form an association and work according to a management plan.

35. In March 1999 the International Labor Organization (ILO) issued a series of recommendations on this case (Tamburini 2000).

36. Possibly the decree was also a reward for support given to *Acción Democrática Nacionalista* (ADN), the main party of President Banzer's governing coalition, during the 1997 elections.

37. Throughout the debate over the Forestry Law the timber industry has lobbied for full private ownership of forest lands (Pavez and Bojanic Helbingen 1998).

38. See Superintendencia Agraria, November 16, 1999, Despacho 715/99.

39. Later the INRA produced maps showing the area claimed by *barracas* and the distribution of communities that had obtained legal personality under the Popular Participation Law of 1994, which are by no means all the existing communities. These maps show clearly the extent to which these rival claims overlap.

40. *Castaña* is the local term for Brazil nuts.

41. *Beneficiadora* owners regularly invoke doom-laden scenarios to defend their interests and threaten to shut down their operations. The support on the part of the President of the Federation of Rubber and Brazil Nut Workers partly reflects the interests of the urban-based workforce that participates in the Brazil nut harvest. It should be noted, however, that both the role and representativeness of this organization are rather doubtful. It holds office in ASPROGOAL that is under the auspices of the employers' organization. The Civic Committee Manifesto mentioned various local NGOs with which it claims to cooperate, but it is far from clear that these organizations would support the manifesto.

42. The stipulation that 500 hectares should be the minimum seems to be the result of a lapse by one of the government delegates during the Montero negotiations. Consultants had recommended that the families should be granted between 300 and 500 hectares.

43. The lack of advance in the Gran Chaco region possibly contributed to the conflict between the emerging movement of landless peasants and allegedly paramilitary "peasants with land," a clash that claimed seven lives in November 2001.

44. Included in the agreement was the fact that at least 50 percent of the land on such farms should be worked. An earlier modification of the regulations already introduced the norm that such properties should be worked with wage labor, that technical/mechanical productive forces should be used, and that production should be destined for the market. As noted, initially the payment of tax was taken as sufficient evidence for the performance of the social economic function.

45. Only part of the workforce employed in the shelling plants is officially registered as such. These workers mostly women are often "helped" by family members who are not themselves officially registered as part of the labor force.

46. Obviously, the scheme is rather questionable. At issue is who really benefited. Clearly, the harvesters receive more, provided that the system works, but the *beneficiadoras* would at the same time receive an indirect subsidy, receiving their raw material at an extremely low cost. On the whole, the scheme proposed could not help but end in a huge fraud.

47. There are pressures from the business lobby to reform the constitution on this point.

48. The argument is not terribly convincing. As we saw, the bottom price for exploitation licenses was set at US$1, and it was expected that it would rise as a result of competition. That has not been the case, since the fee was lowered to promote "economic reactivation."

49. On this point, see Zoomers (2000: 299).
50. On this point, see Carter (2000) and Carter and Salgado (2001).
51. Kaimowititz and Bojanic Helbingen (1998) provide another example. In the late 1990s, when Freddy Hecker was mayor of Riberalta, he proposed that the municipal forest reserve, defined in a way to make it overlap with an indigenous territorial claim, should be exploited by a Cuban enterprise, rather than by local "social associations" of chainsaw operators.
52. This poses a problem. As we saw, parcel sizes in Vaca Díez Province are relatively small. Although until now the communities have sought to accommodate newcomers, the latter receive increasingly smaller parcels, and within the communities some people have no holding at all. Peasant organizations have started to raise the question of a redistribution of land within the communities once they have received their collective title.

References

Allegretti Mary Helena. 1990. "Extractive Reserves: An Alternative for Reconciling Development and Environmental Conservation in Amazonia." In *Alternatives to Deforestation, Steps Toward Sustainable Use of the Amazon Rain Forest*, ed. A. B. Anderson. New York: Columbia University Press.

———. 1994. "Policies for the Use of Renewable Natural Resources: The Amazon Region and Extractive Activities." In *Extractivism in the Brazilian Amazon: Perspectives on Regional Development*, ed. M. Clüsener-Godt and I. Sachs. Paris: UNESCO (MAB Digest 18).

Aramburu, Mikel. 1994. "Aviamento, modernidade e pós-modernidade no interior amazónico?" *Revista Brasileira de Ciências Sociais* 9, no. 25: 82–99.

Assies, Willem. 1997a. *Going Nuts for the Rainforest: Non-Timber Forest Products, Forest Conservation and Sustainability in Amazonia.* Amsterdam: Thela.

———. 1997b. "The Extraction of Non-Timber Forest Products as a Rainforest Conservation Strategy." *European Review of Latin American Studies* 62.

———. 2000. "Multiethnic Constitutionalism, Territories and Internal Boundaries: The Bolivian Case." In *Fronteras: Towards a Borderless Latin America*, ed. CEDLA. Amsterdam: CEDLA.

Barham, Bradford L., and Oliver T. Coomes. 1994a. "Wild Rubber: Industrial Organization and the Microeconomics of Extraction During the Amazon Rubber Boom (1860–1920)." *Journal of Latin American Studies* 26, no. 1: 37–72.

———. 1994b. "Reinterpreting the Amazon Rubber Boom: Investment, the State, and Dutch Disease." *Latin American Research Review* 29, no. 2: 73–109.

———. 1996. *Prosperity's Promise: The Amazon Rubber Boom and Distorted Economic Development.* Boulder, CO, and Oxford, U.K.: Westview Press.

Beekma, Jelle, Armelinda Zonta, and Brigitte Keijzer. 1996. *Base ambiental para el desarrollo; Departamento de Pando y la provincia de Vaca Diez.* Riberalta: SNV (cuaderno de trabajo 3).

Betancur, Ana Cecilia. 2000. "La conversión de la barracas al régimen de concesiones; nueva expropiación a comunidades campesinas e indígenas en el norte amazónico." *Artículo Primero* 4, no. 8.

Bojanic Helbingen, Alan Jorge. 2001. *Balance is Beautiful: Assessing the Sustainable Development in the Rain Forests of the Bolivian Amazon.* Utrecht: Faculteit Ruimtelijke Wetenschappen, PROMAB Scientific Series 4.

Brown, Katrina, and Sergio Rosendo. 2000. "Environmentalists, Rubber Tappers and Empowerment: The Politics and Economics of Extractive Reserves." *Development and Change* 31, no. 1: 201–227.

Calla, Ricardo. 2000. "Indigenous Peoples, the Law of Popular Participation and Changes in Government: Bolivia 1994 1998." In *The Challenge of Diversity: Indigenous Peoples and Re-*

form of the State in Latin America, ed. W. Assies, G. van der Haar, and A. J. Hoekema. Amsterdam: Thela.

Carter, Michael R. 2000. "Old Questions and New Realities: Land in Post-Liberal Economies." In *Current Land Policy in Latin America: Regulating Land Tenure under Neoliberalism,* ed. A. Zoomers and G. van der Haar. Amsterdam and Frankfurt: KIT, Iberoamericana/Vervuert Verlag.

Carter, Michael R., and Ramón Salgado. 2001. "Land Market Liberalization and the Agrarian Question in Latin America." In *Access to Land, Rural Poverty and Public Action,* ed. A. De Janvry, G. Gordillo, J. P. Plateau, and E. Sadoulet. Oxford, U.K.: Oxford University Press.

Chevalier, Jacques M. 1983. "There is Nothing Simple about Simple Commodity Production." *Journal of Peasant Studies* 10, no. 4: 153–186.

CNS. 1991. *Relatório do seminário: alternativas econômicas para as reservas extrativistas.* Rio Branco: Conselho Nacional de Seringeiros.

Coesmans, Karen, and María del Carmen Medina I. 1997. *Entre contradicciones y suerte; una mirada en la realidad cotidiana de las mujeres campesinas y quebradoras de Riberalta y sus alrededores.* Riberalta: Unidad de la Mujer-Radio San Miguel.

Contreras-Hermosilla, Arnoldo and María Teresa Vargas Ríos. 2001. "Dimensiones sociales, ambientales y económicas de las reformas en la política forestal de Bolivia." Center for International Forestry Research, CIFOR working paper.

Coomes, Oliver T., and Bradford L. Barham. 1994. "The Amazon Rubber Boom: Labor Control, Resistance, and Failed Plantation Development Revisited." *Hispanic American Historical Review* 74, no. 2: 231–257.

Costa Sobrinho, Pedro Vicente. 1992. *Capital e trabalho na Amazônia Ocidental.* São Paulo and Rio Branco: Cortez, UFAC.

Dean, Warren. 1989. *A luta pela borracha no Brasil; um estudo de histórioa ecológica.* São Paulo: Nobel.

Deininger, Klaus, and Hans Binswanger. 2001. "The Evolution of the World Bank's Land Policy." In *Access to Land, Rural Poverty and Public Action,* ed. A. de Janvry, G. Gordillo, J. P. Plateau, and E. Sadoulet. Oxford, U.K.: Oxford University Press.

DHV. 1993a. *Desarrollo de la Amazonia boliviana. De la actividad extractiva hacia un desarrollo integral sostenible.* La Paz: DHV.

———. 1993b. *Tenencia de la tierra en la región Castañera de la Amazonia boliviana,* La Paz: DHV

Fifer, Valerie. 1970. "The Empire Builders; a History of the Bolivian Rubber Boom and the Rise of the House of Suárez." *Journal of Latin American Studies* 2, no. 2: 113–146.

Geffray, Christian. 1995. *Chroniques de la servitude en Amazonie brésilienne.* Paris: Karthala.

Genovese, Eugene. D. 1976. *Roll, Jordan, Roll: the World the Slaves Made.* New York: Vintage Books.

Henkemans, Ariënne Bernadette. 2000. "Social Fencing: Forest Dwellers and Control of Natural Resources in the Northern Bolivian Amazon." In *Current Land Policy in Latin America: Regulating Land Tenure under Neoliberalism,* ed. A. Zoomers and G. van der Haar. Amsterdam and Frankfurt: KIT, Iberoamericana/Vervuert Verlag.

———. 2001. *Tranquilidad and Hardship in the Forest: Livelihoods and Perceptions of Camba Forest Dwellers in the Northern Bolivian Amazon.* Riberalta: PROMAB.

Hernáiz, Irene, and Diego Pacheco. 2000. *La Ley INRA en el espejo de la historia; Dos siglos de reformas agrarias en Bolivia.* La Paz: Fundación Tierra.

Holt, J. 1992. "The Brazil Nut Market: An Analysis Prepared by Amazonia Trading Company Ltd for Sr. Victor Flores Veia, Executive Director of INPEX, La Paz, Bolivia."

Jones, James C. 1995. "Environmental Destruction, Ethnic Discrimination, and International Aid in Bolivia." In *The Social Causes of Environmental Destruction in Latin America,* ed. M. Painter and W. H. Durham. Ann Arbor: University of Michigan Press.

Kaimowitz, David, and Alain Bojanic Helbingen. 1998. "Riberalta: extractivistas bajo una elite tradicional." In *Municipios y gestión forestal en el trópico boliviano*, ed. P. Pacheco and D. Kaimowitz. La Paz: CIFOR.

LaFleur, James R. 1992. *Marketing of Brazil Nuts*. Rome: FAO.

Lema Garret, A. M., comp. 1998. *Pueblos indígenas de la Amazonía boliviana*. La Paz: AIP FIDA-CAF.

Lescure, Jean-Paul, ed. 1993. "Les activités extractivistes en Amazonie Centrale: une première synthèse d'un projet multidisciplinaire." Working paper, Paris, ORSTOM/INPA.

Lescure, Jean-Paul, Florence Pinton, and Laure Emperaire. 1994. "People and Forest Products in Central Amazonia: The Multidisciplinary Approach of Extractivism." In *Extractivism in the Brazilian Amazon: Perspectives on Regional Development*, ed. M. Clüsener Godt and I. Sachs. Paris: UNESCO (MAB Digest No. 18).

MACPIO. 2001. *Pueblos indígenas y originarios de Bolivia, diagnóstico nacional*. La Paz: Ministerio de Asuntos Campesinos, Pueblos Indígenas y Originarios.

Martinello, Pedro. 1988. *A "batalha da borracha" na Segunda Guerra Mundial e suas conseqüéncias para o vale amazónico*. Rio Branco: UFAC.

Marx, Karl. 1965. *Pre-Capitalist Economic Formations*, with an introduction by E. J. Hobsbawm, New York: International Publishers.

———. 1974. "Formen, die der kapitalistichen Produktion vorhergehen." In *Staatstheorie; Materialen zur Rekonstuktion der Marxistische Staatstheorie*, K. Marx and F. Engels, ed. von E. Henning, J. Hirsch, H. Reichelt, and G. Schäfer. Frankfurt, Berlin, Vienna: Ullstein.

Mendes, Chico. 1992. "Chico Mendes: The Defence of Life." *Journal of Peasant Studies* 20, no. 1: 160–176.

Nijenhuis, Gery. 2000. "Shifting Borders: The Impact of Bolivia's Decentralization Process on the Local Level." In *Fronteras: Towards a Borderless Latin America*, ed. CEDLA. Amsterdam: CEDLA.

Ormachea Enrique. 1987. *Beni y pando, latifundio y minifundio en el norte boliviana*. La Paz: CEDLA.

Ormachea. Enrique, and Javier Fernández. 1989. *Amazonía boliviana y campesinado*. La Paz: Cooperativa Agrícola Integral "Campesino."

Pacheco, Pablo. 1990. *La situación socio-economico de los trabajadores asalariados de la goma y la castaña*. Riberalta, Guayaramerin: CEDLA.

———. 1992. *Integración económica y fragmentación social: el itinerario de las barracas en la amazonia boliviana*. La Paz: CEDLA.

Pacheco, B. Pablo, and Hernán Ávila. 2000. "Amazonía boliviana." In *Las tierras bajas de Bolivia a fines del siglo XX*, ed. M. Urioste and D. Pacheco. La Paz: PIEB.

Pavez Lizarraga, Iciar, and Alan Bojanic Helbingen. 1998. *El proceso de formulación de la Ley Forestal de Bolivia de 1996*. La Paz: CIFOR, CEDLA, TIERRA, PROMAB.

Paz, Ramiro V. 1999. *Dominio amazónico*. La Paz: Plural.

Pinto, Nelson P. Alves. 1984. *Política da borracha no Brasil: a falência da borracha vegetal*. São Paulo: Hucitec.

Roca, José Luis. 2001. *Economía y sociedad en el oriente boliviano (siglos XVI–XX)*. Santa Cruz: COTAS.

Romanoff, Steven. 1992. "Food and Debt among Rubber Tappers in the Bolivian Amazon." *Human Organization* 51, no. 2: 122–135.

Salvatierra, Hugo. 1996. "Ley INRA; Entre la realidad del latifundio y la necesidad del cambio social en el mundo agrario boliviano." *Artículo Primero* 1, no. 2.

Sanabria Fernández, Hernando. 1988. *En busca de El Dorado*. La Paz: Librería Editorial "Juventud."

Solón, Pablo. 1995. *La tierra prometida; un aporte al debate sobre las modificaciones a la legislación agraria.* La Paz: CEDOIN.

Souza, Marcio. 1980. *Mad Maria.* Rio de Janeiro: Civilização Brasileira.

Stoian, Dietmar. 2000a. "Variations and Dynamics of Extractive Economies: The Rural Urban Nexus of Non-Timber Forest Use in the Bolivian Amazon." PhD thesis. Freiburg: University of Freiburg, Germany.

———. 2000b. "Shifts in Forest Product Extraction: The Post Rubber Era in the Bolivian Amazon." *International Tree Crop Journal* 10, no. 4: 277–279.

Stoian, Dietmar, and Ariënne Bernadette Henkemans. 2000. "Between Extractivism and Peasant Agriculture: Differentiation of Rural Settlements in the Bolivian Amazon." *International Tree Crop Journal* 10, no. 4: 299–319.

Tamburini, Leonardo. 2000. "Otorgamiento de concesiones forestales en territorios indígenas en Bolivia." *Artículo Primero* 4, no. 8.

Urioste, Miguel, and D. Pacheco, eds. 2000. "Land Market in a New Context: the INRA Law in Bolivia?" In *Current Land Policy in Latin America: Regulating Land Tenure under Neoliberalism,* ed. A. Zoomers and G. van der Haar. Amsterdam and Frankfurt: KIT, Vervuert Verlag.

———. 2001. *Las tierras bajas de Bolivia a fines del siglo XX.* La Paz: PIEB.

van Beijnum, Paul. 1996. *Problemática urbana riberalta.* Riberalta: SNV (cuadernos de trabajo 4).

Verheule, Emile. 1998. "Work and Housing in the Periphery of Riberalta." MA thesis, Bolivia. Utrecht: University of Utrecht, Faculty of Spatial Sciences.

Weber, Jutta. 1994. *Población indígena de las tierras bajas de Bolivia.* Santa Cruz: APCOB.

Weinstein, Barbara. 1993. *A borracha na Amazônia: expansão e decadencia (1850–1920).* São Paulo: Hucitec.

Woortman, Ellen F. 1996. "Família, mulher e meio ambiente no seringal." Working paper, ANPOCS.

Zoomers, Annelies. 2000. "Searching for a New Land Policy: Options and Dilemmas." In *Current Land Policy in Latin America: Regulating Land Tenure under Neoliberalism,* ed. A. Zoomers and G. van der Haar. Amsterdam and Frankfurt: KIT, Iberoamericana/Vervuert Verlag.

Part III

Indigenous (Land) Rights

Introduction

André J. Hoekema

Assies's involvement with the social movements of marginalized citizens and their fight against oppressive state policies brought him to the scene of numerous indigenous movements around the world. The next two articles relate the history of these now burgeoning indigenous movements and their plight to obtain recognition as distinct but equally respected communities within a multinational state.

In the first article, "Self-Determination and the 'New Partnership'" (1994), Assies sketches an image of the indigenous awakening all over the world that finally led to the official declaration of the United Nations' Year of Indigenous Peoples (1993). Well-established notions of "the unity of a state" and of the strictly individual nature of citizenship and citizens' rights had to be contested to make way for "new partnership" arrangements that tended to profoundly change state and power constellations. Discussion turned around the notions of internal self-determination and self-government by indigenous peoples. Readers of this article get a forceful impression of the sheer endless debates about these notions and their implications for the dominant political, socioeconomic, and legal setup of states. Some debates have been laid to rest, but many still smolder today. For instance the struggle to get state governments to accept the notion of the collective rights of indigenous peoples as such, as a community, has been won, at least legally. This notion now finds solid support in international law, primarily in the Americas (ILO 169, UN Declaration of the Rights of Indigenous Peoples in 2007, the bold jurisprudence of the Inter-American human rights system). Forms of internal self-government are now accepted in many countries as a means to grant indigenous peoples their collective right to practice self-determination. On the other hand, old debates drag on, for instance about the scope, scale and dimensions of self-government. The political and legal schemes through which this self-government is granted are hedged in with crippling conditions and assailed by constant discussion and infighting as to the scope and domain of its official competences. Think only of indigenous rights to subsoil resources.

Assies not only gives us a complete and solid overview of these still relevant debates and concepts, he also helps us appreciate the links between the way indigenous peoples reorganize themselves and their specific relations to the outside world and not to perceive these communities as closed. He stresses "the dynamic process through which identities are shaped, including the very identification as 'indigenous people.'" Identities and culture are shaped and reshaped in and through the multiple contacts and clashes between these communities and the dominant society. He follows Barth as well as Nagel and Snipp and their concern about ethnic reorganization and therefore also deals with internal stratification and strife, for instance between traditionalists and modernists.

In the second article about Indian justice in the Andes, we move on to ten years later, when the first battle to obtain an official, legal grant of self-government was won, and the indigenous movements had to engage in new struggles. Assies has always been acutely aware of the fact that to win a legal battle and get the wording of a state constitution right is just one small step on a long road. Many new struggles arose over with the way forms of self-government received a state legal expression. Concerning proper Indian justice, for instance, many constitutions establish that indigenous authorities "may exercise jurisdictional functions within their territorial area, in conformity with their own norms and procedures, but always in so far as they are not contrary to the Constitution and the laws of the Republic," as art. 246 of the Colombian Constitution of 1991 states it. This clause can be used to almost completely eliminate this recognition of local, indigenous justice because one of the conditions would then be respect for all human rights that are internationally recognized and ratified by the national state. But this condition, "natural" as it sounds to many Western ears, is thoroughly hostile to local, indigenous justice. An example: any act of justice where the accused is not defended by a professional lawyer of the Western kind would be liable to be declared invalid, in spite of the well-known fact that in such a local, nonstate justice system, the defense of the accused is organized in another way proper to the customs and practices of this specific people. State authorities jump at this difference between the national and the local justice system to frustrate the officially granted right to self-government (in this case: in matters of administering its own justice). The new struggle, then, is about the right type of "coordination laws," the kind that facilitates a serious establishment of official legal pluralism. In this second article Assies covers this follow-up struggle, which is still haunting almost all multiethnic societies. Politically speaking, this topic is far too sensitive to be solved in official law and political regulation, at least when identity-based (often: indigenous) institutions are at stake. As far as I am aware, there is no example available of a well-organized and legally coordinated relation between state and nonstate justice drafted and passed by the legislature of a state, let alone of the kind that would facilitate local justice to develop along its own lines. However, drafts of coordination rules do exist in Colombia, Ecuador, and Bolivia.[1]

Why such coordination laws are so sensitive politically becomes obvious when reading about Colombia, as discussed in this article. The Constitutional Court of Colombia filled the lacunae left by the politicians and very boldly interpreted away the crippling formula quoted above. The judge's saying became famous: in a society pretending to be pluralist, no world view can simply be imposed. Let me add in a very Western-centered fashion: "not even the Western world view." Therefore, regarding limits to indigenous jurisdiction, the court stated that not all constitutional and other legal norms have to be respected "because that would reduce the recognition of cultural diversity to mere rhetoric." On this basis, the court developed a long series of specific coordination rules. This example shows that it is possible to come up with a coordination law that, at least on paper, is not hostile to local indigenous justice but promotes the legal and socioeconomic empowerment of the people involved. All this points to the urgent need to start a new line of research: what is the impact of specific sets of coordination rules and their method of implementation on the opportunities the local communities have to rule themselves and determine their own future? Assies has prepared the scene for this new wave of research into the fate of indigenous peoples in the modern world.

Notes

1. At the time of writing this introduction, an intensive parliamentary discussion was taking place in Ecuador about a proposal for a law to coordinate the indigenous administration of justice and the national one (*Proyecto de ley organica de coordinación y cooperación entre los sistemas de justicia indígena y la jurisdicción ordinaria*).

5 # Self-Determination and the "New Partnership"

5   Self-Determination and the "New Partnership"

The Politics of Indigenous Peoples and States

Under the heading "A New Partnership," the United Nations have proclaimed 1993 the "International Year of the World's Indigenous People." This reflects the increasing success of indigenous peoples in manifesting themselves politically. A central demand of the international indigenous peoples' movement is the right to self-determination. The states into which indigenous peoples have been forcefully incorporated perceive this demand as a threat to their sovereignty and territorial integrity. Moreover, the demand sits uneasily with the universalistic conception of citizenship. Indigenous peoples' movements argue that they do not seek full independence, but arrangements for self-government that would allow them to preserve their ethnic identity. Such arrangements would substantiate the "new partnership." While the political struggle over the content and extent of self-determination goes on, some arrangements allowing greater autonomy for indigenous peoples have emerged, the scope of historically existing arrangements is being expanded, and new arrangements are being negotiated in various countries.

After a brief outline of the emergence of an international indigenous peoples' movement, this paper discusses the problem of conceptualizing indigenous peoples. It is argued that rather than viewing them as "defenders of tradition," more attention should be given to indigenous peoples and their movements as a dynamic contemporary phenomenon. Subsequently, the paper outlines the discussion on self-determination as a concept of international law, and finally some of the critical issues in the implementation of arrangements for self-government are reviewed. A useful distinction can be made between arrangements based on indirect and direct consociation. In the first case administrative reorganization gives indigenous people a greater say in local affairs, while in the second case an indigenous people is recognized as such, and collective rights are involved.

The Emergence of an International Indigenous Peoples' Movement

The attention now being paid to indigenous peoples is the outcome of various developments since World War II. Geopolitics and the search for new resources account for much of the escalation of the number of incursions into indigenous peoples' lands (Burger 1987: 44; ICIHI 1987: 43–90). The post-war process of decolonization in Africa, Asia, and the Pacific left many unresolved questions. Most of the newly independent countries are not linguistically, culturally, or ethnically homogeneous. The new states have sought to assert their authority within the frontiers established by the former colonial powers, often resulting in increased oppression of indigenous peoples. The East-West confrontation also contributed to a preoccupation with frontier security, which turned economically uninteresting areas into areas of military concern. Early warning systems and aircraft testing grounds were installed in northern Canada by NATO, Siberia was militarized, and the Pacific basin was turned into a nuclear testing ground.

Geopolitics overlap and are intertwined with economic considerations. Exploration of forest resources, hydroelectric potential, or subsoil resources contributed to the incorporation of frontier areas, as did colonization and transmigration policies. In South America, for example, settlement of the Amazon basin was promoted as a substitute for land reform.

In the "rich" countries the extension of public services and the welfare state system played a role in stimulating indigenous peoples' mobilization, as in the cases of the Greenland and Canadian Inuit and the Saami in the Nordic countries. Well-intended policies also brought disruption. In the United States the emergence of an Indian movement was related to intensified threats of dispossession and policies aimed at "termination" of Indian status in the 1950s and to the shift in social policies of the Johnson administration that provided new opportunities for resistance.

In the face of the threats to their livelihood and way of life, indigenous peoples have developed new forms of resistance, and since the 1970s an international movement of indigenous peoples has steadily developed. In the early 1970s, indigenous peoples of the Americas, the Arctic, and the South Pacific formed networks, and since then several hundreds of indigenous peoples' organizations have been founded and new regional networks created. In 1977, the International Indian Treaty Council, created on the initiative of the American Indian Movement (AIM) with roots in the United States, was the first indigenous peoples' organization that was granted consultative status in the Economic and Social Council of the United Nations (ECOSOC). By 1989 the number had grown to eleven.

International action, often relying on a "politics of embarrassment" (Dyck 1985: 15), became an effective means to pressurize national governments. Indigenous peoples point to the fact that they were the prior occupants of the land, to the oppression, discrimination and marginalization they suffer, and to their low score on a variety of social indicators. The UN system has become an important platform for the discussion of indigenous peoples' concerns and promotion of their interests. In 1970, the Sub-Commission on Prevention of Discrimination and Protection of Minorities recommended a study on the problem of discrimination against indigenous populations. In 1977 and 1981 nongovernmental organizations (NGOs) organized conferences on indigenous issues in Geneva, and in 1980 the Fourth Russell Tribunal in Rotterdam focused on the rights of the Indians of the Americas. These meetings, and the study by Special Rapporteur José R. Martínez Cobo, which might never have been completed without outside pressure (Morris 1993: 29), contributed to the establishment of the United Nations Working Group on Indigenous Populations in 1982. The Working Group, though operating on one of the lowest levels of the UN system,[1] has become an important forum for the international indigenous peoples' movement (Burger 1987: 44–62, 262–279; Dyck 1985; ICIHI 1987: 31–40, 109–131; Ortiz 1984: 27–123; Morris 1993; Scherrer 1991; Sills 1993).

Indigenous Peoples

What constitutes an indigenous people is a complex question, and there is no generally accepted definition (Burger 1987: 6; Dyck 1985: 21–24; ICIHI 1987: 5). An often quoted working definition has been provided by José R. Martínez Cobo (1987: 29), special rapporteur for the UN Commission on Human Rights:

> Indigenous communities, peoples and nations are those which, having a historical continuity with pre-invasion and pre-colonial societies that developed on their territories, consider themselves distinct from other sectors of the societies now prevailing in those territories, or parts of them. They form at present non-dominant sectors of society and are determined to preserve, develop and transmit to future generations their ancestral territories, and their ethnic identity, as the basis of their continued existence as peoples in accordance with their own cultural patterns, social institutions and legal systems.

As an indicative description, which contains the criteria of preexistence, non-dominance, cultural difference, and self-identification as indigenous (ICIHI 1987: 6; ACM 1993: 12–15), this may serve.

The definition is meant to cover a broad range of situations. In its practical usage, groups within the European continent itself, such as Basques or Catalans, are excluded, as well as for example the Kurds. They are considered national minorities (ICIHI 1987: 8). On the other hand, the Saami in the Scandinavian countries and the Inuit of the circumpolar states and their

Siberian kin are considered indigenous. Furthermore, the definition is meant to include the Aborigines in Australia, the Maoris in New Zealand, and the indigenous peoples of North, Central, and South America. The tribal and nomadic people of Asia also are considered indigenous peoples, and in Africa the term is applied to nomadic pastoralists as well as the San (Bushmen) and the Pygmies. The number of indigenous people is currently estimated at some 300 million.

The definition regards colonization and invasion as constitutive features of indigenous peoples. It should be noted that it does not contain criteria referring to economic organization (e.g., nomadic or seminomadic), political organization (tribal organization, consensus-based decision-making, or degree of centralization of political institutions), or cultural features attributed to indigenous peoples.[2]

Burger (1987: 9) suggests a group of overlapping criteria, of which an indigenous people may contain all or just some. Indigenous peoples:

1) are the descendants of the original inhabitants of a territory which has been overcome by conquest;
2) are nomadic and seminomadic peoples, such as shifting cultivators, herders, and hunters and gatherers, and practice a labor-intensive form of agriculture that produces little surplus and has low energy needs;
3) do not have centralized political institutions and organize at the level of the community and make decisions on a consensus basis;
4) have all the characteristics of a national minority: they share a common language, religion, culture and other identifying characteristics and a relationship to a particular territory, but are subjugated by a dominant culture and society;
5) have a different world view, consisting of a custodial and non-materialist attitude to land and natural resources, and want to pursue a separate development to that of proffered by the dominant society; and
6) consist of individuals who subjectively consider themselves to be indigenous, and are accepted by the group as such.

Other definitions can be found in the ILO Convention Concerning Indigenous and Tribal Peoples in Independent Countries (Convention 169 of 1989) and in the World Bank Operational Directive on indigenous peoples (September 1991). For comment on ILO Convention 169 and the World Bank Directive, in relation to the Draft Declaration on Indigenous Rights, see *Fourth World Bulletin* 2, no. 2. This reflects a certain shift in thinking among indigenous peoples themselves as well as among students of ethnic relations. Thus, Dyck (1985: 24) notes how the World Council of Indigenous Peoples dropped the criterion of continuation of archaic cultures and came to emphasize the status of indigenous peoples as previous occupants of lands taken by colonizing nation-states and as peoples who lack self-determination.

Students of ethnic relations increasingly acknowledge that the interpretation of culture from the standpoint of tradition or continuity over time has its limitations. In a radical essay Barth (1969: 11) argued that common culture should be regarded as an implication or result, rather than as a primary and definitional characteristic of ethnic group organization. In this way attention is shifted away from a supposedly existing, immutable, tore cultural orientation of an ethnic group, to the processes of boundary construction and boundary maintenance that take place between groups. Rather than relating ethnic identity to a "traditional way of life," this way of looking at things makes it possible to see how identities are maintained and reconstructed through processes of change.[3] Pursuing this line of argument, Nagel and Snipp (1993) have advanced the concept of ethnic reorganization. Usually, they argue, four basic processes have been identified in the relations between minority and majority populations: annihilation, assimilation, amalgamation, and accommodation. None of these concepts, however, adequately captures the process experienced by the North American Indians. Hence they propose the concept of ethnic reorganization to account for both the persistence and the transformation of ethnicity. They distinguish various forms of ethnic reorganization. Social reorganization includes the reorganization of community or tribal boundaries, reorganization of marriage rules, reorganization of group or tribal membership rules as well as the reorganization of the larger American Indian ethnic identity, that is, the emergence of supertribal identification. Economic reorganization includes the modification of the community economic base and the reorganization of economic activity itself. Political reorganization involves the restructuring of political organization as well as tribal and supratribal political reorganization, while in the cultural field, processes of revision, blending or revitalization may occur.

One important point is that this approach draws attention to the dynamic process through which identities are shaped, including the very identification as "indigenous people." The definitional problems referred to are related to such issues. Definitions are operational rather than analytical and in fact are at stake in a sociopolitical and discursive process. Thus, the indigenous peoples of North America, the Arctic, and Australia played a vanguard role in the development of the international indigenous peoples' movement, but the inclusion of Indian delegates from South America was fraught with tension. Clearly failing into the category of "indigenous peoples," their experiences and concerns were also different from those of indigenous peoples within liberal democracies. Among the South American indigenous peoples, differences exist between those from the highlands and those from the Amazon basin. The inclusion of peoples from Asia or the Middle East or African liberation movements into the international movement organization is not a matter of course (cf. Dyck 1985). Thus, the labeling as "indigenous people" is often as much a matter of political pressure as of conforming to a legally defined category. Both ascription and identification play a role in the constitution of "indigenous peoples" as an overarching identity covering a great variety.

The argument therefore also applies to the present discourse of indigenousness, and the features and traditions this attributes to indigenous peoples. Whatever the roots in tradition, qualities such as a special nonmaterialist and spiritual relation to the land, consensual decision-making, communitarianism are emphasized and resignified at present. Rather than something like inherent qualities, such features and the discourse by which they are underscored should be viewed as part of the dynamics through which contemporary ethnic or indigenous identity and consciousness are constructed. The stress on certain features constitutes a contemporary and evolving critique of the societies indigenous peoples are facing.

Such an approach brings to light the social processes of reorganization and transformation, which are important to bear in mind in any discussion of indigenous peoples' movements to avoid unwarranted romanticism. With regard to political confrontation Barth (1969: 35) observed that the opposed parties tend to become structurally similar and differentiated only by a few clear criteria. The emergence of the Shuar Federation in Ecuador, which implied the adoption of new forms of political organization and the development of a counterhegemonic discourse challenging the Ecuadorian state, is an illustrative example (Hendricks 1991). Often such processes of indigenous mobilization strongly rely on specific sectors of indigenous society, the youth in particular, and are thus related to processes of stratification within the indigenous society. While invoking the traditional authority of elders, the process of mobilization may pose a challenge to this authority that is not easily resolved (Findji 1992: 117, 130; Jackson 1991). Or it may give rise to new divisions between "progressives" and "traditionalists" within an emerging Indian movement, as for example in the United States (Nagel and Snipp 1993: 218; Forbes 1985: 32). Indigenous peoples cannot be regarded as homogeneous groups without internal divisions. Despite the emphasis on the consensual nature of internal decision-making processes, a system of majority decision making and representation is often adopted, not just as a result of outside pressure by a dominating state that imposes representativity requirements as is often argued, but also in response to internal differentiation among the indigenous people themselves and in relation to the formation of supralocal organizations (Duhaime 1992).

Indigenous peoples differ in their social, economic, political, and cultural organization from the dominant society and, by definition, belong to the most dominated, discriminated, and marginalized groups. The claim to be entitled to special inherent rights as prior occupants of the lands constitutes the main difference from other ethnic groups. In view of their diversity and the dynamics in which they are involved, there is no facile definition, and ascription of all kinds of features should be avoided.

Indigenous Peoples and International Law: From Minority Protection to Self-Determination

For the emerging indigenous peoples' movements the UN has become an important forum, and international law provides a major framework for developing their claims. Certainly, the influence of the North American Indian intelligentsia also played a role in framing the discussion in these terms. Their views and legal reasoning are rooted in the history of treaty making as the basis for interaction between Indian nations and the state (Sills 1993: 17).

When, in 1982, the UN Working Group on Indigenous Populations was set up, one of its tasks was to develop international standards regarding the rights and protection of indigenous peoples under international law. Much of the debate revolves around the stipulations on self-determination and minority protection in the UN Charter and subsequent Covenants and the ILO Conventions on indigenous populations. Through a critique of the assumption that their fate inevitably would be one of assimilation into the national societies, spokespersons of the indigenous peoples have contributed to a shift away from the focus on minority protection toward a claim to self-determination for indigenous peoples. The controversial character of this claim is reflected in the ongoing debate over the question of whether to speak of indigenous populations, indigenous people, or indigenous peoples and the implications this would have for the content and scope of the self-determination they claim.

The UN Declarations and Covenants

Self-determination was enshrined as a "principle" in the 1945 UN Charter, which stated as one of the purposes of the UN

> To develop friendly relations among nations based on respect for the principle of equal rights and self-determination of peoples, and to take other appropriate measures to strengthen universal peace.

The interpretation of the notion of self-determination was strongly related to the post-war process of decolonization. In 1960, the *Declaration on the Granting of Independence to Colonial Countries and Peoples* referred to a right, rather than a principle, stating that

> All peoples have the right to self-determination; by virtue of that right they freely determine their political status and freely pursue their economic, social and cultural development.

At the time it was specified that this right only would apply in cases of a territory geographically separate and ethnically or culturally distinct from the country administering it, that is the "classic" colonial countries separated by "blue water" or "salt water" from their subjugator. In these cases the exercise of the right to self-determination could produce a range of acceptable outcomes, from *sovereign independence* through *free association* with an independent state to *incorporation* within it. Furthermore, following the *uti possidetis* principle that had been developed in the context of Latin American independence, disruption of the territorial integrity of states was ruled out in the UN resolutions and declarations on decolonization (Franck 1992; Hannum 1993: 20–26; Lerner 1991: 100; Lam 1992). The frontiers that had been established by the colonial powers were not to be altered in the process of decolonization. As a consequence a great number of the newly independent countries were not linguistically, culturally, or ethnically homogeneous.

In 1966, however, the right to self-determination made its appearance in the *Covenant on Civil and Political Rights* and the *Covenant on Economic, Social and Cultural Rights* as a general peoples' right, no longer confined to the "classic" decolonization context. It remained unclear, however, what this right would entail in the future, particularly since the meaning of the term "peoples" who are to hold this right was never specified (Lam 1992: 615–616).

While granting a general right of self-determination to "peoples" the Covenant on Civil and Political Rights, in its Article 27, also referred to "minorities" (Hannum 1993: 33–35) providing that:

> In those states in which ethnic, religious or linguistic minorities exist, persons belonging to such minorities shall not be denied the right, in common with other members of their group, to enjoy their own culture, to profess and practice their own religion, and to use their own language.

This article on the protection of minorities is generally regarded as an important instrument for the defense of indigenous peoples, though they were not specifically referred to in the text of the Covenant (Lerner 1991: 100).

The scope of the article, as conceived, is somewhat limited (Rehof 1992: 89; ICIHI 1987: 116). Since it speaks of "persons belonging to minorities" the rights specified tend to be interpreted in individualist terms (ACM 1993: 19). The text, however, leaves some room for a more flexible interpretation. It may be argued that it contains elements of group protection and hence provides some scope for an interpretation in terms of collective rights and that it may allow for positive discrimination of a minority (Brantenberg, n.d.: 85; Lerner 1991: 15). Moreover, in jurisprudence the term "culture" has come to cover traditional economic activities (Rehof 1992: 89; Nowak 1992). In the Norwegian debate on the relevance of this article for the protection of Saami rights, it was concluded that "culture" implies more than creative or artistic activities and institutions and must be understood as including the material basis for culture, i.e., livelihoods and economic conditions (Brantenberg, n.d.: 85).

The ILO Conventions

Among the international conventions applicable to indigenous peoples those produced by the ILO stand out as being specifically dedicated to the issue of the indigenous peoples (Burger 1987: 265; ICIHI 1987: 118). In 1957, the ILO adopted a *Convention concerning the Protection and Integration of Indigenous and other Tribal and Semi-Tribal Populations in Independent Countries* (ILO Convention 107). It aimed to assure

> the protection of the populations concerned, their progressive integration into their respective national communities, and the improvement of their living and working conditions (Hannum 1993: 8–19; ICIHI 1987: 143).[4]

While rather paternalist and oriented toward "integration" and "development," this also was the only international instrument that recognized the right to collective ownership of land which these populations traditionally occupy.

The need for an update and the gradually gathering critique by indigenous peoples and their support groups resulted in a revision of the convention in the course of the 1980s. In 1989 the ILO adopted the *Convention concerning Indigenous and Tribal Peoples in Independent Countries* (ILO Convention 169) (Hannum 1993: 45–59), which purports to eliminate "the assimilationist orientation of the earlier standards." For the first time reference was made to "peoples" rather than to "populations." This was the outcome of heated debate between states that preferred to continue to use the term "populations" and indigenous delegates who argued that the term "population" has no juridical significance in international law (cf. Morris 1993: 26). In the final version of the convention, the term "peoples" was used, but this innovation is immediately followed by a clause stipulating that

> The use of the term "peoples" in this convention shall not be construed as having any implications as regards the rights which many attach to the term in international law.

The convention thus restricts the scope of the right to self-determination usually implied by the term peoples (cf. ACM 1993: 19; Lerner 1991: 102; Morris 1993: 24–28; Rehof 1992: 91).

The convention also remains controversial on a number of other points. It is unclear what scope it leaves for "self-determination." In the text there is no mention of the concept itself, but one finds references to "the right to decide their own priorities," hedged in with a series of conditions (art. 6 and 7). The subordination of indigenous legal procedures to national legislation rather than international standards (art. 8 and 9) is another bone of contention. And the stipulations on the forcible relocation of indigenous people (art. 16) are also ambiguous and contested (Ceinos 1990: 18; Lerner 1991: 107–110; Ministerie van Buitenlandse Zaken 1993: 10).[5]

Toward a Declaration on the Rights of Indigenous Peoples

Since 1985, the UN Working Group on Indigenous Populations has been working on a *Declaration on the Rights of Indigenous Peoples*, intended to be a standard-setting instrument for international law purposes to be adopted by the UN General Assembly. A preliminary version of this declaration (Hannum 1993: 102–112), submitted in June 1992[6] talked about

> the right of self-determination, in accordance with international law by virtue of which they may freely determine their political status and institutions and freely pursue their economic, social and cultural development. An integral part of this is the right to autonomy and self-government.

The introduction to this "working paper," however, makes clear that concepts like "peoples," "self-determination," and "lands and territories" still require further specification. The unequivocal statements about "self-determination, in accordance to international law" meet with the objections of existing states. These insist on their "territorial integrity," seek to limit the rights to "lands and territories" to grants rather than inherent rights and to substitute "self-determination" with terms like "self-governance" or "self-management" (cf. ACM 1993: 55; Daes 1992).

As a result of such objections, the paragraph on self-determination has been rephrased in the latest draft of the declaration (May 1993) (cf. Morris 1993) which now reads

> Indigenous peoples have the right of self-determination, in accordance with international law, subject to the same criteria and limitations as apply to other peoples in accordance with the Charter of the United Nations. By virtue of this, they have the right, *inter alia,* to negotiate and agree upon their role in the conduct of public affairs, their distinct responsibilities and the means by which they manage their own interests.

An integral part of this is the right to autonomy and self-government. This paragraph should be read in conjunction with the paragraph that states that

> Indigenous peoples have the right to autonomy and self-government in matters relating to their internal and local affairs, including culture, religion, education, information, media, health, housing, employment, social welfare, economic activities, land and resource management, environment and entry by non-members, as well as internal, taxation for financing these autonomous functions.

The implication is that the distinction between "internal" and "external" self-determination has been introduced in the drafting of the declaration. Self-determination "in accordance with international law" would include the right to "external self-determination," granting peoples the right to opt between sovereign independence, free association or incorporation into an existing state. This, as we saw, supports the objection of state governments raising the specter of secession, which they claim self-determination inevitably entails. On the other hand, indigenous peoples have repeatedly stated that they do not aspire to independent statehood but seek some form of free association. But "free association" becomes a sham when the option not to associate is barred (Morris 1993: 32–33).

Internal self-determination means that "a people or group possessing a definite territory may be autonomous in the sense of possessing a separate and distinct administrative structure and judicial system, determined by and intrinsic to that people or group" (Martínez Cobo 1987: 20).[7]

The introduction of the distinction between internal and external self-determination seems to constitute an effort to shift the terms of the debate away from "peoples' rights" to the somewhat less controversial "collective rights" to be exercised within existing states. A clear-cut distinction between "internal" and "external" hardly seems possible, however, if internal self-determination is to be related to a specific territoriality.

This is the stake in the debate over the use of the terms "lands" and "territories." "Lands," indigenous peoples argue, constitute generic parcels of real estate that can be owned by anyone in an individual capacity, but which are subject to the overarching jurisdiction of the state. "Territories," in contrast, consist of lands over which sovereign authority can be exercised, and to which indigenous peoples lay claim through aboriginal rights, and over which they should have the power to exercise political and economic authority. The draft declaration states that indigenous peoples have the collective and individual right to own, control and use their lands and territories, and specifies that this means the total environment of the lands, air, water, sea, sea-ice, flora, and fauna that indigenous peoples have traditionally owned or otherwise occupied and used (Morris 1993: 27, 32).

The introduction of the notion of "internal self-determination" furthermore sits uneasily with the draft declaration's assertion that treaties, agreements and other constructive arrangements between states and indigenous peoples should be observed and enforced according to their original intent. The Indian nations of North America insist that these are treaties between sovereign nations and thus pertain to the realm of international diplomacy.[8]

The claims forwarded by the indigenous peoples' movements challenge some of the basic principles of the modern state. Though not aiming for independence, the free association they envision must include both a mutually satisfactory sharing of jurisdiction and the recognition that the indigenous share of that jurisdiction rests upon an inherent right, and not on a revocable grant. These two demands challenge the principles of state sovereignty and exclusive jurisdiction (Lam 1992: 608).

The claim for collective rights is controversial in its relation to citizenship and to internationally acknowledged individual human rights. These include civil rights, political rights, and social rights, usually thought to follow one another in an evolutionary succession. Whereas these rights are individualistic and universalistic, collective rights are particularistic and specific. Some students of human rights legislation fear that according collective rights may contribute to an erosion of individual rights. Collective rights also call into question the presumed equality of citizenship and rights. This not only has met with the objection of states, but also has been a source of friction between, for example, the North American Indian movement and the civil rights movement. Whereas the former demanded a special status, invoking their prior presence in the land and their sovereign status consecrated in treaties, the latter sought equal rights.[9] Similar issues underlie the South American debate on the relation between indigenous struggles and class or popular struggles, some arguing that indigenous struggles are part of a broader movement, others arguing that they represent something like a "third way" in its own right.

While the political struggle and debate over its content and extent continue, the idea that indigenous peoples are entitled to some form of self-determination has gained some acceptance. Indigenous peoples have governed themselves according to customary law and their own ways of doing politics, until they were subjugated by some state which, more or less gradually, sought to incorporate or assimilate them. Such efforts, as we saw, have met with new forms of resistance, as a result of which a search for a "new partnership" has started. This should take more concrete form in systems of self-government or autonomy arrangements that realize the "new partnership" now proposed (Scherrer 1991). While international declarations suggest the orientation and standards for such arrangements, the actual arrangements cannot but be the product of a variety of local situations and experiences. In the case of South America, for example, contemporary practices of self-government often derive in part from the colonial system imposed by the Iberians, and in North America the tradition of treaty making with the colonial powers and their successors provides a framework for the present arrangements.

Systems of Self-Government: Features and Issues

In 1991 the UN Commission on Human Rights organized a Meeting of Experts to review the experience of countries in the operation of schemes of internal self-government for indigenous peoples, in Nuuk, capital of Greenland. In their conclusions and recommendations they included a comprehensive list of desirable features to be included in self-government schemes

> Subject to the freely expressed desire of the indigenous people concerned, autonomy and self-government include, *inter alia,* jurisdiction over or active and effective participation in decision-making on the matters concerning their land, resources, environment, development, justice, education, information, communications, culture, religion, health, housing, social welfare, trade, traditional economic systems, including hunting, fishing, herding, trapping, gathering, and other economic and management activities, as well as the right to guaranteed financial arrangements and, where applicable, taxation for financing these functions.

At the meeting a wide range of experiences purporting to realize some of these requirements to a certain degree were discussed. These included the reservations in the United States, the Home Rule arrangement in Greenland, the Saami parliament in Norway, the *comarea* in Panama, the experiences with regional autonomy in Nicaragua, China, and the Philippines, the 1988 Brazilian Constitution and the *resguardos* in Colombia. This constitutes a rather mixed bag of experiences, each with its own historical context. What they have in common is that they are institutionalized forms of political autonomy of different degrees, as opposed to factual, historical autonomy.

Ethnicity and Territoriality

In practice there seem to be two basic ways to meet the claims to autonomy of indigenous peoples within national states. A distinction should be made according to the subject of this autonomy between territorial or regional autonomy and the autonomy of a people (Willemsen Diaz 2009[1992]: 25). Another way of putting it is to distinguish between direct and indirect consociation as alternative routes to permit the exercise of aboriginal rights. In the case of direct consociation, state ideology expressly acknowledges the existence of various ethnonational collectivities (for example, in constitutional charters), and thus protection is afforded explicitly to the specified (and named) ethnonational communities. In the case of indirect consociation, the ideology does not explicitly protect ethnonational communities. Rather, the philosophy of "universalism" is espoused, and protection is afforded ethnonational communities as a consequence of other principles, such as ensuring that a specified minority ethnonational collectivity forms a majority within a particular political jurisdiction (Asch and Smith 1992).

Where the relationship between ethnicity and territoriality is concerned, we can distinguish between the following situations:

1. Cases of local or regional autonomy where ethnicity formally does not play a role. Administrative boundaries are drawn in such a way that the indigenous population constitutes a majority within them and thus effectively can realize a degree of self-government within the nationally established administrative framework, e.g., municipal councils, provincial councils, federated states (e.g., the Nunavut territory in Canada, Greenland).
2. Cases where ethnicity and territoriality are formally linked in self-government arrangements where, within certain limits as to scope and content, only the indigenous may partake in the government of a territory (e.g., Colombia, the Kuna in Panama or the Indian reserves in the United States).
3. Cases where ethnicity is a criterion without being linked to territory, that is, place of residence. The Saami parliament in Norway is drawn from the national constituency and operates at a national level, where it is involved in representing Saami interests in sectoral policies that even-

tually may become territorialized in their execution. Indigenousness may also be a requirement for welfare entitlements for specific groups such as migrants to urban areas. Such cases put into question the widespread assumption that self-determination is absolutely and necessarily linked to territory (Groves 1990).

The first, indirect approach has the advantage, as Asch and Smith (1992) argue with reference to the Canadian case, that it does not require reshaping of the constitutional order, which in the majority of the present states is based on universalistic principles. The limitations to this approach are firstly, that an indigenous people must have and continue to have the majority of the population on a certain land base and, secondly, that it requires the indigenous people to reduce its view of governance to be established. The Nunavut agreement, which is the case in point, provides for considerable control through current structures of public government without forming an expressly aboriginal government, i.e., self-government exclusively by and for Inuit. The scope of self-government thus is set by the administrative level at which it is exercised, e.g., municipal, provincial. The absence of a "distinct society" concept as a lynch pin of identity may constitute a vulnerability of the arrangement (Haysom 1992: 195).

In the second case, rights are guaranteed explicitly to an ethnonational community notwithstanding the size of its population. This type of arrangement would allow indigenous peoples to govern themselves, within a certain territory and to a specified extent, according to their own political and legal customs.[10] It seeks to institutionalize forms of political and legal pluralism.

The third type of arrangement allows an indigenous people to influence public administration and the execution of certain sectoral policies that affect them in particular. While the Nunavut territorial government basically is a public one, Inuit representatives can participate in a number of management boards and thus, for example, introduce their own wildlife management practices and safeguard priority for Inuit in according hunting licenses. Similar arrangements are conceivable in policy areas such as health care or education. If such sectorwise or participation is embedded in a more comprehensive arrangement, as is the case for the Saatni parliaments for instance, this may tend to a form of self-determination. If not, one should rather think in terms of client-group participation in public policies.

Operationalizations of Ethnicity

The case of Greenland Home Rule, often cited as an example and perhaps a model for indigenous peoples' self-government, does not involve collective rights. Due to its location and population characteristics, there was no problem of fuzzy demarcations, and as Greenland's Premier Lars Emil Johansen (1992: 34) put it, it has thus "to some extent been possible to avoid the unpleasant and difficult task of defining who is a Greenlander and who is not." The right to participate in elections for the Home Rule Assembly is contingent upon the elector having had his permanent residence in Greenland for at least six months (Foighel 1980: 7).

Of the three above-mentioned "ideal-typical" cases, the second and the third require an operationalization of ethnicity in order to specify who is entitled to rights or benefits and who is not. The actual operationalizations of ethnicity provide some illustration of the issue of inter- and intra-group relations and the relation to the state. For the recent (1993) elections for a Saami parliament in Sweden, Saami were defined as those who consider themselves Saami and (1) can prove that he has or has had Saami as his home *language*, (2) can prove that some of his parents, father's or mother's parents have or have had Saami as a home language, or (3) has a parent who is or has been on the electoral list for the Saami parliament (Oreskov 1993). Similar provisions apply in Norway, where a Saami parliament was created in 1989. Thus, in principle, the constituency for the Saami parliament is not related to a specific territory within the Nordic states, but is constituted at a national level. On the other hand, municipalities where Saami constitute a substantial part of the population may qualify for special funding earmarked for Saami. This has influenced registration as Saami and may explain the difference between the number of Saami who registrated and the number actively participating in the elections for the Norwegian Saami parliament (Brantenberg, n.d.: 103–106). The tendencies of registration and active participation in these elections thus reveal the situational character of ethnic identification.

In the United States the Bureau of Indian Affairs (BIA) requires exhaustive documentation to meet seven criteria for recognition as a "tribe." The "tribe" must prove that: "from historical times to the present," it has been identified as Indian; is a community distinct from surrounding communities or descends from Indians of a specific homeland; and holds political authority or influence over its members. The tribe must submit a copy of a governing document and/or criteria for membership, list all current members (who must trace descent from the historical tribe), document that members do not belong to any other tribe, and show that the tribe has not been terminated by Congress. The tribally set rules of enrollment vary from tribe to tribe, but usually involve some designated degree (blood quantum) of tribal or Indian *ancestry, parentage, and/or residency* requirements. According to circumstances tribes may adopt more exclusionary or more inclusionary rules of enrollment as part of their strategies of ethnic reorganization (Nagel and

Snipp 1993: 211). Besides the "federally recognized Indians," entitled to BIA services, one has "non-recognized Indians" and "urban Indians" (Martínez Cobo 1982: 54–55).

In Canada, *genealogical ancestry* also plays a main role in determining who is to be considered aboriginal or not. Aboriginal peoples here include Indians, Inuit, and Metis (persons of mixed Indian and European ancestry). The Indians are further classified into Status Indians, Non-Status Indians, and Treaty Indians (Martínez Cobo 1982: 51; Minister of Supply and Services 1991).

In Colombia, the National Administrative Statistics Department combines the criteria *of self identification* as belonging to a determined ethnic group with a cultural tradition going back to before the Spanish conquest, *and residence*, that is living in a community, i.e., in the territory occupied by the community or group (Arango Ochoa 1991–1992: 226).

The task of determining who exactly belongs to an indigenous people remains controversial, unpleasant, and difficult. It involves a balancing of the requirements of a state, the right of a people to decide whom it includes or excludes, and the right of individuals to decide whether they will be included or excluded. It goes against the almost universal tendency toward legal regimes of governance based on the territoriality of residence of the subject/ citizen rather than "personality" of the individual. These problems are largely avoided in the first type of self-government arrangement mentioned above. A borderline case exists, however, when a long-term residency requirement is used to ensure that an indigenous people remain secure even if they become a minority within the jurisdiction. This is one of the safeguards proposed by the Dene in Canada (Asch and Smith 1992: 108). The second type of arrangement relies on both territoriality and ethnic identification and involves a sort of dual citizenship, whereas the third relies solely on ethnic identification. A major problem with this third type of arrangement is that it may contribute to the dilution of "tribal" content in exchange for a basically "racial" definition of aboriginality (Groves 1990: 238).

The Scope of Self-Government

Some qualitative measures should be employed to sort out the "genuine" arrangements among the broad specter of situations that formally might be regarded as forms of self-government. Bennagen (1992: 72) suggests that certain overarching values have crystallized in the indigenous peoples' movement for self-freedom. Operationally, these would imply:

a) Control of territory (expressed variously as ancestral domain, ancestral homeland, indigenous territory, etc.) and its natural resources, both surface and subsurface;

b) Legislative, executive, and judicial bodies, to include corresponding indigenous institutions;

c) Proper actual representation of the indigenous cultural communities in the various organs of power, not only in the determination, including territorial autonomy and sovereignty, democracy and justice, equity and cultural autonomous territorial unit but also in the national government;

d) Fiscal autonomy, including the power to raise revenues, a just share of national revenues and a capable fiscal administration; and

e) Respect, protection, and development of indigenous cultures.

The above suggestions indicate the dimensions to be taken into account in an assessment of the qualities and limitations of contemporary systems of self-government. A series of more specific questions can be posed concerning the day-to-day practice of operational self-government arrangements, and some examples may illustrate the variety of arrangements and issues to be dealt with. One should bear in mind, however, that the dimensions of self-government are interrelated. Land rights, access to economic and financial resources, political institutions, and legal systems are linked in various ways.

Territory and Land Rights

A first issue is the effective extent of rights to land and the indigenous institutions involved in managing such rights. How are decision-making powers distributed? The Nunavut Agreement is illustrative of some of the complexities of the problem. As noted, the creation of the Nunavut territory is a case of indirect consociation which does not directly involve collective rights. A public government structure will be set up for a certain land area where the majority of the population is Inuit. This political arrangement is linked, however, to a land claim settlement by which an Inuit nonprofit corporation (Tungavik Federation of Nunavut—TFN) receives ownership title to 136,000 square miles of land, of which 14,000 square miles would include ownership of the subsurface. This represents about 18 percent of the land area of Nunavut. Furthermore, Inuit and government will be equally represented on a series of management boards concerned with project screening, planning, wildlife management, water management in the Nunavut territory and on a surface rights tribunal with jurisdiction throughout the Northwest Territories (Fenge 1992).

In the case of Greenland, the question of ownership of land and resources became an important issue in the political debate. Private ownership of land did not exist, but the Danish claim to state ownership was countered with the claim that land should be collectively owned by the population of Greenland. The Home Rule Act provides that Greenland and Denmark shall have equal rights in the use of nonliving resources and that policy decisions should be made jointly. Thus, both parties have a veto power. Where the division and application of revenues from natural resource development are concerned, it was initially argued that the bulk of such revenues should go to Denmark in compensation for previous capital transfers to Greenland, but nowadays the net revenue is equally divided, although the division of as much of the revenue as exceeds DKK 500 million per year is stipulated by legislation, following negotiations between the Home Rule Government and the Danish Government (Greenland Home Rule Authority 1992: 3–4).

While the difference in scale in relation to the above examples should be taken into account, in Colombia, to cite an example of indigenous collective rights, the 1991 constitution stipulates that *resguardo* lands are the collective and nonalienable property of an indigenous community to be managed by a community council (*cabildo*) according to their own habits and customs. In practice, however, families often seem to have acquired rights to certain areas or plots, and such rights can be traded within the community. The exploitation of natural resources will be regulated by law, which also will stipulate the rights of territorial entities to these resources and the mode of repartition of revenues. Such funds are to be used for the promotion of mining, environmental protection and the financing of regional investment projects.

These few examples already indicate that rights to subsurface resources are usually restricted. Surface rights may involve property rights, but these may be restricted, as in the case of Colombia, by the stipulation that land is inalienable collective property, segregated from the market. In still another case only usufruct rights are accorded on what are deemed to be public lands. The geographical extent of jurisdiction over lands is another contentious question. The claim to a territory for indigenous peoples often implies the claim to a contiguous geographical area. States may be inclined to recognize communal holdings, but these would then constitute a more or less fragmented patchwork rather than a contiguous territory. In Nicaragua, to take a notorious example, the Sandinista government was willing to recognize indigenous communities' ownership of their lands, but MISURASATA's claim to extensive jurisdictional powers over about one-third of the land surface of Nicaragua was unequivocally rejected (Burger 1987: 244).

Political Institutions

A second question to be asked concerns the political features of self-government. Which political institutions are prescribed and which are left to the device of the indigenous population, what are their competencies, and what is actually made of them? How do they relate to the institutions of the national state, and what mechanisms for conflict regulation exist? How do they work? How are indigenous peoples, in turn, represented in national institutions?

In his study on treaties between states and indigenous populations, Alfonso Martinez (1992: 17) notes that:

> In general, one can distinguish between societies based on rank, led by elders or "big men," where corporate descent groups play a fundamental role, and societies based on stratification, characterized by marked differences in the attribution of power and wealth among the constituent groups, and often led by hereditary kings. Both are contrasted in turn with so-called egalitarian societies, where authority is related to merit and exercised by some *primus inter pares,* or where leadership is limited to specific functions (e.g. war chief or priest).

Furthermore, he draws attention to the, in comparison to "modern" societies, diffuse character of indigenous legal and political organization, and the multifunctional character of specific actions, roles, and institutions. The ranked societies, he observes, were widespread among the indigenous peoples who entered into treaty relations with European powers, whereas, by contrast, the *primus inter pares-type* societies suffered much pressure, to the point that their political existence and independence were denied for the lack of governing structures identifiable in dominant terms. Nor were treaties concluded with them.

Such observations at least warn us against easy generalizations, a point that obviously is valid for any of the questions discussed in this paper. What Martinez makes clear in any case is that the articulation between widely different policies and the institutionalization of some sort of political pluralism is fraught with difficulties. Indigenous societies characterized by a great diffuseness and decentralization of what we would call "politics" may be vulnerable in the face of state or social violence, but at the same time they may be highly resilient in their resistance as they cannot be attained in some "core." More centralized and stratified societies may be able to field a greater military force, but their resistance may also crumble more rapidly. The degree to which political institutions have been preserved or transformed depends on historical and local circumstances. The present quest for accommodation through self-determination and self-government arrangements usually requires a considerable amount of political reorganization. We already noted Barth's (1969: 35) observation that in a political confrontation the opposed parties tend to become structurally similar and differentiated on a few clear criteria. Such processes are thus accompanied by the adoption of new organizational structures, e.g., the Shuar federation in Ecuador, and quite often by the rise of a new type of leadership competing with the traditional leaders (Chaumeil 1990). Historically, the confrontation that "produced" indigenous peoples has been characterized by asymmetry and only lately is some rectification, contingent upon contemporary processes of ethnic reorganization, taking place, prompting states to propose a "new partnership."

It is beyond the scope of this paper to discuss the present transformations of the "modern state," but we should take note of what Franck (1992) has referred to as a global "afferent/efferent" phenomenon. On the one hand, we can observe a trend toward secessionism, while at the same time we witness the emergence and development of supranational systems. Both tendencies contribute to a redimensioning of what until now has been understood as state sovereignty. In this paper the distinction between direct and indirect consociation provides a framework for the exploration of some features and issues related to the proposed "new partnership."

In the case of indirect consociation the political institutions basically are those of the public administration of the state into which the indigenous people are incorporated, though they form a majority within the jurisdiction. The scope of self-government in such cases is determined by the administrative level, of the jurisdiction, ranging from the municipal level, through the provincial level to federation-type arrangements.

The autonomy statute for the Atlantic coast regions in Nicaragua as implemented after 1987 can be considered an example of indirect consociation. Essentially, it provides for the creation of two administrative regions with a directly elected Regional Council. These councils have administrative powers to participate in the national development plan for the region. Though the Nicaraguan constitution and the Autonomy Statute refer to the multiethnicity of the Nicaraguan people and indicate that the different ethnic groups should be represented in the regional administration, no specific mention is made of the ethnic groups. This contrasts with the demand for recognition as sole representative of the indigenous peoples forwarded by MISURASATA and its successor organization YATAMA, which was founded in 1987. This organization, which won a majority in one of the regional councils in the 1990 elections, purports to function according to traditional political lines, with a council of elders as directing instance. In fact, the extremely complex ethnic composition of the region will make it difficult to arrive at an arrangement that will satisfy Miskito claims for control over their traditional territories, without ignoring the needs of significant mestizo, Creole, and other communities (Hannum 1993: 382; Scherrer 1993).

The *comarca* system in Panama provides a contrast in its recognition of an indigenous political structure that functions alongside the Panamanian state structure. The *comarca* of Kuna Yala (San Bias) can be considered a model for the Panamanian arrangement. In 1925 the Kuna revolted against the attempts at forced assimilation by the Panamanian state. A peace treaty was signed under United States supervision, recognizing the autonomy of the region without much specification. In the wake of their revolt, the Kuna undertook a comprehensive, planned reorganization of their social system under the leadership of their traditional authorities. The reform, which the Kuna referred to as "civilization" (Holloman 1969: 55), included a formalization of the political structure and the creation of new offices and was accompanied by a trend toward secularization. By 1945 the different Kuna factions united and a Kuna constitution specifying the governmental structure of local community congresses and creating a general Kuna Congress was adopted. From the Kuna point of view, this constitution specified the relation to the Republic of Panama. In 1953 a Panamanian law detailed the areas of Kuna autonomy and recognized the political structure as established in the 1945 Kuna constitution. This has provided the framework for a working relationship between the Kuna and the Panamanian state. Some strains on the traditional organization should be noted, however. Secularization, or differentiation between religious and secular leadership at the expense of the former, has proceeded rapidly. This has been accompanied by occupational and educational differentiation among the Kuna. Such tendencies have resulted in splits between the older traditional authorities and younger men and an erosion of the authority of the congress system. Furthermore, new political channels have emerged, such as the political parties and the *juntas locales*, which were introduced in Panama in 1972 and may compete with the local community congresses. Such pressures may result in further adaptations of the Kuna political structure (Holloman 1969; Howe 1986; Prestan 1991).

The Atlantic coast and the Kuna can serve as two examples of self-government arrangements at a regional level. It is difficult to make broad generalizations about political arrangements. The Colombian *resguardos* are to function according to traditional rules, and the new constitution provides that their position will be equal to the municipality the Greenland and Nunavut arrangements operate on a quite different scale.

Conflict mediation and some guarantees that forms of self-government are not simply overruled or eroded by higher level decision-making may constitute other important features of political arrangements. Conflict mediation and settlement can partly take place through ordinary courts or on the basis of administrative law. For conflicts that cannot be resolved through these mechanisms a special board may be set up, as for example in the case of Greenland where it consists of two government appointees, two members appointed by the Home Rule Authority, and three Supreme Court Judges. The arrangement thus seeks to combine political and legal elements.

Guarantees can be provided to a certain extent by including reference to a self-government system in the national constitution. While symbolically important, this usually does not say much about the actual scope and content of self-government. Further guarantees, protecting the indigenous people from majority decisions in national institutions, may be provided by reserving a number of seats in parliament for indigenous representatives. The weight of such seats can be increased by requiring a double majority for legislation affecting the indigenous people, implying that both the assembly as a whole and the indigenous delegates must in their majority vote in favor of such legislation. In Canada the Dene also have proposed that a Dene senate should function alongside the Legislative Assembly for a New Western Territory.

Economic and Financial Conditions

Indigenous peoples, it has been argued in this paper, do not simply defend their traditional ways of life. In the face of assimilationist policies they engage in processes of ethnic reorganization required to reconstruct and maintain borderlines. They claim the right to self-determination and to development on their own terms instead of being sacrificed to imposed forms of development. While the old way of life most often has been destructured beyond retrieval, the proposed self-determined development and self-government require resources to function. The question is, under what economic and financial conditions do such systems of self-government operate? How is access to economic and financial resources for the self-governing territories brought into effect?

As indigenous people have been relegated to a marginal position by the dominant society, tax revenues generated by their own administrative structure will be scant but may contribute to the running of their basic administrative structure. The Kuna, for example, generate money for local activities by levying a wharf use tax on foreign boats, airport taxes, a head tax, rents for the use of buildings by Panamanian government services, fines, income from community enterprises, and assistance from outside agencies.

For the Kayapo in Brazil, the taxing of gold miners and timber companies operating in their territory and the processing of Brazil nuts have become important sources of revenue. In the United States tribal gaming operations have become an important and controversial source of revenue. Furthermore, indemnification for the use of lands or ceding aboriginal title or revenues from the exploitation of surface and subsurface resources may provide a basis for self-determined development projects. In most cases, however, local resources will not be sufficient or need to be developed to meet the requirements of self-determined development.

Resources provided by the state can complement locally generated revenues. In indirect consociation models, the allocation of resources is basically resolved through the redistribution of tax revenues within the state structure. Funds thus distributed may be to a greater or lesser degree at the discretion of the local administrations. In models approaching direct consociation, a similar system may be used, equating the indigenous jurisdiction to one of the state administrative levels. According to the 1991 Colombian constitution, the *resguardos* will be considered as municipalities, and in this condition they will be entitled to a share in the national revenue. On the other hand, indigenous territories may be exempt from some of the state taxes in order to promote economic development, or special funds may be allocated to these territories.

Another problem is that the recognition of communitarian landholding among the indigenous people means that, by law, lands are segregated from the market. Thus, they cannot serve to obtain agricultural credit. While credit supply to smallholders already is quite complicated, this is an additional complication. Special financial schemes may be needed to further indigenous agricultural development.

One should be aware that for indigenous peoples, access to resources to sustain their own development is not a matter of social policy, as states tend to present it. In the United States, for example, the federal government is held responsible for protecting Indian lands and resources, providing social services, and serving tribal autonomy as a result of the promises made in treaties in return for the cession of lands.

Jurisdiction and the Administration of Justice

A fourth question we shall touch upon here is the relation between indigenous legal systems and those of the national state. How are competencies divided, and what are the mechanisms of conflict regulation?

Compared with state systems, indigenous justice and social control often function in a diffuse way through different social institutions and have not been codified. The administration of justice, the classification of crime and regulations concerning land use seem to be among the more controversial issues (Stavenhagen 1990). Orientations in the administration of justice often diverge. Whereas the state system is geared to punishment, indigenous systems are often oriented to conciliation and reestablishing harmony within the local community. Rather than retribution, they may be oriented toward mediation. On the other hand, indigenous systems of coping with crime or some types of crime may conflict with the conception of human rights, and this is one of the issues at stake in the theoretical discussion over the relation between collective rights and individual human rights. In this respect the classification of crimes and offenses is another area of divergence. Western legal systems do not recognize witchcraft as a problem and have no ways of coping with it. From this point of view, the "curing" or killing of a witch is murder. On the other hand, the ritual use of certain drugs may be brandished as a crime. Land-use systems and domestic and family relations may constitute other areas of friction. A most obvious case is the conflict between indigenous systems of land use and allocation and market-based systems rooted in private property. Also, a local land use system may, for example, entail the fragmentation of holdings below minima permitted by national agrarian legislation. Systems of inheritance, forms of adoption, and marriage rules often escape the unitary model states seek to impose.

If states do not simply impose their unitary system and recognize indigenous systems of justice administration and social control, in view of their claim to ultimate authority and the monopoly over violence, they often reserve some areas of justice administration for themselves, as in the case of major crimes in the United States. Lesser crimes may be tried in tribal courts. A further question then is to whom and where the indigenous system should apply. Should it only apply to indigenous people and only within their territory or should it also apply to outsiders in the indigenous territory and to indigenous people outside the indigenous territory? If water rights are involved, do they also apply to upstream water outside the demarcated indigenous territory? Usually such questions are not easily settled and not once and for all. A juridical maze results with ambiguous, precarious, and temporary balances between more or less codified, indigenous customs and state legislation.

Concluding Remarks

This paper started with a brief review of the emergence of an international movement of indigenous peoples. This is the outcome of processes of ethnic reorganization in the face of threats to livelihood and cultures. The context for such developments differs from one continent to another, and though we may speak of an international indigenous peoples' movement, we should be aware that the term covers an amalgam of groups with sometimes converging but also different concerns and often different political orientations.

The emergence of movements and the identification as indigenous peoples form a dynamic social process. In many cases, it is related to the appearance of new modes of organization and action sustained by a new type of leadership. Quite often, literate young people play an important role, and this may be a source of friction within the indigenous societies themselves which, in turn, impacts upon the subsequent dynamic of reorganization. Such processes account for both the persistence and transformation of ethnicity. Instead of viewing indigenous peoples' movements as simple defenders of "frozen" traditions, this alerts us to the contemporary character of the indigenous peoples' movement, its discourse and its claims.

In this paper, attention was focused on the demand for self-determination. The trajectory of this claim and the way it discredited the policies of assimilation and minority protection have been outlined as well as the controversies it gives rise to. States perceive the demand as a threat to their sovereignty and territorial integrity. Furthermore, the claim to a special status as prior occupants of the lands with specific inherent rights sits uneasily with the notion of citizenship and the conceptualization of human rights as they have evolved over the past centuries. Perhaps the framing of the debate in terms of international law and "peoples' rights" entails the risk of becoming diverted or derailed over semantic differences instead of addressing substantial issues. While the development of international standards regarding the rights and protection of indigenous peoples is important, more attention should be given to the way arrangements for self-determination and self-government could be worked out in practice.

Of course it is difficult to generalize with regard to practical arrangements in view of the diversity of situations. The broad definition of indigenous peoples covers groups widely diverging in size, mode of organization, livelihood, etc. A useful distinction can be made between two types of arrangements for increasing the opportunities to influence their own future. Arrangements tending toward indirect consociation avoid many controversial issues. The drawing of administrative borders in such a way that an indigenous people can effectively realize a degree of self-government skirts the problem of collective rights. It may work in situations where an indigenous people constitute a clear majority within a certain area. On the other hand, it is based on the current structures of public government and thus requires the indigenous people to reduce its view of governance to be established. Arrangements tending toward a direct consociation model provide more specific safeguards and require a specification of collective rights as well as an operational definition of the people entitled to such rights. These cases entail an effective institutionalization of political pluralism and are therefore most contentious.

The final sections of this paper discussed some of the dimensions that, in conjunction, constitute the scope of effective self-government. The claim to a territory within which sovereign political and jurisdictional power can be exerted is basic and most controversial. Much depends on the scale of the territorial claim and the extent of sovereignty demanded. Using the distinction between directly and indirectly consociational arrangements, various outcomes of conflicts and negotiations have passed review as illustrative cases. While, in view of the variety of situations, the question of whether such negotiated arrangements are satisfactory can only be assessed for each specific case, they reflect the tendency toward an expansion of the scope of forms of self-government and a substantiation of what the somewhat nebulous notion of "free association" may entail for a "new partnership" between indigenous peoples and states.

Notes

First published in 1994 as "Self-Determination and the 'New Partnership'; the Politics of Indigenous Peoples and State," in *Indigenous Peoples' Experiences with Self-Government*, ed. W. J. Assies and A. J. Hoekema, Copenhagen and Amsterdam: IWGIA and University of Amsterdam (IWGIA Document no. 76), 31–71.We thank André Hoekema and IWGIA for permission to reprint.

1. Its recommendations must pass through the Sub-Commission, then to the Commission on Human Rights, then to the Economic and Social Council (ECOSOC), then to the Third Committee, and finally to the General Assembly.
2. For an extensive discussion of definitional problems and operationalizations various countries, see Martínez Cobo 1982.
3. In the video film *Indian Self-Rule: A Problem of History* (Selma Thomas/ KWSU-TV 1985) Indian participants in a conference on the 1934 Indian Reorganization Act discuss the ambivalent attitudes of White Americans who wish Indians either to be "real Indians" or to assimilate, but cannot acknowledge the existence of "modern Indians." It underscores the dynamism and variability of ethnic group boundaries and the strategic, emergent, situational and, to some extent, volitional features of ethnic identity. Identity thus involves a dialectic of (voluntary) identification and (forced) ascription.
4. ICIHI (1987: 154) also reproduces ILO Recommendation 104 Concerning the Protection and Integration of Indigenous and other Tribal and Semi-Tribal Populations in Independent Countries, which was adopted in conjunction with Convention 107.
5. By June 1992 Bolivia, Colombia, Mexico, and Norway had ratified the convention.
6. This draft constitutes a considerable shift away from the initial draft, submitted in 1985, where controversial claims were avoided and which did not differ much from existing norms regarding minorities (Lerner 1991: 104). The right of "self-determination in accordance with international law" had made its first appearance in the 1991 draft of the declaration, which stated that by virtue of this right "they freely determine their

relationship with the States in which they live in a spirit of co-existence with other citizens and freely pursue their economic, social and cultural and spiritual development in conditions of freedom and dignity" (IWGLA Yearbook 1991: 149–156; Lam 1992: 619).

7. The formulations of the concept of "internal self-determination" are rather elliptic as they refer to "an internal level of national society" as well as to a distinct administrative structure and judicial system determined by and internal, or intrinsic, to a people or group (Martínez Cobo 1983: 41, 44; Willemsen Diaz 1992: 31–32).

8. In 1989 a special rapporteur, Mr. M. Alfonso Martinez, was appointed to make a "Study on treaties, agreements and other constructive arrangements between States and indigenous populations." His first progress report reinforces the principle that treaties and other agreements between indigenous nations and states are based in the equality of nations and remain binding as international agreements (E/CN.4/Sub.2/1992/32).

9. For indigenous people the development of citizenship has often been a rather brutal affair. In the United States, the 1887 General Allotment Act unilaterally bestowed US citizenship on the Indian population, which also made it possible to parcel out their land (Morris 1988–1989). The introduction of individualized property rights, regarded as the foundation of civil freedom, also had detrimental impacts in Latin America from the post-independence period up to the dispossession of the Mapuche in Chili under the Pinochet dictatorship. As noted, in the Nordic countries the development of social citizenship in a welfare state framework, contributed to the mobilization of indigenous people.

10. The opposition between the first and the second type is perhaps most dramatically illustrated in the case of the Nicaraguan Atlantic coast where it constituted a major issue in the conflict. The Autonomy Statute that was accepted in 1987 allows each autonomous region to elect a regional assembly, leaving the ethnic character of the assemblies open. This elected assembly provision clashed with the claim to an ethnic territory and MISURASATA's demand that it be the sole representative of all *costelios* (Diskin 1991: 166; Ortiz 1987: 52).

References

Abelsen, Emil. 1992. "Home Rule in Greenland." Paper presented at the Meeting of Experts, Nuuk, Greenland, September 24–28, 1991.

ACM. 1993. *Indigenous Peoples.* The Hague: Adviescommissie Mensenrechten Buitenlands Beleid (Advisory Report 16).

Alfonso Martinez, Miguel. 1992. "Discrimination against Indigenous Peoples, Study on Treaties, Agreements and Other Constructive Arrangements between States and Indigenous Populations." First Progress Report.

Arango Ochoa, Raúl. 1991–1992. "Situación territorial y tratamiento legal de las areas Indigenas del litoral pacafico y la Amazonia de Colombia." In *Derechos territoriales indigenas y ecologia,* ed. A. Hurtado, E. Sanchez, et al. Bogotá: CEREC, Gaia Foundation.

Asch, Michael, and Shirleen Smith 1992. "Consociation Revisited: Nunavut, Denendeh and Canadian constitutional consciousness." *Etudes Inuit Studies* 16, no. 1–2: 97–114.

Assies, Willem. 1987. *Een land zonder mensen? Inheemse volken en de kolonisatie van het Peruaanse Amazonegebied.* Amsterdam: Werkgroep Inheemse Volken, Peru Komitee Nederland.

Barre, Marie-Chantal. 1983. *Ideologias indigenistas y movimientos Indicts.* Mexico City: Siglo Veitiuno.

Barth, Frederik, ed. 1969. *Ethnic Groups and Boundaries, the Social Organization of Cultural Difference.* Oslo and London: Universitets Forlaget, George Allen & Unwin.

Bayly, John U. 1993. "The Denendeh Conservation Board: An Experiment in Aboriginal Resources and Environmental Management." Paper presented at the 23th International Congress of Anthropological and Ethnological Sciences, Commission of Folk Law and Legal Pluralism; July 29–August 5, Mexico City.

Bennagen, Ponciano L. 1992. "Fiscal and Administrative Relations between Indigenous Governments and States." Paper presented at the Meeting of Experts, Nuuk, Greenland, September 24–28.

Bonfil Batalla, Guillermo, comp. 1981. *Utopia y Revolucion*. Mexico City: Nueva Imagen.

Brantenberg, Odd Terje. n.d. "Constructing Indigenous Self-Government in a Nation State: Same-diggi: The Sarni Parliament in Norway." Mimeo.

Brölman, Catherine, René Lefeber, and Marjolein Zieck, eds. 1993. *Peoples and Minorities in International Law.* Dordrecht, Boston, London: Martinus Nijhoff.

Burger, Julian. 1987. *Report from the Frontier: The State of the World's Indigenous Peoples.* London, Cambridge, MA: ZED, Cultural Survival.

Ceinos, Pedro, coord. 1990. *Minorias etnicas.* Barcelona: Integral.

Chaumeil, Jean-Pierre. 1990. "'Les Nouveaux Chefs. . .' Pratiques politiques et organisations indigenes en Amazonie peruvienne." *Problemes d'Amerique Latine* 96: 93–113.

Churchill, Ward. 1998–1989. "The Black Hills are Not for Sale. A Summary of the Lakota Struggle for the 1868 Treaty Territory." In *Critical Issues in Native North America*, ed. E. Churchill. Copenhagen: IWGIA.

Cohen, Anthony. P. 1985. *The Symbolic Construction of Community.* Chichester, London: Ellis Horwood, Tavistock.

Cohen, Jean. 1985. "Strategy or Identity: New Theoretical Paradigms and Contemporary Social Movements." *Social Research* 52, no. 4: 663–716.

CRTC. 1988. *Cartala de legislacion indigena.* Cali: CRIC.

Daes, Elle. I. A. 1992. "Rapport sur les travaux de la deuxième session du Groupe de travail sur les populations autochtones." E/CN.4/Sub.2/1992/33.

Deloria, Jr., Vine, ed. 1985. *American Indian Policy in the Twentieth Century.* Norman and London: University of Oklahoma Press.

Díaz-Polanco, Héctor. 1987. "Neoindigenismo and the Ethnic Question in Central America." *Latin American Perspectives* 14, no. 1.

Dinstein, Yoram. 1992. "The Degree of Self-Rule of Minorities in Unitarian and Federal States." Paper presented at the Second Amsterdam International Law Conference Peoples and Minorities in International Law, Amsterdam, June 18–20.

Diskin, Martin. 1991. "Ethnic Discourse and the Challenge to Anthropology: The Nicaraguan Case." In *Nation States and Indians in Latin America*, ed. G. Urban and J. Sherzer. Austin: University of Texas Press.

Duhaime, Gerard. 1992. "Le chasseur et le minotaure: itineraire de l'autonomie politique au Nunavik." *Etudes Inuit Studies* 16, no. 1–2: 149–177.

Dyck, Noel, ed. 1985. *Indigenous Peoples and the Nation-State, Fourth World Politics in Canada, Australia and Norway.* St. Johns: Memorial University of Newfoundland, Institute of Social and Economic Research.

ECOSOC/Commission on Human Rights. 1992. "Report of the Meeting of Experts to Review the Experience of Countries in the Operation of Schemes of Internal Self-Government for Indigenous Peoples." Nuuk, Greenland, September 24–28.

Escobar, Arturo, and Sonia. E. Alvarez, eds. 1992. *The Making of Social Movements in Latin America.* Boulder: Westview Press.

Fenge, Terry. 1992. "Political Development and Environmental Management in Northern Canada: The Case of the Nunavut Agreement." *Etudes Inuit Studies* 16, no. 1–2: 115–141.

Findji, Maria Teresa. 1992. "The Indigenous Authorities Movement in Colombia." In *The Making of Social Movements in Latin America*, ed. A. Escobar and S. E. Alvarez. Boulder: Westview Press.

Foighel, Isi. 1980. *Home Rule in Greenland* (Man & Society Series, No. 1). Copenhagen: Nyt Nordisk Forlag.

Forbes, Jack. 1985. "Native American Resistance, 1890–1960: New and Old Indians." *Wampum* 2, no. 1.

Franck, Tom M. 1992. "Postmodern Tribalism and the Right to Secession." Paper presented at the Second Amsterdam International Law Conference Peoples and Minorities in International Law, Amsterdam, June 18–20.

Gerritsen, Rolf. 1990. "Cause for Hope? Aboriginal Self-Management and Local Government in Australia." Discussion paper, Royal Commission into Aboriginal Deaths in Custody, Graduate Program in Public Policy, Australian National University.

Greenland Home Rule Authority. 1992. "Information Memorandum on Greenland." Mimeo.

Groves, Robert. 1990. "Territoriality and Aboriginal Self-Determination: Options for Legal Pluralism in Canada." In *Commission on Folk Law and Legal Pluralism, Proceedings of the VIth International Symposium*. Ottawa: The Commission on Folk Law and Legal Pluralism.

Guinneau-Sinclair, Francoise. 1991. *Legislacion amerindia de Panama*. Panama: University of Panama.

Hannum, Hurst. 1990. *Autonomy, Sovereignty, and Self-Determination: The Accommodation of Conflicting Rights*. Philadelphia: University of Pennsylvania Press.

Hannum, Hurst, ed. 1993. *Documents on Autonomy and Minority Rights*. Dordrecht, Boston, London: Martinus Nijhof.

Harhoff, Frederik. 1993. *Rigsfælleskabet*. Aarhus: Klim.

Haysom, Veryan. 1992. "The Struggle for Recognition: Labrador Inuit Negotiations for Land Rights and Self-Government." *Etudes Inuit Studies* 16, no. 1–2: 179–197.

Hendricks, Janet. 1991. "Symbolic Counterhegemony among the Ecuadorian Shuar." In *Nation States and Indians in Latin America*, ed. G. Urban and J. Sherzer. Austin: University of Texas Press.

Higgins, Rosalyn. 1992. "The Evolution of the Right of Self Determination: Commentary on Professor Franck's' Paper." Paper presented at the Second Amsterdam International Law Conference Peoples and Minorities in International Law, Amsterdam, June 18–20.

Holloman, Regina Evans. 1969. "Developmental Change in San Bias." PhD diss. Evanston, IL: Northwestern University.

Howe, James. 1986. *The Kuna Gathering: Contemporary Village Politics in Panama*. Austin: University of Texas Press.

ICC. 1992. *Inuit Circumpolar Conference: Principles and Elements for a Comprehensive Arctic Policy*. Montreal: Centre for Northern Studies and Research, McGill University.

ICIHI. 1987. *Indigenous Peoples: A Global Quest for Justice*. London and New Jersey: ZED Books.

IWGIA. *Yearbook 1991*. Copenhagen: IWGIA.

Jackson, Jean E. 1991. "Being and Becoming an Indian in the Vaupes." In *Nation States and Indians in Latin America*, ed. G. Urban and J. Sherzer. Austin: University of Texas Press.

Johansen, Lars Emil. 1992. "Greenland and the European Community." *Etudes Inuit Studies* 16, no. 1–2: 33–37.

Jull, Peter. 1990. *Self-Management and Local Government.in Aboriginal North America*. Casuarina, NT: Australian National University, North Australia Research Unit.

Kuppe, René. 1993. "The Indigenous Peoples of Venezuela: Lost Between Agrarian Law and Environmental Law." Paper presented at the 13th IUAES International Conference, Commission of Folk Law and Legal Pluralism, July 29–August 5, Mexico City.

Lam, Maivan C. 1992. "Making Room for Peoples at the United Nations: Thoughts Provoked by Indigenous Claims to Self-Determination." *Cornell International Law Journal* 25, no. 3: 615–616.

Lerner, Norbert. 1991. *Group Rights and Discrimination in International Law.* Dordrecht, Boston, London: Martinus Nijhoff.

———. 1992. "The Evolution of Minority Rights in International Law." Paper presented at the Second Amsterdam International Law Conference Peoples and Minorities in International Law, Amsterdam, June 18–20.

Liberman, Kitula, and Armando Godínez, coord. 1992. *Territorio y dignidad; pueblos indigenas y medio ambiente en Bolivia.* Bolivia: ILDIS, Nueva Sociedad.

Machado, Lia Zanotta. 1993. "L'heterogeneite culturelle et politique en Amerique Latine." In *L'Amerique Latine: vers la democratie?* coord. B. Marques-Pereira. Brussels: Editions Complexe.

Martínez Cobo, José R. 1982. "Study of the Problem of Discrimination against Indigenous Populations." Chapter 18, Political Rights, E/CN.4/Sub.2/1983/21/ add.6.

———. 1987. *Study of the Problem of Discrimination against Indigenous Populations, Volume V, Conclusions, Proposals and Recommendations.* New York: United Nations.

Maybury-Lewis, David. 1991. "Becoming Indian in Lowland South America." In *Nation-States and Indians in Latin America*, ed. G. Urban and J. Sherzer. Austin: University of Texas Press.

Minister of Supply and Services. 1991. *Aboriginal Peoples, Self-Government, and Constitutional Reform.* Canada: Minister of Supply and Services.

Ministerie van Buitenlandse Zaken. 1993. *Inheemse Volken in het Buitenlands Beleid en in de Ontwikkelingssamenwerking.* The Hague: Voorlichtingsdienst Ontwikkelingssamenwerking van het ministerie van Buitenlandse Zaken (Information Bulletin no. 11).

Minugh, C. J., G. T. Morris, and R. C. Riser, eds. 1989. *Indian Self-Governance: Perspectives on the Political Status of Indian Nations in the United States of America.* Kenmore: Center for World Indigenous Studies.

Moody, Roger, ed. 1993. *The Indigenous Voice: Visions & Realities*, 2nd edition. Utrecht: International Books.

Morales, Ascario. 1991. "La Administración de Justicia en las comunidades indígenas kunas y conflictos con el derecho positivo." *Law and Anthropology* 6.

Morris, Glenn. T. 1988–1989. "The International Status of Indigenous Nations within the United States." In *Critical Issues in Native North America*, ed. W. Churchill. Copenhagen: IWGIA.

———. 1993. "International Structures and Indigenous Peoples." In *Indigenous Peoples Politics: An Introduction, Vol. 1*, ed. M. A. Sills and G. T. Morris. Denver: University of Colorado at Denver, Fourth World Center for the Study of Indigenous Law and Politics.

Nagel, Joane, and C. Matthew. Snipp. 1993. "Ethnic Reorganization: American Indian Social, Economic, Political, and Cultural Strategies for Survival." *Ethnic and Racial Studies* 16, no. 2: 203–235.

NAR. 1993. *Briefadvies Inheemse Volken.* The Hague: Nationale Adviesraad voor Ontwikkelingssamenwerking.

Nowak, Manfred. 1992. "The Evolution of Minority Rights in International Law (Comments)." Paper presented at the Second Amsterdam Interna-tional Law Conference Peoples and Minorities in International Law, Amsterdam, June 18–20.

O'Brien, Sharon. 1989. *American Indian Tribal Governments.* Norman and London: University of Oklahoma Press.

Oreskov, Claus. 1993. "Sweden Passes Law for a Sami Parliament." *IWGIA Newsletter 1/93.*

Ortiz, Roxanne Dunbar. 1984. *Indians of the Americas.* London: ZED Books.

———. 1987. "Indigenous Rights and Regional Autonomy in Revolutionary Nicaragua." *Latin American Perspectives* 14, no. 1: 43–66

Pachon César, X. 1980. "Los pueblos y los cabildos indigenas: la hispanizacion de las culturas americanas." *Revista Colombiana de Antropología* 23: 297–326.

Petersen, Robert. 1977. "Continuity and Discontinuity in the Political Development of Modern Greenland." In *Danish Netherlands Symposium on Developments in Greenlandic Arctic Culture.* Groningen: Arctic Centre.

Prestan, A. 1991. "Organizacion social y politica de Kuna Yala." *Hombre y Cultura, Revista del Centro de Investigaciones Antropologicas* 1, no. 2: 107–159.

Prucha, Francis Paul, ed. n.d. *Documents of United States Indian Policy*, 2nd edition. Lincoln, London: University of Nebraska Press.

PNR. 1989–1990. *Cursos de capacitacion en legislacion indigena nacional para autoridades civiles, fuerzas armadas y policia nacional.* Bogotá: Presidencia de la Republica.

Rehof, Lars Adam. 1992. "Effective Means of Planning for and Implementing Autonomy, Including Negotiated Constitutional Arrangements and Involving Both Territorial and Personal Autonomy." Paper presented at the Meeting of Experts, Nuuk, Greenland, September 24–28.

Ribeiro, Darcy. 1970. *Os indios e a civilizacao brasileira: a integractio das populagaes indigenas no Brasil moderno.* Rio de Janeiro: Civilizacao Brasileira.

Scherrer, Christoph. P. 1991. "Selbstbestimmung für indigene Nationalitäten Neuere Entwicklungen im Völker- und Minderheitenrecht." *Widerspruch* 22: 41–50.

———. 1993. *Recognizing Multiplicity, Conflict Resolution in Eastern Nicaragua.* Zurich: Institute of Ethnology, University of Zurich.

Sills, Mark A. 1993. "Political Interaction between States and Indigenous Nations: A Point of Departure." In *Indigenous Peoples' Politics: An Introduction, Vol. 1,* ed. M. A. Sills and G. T. Morris. Denver: University of Colorado at Denver, Fourth World Center for the Study of Indigenous Law and Politics.

SNV. 1993. *SNV-Beleid inzake Inheemse Volken.* The Hague: Stichting Nederlandse Vrijwilligers.

Stavenhagen, Rodolfo. 1990. "Derecho consuetudinario indigena en America Latina." In *Entre la ley y la costumbre,* comp. R. Stavenhagen and D. Iturralde. Mexico and San José: Instituto Indigenista Interamericano, Instituto Interamericano de Derechos Humanos.

Triana Antorveza, Adolfo. 1980. *Legislación indígena nacional.* Bogotá: América Latina.

Trio, Wendel, and Johan Bosman, red. 1992a. *Actuele voorbeelden van inheems verzet in Centraal en Zuid Amerika.* Antwerp: KWIA.

———. 1992b. *Actuele voorbeelden van inheems verzet in de Verenigde Staten en Canada.* Antwerp: KWIA.

Urban, Greg, and Joel Sherzer, eds. 1991. *Nation-States and Indians in Latin America.* Austin: University of Texas Press.

UNPO. 1993. "Self-Determination in Relation to Individual Human Rights, Democracy and the Protection of the Environment." Conference Report, The Hague: UNPO.

Willemsen Diaz, Augusto. [1991] 2009. "How Indigenous Peoples' Rights Reached the UN". In: *Making the Declaration Work; The United Nations Declaration on the Rights of Indigenous Peoples,* ed C. Charters and R. Stavenhagen, Copenhagen: IWGIA. 16–31.

Indian Justice in the Andes

Re-rooting or Re-routing?

Introduction

"That's to say, we thought that when whipping you should lash many times, but the elders said that that should not be done. You should only strike three times: in the name of the Father, the Son, and the Holy Ghost. That is what God forgives." It's April 2001 and some thirty young Indians have come together for a workshop in Peguche, Ecuador, to discuss the findings from their research on Indian justice. A series of sanctions practiced in the communities passed review, such as bathing in very cold water or rubbing the body with stinging nettles. It was also brought up that the number of whiplashes might vary according to the case: "Three, six, up to twelve." Such sanctions go together with counseling, so that the wrongdoer will learn the correct ways. In 1998, a new Ecuadorian constitution had included the right of indigenous authorities to "exercise judicial functions [and] apply their own norms and procedures." More recently, the Department of Law of the Universidad Andina Simón Bolívar had published a draft law on the judicial functions of indigenous authorities (Trujillo, Grijalva, and Endara 2001), which was also discussed at the workshop. It was time to find out what indigenous justice was all about.

One thing the above quote reveals is that "Indian justice" can hardly be understood in essentialist terms. After all, the whip was introduced by the Spaniards, along with the Father, the Son, and the Holy Ghost. On the other hand, the new Ecuadorian constitution was the first Latin American constitution to incorporate a phrase in a language other than Spanish: *Ama quilla, ama llulla, ama shua* (do not be lazy, do not lie, do not steal). Elsewhere in the Andes, in Bolivia, Indian leader Victor Hugo Cárdenas had pronounced the same words upon assuming the vice presidency of that country in 1993 and had added *Ama llunku* (do not be servile).[1] Some of the precepts of Andino normativity have thus acquired a new public prominence.

An increasing number of Latin American countries, including Bolivia, Colombia, Ecuador, and Peru, have recognized the right of indigenous authorities to exercise judicial functions. This recognition of Indian justice is related to the official acknowledgment of the multiethnic and pluricultural character of Latin American countries that has occurred over the past decade and which is further sustained by the ratification of ILO Convention 169 (Assies, van der Haar, and Hoekema 2000; Van Cott 2000). The new constitutions as well as Convention 169 provide a certain support for the recognition of indigenous forms of organization and authority and their ways of doing justice.[2] What was once considered marginal, if not illegal, has thus become a right.

This development has opened up a new and highly dynamic field of inquiry into its legal and political aspects from various disciplinary perspectives, and it gives rise to new questions regarding competencies and the limits to the application of "their own normative systems." One of the issues that emerges is how to develop "laws of coordination and compatibilization" as they are foreseen in various Latin American constitutions. This involves questions regarding the delimitation of indigenous jurisdiction, its relation to state law or positive law (Hoekema 1998), and how to navigate between cultural relativism and human rights (Bronstein 1999: 38). Advances in elaborating "coordination laws" have been few, however.

In this article I will focus attention on the jurisprudence developed by the Colombian Constitutional Court, which in fact substitutes a law of coordination as foreseen in the constitution.[3] The presentation of some cases handled by the court and the manner of proceeding adopted provide a perspective on the dilemmas that arise. I shall then briefly present the attempt at unification of its doctrine by the Colombian court as well as the draft "coordination laws" currently under discussion in Bolivia and Ecuador. In the concluding section, I will comment on the development of indigenous jurisdiction in these three Andean countries and discuss some of the theoretical problems that arise in applying Kymlicka's (1995) well-known liberal approach to group-differentiated rights, which often serves as a source of inspiration in the development of legislation and jurisprudence.

Colombia: The Constitution and the Doctrine

With reference to the limitations on indigenous jurisdiction in Latin America various formulas are used (Yrigoyen Fajardo 2000). Whereas the 1993 Peruvian constitution refers to "the fundamental rights of the person," the constitutions of Colombia, Ecuador, and Bolivia establish that indigenous jurisdiction should not contravene "the Constitution and the laws." Article 246 of the Colombian constitution, for example, reads:

> The authorities of the indigenous peoples may exercise jurisdictional functions within their territorial area, in conformity with their own norms and procedures, but always insofar as they are not contrary to the Constitution and laws of the Republic. The law will establish the forms of coordination of this special jurisdiction with the national justice system.

This formulation gives rise to a dilemma that was promptly recognized by the Colombian Constitutional Court. In its verdict in *tutela* case T-349 in 1996,[4] the court stated the following:

> Of particular interest here is to examine the limits that can be established regarding the exercise of the jurisdictional faculties expressly conferred to the authorities of the indigenous communities as a consequence of the principle of cultural diversity since, although the Constitution generically refers to the "Constitution and the law" as parameters of restriction, it is clear that this cannot mean all the constitutional and legal norms, because that would reduce the recognition of cultural diversity to mere rhetoric.

Verdict T-349 was one in a series in which the Constitutional Court gradually, and not without contradictions, sought to develop a doctrine regarding the scope and limits of indigenous jurisdiction. Here I will discuss some cases that prompted the development of such norms.

Case T-349 and the Limits on the Autonomy of Indigenous Jurisdiction

One of the cornerstones of the doctrine developed in Colombia is that the autonomy of indigenous peoples should be maximized to assure their cultural survival. In applying their own justice therefore, they can only be required to respect a core of the most fundamental human rights and a form of due process. This part of the doctrine was formulated in 1996 when the Constitutional Court reviewed a lower court verdict over a *tutela*-demand filed by an Embera-Chamí Indian.

In September 1994, Ovidio González Wasnora and another Indian were arrested by the *auxiliares locales* of the Cabildo of Purembará on the charge of having been involved in the murder of Jesús Edgar Niaza Dobigama of the same Embera-Chamí community. After their version of the occurrences had been registered, the two were locked up in the local *calabozo*. A week later they escaped and voluntarily handed themselves over to the *Fiscalía 24* in Belén de Umbría, alleging that they had received death threats from members of the community and that they had been tortured. The Fiscalía began an investigation and kept only González Wasnora in custody, releasing the other prisoner for lack of evidence.

In January 1995, the Cabildo Mayor Único de Riseralda, a recently created indigenous organization, notified the prison of the Pereira Judicial District where González Wasnora was held that they had condemned him to "8 years imprisonment." Once it had been informed of this decision, the Fiscalía stopped its own investigation. On the other hand, representatives of the *Defensoría del Pueblo* in Mistrató unsuccessfully tried to convince the community to modify its verdict and to have a retrial, so that the accused could be present as well as a lawyer.

In February 1995, however, a General Assembly of the community reviewed the sentence of the Cabildo Mayor Único and increased the sanction to twenty years imprisonment. At the assembly, both the family of the victim and the family of the convict were present and all agreed on increasing the sentence. This severity corresponded to the fact that the victim was considered to be a young, very honest, and hard-working man without any antecedents, whereas González Wasnora was a notorious troublemaker who earlier had been involved in another murder case.

The *Defensoría del Pueblo* again sought to mediate without success, and González Wasnora decided to file a *tutela* writ against the General Assembly of Cabildos of the Community as well as against the Cabildo Mayor Único de Riseralda. According to the plaintiff, his constitutional rights to due process, to a defense, to his life and to his physical integrity had been violated. The first instance Municipal Tribunal at Riseralda conceded the *tutela* and ordered the cabildo to turn over all documentation to the ordinary justice system in order to reopen the case. Among other considerations, the tribunal argued that the community did not possess preexisting norms to deal with homicide cases, that the accused had not been present at the trial and thus could not defend himself—whereas the family of the victim had been present and participated in the judgment—and that the accused had been condemned twice for the same acts. A year later, the Constitutional Court reviewed the verdict of the Riseralda Tribunal.

The Review by the Constitutional Court: The Doctrine

According to the Constitutional Court, the central question in this case was "What are the concrete limits the constitution establishes regarding the exercise of jurisdictional faculties by the authorities of indigenous communities, and specifically in the case of judging the conduct of one of its members against another within the community's own territory?"

In view of the constitutional recognition of the inherent value of cultural diversity, the court argued, the rule for interpretation should be that of maximum autonomy of the indigenous communities as a guarantee for their cultural survival. Restrictions should be limited to those that are indispensable for assuring hierarchically superior interests, such as internal security, and should be as little onerous as possible where the autonomy of the communities is concerned.

Once this principle had been established, the court turned to interpreting Article 246 of the constitution and its stipulation concerning the "Constitution and the laws." Considering that the full application of all laws would reduce autonomy to mere rhetoric, the court argued that the principle of maximization should apply and that it was particularly important in this case, which concerns a problem fully internal to the community. It could be assumed, therefore, that all involved share, in principle, the same tradition. In such purely internal cases, the court argued, the principle of maximum autonomy is paramount, since preservation of the cultural identity and cohesion of the group depends on its capacity to regulate internal affairs. Therefore,

> [T]he limitations on the forms in which this internal control is exercised should be the acceptable minimum; that is, they can only refer to what is really intolerable for violating what is most precious to humankind.

In the view of the court, this core of intangible rights only includes the right to life, the prohibition of slavery, and the prohibition of torture. There are two arguments that lead to this conclusion: in the first place, the recognition that it is only in regard to this core that a real intercultural consensus exists. In the second place, the fact that this group of rights is included in the core of intangible rights recognized in all human rights treaties as rights that cannot be suspended, not even in situations of armed conflict.

To this group of rights the court added the requirement of due process in the sense that the judgment should conform to the "norms and proceedings" of the indigenous community, as stipulated in the constitution. On this point, the court clarified that this requirement only meant that the reaction of the indigenous authorities to an offense should be foreseeable. Otherwise, it would lead to a complete denial of indigenous forms of norm development and rituals of judgment, which is exactly what should be preserved. Indigenous authorities may not act arbitrarily, but the court was careful to stipulate that this does not imply that traditional norms should become completely static, given that "every culture is essentially dynamic."

Applying the Doctrine

To take into account the specificity of the social and political organization of indigenous communities, the Colombian judiciary often relies on a series of studies that the Colombian Anthropological Institute was commissioned to carry out after the adoption of the 1991 constitution in order the prepare the magistrates for their new tasks (Perafán Simmonds 1995; 1996). The studies of the Embera-Chamí, as well as other information collected by the court, suggested that the Embera-Chamí politico-legal order can be classified as essentially a segmentary system. The parties involved in a conflict (families, patrilineages) negotiate the sanction to be imposed on the offender or the compensation to be paid in order to avoid escalation of the conflict into blood vengeance or feuding.

However, the recent creation of the cabildos implies that besides this segmentary system, a centralized system is emerging that operates through meetings of the inhabitants of the *veredas* (valleys, sections of the *resguardo* or "reserve") or through general assemblies (*reuniones de todos*) of the resguardo. A crucial requirement for the working of this arrangement is the articulation between the two systems. To be effective, the cabildo system requires that all extended families involved in a conflict be present at the meetings. Therefore, the *vereda*-meetings only deal with matters that involve parties belonging to that same *vereda*. Otherwise, the deciding instance is the general assembly. This assembly also is the instance that deals with grave crimes. Still more recently, however, a new instance, the Cabildo Mayor Único de Risaralda, has emerged and begun to exercise jurisdictional functions. This Cabildo Mayor, however, does not rely on large assemblies, nor does it consult the patrilineages of the parties involved in conflicts. This has generated a series of problems, including in the case under discussion. As we saw, the Cabildo Mayor Único had condemned González Wasnora to "8 years of prison," a verdict that was subsequently modified by the General Assembly.

Where sanctions on homicide are concerned, the anthropological studies showed that in the Embera-Chamí communities it is punished by a combination of forced labor in benefit of the community during the day and the application of the *cepo* (pillory) during the nights for periods from three to eight years, depending on contextual factors. Only exceptionally the suspect of a homicide is handed over to the ordinary justice system.

On the basis of the doctrinary considerations and the anthropological information, the court proceeded to examine the claims made by González Wasnora in his *tutela* demand. Had the constitutional limits on the jurisdictional faculties of the indigenous communities been transgressed? Where the right to life is concerned, the court established that the Embera-Chamí legal order does not include the death penalty and that if threats had been made, they had not come from the community authorities who would be quite capable of preventing acts of vengeance. The authorities themselves affirmed that it was rather González Wasnora himself who was a nuisance and who had threatened the people.

In relation to the issue of the integrity of the person González Wasnora had claimed that condemnation to the *cepo* constituted a "cruel and inhuman treatment." The court, however, considered that it is a form of corporal punishment which is part of local tradition and is highly valued by the local community for its great degree of intimidation. Although it implies physical suffering, it is applied in a manner that does not damage the integrity of the condemned. It cannot be considered cruel or inhuman since it is neither a disproportionate or useless form of punishment nor one that produces any grave physical or mental damage. Moreover, the court argued, González Wasnora had occupied one of the communal leadership positions and at the time he had never done anything to abolish the practice, although he could have done so: "[O]nly now, surely after counseling by the 'whites' and expecting that he could draw a profit from it, has he decided to accuse his community of dealing out inhuman treatment to its members by practicing the use of the *cepo*."

Third came the question of due process. As noted, González Wasnora was first condemned to eight years imprisonment by the Cabildo Mayor Único, but then a General Assembly decided on twenty years of imprisonment. Although no second instance is known in the Embera-Chamí legal order, the fact that the case was judged twice could not be considered a transgression of traditional normativity, the court opined. Quite to the contrary, the second trial sought to remedy the failures of the first one. The Cabildo Mayor Único had not consulted the patrilineages involved and therefore its proceedings lacked legitimacy. The second trial by the General Assembly was a logical consequence of the first and an effort to adhere to local custom. The community exercised its jurisdictional faculties strictly according to its own legal order and this can only be qualified as a form of "due process."

The related issue of the right to defense led the court to consider that "for them" this does not exist in the way "we" consider it. The Embera-Chamí system does not protect individual values as a matter of priority. According to their cosmovision, a homicide threatens peace and may trigger a conflict between families that can only be prevented if the patrilineages involved reach an agreement. It was exactly for this reason that the second trial by the General Assembly was held. Since the patrilineage of the accused was present at this assembly it could be assumed that his interests were represented.

Finally, the court considered the legality of the crime and the punishment. The anthropological information made clear that the Embera-Chamí communities prohibit and sanction homicide and that their members are well aware of the norms in this regard. Where the punishment was concerned, it was clear that the traditional punishment for the case at hand was at least three years of forced labor in combination with the *cepo*. The other option would have been to hand the case over to the ordinary justice system. The community, however, took a completely unforeseeable route in condemning González Wasnora to twenty years imprisonment in a "white" jail.

The court concluded that the *tutela* should be granted, since the community had abused its jurisdictional faculties. To guarantee the rights of the accused as well as the autonomy of the community, the court resolved to ask the community to try the case again and to impose a traditional sanction, or otherwise hand it over to the ordinary justice system. If the community, in a General Assembly, should decide to try the case again, the ordinary justice system would bring the accused to the community territory. Meanwhile, González Wasnora had enjoyed the benefit of provisional liberty since Fiscalía 24 in Belén de Umbría had failed to come up with a proper accusation. A warrant for his arrest had been issued, however.

Case T-523, the "Case of the Whip"

In 1997, the court further specified its doctrine. This time the key question was whether whipping and expulsion from the community could be admitted in light of the constitution.

In August 1996, Marden Arnulfo Betancur, at the time Mayor of the Jambaló municipality in the Cauca region, was murdered. Some days later, the governors of the indigenous Cabildos of the Northern Cauca Zone decided to "investigate and sanction those responsible for this assassination." They ordered the arrest of Francisco Gembuel and five other persons, whom they accused of having instigated the murder by denouncing Betancur to the guerrillas as a member of a paramilitary group and accusing him of embezzling public funds.[5]

In the course of the proceedings, Gembuel's testimony was taken as well as that of various community members who affirmed that they had seen him talking with the guerrillas. The site where this talk had supposedly taken place was visited. The commission also considered Gembuel's request to be defended by a lawyer and responded that he could have a defender if—and only if—he named a permanent member of the Jambaló community who was knowledgeable regarding local customs. Written acts were drawn up of all of these proceedings.

Next, the investigating commission called a General Assembly of the community to present its findings. One day before this meeting took place, however, a local newspaper published an article in which the guerrilla accepted responsibility for the murder. Gembuel then launched a *tutela*-procedure against the governor of the Jambaló cabildo and the president of the Association of Cabildos of the Northern Cauca. He argued that the local authorities had not taken into account that the guerrillas had formally accepted responsibility for the murder and that, moreover, his right to due process was being violated. The evidence against him was kept secret so that he could not dispute it, and those in charge of the investigation were his political enemies. Finally, the indigenous community could not judge him since, according to Gembuel, it had no customs in dealing with homicide. The indigenous authorities, therefore, should call off the assembly and hand over their findings to the ordinary justice system.

Five days later, while a verdict in the *tutela*-procedure was still pending, the Assembly of the Northern Zone took place in Jambaló, with the participation of members from all the *resguardos* of the Northern Zone. The commission presented its findings and conclusions and the incriminated were allowed to present their arguments. Gembuel only stated that he had filed a *tutela*-writ and that he would act according to the outcome of that procedure. After deliberations, the assembly decided that Gembuel was responsible and condemned him to sixty whiplashes, expulsion from the community, and the loss of his political rights in the community. However, at the moment when the public whipping was about to begin, members of Gembuels's family caused a disturbance and the execution of the sanction was suspended.

Meanwhile, the local tribunal worked on the *tutela*-demand and finally decided in favor of Gembuel. Although it recognized the competence of the indigenous community to carry out the process, it considered that the right of defense had been violated and that the sanctions imposed threatened the life and personal integrity of the accused. It therefore ordered that the decisions of the assembly be left without effect and that the investigation by the indigenous authorities be reopened. Some weeks later, in February 1997, this verdict was confirmed by a second instance tribunal.

Review by the Constitutional Court

In October 1997, the Constitutional Court reviewed the *tutela* verdicts. The two questions to be resolved, in the opinion of the Court, were:

A. Does the procedure followed by the authorities of the Indigenous Cabildos of the Northern Cauca correspond to the characteristics of the juridical order of the Paéz of Jambaló?

B. Do the sanctions imposed by the General Assembly go beyond the limits imposed on the exercise of jurisdictional faculties by the indigenous authorities?

The court took its earlier arguments concerning the scope of indigenous jurisdiction, as developed in case T-349, as a starting point. It also heard the opinion of some experts as well as the explanation by the governor of the indigenous Cabildo of Jambaló.

One of the experts, anthropologist Esther Sánchez Botero, argued that the Paéz have preserved various cultural features, among them their juridical order based on procedures to investigate occurrences that upset the equilibrium in the community.[6] The procedure begins when the family or the social segment to which the victim belongs demands that the cabildo investigate the facts and sanction the guilty party. The cabildo then appoints an investigation commission, made up of persons of prestige within the community, which should establish the faults committed and "find the lies in the words of the accused" (*encontrar la mentira en la palabra de los acusados*).

The commission begins by citing the accused to hear their version of the facts. If they accept responsibility, the commission takes no further steps; otherwise the investigation continues by hearing witnesses and visiting the site of the events. Next, the cabildo evaluates the findings of the commission. If a *mentira* is detected, a General Assembly is called as the highest authority to decide the case. At the assembly, a public confession by the accused is demanded, and a *careo* or confrontation between the statements of the accused and the testimonies against him is staged. In its judgment, the Assembly not only considers the occurrences that directly caused the damage but also those that in some way have permitted or facilitated the "upsetting of harmony."

The sanction is regarded as a means of reestablishing harmony. As it is applied in public it serves to dissuade other community members from committing offenses in the future and the accused from repeating. The most common sanctions among the Paéz are public whipping, forced labor in community enterprises, the indemnification of the person or family affected, and expulsion from the community. As to whipping, the anthropological expert affirmed that, while introduced in colonial times, the practice has been incorporated in Paéz culture. They liken it to lightning, which mediates between light and dark, and view it as a form of purification. Expulsion, on the other hand, is the most severe punishment, and it is only applied in cases of recidivism or when the authority of the cabildo is not accepted. Although sanctions are personal, in some cases they may be extended to the family, if it has not contributed to preventing the crime. Among the Paéz, one of the principal responsibilities of the family is to know what its members are up to.

After these explanations, the court proceeded to review the course of action taken by the Association of Cabildos. The first issue concerned the competence of the community to judge Gembuel. The question arose because in his first declaration he had stated that he belonged to the community, although he later denied that. The court opined that this reflected an opportunist attitude on the part of Gembuel, who in fact had been one of the most important leaders of the community. One cannot say one belongs to a community at one moment and then renounce at one's own convenience.

As we saw, according to the court the right to due process should be considered within each specific cultural context. In this case, the family of the victim had brought the case to the cabildo, which assumed the investigation. Contrary to Gembuel's affirmation that guerrilla responsibility had only become clear through a newspaper article, it had been assumed from the start that it had been the guerrilla who killed Betancurt. The fact that the Jambaló governor had invoked the assistance of the other cabildos of the Northern Zone was not anomalous either. In 1984 the cabildos had agreed to cooperate in cases that involved armed groups. The procedure of investigation, gathering testimonies and visiting sites, was fully regular.

Gembuel had affirmed that his defense rights had been violated since the community had rejected the presence of a lawyer, an argument that had been accepted by the first and second instance courts. The Constitutional Court decided otherwise arguing that the means to exercise the right to defense do not necessarily have to be those mentioned in national norms or international treaties. The community norms and procedures should have precedence. In Jambaló a community member with good knowledge of the language and customs would be allowed to take up the defense. The accused also could personally defend himself during the assembly. Thus the right to defense had not been violated. Moreover, after the second *tutela* verdict, the community had convoked a new assembly to hear the case, and Gembuel had freely responded to questioning on that occasion.

Finally, the court decided on the legality of the sanctions: flogging and expulsion. The whipping revealed the tension between the views of majority society and those of the Paéz, the court argued. Whereas the former punishes because a crime has been committed, the latter sanctions to reestablish the order of nature and to dissuade community members from committing crimes in the future. Whereas the former rejects corporal punishment as a violation of dignity, the latter considers it a purifying element that helps the convict to liberate himself. In the face of these divergent views, the court sustained the argument elaborated in case T-349 that in a society that pretends to be pluralist, no worldview can be simply imposed. The indigenous worldview merits maximum respect. The only restrictions are the right to life and the protection from slavery and torture. The question then is whether whipping constitutes torture.

The court revised some international norms and considered that among the Paéz the flogging is done on the lower part of the legs with a cattle whip. This sanction is considered less severe than the *cepo*. The objective is not to cause excessive suffering but to purify the individual and reestablish harmony. The physical consequences are not such that one can speak of torture. Neither is the punishment humiliating since it is not meant to expose the convict to public ridicule, but to allow the individual to return to the community. Moreover, none of the condemned had questioned the sanction.

The sanction of expulsion from the community also was condoned, although the constitution prohibits banishment. International pacts, however, define banishment as expulsion from the national territory, and this was not the case here.

The court thus concluded that the rights to defense and to due process had not been violated and that the sanctions imposed did not surpass the limits of indigenous jurisdiction. They were foreseeable and did not violate the right to life or the prohibitions on slavery and torture.

Systematizing the Doctrine, Sentence U-510

To illustrate the way in which the Constitutional Court seeks to develop a jurisprudence that in fact substitutes a coordination law I have presented two cases that allowed the court to develop some basic features of its doctrine concerning the scope and limits of the constitutionally recognized "special indigenous jurisdiction." In 1998, the court has sought to unify its jurisprudence regarding indigenous jurisdiction. On the occasion it confronted the question whether an indigenous community, in this case Arhuac, could prohibit the activities of the *Iglesia Pentecostal Unida de Colombia* in its territory. In other words, it raised the issue of the legitimacy of the restriction of religious liberty as a means to protect cultural integrity and, if legitimate, whether the measures taken by the Arhuac authorities are allowed by the constitution. A further question was whether Arhuac authorities could prohibit religious congregations to enter their territory. Here I only will outline the effort at systematization of the doctrine. In the concluding section I will develop some further comments.

The effort at systematization can be summarized[7] as follows:

1. The Colombian constitution starts from the (liberal) premise that in the course of their life individuals establish links of association and belonging to various forms of association or community. Generic citizenship is compatible with such forms of belonging. Belonging to an indigenous community, however, means being entitled to a special status. The constitution recognizes a bundle of group-differentiated rights of indigenous communities, based on the principle of self-determination. In contrast to other, contingent, forms of association individuals may engage in, belonging to an indigenous community is a matter of birth. Indigenous people therefore are entitled to two forms of original belonging: to the Colombian state and to their traditional community.

2. The court recognizes that this double condition is not exempt from tensions. In the sphere of liberties the court has sought to privilege the principle of *pro libertate* but it also has sought to maximize the autonomy of indigenous peoples according to the *pro communitas* principle, without losing sight of the limits established in the constitution.

3. The two principles should be combined harmoniously but there is no abstract formula to resolve conflicts between them so that solutions should be found for each particular case.

4. The constitutional recognition of multiculturalism should have concrete effects, which implies accepting worldviews distinct from the occidental one.

5. Indigenous communities are subjects of fundamental rights. The rights of indigenous communities should not be confounded with the collective rights of other human groups in the sense that the indigenous communities are *collective subjects* and not the sum of particular individuals who share some diffuse rights.

6. The limits to diversity are defined, in principle, in constitutional Article 1 which defines Colombia as a unitary State and by the requirement that the indigenous communities respect the "Constitution and the law."

7. The court recognizes the tension between the recognition and valorization of diverse worldviews and value systems and transcultural universal norms. In the face of this disjunctive the constitution takes an intermediate position, neither opting for extreme universalism nor for unconditional cultural relativism.

8. To achieve a balance between these sets of rights the right to cultural diversity should prevail over constitutional interests of a lower order. On the other hand, the core of fundamental rights and contextually understood due process should be respected. These rights constitute the minimal requirements for intercultural dialogue.

9. The more the traditional culture is preserved, the greater the autonomy that should be granted.[8]

The Colombian Constitutional Court thus has developed a jurisprudence that seeks to maximize the autonomy of indigenous communities and to respect their ways of doing justice without embracing an unconditional cultural relativism. It recognizes indigenous communities as subjects of rights, which are distinct from the rights of individual members. Although the doctrine is for a good part inspired by Kymlicka's (1995) liberal theory of group-differentiated rights it also raises some important questions regarding the applicability of this theory in the Andean context. Before turning to such issues we should have a brief look at the draft "coordination laws" currently under discussion in Bolivia and Ecuador.

Bolivia and Ecuador: Draft Coordination Laws

Both Bolivia and Ecuador have constitutionally recognized indigenous jurisdiction, albeit in somewhat different terms, the Ecuadorian formula being definitely more affirmative.

Bolivia: Constitution, 1994	Ecuador: Constitution, 1998
Art. 171 . . . The natural authorities of indigenous and peasant communities may exercise the functions of administration and application of their own norms as an alternative solution to conflicts, in conformity with their uses and procedures, provided that these are not contrary to this Constitution and the laws. The law shall make such functions compatible with the attributions of State authority.	Art. 191 . . . The authorities of the indigenous peoples shall exercise judicial functions [and] apply their own norms and procedures for the solution of internal conflicts in conformity with their customs or customary law, provided that these are not contrary to the Constitution and the law. The law shall make those functions compatible with the national judicial system.

A notable feature of the Bolivian formula is that it refers to the "alternative resolution of conflicts," a formula that is not found in any other Latin American constitution and that probably is inspired on the popularity of alternative conflict resolution mechanisms in the United States, and among multilateral development agencies who regard it as a sort of privatization of justice. In any case, it introduces an element of ambiguity into the recognition of an indigenous jurisdiction. Both countries employ the restriction that indigenous jurisdiction should "not be contrary to the Constitution and the law(s)" and both constitutions foresee the elaboration of a law of compatibility.

A central question in discussing such coordination laws[9] concerns the scope of indigenous jurisdiction or the different dimensions of competency involved: the competence in legal matters, personnel and territorial competencies. In other words: what may be judged, who may be judged, and what is the territorial extent of jurisdiction? In view of the "the Constitution and the law(s)" formula it furthermore is interesting to have a look at the way the limits of indigenous jurisdiction are defined and how coordination mechanisms are conceived of (Yrigoyen Fajardo 1999; 2000).

A first thing to note is that both draft laws are brief and rather concise, though the articles of the Ecuadorian draft are more elaborate and specify some important issues. As to the object of recognition, both proposals refer to the authorities of the indigenous peoples and recognize them as public servants. The Ecuadorian proposal contains stricter norms of registration of these authorities and an article on usurpation of functions. Both proposals recognize customary law.

The competency regarding legal matters is defined differently in the two cases, the Bolivian case being more restrictive in stipulating that indigenous authorities may judge any matter "regulated by their own norms." The Ecuadorian proposal expressly refers to innovations in response to new needs and requirements. The issue is not without importance since indigenous systems often lack "administrative law" (Perafán Simmonds 1995), which is considered of prime importance for public administration.

Both proposals include the mandatory character of indigenous jurisdiction and thus make sure that it is not merely subsidiary. In the Bolivian case this may well require a modification of the constitution, which refers to "alternative" resolution of conflicts.[10] However, whereas the Bolivian proposal exempts nonindigenous persons living within the indigenous territories, the Ecuadorean proposal expressly includes them and contains a series of stipulations for handling such cases. The point is important since exemption of nonindigenous residents may drastically undermine governability of the community or the territory (Hoekema 2000: 824). The Ecuadorean proposal is more congruent in relating territorial and personal competency. It furthermore contains a procedure to resolve cases in which a person denies belonging to an indigenous community, which as we saw in the Colombian cases, is not an unimportant issue. The Ecuadorian draft proposes that such cases should be resolved by the *Defensoría del Pueblo*. Finally, the Ecuadorian draft contains some noteworthy stipulations regarding conflicts that occur "outside the collectivity" and seeks to guarantee "due process" in these cases. Clearly, the question of "due process" is not merely an issue to worry about where indigenous justice is concerned but also, and perhaps even more so, when indigenous people face the "ordinary" justice system.

The Ecuadorian proposal also is more specific about how to resolve conflicts between different indigenous collectivities or between indigenous persons belonging to different collectivities. In both cases, however, the principle is that the conflict should be resolved by indigenous organizations, unless they decide otherwise.

A further interesting feature of the Ecuadorean draft is its stipulations regarding the relations between indigenous authorities and the ordinary judicial, police and administrative system, which it obliges to cooperate with the indigenous authorities and to follow their instructions.

Finally, what about the "Constitution and the law(s)"? The Bolivian draft suggests that indigenous justice should respect "what is established in the Political Constitution of the State and the international human rights treaties ratified by the Bolivian State." The formula is less restrictive than the constitutional stipulation and potentially permits to leave aside the laws of the Republic. An ambiguity remains, however, in the reference to the constitution, since this same constitution contains the problematic formula. This probably requires amending the constitution on this point. The Ecuadorean draft contains a somewhat similar formula in referring to the constitution and the international instruments in vigor in the country while stipulating that the dignity of the person should be respected and that to do so the facts and the law should be given an intercultural interpretation.[11]

Both proposals foresee a role for the Constitutional Court as an instance of appeal. The Ecuadorian draft, however, is interesting in that it provides for the presence of judges (*conjueces*) selected by national-level indigenous organizations. In this way it goes a step toward a mixed composition of the court when it rules in cases of conflicts between the indigenous jurisdiction and the rights guaranteed by the constitution and international norms. This would be one more important step toward an equitable recognition of indigenous jurisdiction and normativity (Hoekema 1998).

By Way of Conclusion

In this essay I have reviewed some of the efforts made in three Andean countries to construct a new and more equitable multiethnic order. The proposals reviewed and the jurisprudence of the Colombian Constitutional Court suggest that the recognition of indigenous jurisdiction involves much more than allowing them to resolve cases of chicken theft. If the proposals reviewed provide anything to go by they imply a significant restructuring of state powers and an important empowerment of indigenous authorities, both in relation to the state and to the members of their communities. The process throws up a series of dilemmas for the national judiciary as well as for the indigenous peoples. Here I will first address some theoretical issues and then turn the attention to the ongoing debates among indigenous people(s) and with society "at large."

One of the major sources of inspiration in the present debate is Kymlicka's (1995) work in which he seeks to develop a liberal theory of group differentiated rights. A basic feature of his theorizing is the distinction between "external protections" and "internal restrictions." External protections involve inter-group relations and are intended to protect a minority from the impact of external decisions of the larger society. Kymlicka mentions special group representation rights, self-government rights, and polyethnic rights, which protect specific religious and cultural practices. Internal restrictions, by contrast, involve the claim of a group against its own members and are intended to protect the group from internal dissent. They curtail the civil and political liberties of group members. According to Kymlicka external protections can be justified from a liberal point of view, but internal restrictions cannot. His view "requires *freedom within* the minority group, and *equality between* the minority and the majority groups." There is one exception. Under extreme circumstances internal restrictions may be justified on a temporary basis, where they are required to protect the society from literal disintegration (Kymlicka 1995: 152n).

In the foregoing I briefly referred to the case of the Arhuac and the Pentecostal Church, which provided the occasion for the Colombian Constitutional Court to unify its doctrine. The court ruled that the expulsion of the Pentecostal Church and sanctioning of its adherents, prohibiting collective rites and discriminating in the distribution of goods and resources, was justified since its activities threatened the core values of the Arhuac theocentric culture. In this particular case the replacement of Arhuac religion did not mean that only a segment of their culture is affected, but the totality, including its political and family structure.

The crucial issue here is that the court ruling is based on the argument that Arhuac cultural survival was at stake. The ruling thus is assimilated to what Kymlicka (1995) would consider exceptional circumstances that temporarily justify internal restrictions (Bonilla 1999). In other words, if the court had found that cultural survival was not at stake, would it have decided otherwise? The decision sits uneasily with the recognition of equal dignity of all cultures and the idea that indigenous communities are collective subjects, more than the sum of their members. After all, Kymlicka requires freedom, understood in classical liberal and individualist terms, within the minority group. Bonilla (1999: 84) argues that the courts' doctrine "implies the affirmation that the constitution does not recognize all cultures existing in our country, but only the equality and dignity of *liberal* cultures."[12] Kymlicka's approach implies that the recognition of cultures is conditioned on a substantial modification their internal norms and practices, which would in fact undermine their self-governing capacities (Assies, van der Haar, and Hoekema 2000b: 303–304). To put it otherwise, although he refers to self-government rights Kymlicka only would accept forms of "indirect consociation" that ensure that an ethnic collectivity forms a majority within a particular political jurisdiction while upholding the philosophy of "universalism." "Direct consociation," by contrast, involves the explicit recognition of distinct political and legal customs (cf. Assies 1994: 45–46). Kymlicka thus provides an uneasy guideline to confront Latin American realities but at the same time raises important questions for the indigenous peoples, among others.

I started this essay with the image of some thirty young Indians coming together to discuss traditional ways of doing justice on which they had interviewed the elderly. It is only one instance of a vivid debate that has taken new force with the recognition of indigenous jurisdiction in Latin America. The quest for the roots is complex and multifaceted. We have seen that one of the rules developed by the Colombian Court is that autonomy should be granted in function of the preservation of traditional culture and in passing I noted that this is a quite slippery requirement, which moreover, is difficult to apply. One effect of the requirement can be that ways of justice that have fallen into disuse are resurrected. Reportedly, the Inga of the lower Putumayo in Colombia reintroduced the *cepo* to prove their traditionality (Sánchez Botero and Jaramillo Sierra 2000: 65). On the other hand, take the search for roots in a recent Bolivian publication on Aymara justice, self-proclaimed as "one more means of anti-colonial struggle." It describes harsh punishments, seems to condone the "popular" view that human rights only serve to protect criminals, and suggests that human rights only serve as a pretext for state paternalism and interference (Fernández 2000; Clavero 2001).

Human rights nonetheless are an important reference for the indigenous people's movements, also in their debates over Indian justice. The "case of the whip" generated ample public reaction, and Amnesty International accused the Jambaló cabildo of condoning torture, triggering debate among the indigenous movement itself. At the same time, the case caused concern over state interference in what indigenous activists considered an internal affair. One reaction has been that indigenous organizations have sought to strengthen their own justice system, including the concern for human rights, and to devise mechanisms to review controversial cases without resort to nonindigenous courts. At the same time, the Constitutional Court jurisprudence has effects within the indigenous jurisdiction. In 1999 a homicide occurred in the vereda El Tablón of the Jambaló resguardo. The victim was accused of witchcraft. The Jambaló cabildo investigated the case and decided to sanction those responsible with five minutes in the *cepo* and forty-eight whiplashes. Doing so, it overruled the decision of the local cabildo to sanction them with only five lashes. In its resolution the cabildo stated that "[It] is unacceptable that a community condones homicide on the single argument that the victim was a witch, since this violates the Right to Life and Human Rights." At the same time the cabildo affirms its jurisdictional faculties invoking not only the constitution and Law 89 of 1890, but also Constitutional Court Verdict T-523.[13]

Thus the recognition of indigenous jurisdiction may well imply that indigenous authorities are held increasingly accountable for their actions, both by outsiders and inside their jurisdictions. Often emphasized features of indigenous justice systems are that they are predominantly oral, flexible, and integral (somewhat like "total social facts"), that decisions are taken collectively and in a participatory manner, and that they are swiftly applied. Moreover, it is often asserted that, rather than punishing, indigenous justice seeks compensation and reconciliation and the reestablishment of harmony. Such assertions do not have to be taken at face value, and the features mentioned should be understood in the proper context of indigenous justice systems (Assies 2000). The interesting point is the emergence of a discourse on Indian justice, which is shared by indigenous activists throughout Latin America. It should be understood as a counterhegemonic discourse elaborated in an ongoing confrontation and critical dialogue with other social actors in the context of the by now celebrated "pursuit of alternative modernities."

Notes

In 2003, this chapter was published as "Indian Justice in the Andes: Re-rooting or Re-routing?" in *Imaging the Andes: Shifting Margins of a Marginal World*, ed. T. Salman and A. Zoomers, Amsterdam: Aksant. We thank CEDLA and Aksant for their permission to republish.

1. This phrase would eventually be held against him since during his time in office he never spoke out against the neoliberal policies of the Sánchez de Lozada administration (1993–1997), which fell rather hard upon his brethren.
2. Convention 169 states that "[T]o the extent compatible with the national legal system and internationally recognized human rights, the methods customarily practiced by the peoples concerned for dealing with offenses committed by their members shall be respected" (art. 9.1).
3. In 1991, the national indigenous organization presented a proposal, which was not approved. It included the idea of elaborating an indigenous penal law, a proposal that was considered restrictive by specialists who pointed out that the constitution did not require formalization of indigenous law and procedures. A year later, the Ministry of Justice elaborated a draft that was harshly criticized for defining too many things and basically following the occidental legal tradition. The proposal was withdrawn (Perafán Simmonds 1995: 19–20).

4. The *acción de tutela* is a simple procedure introduced by the 1991 Colombian constitution. It allows any person to denounce a violation of his or her constitutional rights and stipulates that a verdict should be given by the judge or the court where the complaint was filed, within ten days.

5. These accusations were made in a context of factional struggle. Gembuel and Betancur belonged to different factions of the regional indigenous organization CRIC and had participated in the 1994 municipal elections. Betancur had won the election, but contrary to custom had not included the losing slate in a secondary position when distributing municipal *cargos* (Van Cott 2000: 114–116).

6. "Concepto Antropológico, Esther Sánchez Botero, Agosto de 1997." Reproduced in Sánchez Botero (1998: 331–339).

7. For a somewhat different summary see Bonilla (1999: 72–73).

8. This is a quite slippery and hardly applicable requirement. Exemption from military service, for example, was made conditional on residence in the indigenous territory and preservation of their "cultural, social and economic integrity," which in fact discriminates against Indians who study outside the territory (Sánchez Botero and Jaramillo Sierra 2000: 55).

9. The Bolivian project counted with World Bank funding, whereas the Inter-American Development Bank contributed to the Ecuadorian project. The projects are embedded in a much more comprehensive drive to overhaul the judiciaries and their final destiny will depend much on the support by indigenous peoples' organizations.

10. Ramiro Molina R., director of the communitary justice project, personal communication, March 2000.

11. An earlier draft referred to "moderate relativism" (see Trujillo, Grijalva, and Endara 2001: 35), but the notion was dropped since "people did not understand it" (Ximena Endara, personal communication, April 2001).

12. Although Kymlicka condemns the injustice of internal restrictions, he would not condone coercive imposition of liberal norms. For a discussion of the issue see James (1999).

13. Cabildo Indígena Resguardo Jambaló Cauca Colombia, Resolución Nro. 3, March 6, 1999 (copy provided by Esther Sánchez Botero). Since some of the *vereda* population commented its intervention the Jambaló cabildo also sanctioned the community by suspending various ongoing projects.

References

Assies, Willem. 1994. "Self-Determination and the 'New Partnership,' the Politics of Indigenous Peoples and States." In *Indigenous Peoples' Experiences with Self-Government*, ed. W. Assies and A. J. Hoekema. Amsterdam and Copenhagen: University of Amsterdam, IWGIA.

———. 2000. "La oficialización de lo no-oficial: ¿Re-encuentro de dos mundos?" Text presented at the post-congress Identidad, autonomía y derechos indígenas: Desafíos en el Tercer Milenio, March 18–22, Arica, Chile.

Assies, Willem, Gemma van der Haar, and André J. Hoekema, eds. 2000a. *The Challenge of Diversity: Indigenous Peoples and Reform of the State in Latin America*. Amsterdam: Thela Thesis.

———. 2000b. "Diversity as a Challenge: A Note on the Dilemmas of Diversity." In *The Challenge of Diversity: Indigenous Peoples and Reform of the State in Latin America*, ed. W. Assies, G. van der Haar, and A. J. Hoekema. Amsterdam: Thela Thesis.

Bonilla, Daniel. 1999. *La ciudadanía multicultural y la política del reconocimiento*. Santa Fe de Bogotá: Ediciones UNIANDES, Facultad de Derecho.

Bronstein, Arturo. S. 1999. "Hacia el reconocimiento de la identidad y de los derechos de los pueblos indígenas en América Latina: Síntesis de una evolución y temas para reflexión." In *Memoria del segundo seminario internacional sobre administración de justicia y pueblos indígenas.* San José: IIDH.

Clavero, Bartolomé. 2001. "La ley del Ayllu (Book Review)." *T'inkazos* 8: 167–173.

Fernández, O. Marcelo. 2000. *La ley del Ayllu; Práctica de jach'a justicia y jisk'a justicia (Justicia Mayor y Justicia Menor) en comunidades aymaras.* La Paz: PIEB.

Hoekema, André. J. 1998. "Hacia un pluralismo jurídico formal de tipo igualitario." *América Indígena* 58, no. 1–2: 261–300.

———. 2000. "La sociedad mayor frente a la justicia de pueblos indígenas." In *Congreso Internacional Derecho Consuetudinario y Pluralismo Legal: Desafíos en el Tercer Milenio,* ed. C. Lucic. Santiago: University of Chile, University of Tarapacá.

James, Michael Rabinder. 1999. "Tribal Sovereignty and the Intercultural Public Sphere." *Philosophy and Social Criticism* 25, no. 5: 57–86.

Kymlicka, Will. 1995. *Multicultural Citizenship.* Oxford, U.K.: Oxford University Press.

Perafán Simmonds, Carlos Cesar., et al. 1996. *Sistemas jurídicos tukano, chami, guambiano y sikuani.* Bogotá: COLCIENCIAS, ICAN.

Perafán Simmonds, Carlos Cesar. 1995. *Sistemas jurídicos paez, kogi, wayúu y tule.* Bogotá: Instituto Colombiano de Antropología-COLCULTURA.

Sánchez Botero, Esther. 1998. *Justicia y pueblos indígenas de Colombia.* Bogotá: National University of Colombia, UNIJUS.

———. 2000. "The *Tutela*-System as a Means of Transforming Relations between the State and the Indigenous Peoples of Colombia." In *The Challenge of Diversity: Indigenous Peoples and Reform of the State in Latin America,* ed. W. Assies, G. van der Haar, and A. J. Hoekema. Amsterdam: Thela Thesis.

Sánchez Botero, Esther., and Isabel Christina. Jaramillo Sierra. 2000. *La Jurisdicción Especial Indígena.* Bogotá: Procuraduría General de la Nación.

Trujillo Vásquez, Julio César, Ximena Endara Osejo and Agustín Grijalva. 2001. *Justicia indígena en el Ecuador.* Quito: Universidad, Andina Simón Bolívar.

Vadillo, Alcides. 1997. "Constitución política del estado y pueblos indígenas: Bolivia, país de mayoría indígena." In *Derecho indígena,* coord. M. Gómez. Mexico: INI, AMNU.

Van Cott, Donna Lee. 2000. *The Friendly Liquidation of the Past: The Politics of Diversity in Latin America.* Pittsburgh: University of Pittsburgh Press.

Yrigoyen Fajardo, Raquel. 1999. *Pautas de coordinación entre el derecho indígena y el derecho estatal.* Guatemala: Fundación Myrna Mack.

———. 2000. "The Constitutional Recognition of Indigenous Law in Andean Countries." In *The Challenge of Diversity: Indigenous Peoples and Reform of the State in Latin America,* ed. W. Assies, G. van der Haar, and A. J. Hoekema. Amsterdam: Thela Thesis.

Part IV
Ethnicity and Citizenship

Introduction

Salvador Martí i Puig

I met Willem Assies in Barcelona in May 2004 when he participated in a seminar that I was coordinating: "Indigenous Peoples in Latin America: The Current Situation and Their Challenges." However, as often happens in these cases, I had already been familiar with his work for some time.

The first time I read one of his texts was in the 1990s, when I was carrying out research on the Sandinistas' agrarian reform and the peasant *contra*. At the time, Willem Assies was involved in the agrarian debates that set those supporting the peasants against those who supported the pro-development industrialists, and he was always in favor of the former. I found his arguments interesting due to his heterodox perspective, his rejection of any type of dogmatism, and the importance he attached to real life peasants above any other consideration. Assies' texts on the worlds of peasants turned out to have enormous usability when interpreting the processes of "modernization from above" and processes of mobilization of workers in the rural area. The differences signaled by Assies in interests, habits, and networks between day-workers, small, medium, and large landowners, and their relation with bureaucrats and political authorities out turned out to be crucial when interpreting realities that had often remained concealed because of the noise produced by ideological debates.

Apart, however, from his work on peasant issues, some years later, when I became interested in researching the emergence of indigenous peoples in Latin America I yet again came across Assies's work. However, this time his studies not only took part in the debates, but in fact were obligatory reading material for researchers interested in the topic.

His works on the participation of indigenous peoples in Latin American politics, on their claim to land and territory, on constitutional multiculturalism, and the lack of willingness on the part of governments to respond to indigenous demands were already a reference point. However, these studies had something in common with his previous work: they rejected any type of dogmatism and emphasized the interests of the real life indigenous communities over any other consideration. Furthermore, his studies on indigenous peoples reflect a concrete, pragmatic, and firsthand knowledge of the reality of the communities involved. Precisely for that reason, the indigenous peoples in his studies belong to a specific and unique sociocultural context but who also have needs, interests, contradictions, and dilemmas.

This way of approaching indigenous reality was in keeping with his personality and way of working, since his studies always tried to understand "the underdogs" and their ways of life. With this aim Assies aimed to explain and relate the desire and tenacity of the subordinated to resist arbitrary power (and the powerful). For that reason, during his long stay in Michoacán (Mexico), it was natural and logical that Assies should become interested in indigenous peoples, just as he has become interested in *favela* inhabitants who fought for better living conditions in Brazil or in peasants who demanded land in Peru.

Consequently, in contrast to other academics, Assies did not penetrate the indigenous world attracted by the wave of interest during the "International Decade of Indigenous Peoples" in the 1990s. Precisely for that reason his perspective was original, critical, and bold. Assies always treated with some caution the grand, official declarations of international organizations, the manifestoes written in conferences, the legal innovations and governmental promises about indigenous autonomy. This does not mean that he felt that the struggles of indigenous peoples had been in vain, but he always analyzed them with caution showing at times a contradictory spirit, as can be seen in the texts that are edited in this section.

The two texts that are included in this section are representative of this critical perspective and the impressive data, the quality of information and analytic capacity of Assies. The text "The Limits of State Reform and Multiculturalism in Latin America," which was published five years later, is representative (and to a certain extent conclusive) of his studies on the impact of indigenous demands in Latin American systems. This essay reflects his critical vision of the processes of multicultural reform of Latin American states. This vision is based on a detailed analysis of the meaning of multicultural reforms in the region and the degree to which they can be applied (with special emphasis on Bolivia, Colombia, and Mexico). As a result, he argues that the expectations of a new multiculturalism (which was so highly celebrated at the start of the 1990s) had pretty much vanished as of 2010.

The second text, "Two Steps Forward, One Step Back: Indigenous Peoples and Autonomies in Latin America," which was published in 2005, is an essay that analyses with some detail two interrelated issues. The first is the "multicultural" transformation of the majority of Latin American constitutions, as a result of the ILO's Convention No. 169/80 and the mobilizations of the region's indigenous movements, and the second issue is that of the autonomous territories that are enshrined in the constitutions and legal texts of Nicaragua, Colombia, and Ecuador. The great contribution of this text is the valuable information it offers to the panorama in Latin America more generally and the three cases more specifically, as well as the critical perspective with which it interprets not only the new legality but also its lack of effectiveness when responding to the interests and concrete demands of indigenous peoples beyond legal changes.

Consequently, Willem Assies puts two issues on the table at an early stage: the implementation gap and the dangers (and false expectations) brought about by "neoliberal multiculturalism." With the concept of "neoliberal multiculturalism" Willem Assies does not aim to highlight that the conquests of Latin America's indigenous peoples are a fiction or a tall story. Rather, he wants to warn us that we cannot and should not take the "official discourse" as fact, since real and profound changes are not the result of declarations, fashions, or juridical changes, but rather of new correlations of forces that in turn are a result of new alliances, sensibilities, and tensions. However, Assies does not present this argument in an aggressive or dogmatic manner, nor does he aim to make his ideas a battle cry. Rather, he simply offers his opinion to whoever might be willing to listen.

Apart from these views on the nature of Assies's contributions, they have also proved most helpful in interpreting the realities of indigenous communities today. This is important because after a decade in which many scholars and activists advocated the indigenous cause, voices criticizing the indigenous have emerged. Moreover, indigenous struggles now seem to have become fragmented, and their demands seem to have lost visibility and allies—even if they have remained protagonists in determined efforts to defend their cultures, resources, habitat, and interests.

These interests, as Assies observed, do not always coincide with what is considered politically correct or compatible with imagined quests for "modernity." In all likelihood, either they do not always coincide with the views held by scholars who believe themselves to be fellow travelers, or they are simply not very explicit nor public. In the past, secrecy was often been a key social instrument for vulnerable groups. Perhaps it is for that reason that some indigenous groups have moved from public manifestation to silent resistance. Understanding and analyzing changes in the dynamics of indigenous struggles will not be an easy task, but Assies's sharp and lucid insights can and will provide inputs to explore new tendencies and the ongoing developments in the indigenous longings and dreams.

<table><tr><td>7</td><td>

The Limits of State Reform and Multiculturalism in Latin America

Contemporary Illustrations
</td></tr></table>

Three Decades of Indigenous Struggle

In early 2000, the city of Cochabamba, Bolivia, was the scene of a pitched battle known as the Water War. *Aguas del Tunari* Company, a Bolivian corporation linked to the multi-national consortium Bechtel, won water development and distribution rights in Cochabamba through a shady process, and then boosted city water rates supposedly to help finance improved services. The protest that followed was not just an urban consumer revolt or an isolated event. Irrigators in the region who saw their rights to water threatened were also involved and the Water War ultimately resulted in a substantial amendment to the Drinking Water and Sanitary Sewerage Law, which had been enacted a few months before. Multi-lateral agencies had promoted the law to privatize water supply in large cities and turn water into a commodity. The opposition considered water to be a fundamental right and a public good. The Cochabamba Water War was the most heated example of the Bolivian people's broad-based opposition to the neoliberal model, and was considered the first victory after a decade and a half of defeats (Assies 2001).

This confrontation marked the start of a cycle of protests about management of the country's resources under the neoliberal model which was imposed beginning in 1985. These protests eventually led to the flight of President Gonzalo Sánchez de Lozada[1] and the resignation of President Carlos Mesa in June 2005. In January 2005, the people of the city of El Alto had forced the Carlos Mesa government to rescind a contract with *Aguas de Illimani* (a company that is part of Suez Lyonnais des Eauxs de France) for its resistance to extending service to the poorer parts of that city.

Conflicts over water and other natural resources were the focus of popular and indigenous movements in Bolivia and other Latin American countries. The new political context inaugurated by the government of President Evo Morales (January 2006) created an historic opportunity to transform protest into state policy and design a new regulatory framework for natural resource management. With the support of rural, indigenous and grassroots organizations for its working agenda, including promotion of indigenous and peasant "uses and customs" regulating water management, Bolivia's new government now faces a huge political, ideological, and legal challenge to reconfigure water norms and management.

For the last few decades, indigenous movements have become major societal and political stakeholders in the Latin American arena. What has been called "indigenous emergence" began in the late 1960s and expanded throughout the following decade (Bengoa 2000). The relationship between ethnicity and class was revisited, and ethnic identity was revalued. The Shuar Federation in Ecuador, the Katarist movement in Bolivia and the Indigenous Regional Council of Cauca Valley (CRIC) in Colombia, are a few of the movements considered to have led the way. These movements shared two key characteristics: they rejected concepts of political identity derived exclusively from economic class and they emphasized the importance of ethnicity in defining political identity. The first CRIC training workbook in 1973 entitled *Our Struggles, Yesterday and Today*, taught that "we are peasants" and "we are Indians." Similarly, the Shuar Federation stressed, "we cannot agree with the conclusions of people who view Indians just as miners, peasants, or exploited laborers, as the case may be. A Shuar and a non-native tenant are not the same (even if the latter is exploited along with the Shuar), nor is a Shuar chauffeur the same as a *cholo* chauffeur (although both have the same job)." In Bolivia, the Tiawanacu Manifesto stated "We feel economically exploited and culturally and politically oppressed" (cf. Bonfil Batalla 1981: 216–223, 279–296, 321–324).

The 1970s and 1980s witnessed the emergence of indigenous movements in Latin America that often built local networks before attempting to organize on the national level. A major landmark was the revision of the 1957 Convention 107 of the International Labor Organization (ILO) in 1989. The revision, now embodied in Convention 169, rejected the assimilationist orientation of the previous version and despite multiple constraints, proposed rights geared toward indigenous autonomy within nation-states. Convention 169 has been ratified by a dozen Latin American countries, which have thereby made the commitment to reconcile their national legislation with the Convention's premises. Similarly, beginning in the mid-1980s, the same number of countries in the region amended their constitutions to recognize the multi-ethnic, pluri-cultural composition of their populations, formally departing from the homogenizing concept of the melting-pot nation-state. Indigenous movements picked up momentum when the United Nations declared the year and decade of Indigenous Peoples in 1993 and 1994, respectively. Commemoration of the five hundredth anniversary of the Spanish invasion also gave rise to international gatherings of indigenous movements.

In the closing decades of the twentieth century emergent indigenous movements practiced "identity politics" and the Latin American states responded with "recognition policies." Dialectic between identity politics and recognition policies encouraged expectations and raised hopes about a "friendly liquidation of the past" (Van Cott 2000). This process took place under the "dual transition": toward civil governments and toward a new development model and was promoted through structural adjustment policies inspired by neoliberalism. This dynamic then spread and deepened under globalization as *market democracies* emerged: the rise of formal, electoral democracy alongside market liberalization.

After several decades of multi-cultural policies, there are new questions and issues about the future course of indigenous movements and the scope of Latin American recognition policies. Constitutional amendments and ratifications of Convention 169 suggested a new direction in relationships between indigenous peoples and states, including recognition of territorial rights, indigenous jurisdiction within indigenous territories and a degree of political autonomy. These calls for recognition of peoples' identities and for greater political and regulatory autonomy are related to the struggle for fairer distribution of resources and means of production and also deeply entwine with the issues of water control, water rights formulation, and water policy implementation.

Evaluating the New Multi-Culturalism

Initial optimism about new "pluri-multi-coexistence" appears to be fading. Stavenhagen has argued that for indigenous movements the "going will be rough from now on" because "redress for historical grievances—which is what originally started the movement—is a limited objective in the long run. . . . It has now become clearer that what began as demands for specific rights and compensatory measures has turned into a new view of the nation and the state" (Stavenhagen 2002: 34, 41; cf. Iturralde 1997).

Some authors have suggested that recognition policies in an era of globalization should be understood in the context of large-scale transformations of states, leaving behind the 19th century model of nation-states and the mode of territoriality that they entail.[2] The "homogeneous" state is transformed as overlapping local, national and global jurisdictions emerge with different loyalties, creating a new legal and political pluralism. Potentially, or perhaps ideally, such "dis-aggregation" of the state could accommodate indigenous demands for autonomy; however, these demands face accusations of "Balkanizing" the country. Yet this argument denies actual indigenous claims and reality. Moreover, if the concern were the integrity of the country, it would also seem to militate against those policies and politicians who bargain away resources to transnational corporations with special jurisdiction arrangements over their "concession areas" under free trade agreements (e.g. international arbitration, application of metropolitan norms for dispute-resolution, and keeping litigation out of national courts).

The shift toward multi-cultural policies not only occurred in the context of democratic transitions but also in the shift from the national-development model toward the neo-liberal development model. Neoliberalism extends beyond economics to culture, involving a redefinition of "citizenship." A neo-liberal criticism of nation-state development is that it produces "dependent" citizens expecting the state to solve all their problems. Neoliberalism argues that states should stop being "paternalistic" toward the citizenry and give them back responsibility for their own well-being.

Following on my reflections on the "cultural project" of neoliberalism (Assies 2000), Hale (2002) has proposed a theoretical framework that could be used to evaluate the scope of recognition policies within the neoliberal framework. In order to distinguish between managed multiculturalism and transformative multiculturalism, he asks to what degree "neoliberal multiculturalism" truly involves redistribution of power and resources to indigenous people. Managed multiculturalism celebrates cultural plurality but without concrete, lasting effects for the members of the oppressed cultural group. By contrast, transformative multiculturalism truly redistributes power and resources. One model is "top-down" and the other is "bottom-up"; the former reinforces limited, essentialist expressions of group identities whereas the latter would build on key elements from progressive identity politics such as "heterogeneity" and "hybridity" as well as redistribution of resources and means of production to groups affirming their identity.

Building on Foucault's reflections on governance and the "production of subjects," Hale (2002) proposes to evaluate the consciousness of those struggling for cultural rights. Classical liberalism, which sought to "liberate" individuals from community and corporate bonds, may be distinguished from present-day neoliberalism, which paradoxically applauds non-governmental entities such as community, civic and volunteer organizations, and churches that "rescue" the individual. The neoliberal state expects its citizen-subjects to resolve their own problems, whether daily or epochal. As individuals or members of volunteer associations, they have to assume their "responsibilities" and this makes them vulnerable to "top-down" policies seeking to tap, circumscribe and shape this "participation." Professionalized NGOs would be the vehicles *par excellence* to achieve this new governance. Therefore, the neoliberal state does not simply "recognize" the community, civil society, or indigenous culture, but reconstructs them after its own image, making distinctions, for example, between "good" and "bad" Indians. A "good Indian" presents "cultural" demands compatible with the neoliberal project and thus may become what Hale (2004) has called the "Indio Permitido," whereas the "bad Indian" is the "radical" calling for power and resource redistribution.

Although the neoliberal project speaks of decentralization and respect for multiculturalism, the latter is allowed so long as it does not get in the former's way. Respect for certain cultural traits like old-fashioned valuing of "folk" culture is no problem, but if the idea is to manage resources differently than market logic it is another matter. The struggles over water control and water policies constitute a powerful example. Decentralization and transferring management of water use systems to the users in the neoliberal mode usually do not involve the transfer of autonomy of rule-making regarding water control and water rights to these users according to their own practices, demands and traditions. The paradox of this kind of decentralization is that it allows natural resource management only when it fits centralized guidelines that are promulgated without consulting affected local stakeholders.

Hale also argues that in Latin America, the neoliberal movement faces autonomous, volatile and variable civil-society organizations that allow for creation of transformative projects. He further argues against the choice between frontal rejection and total acceptance of the neoliberal project. According to Hale, there are not many alternatives to accepting the existence of "neoliberal multiculturalism." Although there may be room to maneuver because of the volatility and variability of civil-society organizations in Latin America, the possibilities and potential for struggles "from within" should not be over-estimated. It all depends on a well-articulated strategy to achieve transformative multiculturalism that will transcend neoliberal multiculturalism and its mechanisms for resource and power allocation. Such a strategy also involves the relationship between indigenous "cultural" demands (including "radical" demands to redistribute resources and power) and "popular movements."

This gives us some background to discuss the achievements and limitations of the new indigenous movements and new recognition policies in terms of affirming legal pluralism and autonomy, or territorial self-management, by indigenous peoples. This will also help to analyze structural tensions that governments such as President Evo Morales's administration experience when pursuing multiculturalism. This analysis applies not only to the government but also to relations among the Bolivian indigenous movement and the international cooperation agencies and multilateral entities that all work with different definitions of "good (or allowed) Indians" and "bad Indians."

Multicultural Policies in Latin America

Although the figures are disputed, the number of indigenous peoples in Latin America is estimated at 34–40 million, i.e., about 8–10 percent of the total population (Psacharopoulos and Patrinos 1994). The figures gloss over a great diversity of situations, from sedentary farmers with variable historical relations to the state and market in the Andean and Meso-American region, to relatively isolated hunter-gatherer peoples some of whom are isolated in the Amazon region and other "peripheral" areas. Indigenous people can remain "invisible" until their renewable or non-renewable resources are discovered and they are incorporated into the national arena for economic or geopolitical reasons.

In the 1960s and 1970s large-scale land reforms aimed to give "land without people to people without land," but failed to realize any genuine redistribution of land from hacienda owners to indigenous and peasant populations. In many cases, limited redistribution was attempted in order to help "modernize" large landholdings (the "Junker way") while seeking to redirect redistribution (the "peasant way") toward colonizing "land without people." Renewable resources were discovered (forests and water, mostly), as well as non-renewable resources (oil, gas, minerals, etc.). These geo-political processes provoked objections to disposal of resources, and gave rise to differing notions of "territory" in indigenous movement discourse.

Although Amazon peoples occupy land differently from Andean peoples, their notion of "territory" was soon also adopted by Andean peoples. Territory is currently a major theme in indigenous movement discourse, involving space and resources as well as jurisdiction and political authority as foundations for autonomy. The territorial claim is also supported by International Labor Organization Convention 169, which states in Article 13–2 that use of the term "land" must include the concept of territories. And the UN Declaration on the Rights of Indigenous Peoples which was finally adopted by the General Assembly in September 2007 recognizes indigenous peoples' right to self-determination and autonomy or self-government and contains important stipulations regarding territories and natural resources. Shortly thereafter Bolivia adopted this declaration as national law.

Bolivia: Community Land of Origin and People's Participation

The 1952 revolution in Bolivia triggered agrarian reform. A 1953 Agrarian Law introduced the concept of the land's "social function." In the Andean west and the central valley region, this process led to land redistribution. In the tropical Oriente, by contrast, agrarian policies adopted by revolutionary and post-revolutionary governments consolidated and modernized the large plantations and cattle ranches. In the Santa Cruz region, an agro-industrial complex arose, initially grounded in production of rice, sugar cane and cotton, expanding into soybeans by the late 1960s. In Santa Cruz and in other Oriente regions cattle-raising played a major role and woodlands were pursued by logging companies.

Beginning in the 1980s, the indigenous peoples of the Oriente, constituting some thirty groups and nearly two hundred thousand people, organized and created the Confederation of Indigenous Peoples of the Bolivian Oriente (CIDOB) in 1982. In 1990 the indigenous peoples of the Beni region held a March for Territory and Dignity as a protest against logging activities in their territories. This highly publicized march reminded the country that there were indigenous peoples in their lowlands. President Jaime Paz-Zamora went personally to meet with the indigenous protestors but was unable to persuade them not to continue to La Paz. By late September, Paz-Zamora had signed the first four Supreme Decrees recognizing indigenous territories, later followed by another four.

After the 1952 Revolution two agrarian reform institutions (the National Agrarian Reform Council (CNRA) and the National Colonization Institute) had distributed land and granted land titles, sometimes issuing several overlapping titles for the same land. Moreover, they also turned over huge pieces of land under questionable circumstances during the *de facto* government of Hugo Banzer (1971–1978) and the following military regimes. This led to new agrarian legislation being considered in 1994 under the government of Sánchez de Lozada (1993–1997) as well as a counter-proposal by indigenous peasant organizations. Negotiations among the parties achieved a consensus that was then repeatedly ignored by the government. This led indigenous and peasant organizations to mobilize and press for enactment of the proposed Law of the National Agrarian Reform Service (SNRA), immediate recognition of indigenous territories and other demands. The government's offer to recognize territories in the lowlands, however, fractured the movement. Moreover, business organizations, supported by the Civil Committee of Santa Cruz, pressured for amendments that would favor their interests.

Finally, in August 1996 the SNRA Law was enacted which conceded to several indigenous demands. The government and the World Bank had initially foreseen opening up the land market, but the new law maintained the distinction between land's social function and its economic-social function, resulting in some lands being unmarketable. The former category includes two forms of collective property: community lands of origin (TCO) and community lands, in addition to individual peasant housing plots and small properties. These types of socially important property are non-transferable or only transferable under certain conditions. It was also established that certain territories already recognized by a Supreme Decree should be granted title under the TCO mode; another sixteen demands were covered, while opening up the possibility for new demands to be presented.

Interestingly, the TCOs provide to "indigenous and original communities and peoples collective ownership of their land, granting them the right to share in the use and sustainable utilization of renewable resources present there."Under the law, distribution and redistribution for use within TCOs "shall be governed by community rules, according to their norms and customs" (SNRA Law, Article 3-III). However, use of non-renewable resources in TCOs is governed by the Constitution and special norms regulating them. This has made it possible for mining and petroleum concessions to overlap TCOs resulting in land and water pollution and use of resources according to a market approach that fails to consider the cultural interests of people living in TCOs.

Another issue is that TCOs are not jurisdictional or political entities but rather fall under the jurisdiction of municipalities or provinces. However, the amended 1995 Bolivian Constitution, while recognizing the multi-ethnic, pluri-cultural nature of the country in Article 1 stated in Article 171 that: "Natural authorities of indigenous and peasant communities may perform administrative functions and apply their own norms as a form of alternative conflict resolution, in keeping with their customs and procedures, providing they do not contradict this Constitution or the Law. Laws will make these functions compatible with the powers of the branches of the State." In this same article, the Constitution recognized the legal status of indigenous and rural communities, associations and unions. This expression of multiculturalism, however, was not implemented by the state in good faith.

The People's Participation Law (LPP) of 1994 recognized indigenous authorities. This opened up the possibility of creating Indigenous Municipal Districts (DMI). In a DMI, the indigenous authority would be recognized as a sub-mayor. Although DMIs are institutionally weak since their jurisdiction is not defined and they depend on the goodwill of the municipal mayor, it would be an interesting arrangement for indigenous territorial reconfiguration strategies.

TCOs were recognized through the agrarian law and not through the LPP because the state sought to prevent any connection between the notions of territory and jurisdiction, alleging that this would lead to "Balkanizing" the country. In this regard, Calla has suggested that the mid-1990s involved a silent and largely unperceived dual decentralization process: (1)

the territorial decentralization is driven by TCO demands which have arisen in the last few years in the highlands, and (2) the municipal decentralization process driven by the LPP (Calla n.d.). The indigenous peoples pursue strategies to make the two legal frameworks converge. An example is the community of Raqaypampa in the Department of Cochabamba, municipality of Mizque, which has a Quechua population of about eleven thousand. By the late 1990s the indigenous population in the Mizque municipality was organized into unions, sub-centrals, and a Regional Central and in 1997 the Indigenous Municipal District of Raqaypampa was created. In 2001, they prepared regulations for governance of the DMI that were approved by the Municipal Council of Mizque. The unions also discussed the SNRA Law and in early 2002 applied to the departmental INRA for recognition of the TCO coinciding with the DMI's area.

The next step in this strategy would be to make the DMI into a municipality under the 1999 Municipalities Law. That would effectively integrate the indigenous government into the structure of the Bolivian government. Similar efforts were underway in many other parts of the Andean region, sometimes with clear ethno-nationalistic overtones, such as in certain Aymara areas. The territorial recomposition can extend beyond the local community based on the union organization as in Raqaypampa and in other cases based on reorganized *ayllus*. In his assessment of the process—which was written years before the election of Evo Morales—Calla pointed out that little thought had been given to the significance of such processes or their possible consequences for Bolivia's political and administrative structure or distribution of governmental resources.

With the election of Evo Morales and the drafting of a new Constitution, which was approved in a popular referendum in January 2009, conditions have significantly changed. The new Constitution foresees the creation of indigenous autonomies. How this will work out in practice and how further legislation will take shape remain to be seen.

Finally, the debate about a new water law that was suspended after the 2000 "Water War" is again a hot issue in Bolivia. This is because of controversial attempts to sell water from the Department of Potosí to northern Chile supposedly to benefit urban populations in that region but also to benefit mining companies thirsty for water for industrial use. Moreover, after a "gas war" in October 2003 over developing and exporting natural gas, the natural resource use issue and the neoliberal model in general have come to occupy an even more prominent place in national debate. Indigenous movements are major protagonists in challenging the market model and proposing that water and other resources be treated as public goods and handled according to criteria of equity, social justice and respect for multiculturalism.

The new Bolivian government, for example, has created a Water Ministry—an unprecedented decision for Latin America—and also intends to develop participatory, decentralized public policy that will go beyond centralized, bureaucratic management of water resources. This proposal entails challenging the patterns of "rationality" imposed by hegemonic discourse and multilateral agencies. A first step in this direction was the approval of regulations of the Irrigation Law of 2004 which clearly depart from the market logic and stipulate that water and water rights are not marketable. The regulations also stipulate the use rights of indigenous-peasant communities and families and deal with their registration. Bolivia's new constitution defines access to water and sewerage as human rights and forbids their concession or privatization.

Colombia: From Hope to Despair

Colombia along with Bolivia was studied by Van Cott in her 2000 book *The Friendly Liquidation of the Past*, a title reflecting the optimism of the time regarding emerging multiculturalism in Latin America. The 1991 constitutional reform in Colombia gave rise to major hope for the country's indigenous people. Although indigenous people comprise only 2 percent of Colombia's population (compared to 62 percent for Bolivia), participation of indigenous people in the 1991 Colombian constitutional reform process generated great expectations. Not only were their presence and performance noteworthy, but they also succeeded in getting a series of stipulations in the new constitution (Van Cott 2000). Their *resguardos* (reservations) were recognized as collective, inalienable property governed by indigenous councils set up according to local customs. Unlike the Bolivian case, there was no governmental strategy to separate territory and jurisdiction. Theoretically, the rights set forth in the Colombian Constitution are more coherent and solid.

The *resguardos* were created in Colombia during colonial times. In the course of the nineteenth century, as in other countries, there were attempts to dissolve them and encourage private property, a process that was stopped for a time when Law 89 was enacted in 1890, which momentarily recognized the reservations and their councils. However, pressures to dissolve them continued, leading to a resistance movement, including armed resistance led by Quintín Lame in Cauca Valley from 1910 to 1918. Despite resistance, by 1960 there were only some 70 reservations left. In 1961, under the auspices of the Alliance for Progress, an Agrarian Reform Law was enacted and the Colombian Agrarian Reform Institute (INCORA) was created, but the law was not implemented until the end of the decade when peasants and indigenous people began recovering land.

By 1980, existing reservations, including extensive reserves created in the tropical eastern area since the 1960s, were consolidated and new ones established. After enacting the new 1991 Constitution, these reservations were also granted *resguardo* status, which provides stronger legal protection for lands. The number of reservations increased, reaching 638 in 2001 and covering some 25 percent of the national territory, much of it in the Amazon region. It is estimated that now almost 90 percent of the indigenous people live on reservations (Arango and Sánchez 2002; Pineda 2001: 36–37).

The 1991 Constitution consolidated reservations and also formalized indigenous jurisdiction, regulation of land distribution within reservations, design and implementation of development plans, promotion of public investment and representation for dealing with the national government. It also addressed without clear articulation the concept of territorial entities under state law (municipalities, etc.) and indigenous territorial entities (Van Cott 2000: 94–95). The constitution was supposed to create regional autonomy for several reservations and an Organizational Law for Territorial Distribution was intended to regularize self-government and expand indigenous jurisdiction. Secondary legislation was needed to stipulate which reservations qualified to receive a portion of the national budget as municipalities within the state structure.

Indigenous people influenced the 1991 Constitution and achieved public prominence and highly significant moral leadership. Social movements also played a role along with the Liberal Party and the neoliberals in promoting decentralization for different reasons. Therefore, recognition of indigenous autonomy was part of a broader context of decentralization and attempts to put an end to violent conflicts in Colombia.

In 1994, funds began reaching reservations. They came through non-indigenous mayors and departmental governors on the basis of investment and development plans that had to be presented by reservations. Funding was accompanied by time-consuming training programs, prompting one indigenous leader to remark "nowadays, you need a lot of time to be indigenous" (Padilla 1995: 147). Perhaps conforming to the Colombian government's procedures is not merely inconvenient but, as Padilla suggests, doing so may actually increase the possibilities for state and para-state intervention in the internal affairs of the indigenous peoples through NGOs. Indeed, it appears to be an effort to "standardize" government procedures, effectively impeding the capacity of indigenous people to govern themselves (Hale 2002; Hoekema 1996).

While the César Gaviria government showed some affinity for the indigenous cause (Van Cott 2000), subsequent governments have been much more interested in implementing "mega-projects" to extract natural resources (oil, minerals, hydropower, African palm plantations). Implementing such projects often affects indigenous populations in several ways, such as by polluting the water, competing for water resources to irrigate monocrops for export and building hydropower projects.

A notorious case is the struggle by the Embera Katío people in northwestern Colombia against building of the Urrá I and II dams in their territory. That project would benefit agricultural businesses in the region and generate electricity for Bogotá, but would also affect indigenous fishing areas. Recognition of reservations and indigenous rights have been conditioned upon and subordinated to the creation of "strategic alliances" with the private sector under "Plan Colombia," which attempts to pacify the country and eliminate drug traffic by promoting business sectors at the expense of more vulnerable groups. Indigenous territorial rights are restrictively interpreted. Such policies along with increased violence related to drug wars jeopardize indigenous peoples' existence. Violence against indigenous people and their allies has been the subject of judicial proceedings in Colombia and before the Inter-American Human Rights Commission. The Colombian government, however, has disregarded the Commission's recommendations.

Colombia's new 1991 Constitution declared Colombia a "social State under the rule of law" and recognized indigenous rights. The constitutional process offered hope for pacifying the country. However, some portions of the Constitution were ambiguous and the sections on economic issues were heavily influenced by the neoliberal model. The gap between what the Constitution said about indigenous rights and actual practice has been growing as guerrilla conflicts and efforts to combat drug trafficking have put pressure on policies advancing indigenous rights. Especially under the government of Álvaro Uribe systematic efforts have been made to roll back the advances made in 1991. Neoliberal policies were deepened. In 2007 all dialogue between the government and indigenous organizations came to a virtual standstill when it became known that Colombia was the only Latin American country that had abstained from the vote over the UN Declaration on the Rights of Indigenous Peoples. Meanwhile, new legislation on rural development and projects for oil and mineral exploitation constitute a serious threat for the *resguardos* and the share in tax revenues to local governments, among them the *resguardos*, has been reduced.

Mexico: The Reform, Betrayed

Mexico was one of the countries that incubated "indigenism," a current of thought that revisited "indigenous affairs" in the 1920s and 1930s.The concept was institutionalized with the Patzcuaro Congress in 1940, which gave rise to the indigenist institutions, both nationally and at the inter-American level. Indigenism was considered progressive because it criticized racist theories, but it became a means of denying diversity by seeking cultural and racial mixing and assimilation. In the 1970s the assimilation aspect began to be abandoned, at least in theory.

In Mexico, the "indigenism of participation" arose in part to contain the emergence of independent movements. For each of the 56 peoples officially recognized, a congress was held which was supposed to lead to the creation of a Supreme Council. One example was the famous Indigenous Congress in Chiapas in 1974. The local government put the Archbishop of Chiapas Samuel Ruiz in charge of organizing the congress. But contrary to official objectives, the congress escaped government control and became an occasion for the area's indigenous groups to meet and discuss their common problems and ways to address them. From the local congresses and Supreme Councils a National Council of the Indigenous Peoples was created in 1975. However, this renewed indigenism soon showed its limits and the attempt to incorporate the indigenous movements into the state system largely failed.

When the ILO adopted its new Convention 169, Mexico was eager to appear progressive and became the first Latin American country to ratify it. Within the country, ratification went virtually unnoticed, however. Mexico amended its constitution in early 1992 to implement Convention 169 by recognizing the pluricultural composition of the nation. But, at the same time, Article 27 of the constitution which had provided the framework for agrarian reform after the Mexican revolution (1910–1927) was also amended. The land reform process thus was officially ended and the amended Article 27 was at odds with Convention 169 by opening the way for the privatization of community lands.

The Salinas government (1988–1994) sought to present Mexico as a "first-world" country by negotiating the North American Free Trade Agreement (NAFTA). While negotiating NAFTA, Mexico agreed to put an end to agrarian redistribution, to open up the land market, promote individual property titles for collective *ejidos* and agrarian communities and remove prohibitions against dissolving (formerly inalienable) *ejidos* and communities. A new agrarian law included reference to the protection of the land of "indigenous groups" pursuant to the constitution, but the constitution referred to protection pursuant to the law and there was no mention of territories in the agrarian law. Therefore, the issue of indigenous land remained in a legal limbo. Later in 1992 the government also passed a new forestry law and new water legislation. The water law reversed the social orientation of previous legislation which protected irrigated agriculture and accorded priority to *ejidos* and agrarian communities over industrial water use and use for electricity generation. With the new law the government sought to create a market in water rights and strongly reduced the role of the state in water management.

Such neoliberal policies created the climate for the outbreak of the Chiapas rebellion in January 1994 (Harvey 1998). Several days of combat ended in a cease-fire and lengthy negotiations began between the Zapatistas and the Zedillo government (1994–2000). The dialogue bogged down because of a lack of government interest. To resume the peace process, in 1996 the Concord and Pacification Committee (COCOPA) of representatives from the local and national congresses drafted a proposal to amend the federal constitution. The Zapatistas agreed to this with some reservations. The government also agreed initially, but then presented a series of "observations" that distorted the proposal and precipitated a crisis. While the constitutional amendment was pending, the Zapatistas moved back into their municipalities and communities to consolidate their autonomous governments and strengthen their ties with national and international "civil society."

Chiapas was one of the central issues in the 2000 presidential election. Candidate Vicente Fox, of the National Action Party (PAN), at one point declared that he would settle the matter in "fifteen minutes" and promised that, if elected, he would send the COCOPA proposal to Congress. The July elections yielded the historic defeat of PRI and once he took office in late 2000 President Vicente Fox did, in fact, send the COCOPA proposal to Congress. In response, in February–March 2001 the Zapatistas organized a caravan that crossed the country and finally reached the federal capital where they made an historic appearance in Congress to support the COCOPA reform.

However, in April 2001 Congress passed a constitutional amendment that fell short of the COCOPA proposal. The wording recognized the rights of indigenous peoples and communities to self-determination "in a constitutional framework of autonomy that will assure national unity." Nonetheless, instead of recognizing indigenous peoples as legal entities, it recognized them as "public-interest entities," that is, as recipients of state care rather than subjects with rights. The concept of territories was eliminated, while maintaining a reference to Article 27.Communities were also allowed to associate with one other, but only within municipalities. An amendment to Article 115 of the constitution on municipal organization was left out so indigenous municipalities cannot be created. Supporters of these provisions cited "the nation's unity and indivisibility." Over three hundred municipalities challenged the law in the National Supreme Court of Justice, which declared the challenges out of order for technical reasons. Despite widespread rejection by indigenous movements, the revised amendment was ratified by sixteen state congresses—the states with the lowest indigenous populations. In August 2001, President Vicente Fox signed the amendment decree.

While this tug of war was going on at the federal level, a number of states amended their constitutions and in some cases passed secondary laws. Out of Mexico's thirty-one states, more than seventeen have amended their constitutions to foster multiculturalism, as has the Federal District. Various states have enacted secondary legislation, including indigenous rights and culture laws. Except for a few positive features, the reforms have no significant consequences.

Legal protection for territories and natural resources is weak and conflict is common. For example, in 2004, the Community Front to Defend Human Rights and Natural Resources of the Mazahua people in the State of Mexico organized several protests against taking water from the Mazahua communities for the thirsty Federal District without compensation. Protests continued because negotiations and promises by government agencies produced no concrete actions to benefit Mazahua communities in such areas as sanitation, drinking water supply and rehabilitation of irrigation systems. These protests continued during the following years and in March 2006 the Mazahua Women's Army in Defense of Water presented the case at the World Water Forum in Mexico City. It is just one example of indigenous peoples' involvement in conflicts over water resources throughout Mexico.

Conclusion

After this tour of the reform processes in three Latin American countries, we have to conclude that the results of the new multiculturalism have at best been mixed. The policies were introduced in a context of structural adjustment measures. Neoliberal multiculturalism or what has been called "neoindigenism" (Hernández, Paz, and Sierra 2004) supplanted the old indigenism and its openly assimilationist policies in an effort to develop new forms of governance under the guidance of the multilateral development agencies. At the same time, macroeconomic policies contributed to the poverty of vulnerable social groups, including indigenous peoples and income distribution tended to become more inequitable. Free trade policies and the opening up of the national economies went in tandem with the introduction of market-oriented policies regarding natural resources including water, and an intensification of natural resource exploitation.

The new multiculturalism fitted into the process of dismantling the state and transforming social policies which were already deficient into targeted programs aiming to "help the poor help themselves." Within this framework the new multiculturalism purported to be culturally sensitive, but this sensitivity goes hand in hand with regulating the lives of aid program beneficiaries.[3] "Participation," "human capital," and "social capital" became key words in the new discourse. Mexican "neoindigenism" (Hernández, Paz, and Sierra 2004) is emblematic in this sense. The projects promoted by Mexican regional development funds, for example, are often business-oriented, and seek to transform communities into community enterprises. These projects ignore alternative visions of development based on organic agriculture, notions of territoriality, food security and collective rights to natural resources, as well as local forms of water management.[4] In Colombia the hopes generated by the 1991 constitutional reform have been dashed and indigenous access to territories has increasingly become conditioned upon accepting development projects in cooperation with the private sector. In Bolivia, mining, petroleum, and forestry concessions frequently overlapped with the TCOs. In both Colombia and Mexico megaprojects such as the development of the Pacific Coast or the Puebla-Panama Plan threaten indigenous and other rural peoples and their livelihoods.

The case of Bolivia, however, is suggestive of the shift in policy orientations that is occurring in the region. The *Movimiento al Socialismo* (MAS) is an exponent of the "New Latin American Left" and the search for alternatives to the hitherto dominant neoliberal model. The new Latin American left is extremely diverse and the search for alternatives is an ongoing process (Barrett, Chavez, and Rodríguez-Garavito 2008). Some elements, however, seem to emerge: a newly enhanced role for the state in the economy and in natural resource management and the distribution of benefits, a renewal of social policies and efforts to create a more beneficial economic climate for the poorer sectors of the population, experiments with forms of democracy that complement electoral democracy and a more beneficial stance toward indigenous peoples that may go beyond neoliberal multiculturalism. This chapter has discussed the example of the Bolivian irrigation legislation. More broadly, one might point to the processes of constitutional reform in countries like Ecuador or Bolivia. As in Bolivia, however, the new Ecuador Constitution defines the right to water as a fundamental human right, indispensable for "living well." Whether that results in concrete policies remains to be seen. In the case of Ecuador, for example, the relationship between the indigenous movement and the Rafael Correa government is rather tense, particularly due to disagreements over natural resource management and exploitation.

Notes

First published in 2010 as "The Limits of State Reform and Multiculturalism in Latin America: Contemporary Illustrations," in *Out of the Mainstream: Water Rights, Politics and Identity*, ed. R. Boelens, D. Getches, and A. Guevara-Gil, London, Washington D.C.:

Earthscan. Our gratitude goes to Earthscan and the book editors for granting permission to republish this book chapter.

1. The departure of President Gonzalo Sánchez de Lozada was also provoked by the Gas War in October 2003.
2. See Assies (2000). Castells (1998) has called this the "Network State"; others have referred to it as the "new medievalism." Cf. Held, McGrew, Goldblatt, and Perraton (1999: 85).
3. Laws on indigenous rights and culture in Mexico, for example, include lengthy sections to circumscribe indigenous jurisdiction and reduce it to cases of "chicken theft."
4. An issue that is profoundly examined in, for example, multiple studies and debates by the WALIR program (see, for example, http://www.eclac.cl/drni/proyectos/walir or the WALIR book series with IEP Lima).

References

Albert, Bruce. 1997. "Territorialité, ethnopolitique et développement: à propos du mouvement indien en Amazonie brésilienne." *Cahiers des Amériques Latines* 23, no. 3: 177–210.

Arango, Raúl and Enrique Sánchez. 2002. *Los pueblos indígenas en el umbral del nuevo milenio.* Bogotá: National Planning Department, http://www.dnp.gov.co /01_CONT/DES_TERR /DIV_ET.HTM#8. Accessed August 15, 2005.

Assies, Willem. 1994. "Self-Determination and the 'New Partnership'; The Politics of Indigenous Peoples and States." In *Indigenous Peoples' Experiences with Self-Government*, ed. W. Assies and A. J. Hoekema. IWGIA Document no. 76. Copenhagen and Amsterdam: IWGIA and University of Amsterdam.

———. 2000. "Indigenous Peoples and Reform of the State in Latin America." In *The Challenge of Diversity: Indigenous Peoples and Reform of the State in Latin America*, ed. W. Assies and G. van der Haar. Amsterdam: Thela Thesis.

———. 2001. "David vs. Goliat en Cochabamba: los derechos del agua, el neoliberalismo y la renovación de la protesta social en Bolivia." *T'inkazos* 8: 106–131.

Assies, Willem, Gemma van der Haar, and André Hoekema, eds. 2000. *The Challenge of Diversity: Indigenous Peoples and Reform of the State in Latin America*. Amsterdam: Thela Thesis.

Barret, Patrick, Daniel Chavez, and César Rodríguez-Gavarito, eds. 2008. *The New Latin American Left: Utopia Reborn*. London: Pluto Press

Bengoa, José. 2000. *La emergencia indígena en América Latina*. Mexico City and Santiago: Fondo de Cultura Económica.

Bonfil Batalla, Guillermo. 1981. "Lo propio y lo ajeno: una aproximación al problema del control cultural." In *Pensar nuestra cultura*, ed. G. Bonfil Batalla. Mexico: Alianza Editorial.

Calla, Ricardo. n.d. "Derechos territoriales de los pueblos indígenas en los Andes de Bolivia, Perú y Ecuador: una exploración preliminar." In *Avizorando los retos para los pueblos indígenas de América Latina en el nuevo milenio: territorio, economía, política e identidad* (CD-ROM). OXFAM.

———. 2000. "Indigenous Peoples, the Law of Popular Participation and Changes in Government: Bolivia, 1994–1998." In *The Challenge of Diversity: Indigenous Peoples and Reform of the State in Latin America*, ed. W. Assies, G. van der Haar, and A. Hoekema. Amsterdam: Thela Thesis.

Castells, Manuel. 1998. *End of Millenium*. Malden, MA, and Oxford, U.K.: Blackwell Publishers.

Hale, Charles R. 2002. "Does Multiculturalism Menace? Governance, Cultural Rights and the Politics of Identity in Guatemala." *Journal of Latin American Studies* 34: 485–524.

———. 2004. "Rethinking Indigenous Politics in the Era of the 'Indio Permitido." *NACLA Report on the Americas* (September/October): 16–21.

Harvey, Neil. 1998. *The Chiapas Rebellion: The Struggle for Land and Democracy*. Durham and London: Duke University Press.

Held, David, Anthony McGrew, David Goldblatt, and Jonathan Perraton. 1999. *Global Transformations: Politics, Economics and Culture*. Cambridge, U.K.: Polity Press.

Hernández, Rosalva Aída, Sarela Paz, and María Teresa Sierra, eds. 2004. *El Estado y los indígenas en tiempos del PAN: neoindigenismo, legalidad e identidad*. Mexico: CIESA, Miguel Ángel Porrúa.

Hoekema, André J. 1996. "Autonomy and Self-Government: A Fundamental Debate." Internal memo, Amsterdam: University of Amsterdam, Department of Sociology and Anthropology of Law.

Iturralde, Diego. 1997. "Demandas indígenas y reforma legal: retos y paradojas." *Alteridades* 7, no. 14: 81–98.

Padilla, Guillermo. 1995. "What Encompasses Goodness, the Law and the Indigenous People of Colombia." In *Ethnic Conflict and Governance in Comparative Perspective*. Latin American Program Working Paper Series, no. 215, The Woodrow Wilson Center, Washington.

Pineda, Roberto. 2001. "Colombia y el reto de la construcción de la multiculturalidad en un escenario de conflicto." In *Multiethnic Nations in Developing Countries*, ed. M. J. Cepeda Espinosa and T. Fleiner. Basel, Geneva, Munich: Helbing & Lichtenhahn (Institut de Fédéralisme Fribourg Suisse).

Psacharopoulos, George, and Harry Anthony Patrinos, eds. 1994. *Indigenous People and Poverty in Latin America: An Empirical Analysis*. Washington: The World Bank.

Stavenhagen, Rodolfo. 2002. "Indigenous Peoples and the State in Latin America: An Ongoing Debate." In *Multiculturalism in Latin America: Indigenous Rights, Diversity and Democracy*, ed. R. Sieder. Houndmills, Basingstoke, Hampshire: Palgrave Macmillan.

Van Cott, Donna Lee. 2000. *The Friendly Liquidation of the Past: The Politics of Diversity in Latin America*. Pittsburgh: The University of Pittsburgh Press.

Wade, Peter. 2006. "Etnicidad, multiculturalismo y políticas sociales en Latinoamérica: Poblaciones afrolatinas (e indígenas)." *Tabula Rasa* 4: 59–81.

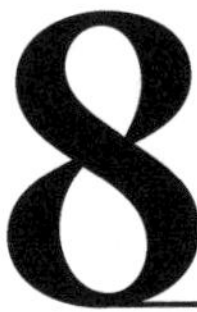

Two Steps Forward, One Step Back

Indigenous Peoples and
Autonomies in Latin America

Introduction

The last three decades of the past century have seen a remarkable surge of activism by and on behalf of indigenous peoples in Latin America. States, in turn, have responded by formally abandoning the integrationist and assimilationist policies of *indigenismo* and have reformed their constitutions to recognize the pluriethnic and multicultural composition of their populations.[1] The region furthermore stands out for the fact that among the seventeen countries that ratified ILO Convention 169 (1989) thirteen are Latin American.[2] The constitutional reforms and the ratification of ILO Convention 169, one might surmise, provide a legal framework for the emergence of autonomy regimes for indigenous peoples.

The dialectics between the identity politics practiced by indigenous peoples' movements and the politics of recognition that have been adopted by the states have certainly contributed to the dynamism of what has been called the "indigenous emergence" (Bengoa 2000). Indigenous peoples' demands and the responses to these demands have become important elements in the ongoing processes of transformation of the Latin American states which, it has been suggested, may point to the emergence of a "multicultural regional model" (Van Cott 2000: 265; Sieder 2002). Indigenous peoples, however, are not the only actor in these transformation processes and the emergence of autonomy regimes is far from a smooth process and in fact is mostly rather conflictive and contested. Nonetheless, the processes of state transformation suggest a significant departure from the nation-state model as it emerged in the nineteenth century and will have profound implications for the concepts of citizenship, democracy, development, and human rights predicated upon this model.

This chapter seeks to place indigenous peoples' movements in a broader context and to examine their role in the process of state transformation in order to assess the scope of emerging autonomies and some of their possible implications. First, I will briefly discuss the Latin American context. Then

I will examine the emerging legal framework and discuss some aspects of autonomy regimes. In the third section of the chapter I will first provide a general overview of the constitutional reforms that have taken place in Latin America and then examine four cases in which stipulations regarding a formal political autonomy regime were included in the constitution: Panama, Colombia, Ecuador, and Nicaragua. The final section offers some reflections on these cases and the process of state transformation in Latin America.

Indigenous Peoples and Movements in Latin America

Estimates of the indigenous population of Latin America are highly variable. Generally it is assumed that there are between 30 and 40 million indigenous people, corresponding to about 8 to 10 percent of the total population, and that there are some four hundred indigenous peoples (Hopenhayn and Bello 2001: 13–15; Psacharopoulos and Patrinos 1994: 21–54). In Bolivia, Guatemala, and Peru indigenous people constitute the majority of the population. In Ecuador they make up between 30 and 40 percent of the population, in Mexico and Belize between 15 and 20 percent and in the remaining countries they would be less than 6 percent of the total population. A major problem is the friction or mismatch between the ways states classify and count their populations and the ways these populations define themselves. In Mexico, for example, the official number of indigenous groups has been fifty-six for decades, but the groups and the way they were counted changed from year to year (Levi 2002: 6–7). On the other hand, according to the 2000 Brazilian census, the number of people identifying themselves as "Indian" was 701,462; that is twice as much as in the previous 1991 census. Natural growth by itself cannot explain such outcomes, which suggest that an increasing number of people somehow identify themselves as "Indian" (Brackelaire 2002: 34). Such numbers, it should be noted moreover, cover a wide range of situations, going from still relatively isolated hunters and gatherers, through settled indigenous peasantries to the rapidly increasing numbers of indigenous peoples living in urban areas.

From the 1960s onward new movements of indigenous peoples have emerged. Various developments contributed to this dynamic and the manner in which these movements framed their discourses. Let me just mention a few:

- The indigenist education policies had the, perhaps paradoxical, effect of contributing to the emergence of a new generation of indigenous intellectuals capable of articulating a discourse that found resonance both with the indigenous people(s) and with sectors of the "national" society and, perhaps even more importantly, in the transnational arena. In the course of the 1970s a transnational movement emerged that skillfully articulated a "politics of shame" in this arena;

- New links emerged between rural and urban areas as a consequence of the increased mobility of rural populations;
- The agrarian reforms of the 1950s to 1970s often broke up rural power structures and contributed to the consolidation of holdings of the indigenous peasantries;
- The accelerated occupation of the Amazon region, the "last frontier," through policies of colonization and the search for natural resources triggered the concern of ecologist movements and directly affected the hitherto relatively isolated indigenous peoples of the region. An emerging alliance greatly contributed to the "visibility" of the indigenous peoples of the region and brought new items to the agenda. On the one hand it resulted in an often highly problematic, convergence of indigenous and ecologist discourses. On the other, it brought a concern with "territory." Whereas the indigenous-peasant populations of the Andean highlands and parts of Meso-America had become accustomed to articulate their demands largely in terms of "land" in the context of state-sponsored agrarian reform policies, those of the Amazon region would formulate their demands in terms of "territory" and this would infuse indigenous movements' demands with a new dynamic;[3]
- Liberation Theology[4] as well as the emergence of human rights movements in the context of the "democratic transitions" brought new allies to the indigenous cause. The end of the authoritarian regimes opened further political spaces for indigenous peoples' movements;
- The end of the Cold War meant that the formerly quasi-automatic polarization in terms of a class struggle discourse weakened and that campesinos (peasants) could become *indios otra vez* (Indians again);[5] a process that received further impetus as result of the celebration of diversity, by both neoliberals and postmodernists;
- The celebration of the "Encounter of two worlds" in 1992[6] rapidly was transformed into a commemoration of "500 years of resistance," which through the organization of continental encounters contributed to the strengthening of networks and interchanges among indigenous organizations and to an enhanced visibility.

The conjunction of such developments accounts for the emergence of vibrant and varied indigenous movements in the region and their becoming prominent social and political actors. In the course of this process demands have increasingly centered upon autonomy claims in the sense of coupling territorial demands with claims to the recognition of their own ways of doing politics and their own ways of imparting justice. Such claims are partly sustained by ILO Convention 169, which in the course of time has been ratified by a significant number of Latin American countries.

ILO Convention 169, Self-Determination and Autonomy

ILO Convention 169 has become a key element in framing indigenous demands in Latin America and in the struggle for reform of Latin American constitutions. Ratification means that the Convention acquires the status of domestic law.[7] It therefore is worth briefly discussing it. The Convention defines indigenous peoples as

> Peoples in independent countries who are regarded as indigenous on account of their descent from the populations which inhabited the country, or a geographical region to which the country belongs, at the time of conquest or colonization or the establishment of present state boundaries and who, irrespective of their legal status, retain some or all of their own social, economic, cultural and political institutions.

The Convention furthermore states that self-identification is to be regarded as a fundamental criterion for determining the groups to which the Convention applies. Albeit hedged in with qualifiers, the Convention contains stipulations regarding the "right to retain their own customs and institutions" (art. 8), respect for "the methods customarily practiced by the peoples concerned for dealing with offences committed by their members" (art. 9), and the recognition of "the rights of ownership and possession . . . over the lands which they traditionally occupy" (art. 14) and it stipulates that the term "'lands' shall 'include the concept of territories, which covers the total environment of the areas which the people concerned occupy or otherwise use" (art. 13).[8]

A notable feature of the Convention is that it is the only international legal instrument that uses the term "peoples" in relation to indigenous peoples. This, however, is immediately followed by the stipulation that the "use of the term 'peoples' in this Convention shall not be construed as having any implications as regards the rights which may attach to the term under international law" (art. 1). Thus, although under the pressure of indigenous delegates who participated in the drafting of the Convention the terms "populations" and "minorities" were avoided at the same time indigenous peoples were denied the right of peoples under international law, that is the right to self-determination by virtue of which they "freely determine their political status and freely pursue their economic, social and cultural development."

Self-determination under international law would include the right to sovereign independence and this met with the objection of state representatives.

In the debates over a UN Declaration on the rights of indigenous peoples the controversy over terms and the issue of "self-determination" is ongoing. In such debates the notion of "internal self-determination" has cropped up.[9] Martínez Cobo (1987: 20) once defined it as meaning that "a people or group possessing a definite territory may be autonomous in the sense of possessing a separate and distinct administrative structure and judicial system, determined by and intrinsic to that people or group."

Some years later, at the expert meeting on internal self-government in Nuuk, Greenland, Bennagen (1992: 72) outlined five operational features of such self-government:

- control of territory (expressed variously as ancestral domain, ancestral homeland, indigenous territory, etc.) and its natural resources, both surface and subsurface;
- legislative, executive, and judicial bodies, to include corresponding indigenous institutions;
- proper actual representation of the indigenous cultural communities in the various organs of power, not only in the autonomous territorial unit but also in the national government;
- fiscal autonomy, including the power to raise revenues, a just share of national revenues, and a capable fiscal administration; and
- respect, protection, and development of indigenous cultures.

More recently, Hoekema (1996) has sought to further develop the concept of internal political autonomy and self-government—the institutionally guaranteed capacity of a social entity or territory to rule itself within the ambit of sovereignty of a state—and to develop some criteria for the assessment of such an arrangement. In the first place he addresses the aspect of *formal political autonomy*, which he defines as a legal regime, whereby (revocable or irrevocable) powers of self-government, including legislative competence, concerning one or more specified areas—within the overall constitutional makeup of the state in question—are conferred on a distinct group of individuals (defined by their ethnic origin and/or language, etc.) or on inhabitants of a specific and distinct territory.[10] Here political autonomy refers to a concept in constitutional law. The addition of a reference to a territorial form of self-government is meant to highlight the fact that self-government can come in several forms. One form is nonterritorial, conferring some rights on an indigenous people independent of the place of residence, for example, through mechanisms of positive discrimination where an indigenous council has a say in the implementation of such policies. The Saami parliaments in

Scandinavia, which have some say in sectoral policies, are an example of such delinking between self-government and territoriality.[11] The territory-based type of self-government can take two forms. One is what Hoekema calls "ethnic self-government" in which, we might say, legal pluralism and the diversity of political institutions are institutionalized. The other form relies on the drawing of administrative boundaries in such a way that in practice chances are great that indigenous persons exercise the authority. Such a territory is seen as deserving a special status, although the institutional structure is modeled after established public bodies. This distinction corresponds largely to the distinction between direct and indirect consociation (cf. Assies 1994).

Such arrangements, Hoekema argues, can be of a federal type or be adopted in a unitary state; a distinction that again converges with the distinction between direct and indirect consociation. In a federal state all constituent parts have a special status and are not subordinated to the central government but to the constitution. A variant is where one or some specific regions constitutionally receive a special status. Within unitary states, by contrast, decentralization would be the mechanism but then the powers delegated to local authorities can be diminished or even (formally) abolished by the central government and/or legislature.

A second level of analysis is that of *effective political autonomy*, which refers to the way in which real decision-making powers are distributed among indigenous incumbents of official positions, as well as (other) indigenous leaders on the one hand, and outside authorities and functionaries on the other. The point of making the distinction between formal and effective political autonomy is that one can come across cases of effective autonomy without much formal autonomy as well as cases of hardly effective formal autonomy.

A third level of analysis is that of *autonomy as the freedom of a social collectivity to choose its own destiny* and concerns the process of being autonomous, the exercise of autonomy itself. This is a sociocultural criterion to assess if effective political autonomy reflects and promotes a social process of self-determination of the people in question. Does it serve the best interests of the people? Are the people "really" choosing freely their own destiny? Of course, Hoekema points out, answering such questions is fraught with practical and epistemological problems, but these are questions that have to be posed. What if, for example, effective political autonomy benefits only a tiny elite or promotes the displacement of traditional authorities by younger indigenous people more capable in dealing with the administrative structures and functionaries of the state? Could this not result in more subtle forms of domination than outright oppression through a sort of "colonization of the mind" and, to put it otherwise, a disempowerment of a people in choosing their own destiny?

Such an approach seems to be useful. One might argue, for example, that until now indigenous communities or peoples have managed to maintain a certain effective autonomy despite efforts by the state to encroach upon it. States now have opted for formal recognition. Does this make autonomy more effective and does it augment the scope for self-determination?

This type of question also informs the current debate over "neoliberal multiculturalism" (Gustafson 2002; Hale 2002) in which the recognition of indigenous peoples' rights is embedded in, and restricted by, the policies of decentralization recommended by the multilateral development agencies as part of their post-Washington Consensus "second generation" structural adjustment policies.

Mechanisms like ILO Convention 169 and constitutional reforms provide the legal framework through which the politics of recognition are operated. They suggest some degree of recognition of territorial claims and claims to recognition of indigenous systems of authority and forms of administering justice. This would occur through the formalization of regimes that outline the competencies, ambit and scope of "internal autonomy" and its relation to the state.

Constitutional Reforms and Autonomies

In her overview of Latin American constitutions and indigenous rights Van Cott (2000: 266–268) finds that only in four cases is an autonomy regime included, while in a later article she identifies five cases (Van Cott 2001). More recently, Mendoza (n.d.: 8) has presented an overview similar to the one drawn up by Van Cott (2000: 266–268). The overview I present in Table 8.1 here is inspired by these overviews but has been revised and updated with the help of the database on indigenous legislation of the Inter-American Development Bank (IADB 2003).[12]

It should be clear that in many cases we confront a situation of what Van Cott (2000) calls a "rhetorical recognition of multiculturalism."[13] In my representation the recognition of territorial autonomy in Venezuela has received the benefit of the doubt. The 1999 Venezuelan constitution includes an article that makes it possible to create a special regime for municipalities with an indigenous population (art. 169). It is not very clear what this eventually may imply. As we shall see, the wording used in constitutions often is deliberately ambivalent[14] and Venezuela's Article 169 is no exception, but read in conjunction with other articles it suggests that formal political autonomy may be granted.[15] Eventually the constitutional provision might, for example, have important effects in the state of Amazonas

Table 8.1. Latin American Constitutions and Indigenous Rights

	Venezuela	Ecuador	Colombia	Nicaragua	Peru	Paraguay	Brazil	Mexico	Panama	Guatemala	Bolivia	Argentina	Total
Recognition of collective property of indigenous lands	yes	yes	yes	yes	yes	yes	yes	yes	yes	yes	yes	yes	12
Recognition of multiethnic and pluricultural reality	yes	yes	yes	yes	yes	yes	yes	yes	yes	yes	yes	no	11
Bilingual education	yes	yes	yes	yes	yes	yes	yes	yes	yes	yes	no	yes	11
Recognition of customary law	yes	yes	yes	yes	yes	yes	no	yes	no	no	yes	no	8
Official indigenous languages	yes	yes	yes	yes	yes	yes	no	no	no	no	no	no	6
Consultation for natural resource exploitation	yes	yes	yes	no	no	no	yes	no	no	no	yes	yes	6
Territorial autonomy	yes	yes	yes	yes	no	no	no	no	yes	no	no	no	5
Protection of collective intellectual property rights	yes	yes	no	no	no	no	no	no	no	no	no	no	2
Political participation and representation[a]	yes	no	yes	no	no	no	no	no	no	no	no	no	2
Number of reforms adopted by each state	9	8	8	6	5	5	4	4	4	3	3	3	

a. Institution of an "indigenous circumscription" granting participation in the national congress.

where nearly half of the population is indigenous and rural municipalities are overwhelmingly indigenous.

We thus find five cases where territorial autonomy is reflected in the constitution: Ecuador, Colombia, Nicaragua, Panama, and Venezuela. The Panamanian and Colombian arrangements are examples of "ethnic autonomy," whereas Nicaragua is a case of indirect consociation, while the case of Ecuador is inconclusive, as is the case of Venezuela. I will discuss the debate that is ongoing in Ecuador, but I will not discuss the Venezuelan case since at this stage hardly anything is known about the terms of debate over the possible implementation of some sort of autonomy regime.

Panama

Panama's first *comarca* was created in the wake of the 1925 Kuna revolt against the attempts at forced assimilation by the Panamanian state (Howe 1998).[16] A peace treaty was signed under US supervision, recognizing the autonomy of the Kuna region without much specification. In 1930 a reserve was created, which eight years later was transformed into the Comarca de San Blas. It comprises some fifty small islands and a strip of land on Panama's east coast, ending at the Colombian border. Meanwhile, in the wake of the revolt the Kuna undertook a comprehensive, planned reorganization of their social system under the leadership of their traditional authorities. After factional divisions had been overcome, in 1945 this process resulted in the drawing up of an Organic Charter of San Blas, which specified the governmental structure of the local community congresses, stipulated that there would be three principal *caciques* and created a Kuna General Congress.[17] In 1953 a Panamanian law organized the San Blas Comarca (or Kuna Yala),[18] detailed the areas of Kuna autonomy, and recognized the political structure as established in the 1945 Organic Charter. The comarca is officially administered by a government appointed *Intendente* while the Kuna authorities, according to rank, were given the status of "police inspectors" on the state payroll (*América Indígena* 1995; Pérez Archibold 1998; Turpana 1994).

Although this construction has been a source of friction, the Kuna have managed to defend their land and self-government. Kuna autonomy has regularly come under pressure from different sides. Tourism is one of the problems that generated tensions from the 1960s onward. North American tourist ventures were established in the late 1960s with the permission of the Kuna chiefs, but without permission from the General Congress. By 1981 the two resorts were closed after having been attacked and torched by groups of Kuna. Similarly, the Panamanian government has sought to sponsor large-scale projects such as a resort hotel on an artificial island in Kuna territory, which in the late 1970s led to a deep crisis between the government, the Kuna Congress and the *caciques*, who had endorsed feasibility studies without Congress permission. By the mid-1990s the government developed plans to construct a military base in Kuna territory to counter drug trade and armed intrusions from Colombia. As a result of opposition from the Kuna the project finally was shelved. Intrusions by Colombian guerrilla bands, groups of gold-miners and drug-traders constitute further problems, as well as the incursions of mestizo peasants in search of land. The latter problem was countered with the much-praised PEMASKY project, a cooperative effort between the Kuna Congress and environmentalist NGOs to establish a self-managed forest-reserve. The project managed to halt the invasion by peasants and buy out those already established, but failed to achieve its broader aims (Arias and Chapin 1998; Howe 2002).

Meanwhile, the Kuna are attempting to strengthen their self-government structures and improve administrative continuity. Also, at least since the early 1980s attempts have been made to update the Kuna Organic Charter and the 1953 enabling legislation, but such attempts have not met with government support (*América Indígena* 1995; Howe 2002). Neither has the government been responsive to demands that it ratify ILO Convention 169.

The Comarca Kuna Yala and its mode of governance have stood as a model for the creation of other *comarcas* in Panama, which by 2000 numbered five. Two of them are Kuna *comarcas* (1996; 2000) on the mainland and two others were created for the Emberá-Wounaan (1983) and the Ngöbe-Buglé (1997). One of the problems with introducing this form of self-government for the latter groups is that the governance structure of the Kuna Organic Charter was copied, although it does not fit their modes of social and political organization.

Colombia

Colombia is the other case where we find a direct consociation model of formal political autonomy, which was instituted through the 1991 Constitution.[19] That same year the country ratified ILO Convention 169. Colombia counts over eighty indigenous peoples, which together count a little under eight hundred thousand persons and make up nearly 2 percent of the total population. Despite this small number indigenous representatives came to play a key role in the constitutional process and Colombia's indigenous peoples gained an important set of rights (Van Cott 2000). The *resguardos* were recognized as inalienable collective property governed by indigenous *cabildos* (councils) according to the regulations and customary practice of the indigenous communities.

Resguardos, governed by *cabildos*, had first been created under colonial rule. During the nineteenth century attempts were made to extinguish them until, in 1890, the process was temporarily stalled by Law 89, which recognized the existence of the *resguardos* and *cabildos* for the time being. Nevertheless, *resguardos* continued to be divided up[20] and by the 1960s only some seventy still existed. In 1961, encouraged by the Alliance for Progress, an agrarian reform law was passed and a year later the *Instituto Colombiano de Reforma Agraria* (INCORA) was created. In the late 1960s the new institute became more active under the pressure of emerging indigenous and peasant movements that started to implement a land reform of their own through invasions.[21] Beginning in the early 1980s the still existing *resguardos* were consolidated and new ones were created.

Besides the *resguardos*, from 1967 onward often very large "reserves" were formed in the Amazon region, sometimes containing various indigenous peoples. After the promulgation of the 1991 constitution these "reserves" were converted into *resguardos* and thus became the collective property of their inhabitants. By the early 1990s some 400 *resguardos* existed and after the promulgation of the new constitution the number grew to 638 in 2001. By then, the *resguardos* covered some 31 million hectares, about a quarter of the national territory. Eighty-five percent of this total is located in the Amazon region, which houses 9 percent of the total indigenous population, divided into fifty-eight peoples.[22] It is estimated that 87 percent of the indigenous population lives in the *resguardos* (Arango and Sánchez 2002; Colombia 1995; Pineda 2001: 36–37).

The 1991 constitution not only consolidated the *resguardos* and recognized *cabildos*, but specified a further set of rights. Indigenous authorities have the right to exercise jurisdiction in the *resguardos* according to their own norms and procedures (special jurisdiction) (art. 246), to apply legal norms of land use and population in their territories, to design and implement development plans, to promote public investment, to receive and administer (financial) resources, to conserve natural resources, to coordinate projects of the communities in their territory, to cooperate with the maintenance of public order following the instructions and dispositions of the national government, and to represent their territories to the national government (art. 330). Furthermore, it was stipulated that statutory law should determine which *resguardos* will be given a status equal to that of the municipalities and in this way receive a portion of the national income.[23] The share of national income going to municipalities or their equivalents would rise to 22 percent in 2002 (art. 357).

According to another article in the constitution departments, districts, municipalities, and indigenous territories are considered *entidades territoriales* and will be autonomous within the limits set by the constitution and the law (art. 286). They are entitled to: (1) govern themselves through their own authorities; (2) exercise the competencies that correspond to them; (3) administrate resources and establish taxes necessary to fulfill their functions; and (4) partake in national tax-revenues (art. 287). The constitution as well envisions the creation of *Entidades Territoriales Indígenas* (ETIs) (art. 329) in the context of a *Ley Orgánica de Ordenamiento Territorial.* The idea was that the ETIs would be something like autonomous indigenous regions and this was strongly advocated by indigenous representatives in the constituent assembly (Cepeda 2001: 160–170). The proposal, however, met with strong opposition and was only introduced in the constitution at the last minute in very ambiguous terms (Van Cott 2000: 94–95).

The new constitution also created a special electoral district by which two seats in the national senate are reserved for indigenous representatives (art. 117).[24] Colombia's constitutional process responded to the mounting crisis in the country (Van Cott 2000) and was not only influenced by indigenous delegates and their allies in the constitutional assembly but also by social movements, liberals and neoliberals who, for diverse motives, pushed for decentralization. The recognition of indigenous autonomy therefore should be viewed in this broader context of a decentralization drive and the attempts to end the violent conflicts plaguing the country.

Implementation of the reforms was facilitated by government commitment to the reform agenda, the rulings of the new Constitutional Court that often were in favor of indigenous peoples, and the strength of the indigenous movement and related political parties (Cepeda 2001; Van Cott 2000; 2002). Funds started to be disbursed in 1994 and by 1997 the *resguardos* were receiving approximately US$61,000 on average. This also has resulted in difficulties, however. Nonindigenous mayors or departmental governors act as intermediary recipients of the funds and the *resguardos* have to present an investment plan. In some cases these have not been duly transferred to the *resguardos* (Arango and Sánchez 2002; Van Cott 2002: 50–51).[25] Within the *resguardos* themselves the administrative capacity is unequal. The start of the transfers was accompanied by a series of seminars, workshops, etc., which made one indigenous leader remark that "nowadays, one needs a lot of time to be an Indian" (Padilla 1995: 147). Such accommodation to administrative norms of the state perhaps is not simply bad in and of itself but, as Padilla (1995) argues, it has its drawbacks in that it tends to increase the possibilities for state intervention in the internal affairs of indigenous peoples and in requiring them to act according to state norms in the management of budgets, projects, and development plans. Traditional knowledge and authority figures tend to be set aside and younger people, or even NGOs, assume the management of indigenous affairs (Padilla 1996). Such "normalization" diminishes the possibilities for freely choosing their own destiny. The delegation of administrative affairs to the *resguardos* is based on the assumption that their self-government is organized according to the *cabildo*-model that has emerged in the Andes region since colonial times.

This, however, is not always the case and, particularly in the Amazon region, this has created problems. Another case is that of the Wayúu who do not have a centralized political organization. The availability of funding triggered a genuine regional crisis when some Wayúu groups were qualified and others excluded (Pineda 2001: 50).

This form of autonomy, in the context of state decentralization, thus may come as a mixed blessing. On the other hand, while the Gaviria government showed some commitment to the indigenous cause, since 1994 the hopes generated by the new constitution have been dashed. In the context of neoliberal policies and in response to the growing fiscal and political crisis the Colombian governments have sought to implement mega-projects for natural resource exploitation (oil, minerals, hydroelectricity, African palm) that often affect indigenous peoples. By the late 1990s the requirements for granting licenses for natural resource exploitation on indigenous territories were relaxed and the government sought to condition the granting of *resguardo* lands to the prior approval of production projects based on "strategic alliances" with the private sector. Agroindustrial projects have become key to the Plan Colombia.

Such policies and above all the escalation of armed conflict threaten the very existence of the indigenous peoples of Colombia (Jackson 2002). On the other hand, as noted, the 1991 constitution foresees the creation of a new type of territorial entity, the ETI, albeit in very ambiguous terms. Some efforts to define such ETIs were made with the support of the PNUD and in cooperation with the ONIC but soon the process stalled. By 2001, however, the government had launched a new initiative to formulate a *Ley Orgánica de Ordenamiento Territorial* (LOOT). This initiative plays on the ambiguity of the constitution. Whereas the ONIC would argue that Article 286 implies the automatic recognition of *resguardos* as indigenous territorial entities and that Article 329 provides for the creation of regions comprising several *resguardos* or perhaps some sort of multiethnic regions, the government project argues that the two articles should be related, with nefarious implications for the status of the *resguardos* because it introduces population size (>3,000 inhabitants) or surface (>80,000 hectares) as criteria for the recognition of territorial entities of whatever type.[26] Only seventy-four *resguardos* comply with one or both of these criteria. They house nearly 70 percent of the people living in *resguardos* and represent some 85 percent of the total area covered by *resguardos*. Forty percent of the indigenous population of the country, that is including those not living in *resguardos*, would be barred from the possibility to live in an *Entidad Territorial Indígena* (ETI) (Arango and Sánchez 2002). This is what might be called a "bitter harvest" of indigenous participation in the confection of the 1991 constitution and the subsequent neoliberal and increasingly right-wing implementation of this constitution.

Ecuador

Ecuador's indigenous peoples began creating new organizations in the 1960s and in 1986 formed the umbrella organization *Confederación de Nacionalidades Indígenas del Ecuador* (CONAIE), one of the strongest indigenous organizations in Latin America.[27] In 1990 a *Levantamiento General* made the indigenous cause a national concern and was followed by various other large mobilizations throughout the decade. In 1994 the organization launched its political platform in which it demanded a new constitution (CONAIE 1994). CONAIE played a key role in the ousting of President Abdalá Bucaram in 1997 and, through the related Pachakutik political party, successfully pressured for the convocation of a constituent assembly that produced a new constitution in June 1998 (Espinosa 2000; Macdonald 2002; Van Cott 2002). ILO Convention 169 was ratified that same year.

To pressure for the convocation of a Constituent Assembly CONAIE and other social movements organized a "People's Assembly" of their own to develop a proposal for a new constitution. The assembly started its work on October 12, Columbus Day, and by mid-December, just before the official Constituent Assembly began to meet, the People's Assembly approved a *Proyecto de Constitución del Estado Plurinacional de Ecuador* (CONAIE 1998). In early January this project was officially presented in the National Constituent Assembly.

As a result of such pressure and the presence of Pachakutik delegates in the official assembly the new constitution came to include some of the viewpoints of the indigenous movement. In its first article it declares the Ecuadorian state to be pluricultural and multiethnic. It also is the first Latin American constitution that includes the Quechua moral principles *ama quilla, ama lulla, ama shua* (don't be lazy, don't lie, don't steal) (art. 97). The idea of a multinational state advocated by CONAIE, however, was only vaguely reflected in an article, which speaks of "indigenous peoples, who define themselves as nationalities" (art. 83). The next article stipulates a series of collective rights of indigenous and Afro-Ecuadorian peoples (art. 84) and the chapter on the territorial organization of the state and decentralization introduces the possibility of creating ethnically defined territorial circumscriptions (art. 224).

Despite the multinational rhetoric of CONAIE and its allies and despite the fact that the proposal of the People's Assembly spoke of the "territories of the indigenous nationalities" and of "territories of the black *comarcas*," very little of all this was concretely reflected in the new constitution except for the mention of the "territorial circumscriptions" to be created by law. Overall, however, the new constitution is more concerned with decentralization and hardly modifies the territorial organization of the state. This can be attributed to various factors. For most political actors in Ecuador the theme of decentralization was secondary and was mostly promoted by the multilateral banking agencies. In 1997 a law was adopted according to which by 2000, 15 percent of the national budget was to be assigned to the "sectional governments."[28] As far as the autonomy theme is present, it is mostly related to Guayaquil regionalist demands for autonomy for the Guayas Province motivated by the wish not to share taxes generated there with the other provinces. This may be one reason for the indigenous movement not to play out the autonomy theme.[29] Although there is quite some debate over decentralization and a reordering of the country's administrative structure there is hardly any consensus, and in the end the Constituent Assembly left the existing structure of provinces, cantons, and *parroquias* (parishes) untouched. It only attempted a somewhat more specific definition of competencies, but they remain vague and ill defined (León Trujillo 1998). On the other hand, there is no consensus within the indigenous movement and a variety of proposals to implement "territorial circumscriptions" is in circulation. The lack of consensus is related to rivalries within and between movements and to different views of a possible autonomy regime.[30] Proposals that go in the direction of democratization and multiethnicity vie with proposals that are based on a monoethnic vision.[31] Neither is it clear whether the circumscriptions should coincide with one of the existing levels of the administrative structure or constitute a new level with distinct functions (Trujillo 2000; Van Cott 2002). This is further complicated by regional differences. While in some regions, especially the Amazon region, indigenous peoples occupy continuous territories, the situation is much more complex in the highlands.[32] While debate is ongoing the Pachakutik party has made important electoral gains, both on the national and the subnational level. In 2000 it won the elections for prefects in five provinces as well as twenty-seven municipalities giving rise to attempts to create alternative forms of local government without modifying the institutional structure of the provinces and cantons. In this context the tendency seems to be to assimilate the indigenous territorial circumscriptions to the local community level and the *juntas parroquiales*.[33] Meanwhile, the trajectory of the indigenous movement has been marked by the January 2000 uprising, which ended the Mahuad government and briefly brought CONAIE leader Antonio Vargas to the presidency.

New protests against the neoliberal policies of the Noboa government took place in February 2001 and in the 2002 elections Lúcio Gutiérrez, the colonel who had led the lower-rank military in the ousting of Mahuad, was elected to the presidency with strong support from the indigenous population. The initial honeymoon soon was over, however, and by April 2003 the indigenous movement started to pressure its representatives within the new government to withdraw if no clear break was made with IMF policies and free trade area initiatives. A few months later the alliance with Gutiérrez broke down.

Nicaragua

Nicaragua's Atlantic coast region, which comprises about half of the country's surface, has had a history that sets it apart from the rest of the country. Whereas the west of the country was occupied by Spanish colonial forces on the less accessible Atlantic coast the indigenous population forged alliances with pirates from various European countries and in 1687 the British crowned a Miskito "king" whereby the region became a British protectorate. That ended in 1860 when, after rivalries with the United States, the British signed a treaty by which the region was returned to Nicaragua. A border conflict with Honduras in 1894 spurred the military incorporation of the region and brought an end to the Miskito "kingdom." By the mid-nineteenth century the Moravian Church established itself in the region and became a principal structure of governance. The regional economy was largely dominated by US interests that exploited wood and minerals and established banana plantations (Standard Fruit).

The autonomy regime for the region is the outcome of the conflict with the Sandinista revolutionary government that replaced the Somoza dictatorship in 1979. Although relations with the Sandinistas initially seemed promising they soon deteriorated. The introduction of Spanish language alphabetization in a region where indigenous languages and English predominated was one issue; attempts to incorporate the region and its natural resources to the benefit of the revolutionary nation was another. Suspicions about local separatism led the Sandinistas to arrest local indigenous leaders and tensions were exacerbated by the 1982 Sandinista decision to evacuate Miskito villages in the border region with Honduras, which had become a center of *contra* attacks and alliance-making with the indigenous leadership, sponsored by the Reagan administration.[34] In response the Sandinista government changed its attitude and started negotiating an autonomy statute for the region in the context of a pacification strategy (Scherrer 1994).

The changes in the constitution and the autonomy statute were achieved in 1987.[35] Initial high-level negotiations between the government and one of the indigenous organizations broke off five months after the cease-fire in 1985. Both the Sandinistas and the leadership of the organization had their reasons for not continuing these negotiations. The Sandinista then initiated a broad consultation process with the local population, which although skeptical was willing to accept what the government had to offer (Hale 1996). The outcomes of the process were approved during a mass meeting in April 1987.[36] The autonomy statute created two 45+ seat[37] autonomous regional councils to govern the autonomous regions of the north Atlantic coast (RAAN) and the south Atlantic coast (RAAS), to be elected by popular vote. The councils, in turn, elect a governing board and a coordinator (*gobernador*). Each of the indigenous peoples in the regions, four and six in RAAN and RAAS, respectively, should have at least one representative on the governing board to assure representation of the smaller groups.[38] Candidates can either be presented by political parties or by *grupos de suscripción popular* (popular lists), which was meant to allow for the formation and participation of regional political organizations. The regions, in turn, are subdivided into municipalities. The statute furthermore incorporates a series of economic, cultural, juridical, and ecological rights.[39] The statute is only a first step and should be complemented by further regulatory legislation. The autonomy granted by the statute is rather relative. The regional councils do not have a budget of their own but present a proposal to the central government. They may initiate social, cultural, and economic projects, but only on the basis of regional taxes to be established conforming to state laws and the promotion of regional market integration. For other development programs they participate in design or execution or administrate programs in coordination with state agencies. The regions share in the benefits deriving from natural resource exploitation, but the share they receive is not specified. And although mention is made of "communal authorities" this does not go beyond a token recognition of indigenous authorities or political institutions (Acosta 1996; Cunningham 1998; Scherrer 1994).

Implementation of the autonomy regime only slowly got under way due to the difficult circumstances in the region and factional struggles among indigenous organizations, some siding with the Sandinistas and others with the opposition. For their part, the Sandinistas had an interest in postponing elections for the councils and implementing development projects and social services in the meantime to garner sympathy among the population.

The elections were only held in 1990 and then coincided with the national elections in which the Sandinistas were defeated by the *Unión Nacional Opositora* (UNO) coalition. None of the parties in the new government coalition had any sympathy for the autonomy statute. Moreover, at the regional level, one of the leaders of the autonomy movement, Brooklyn Rivera, had at the last moment declared support for the UNO in return for promises to gain a cabinet post. Rivera became minister of a new government agency, the *Instituto Nicaragüense de Desarrollo de las Regiones Autónomos* (INDERA). INDERA was not only assigned a budget beside which the budget allocated to the regional councils paled but it also was given decision powers over natural resources in the autonomous regions which turned their autonomy into a scam. The effective implementation of an autonomy regime under new governments of a neoliberal, and paradoxically[40] centralizing, orientation thus was prone to generate a series of conflicts and crises.

The first years after the 1990 election of regional councils were characterized by strong polarization. In the RAAS the UNO majority rejected any cooperation with the nearly equally strong Sandinista delegation. Although in subsequent elections, held every four years, *grupos de subscripción popular* gained some influence national-level parties continued to dominate regional politics. A crisis in the RAAN council, which failed to meet throughout May 1999 to May 2000, reflected national level rivalries and was finally resolved through a pact between the Sandinistas and the *Partido Liberal Constitucional* (PLC). Similarly, conflicts between the councils and the coordinators reflected national level loyalties. Such political polarization often virtually paralyzed the regional councils and led traditional authorities, Councils of Elders, to call for solutions. Thus, paradoxically, the nonrecognition of traditional authorities enhanced their respectability.

Despite such problems the regional councils did not altogether fail to function and in 1993 they proposed regulatory legislation for the 1987 autonomy statute. In 1998 a new proposal was presented as a citizen's initiative, supported by twelve thousand signatures, but national governments have until now lacked the political will to consider the proposal. The absence of regulation translates into problems of institutionalization and accountability of the autonomous governance structure. It also is reflected in the relations between the regional structures and the central government, which became more conflictive under the Alemán government (1997–2001) that sought to recentralize power in the executive (Cunningham 1998; Díaz-Polanco 1999; MIN/CALPI 2000; Ortega Hegg 1996).

Natural resource management, in particular, is an area of conflict. One of the best-known cases is that of the community of Awas Tingni, which saw its lands invaded by the Korean lumbering enterprise SOLCARSA. A concession had been granted by the Ministry of the Environment and Natural Resources (MARENA) with the support of the governing board of the RAAN. Although the Supreme Court of Justice decided in 1997 that the concession was illegal, MARENA pressured the RAAN regional council into endorsing it. In the face of the laxity of the justice system, to which it appealed on various occasions, the Awas Tingni community appealed to the Inter-American Commission for Human Rights. In an unprecedented decision in 2001 the commission ruled in favor of the community and ordered the Nicaraguan government to delimit and title community lands (Acosta 2000). To date the government has failed to do so.[41] Nonetheless, by the end of 2002 a law on demarcation and titling of communal lands was approved and is expected to have some beneficial effects in the long run.

Conclusion

The last decades of the past century have seen important changes in the relation between indigenous peoples and the Latin American states. Formally, at least, the multicultural and pluriethnic composition of the populations has been recognized, but as Stavenhagen (2002: 34) has put it, after these promising beginnings "the going will be rough from now on." The foregoing discussion confirms this view. In this chapter I focused on four cases of formal political autonomy regimes in Latin America. It should be noted, however, that there are other types of legislation that purport to enable indigenous self-determination. The 1994 Bolivian Law of Popular Participation is a case in point. However, although this law opened up some space for indigenous participation in local government it is essentially a decentralization measure in the context of neoliberal "second generation" reform policies (Albó 2002; Calla 2000). Another example might be the Mexican state of Oaxaca, which in 1995 recognized the right of indigenous communities to elect their authorities according to customary practice. On the other hand, we might mention the self-styled effective autonomy of the Zapatista communities and the *Regiones Autónomas Pluriétnicas* in Chiapas, which are inspired by the Nicaraguan model (Díaz-Polanco 1997; López y Rivas 1995; Mattiace, Hernández, and Rus 2002).

Let us try to summarize some of the main points that emerge from the foregoing discussion in the light of the theoretical framework developed in the first part of this chapter, looking at the formal aspect, the scope of effective political autonomy and autonomy as empowerment or the freedom of a population to choose its own destiny (Table 8.2).

Table 8.2. Comparison of Autonomy Regimes in Latin America

	Panama	Colombia	Ecuador	Nicaragua
De jure Level of autonomy	Regional	Local, ETIs not implemented	Local, status of territorial circumscriptions unclear	Regional
Type of autonomy	Direct consociation	Direct consociation	Indirect consociation	Indirect consociation
De facto control of territory	High	Declining	Moderate	Low, but perhaps increasing moderately
Institutional Representation	High, through established party system	Formally high, electoral district and own parties at national and municipal level	Not formal but in practice, through own political and representation in government agencies	Low, through established parties but also through regional "popular lists"
Fiscal Autonomy	Somewhat	Formally recognized but declining	Municipal level, "alternative" government	Low
Respect	Moderate	Declining on the part of the state	Moderate	Low, largely depending onpaltry allocations
Empowerment	Reasonable, probably increasing	Tenuous in a context of violence	Increasing	Low and disputed

The comparison presented here is, of course, extremely crude, but nevertheless suggestive. In Panama we find an autonomy regime that has taken form since the 1920s, in the case of the Kuna, and which has allowed them to exercise a relatively high degree of what Bonfil Batalla (1981) has called "cultural control." Bonfil Batalla's scheme (Table 8.3) is helpful in framing the issues at hand.

The framework proposed by Bonfil Batalla can be combined with Barth's (1969) perspective on interethnic relations, which was subsequently taken up by Nagel and Snipp (1993) in their discussion of "ethnic reorganization," which includes forms of social, economic, political, and cultural reorganization. Such frameworks highlight the dynamics of intercultural interaction and the degree of control over cultural change, or "agency," exercised by the "subaltern" population. If we look at the cases under study from this

Table 8.3. "Cultural Control"

Cultural elements	Decisions	
	Own	**Alien**
Own	Autonomous culture	Alienated culture
Alien	Appropriated culture	Imposed culture

Source: Bonfil Batalla 1981: 50.

perspective it becomes clear that the Kuna have achieved a relatively high degree of cultural control, blending autonomous culture with appropriated elements in a process of comprehensive reorganization of their social and political system led by their traditional authorities. Currently they are pushing for further internal reform and a clarification of their relation to the Panamanian state, a process that affects the framing of issues for the other indigenous peoples in the country who, more recently, saw their autonomy condoned.

If we look at the formal aspects of the four cases presented here we should first of all note the difference in scale. In Panama and Nicaragua we find regional level autonomy, in the first case monoethnic and in the second case pluriethnic. In Colombia we have an intermediary situation in the sense that some *resguardos* are quite large, comprise several communities, and sometimes are pluriethnic. The promise held out by the ETI formula however did not materialize and, as we saw, may actually be turned against *resguardo* autonomy. In the case of Ecuador the status of indigenous territorial circumscriptions remains undefined, but we have noted that, particularly in the Andes region, they tend to be assimilated to the lowest level of the institutional state structure. It would rather be a matter of labeling specific *parroquias* "indigenous."

To be sure, each of these cases should be considered against the background of the specific national context. That might explain, for example, why in Ecuador regional autonomy is not a big issue in the Andean context and working through the existing institutional structure of municipal government seems to be a viable option. Moreover, the indigenous movement is strong at the national level and heavily engaged in national politics and in the implementation of policies through CODENPE, where it is strongly represented on the governing board. The engagement in national politics also means that popular demands and demands for democratization are balanced with specific ethnic demands. The issue of the scale of autonomy, however, is not altogether irrelevant. Díaz-Polanco (1997: 27–31) talks of the "myth of the invincible community" to argue in favor of regional autonomy. The community, he argues, is not as invincible as some would claim but rather is a last line of resistance. Creating an additional level of supra-community administrative organization would contribute to strengthening the local level and thus contribute to effective autonomy; hence his defense of regional autonomy schemes.

Looking at the question of effective autonomy we can combine the notion with Bennagen's operational features of self-government. Probably we should say that the Kuna have succeeded in defending a rather high level of effective autonomy while at the same time establishing a pragmatic, though not tension-free, working relationship with the Panamanian state. Above all they have managed to ward off state-imposed projects for natural resource exploitation and tourism development. They also largely control their internal structures of governance and the way they adapt them to changing circumstances. They have some capacity to raise local taxes and to demand compensation for certain uses of their territory (e.g., telephone or electricity cables). By contrast, natural resource use is a highly contested issue in Nicaragua where the autonomy regime is weakly institutionalized and poorly respected by the national governments. Some advances can be signaled (e.g., local universities) and political and interethnic polarization has been held in check (Cunningham 1998). Nonetheless, the political infighting and the consequent virtual paralysis of the autonomous councils is resulting in a decreasing interest among the local population, which is reflected in the abstention rates in regional elections, which went from 22 percent in 1990 to 63 percent in 2002, though it should be noted that abstention is significantly higher among the mestizos than among the indigenous population. The difficulties in substantiating autonomy and the increasingly tense relations with the national government have led the Miskito Council of Elders to adopt a radical stance advocating the creation of an independent state (Marshall and Gurr 2003: 58).

In Colombia and Ecuador issues of natural resource use also are prominent. In both cases consultation procedures have been introduced. How sound such procedures are is controversial. In the case of the U'wa in Colombia a ruling by the Constitutional Court in favor of the U'wa, who rejected oil exploration in their territory, was overruled by the Council of State in 1997. As noted, since 1994 Colombian governments have sought to reverse and reduce the advances made possible by the 1991 constitution and their policies may be characterized as a case of "neoliberal multiculturalism" and token recognition of the rights of indigenous peoples.

While in nearly all cases the exploitation of subsoil resources is a source of conflict, the overlap of conservation areas and national parks with indigenous territories is another source of friction and dispute over the management of surface resources.

With regard to natural resource use and previous consultation the "colonization of the mind" theme has recently been taken up by Ramírez (2002), in a, in my opinion, somewhat perverse way, in relation to oil exploitation in Colombia. She argues that in such consultations local leaderships and traditional authorities tend to be displaced by new "'indigenous elites'—state sponsored leaders," and that regional and national level leaders overruled the decisions made by local traditional authorities. A local organization had negotiated a US$25,000 "major integral development plan"[42] with an oil company in exchange for allowing exploitation. This was vetoed after the intervention of a national-level ONIC leader. It is not the place here to go into the details of the case, but rather to point to Wray's (2000) discussion of the logic of previous consultation in Ecuador. She shows how oil companies seek to present segmented information that does not reveal the full potential impact and how they seek to come to agreements with different groups, playing them off against each other. In such circumstances one cannot be too sure that the outcome is in the best interest of a local community and the intervention of a higher-level organization may well be desirable. That is to say that somewhat colonized minds may be required to see the dangers of negotiating with powerful interested parties. The improvement of previous consultation procedures is an ongoing and controversial process and a strengthening of the parties that negotiate from a disadvantaged position is badly needed to assure that they have more effective control over their destiny.

The recognition of indigenous institutions is related to the formal features of the autonomy regime, whether it follows a direct or indirect consociation model. The situation on the ground can be highly complex, however. While in Panama and Colombia a direct consociation model has been adopted formally, we also have noted that the Kuna charter with its congress model and the *cabildo* form of government have provided models that have been applied to situations where other forms of indigenous organization exist. On the other hand, in Ecuador indigenous forms of organization coexist and interact with municipal organization, while in Nicaragua the relation between indigenous institutions and the regional and national government is fraught with tension and conflict. While we can say that much, it should be noted that it is difficult to generalize because situations vary by region, particularly in the cases of Ecuador and Colombia where the differences between the Andean highlands and the Amazonian lowlands with their distinct modes of indigenous organization should be taken into account. Furthermore, regarding the Colombian case we have noted that the possibilities for effective self-government tend to be undermined by new legislation and the freedom of peoples to choose their own destiny is increasingly hedged in by the attempts to incorporate the *resguardos* into the formal administrative structure of the state and its supervisors. Although more funding has been reaching the *resguardos* and has contributed to the improvement of some conditions it tends to come at the price of an imposed administrative culture, particularly in the Amazon region. The escalation of violence further reduces the scope for effective self-government and the pursuit of a self-chosen destiny.

As to political involvement and representation in state structures Iturralde (1997) has pointed to the dynamic of indigenous political organization and argues that the articulation of a political platform tends to involve a maximization and juridization of demands and that this creates tensions with the local organizations characterized by more immediate production and welfare oriented concerns. More generally, the process of political organization is fraught with paradoxes and presents the indigenous movements with a series of challenges. It is beyond the scope of this article to fully discuss such issues, but let me briefly enumerate some. For one thing, there is the relationship between leadership and bases. This involves the process of class differentiation among indigenous peoples. The emergence of the new movements was related to the emergence of something like a native middle class, which certainly is being empowered through the dialectics between identity politics and the politics of recognition.

At the same time this affected organizational structures and created tensions between traditional authority structures and emerging leaderships of new organizations. In his classic essay Barth (1969: 35) had already observed that in situations of conflict the opposed parties tend to become structurally similar and differentiated only by a few clear criteria. One paradox here seems to be that while this creates tensions between traditional authority structures and emerging organizational structures it also spurs "strategic essentializing" and a renewed emphasis on "tradition," which, formally at least, might empower traditional authorities.[43] The tension between the Kuna Congress and their traditional authorities illustrates the complexity of the issue and it refers back to my discussion of the dynamics of previous consultation. The Kuna Congress repeatedly disavowed decisions made by the traditional authorities and this highlights the issue of internal democracy of the indigenous movements, or more precisely what the Zapatistas call *mandar obedeciendo.* In the case of the Kuna Congress we might say that on some occasions the voice of those whose minds were a bit more "colonialized" strengthened self-determination.

These considerations bring us back to Hoekema's (1996) thoughts on empowerment. Does the recognition of indigenous rights really enfranchise a "people" or does it only benefit a small elite? Again, it is difficult to generalize. As has been noted, the emergence of the new indigenous movements was related to processes of internal differentiation among indigenous peoples and to the rise of a new generation of indigenous intellectuals. At the same time the formation of the new movements imply processes of ethnic reorganization.

Such processes are not tension-free and often involve a questioning of traditional power structures and the emergence of new power groups. How this actually works out can only be assessed on a case-by-case basis. Quite probably the difficulties in institutionalizing the Nicaraguan autonomy regime are related to interethnic and intraethnic friction, fuelled by the state and the party system. On the other hand, in the other three cases more solid forms of organization seem to balance or check such tensions, often through the introduction of elements of democracy, as is the case in the reorganization of Kuna governance and the establishment of the congress system. The involvement with "wider society" and in the struggle for democracy and respect for human rights furthermore influences the processes of ethnic reorganization and it is in such a context that one can speak of "reflexive identity politics" (Eriksen 2001: 45). Such reflexivity leads to a questioning of certain features of indigenous cultures and issues like the position of indigenous women, human rights or the relation between ethnicity and class[44] are a matter of debate within indigenous movements.

Finally, one important feature of autonomy is that it is not about isolation but rather about the conditions for participation (Assies, van der Haar, and Hoekema 2000: 301). As noted, Colombia has reserved two seats in the senate for indigenous representatives. In that country indigenous political parties do reasonably well on the national level due to the sympathy vote of the urban electorate and actually three more indigenous senators have been elected while on the local level indigenous people have been elected mayor and into municipal councils (Arango and Sánchez 2002). In Ecuador the Pachakutik party has become a strong political player. In Nicaragua and Panama indigenous representation is channeled through the established party system and we have noted the problems this can create in the case of Nicaragua. One challenge for such political involvement is to go beyond formulating national proposals for indigenous issues and to come up with indigenous proposals for national problems (Iturralde 1997). Another, related, challenge is not to get trapped in the juridization of discourse. The framing of demands in terms of self-determination and the rights of peoples in quasi-international relations terminology may be helpful but it also has its limitations. One of these limitations is that the autonomy discourse makes it difficult to address the structural concerns that determine the role of indigenous peoples, such as overall fiscal, agrarian, transport, housing, educational, and other economic and social policies (Plant 2000: 42). In particular, the autonomy discourse, with its oftentimes rural bias, does not address the concerns of the increasing number of indigenous people living in urban areas. Such issues, as well as the question of the construction of pluriethnic regions, suggest that while autonomy and self-determination may be important, they should be embedded in a broader process of democratization, both formal and substantive, that empowers people to challenge "neoliberal multiculturalism" as well as neoliberalism as such.

Notes

This chapter was first published in 2005 as "Two Steps Forward, One Step Back: Indigenous Peoples and Autonomies in Latin America," in *Autonomy, Self-Governance and Conflict Resolution: Innovative Approaches to Institutional Design in Divided Societies*, ed. S. Wolff and M. Weller, London and New York: Routledge. We thank the editors and Taylor & Francis for their kind permission to republish.

1. Guatemala (1985), Brazil (1988), Nicaragua (1987, 1995), Colombia (1991), Mexico (1992, 2001), Paraguay (1992), Peru (1993), Argentina (1994), Bolivia (1994), Panama (1997), Ecuador (1998), and Venezuela (1999). Chile adopted special legislation in 1993.
2. ILO Convention 169 was ratified by Mexico (1990), Norway (1990), Colombia (1991), Bolivia (1991), Costa Rica (1993), Paraguay (1993), Peru (1994), Honduras (1995), Denmark (1996), Guatemala (1996), the Netherlands (1998), Fijí (1998), Ecuador (1998), Argentina (2000), Venezuela (2002), the Dominican Republic (2002), and Brazil (2002).
3. This reflects one of the very gross distinctions often made between the peoples of the highland regions and Meso-America and those of the Amazon region. The former often have extensively been involved in market relations and in forms of peasant trade unionism, either promoted by left-wing organizations or by developmentist states. The latter often are not sedentary, have not been involved in market relations on the same scale, and have had little experience with peasant unionism. Their emergence and new visibility dates from the 1970s.
4. Liberation Theology is a current within the Catholic Church that emerged after the Second Vatican Council (1962–1965), which opened the way for dialogue with Marxism and dependency theory. In the late 1960s the Latin American Church officially adopted a "preferential option for the poor." Liberation Theology was extremely important in the opposition against authoritarian rule in a country like Brazil and the rights of indigenous peoples figured prominently on the agenda. One should also remember that the ground for the Chiapas rebellion in Mexico was partly prepared by Liberation Theology inspired missionary labor.
5. This, however, should not lead us to reduce the issue to ethnic identity and deny that class or other dimensions play a role. It is rather the intersection between different aspects such as ethnic identity, class, gender, religion, etc. that should be taken into account. The notion of "being Indian again" is taken from Vázquez León (1992).
6. Christopher Columbus "discovered" the Americas in 1492. To celebrate the event Ibero-American diplomacy invented the lavishly funded "encounter," which was an occasion for indigenous peoples and their allies to drum up (often literally) support for countermanifestations and international networking.
7. This depends on the national constitutional systems of the respective states, and the way they address the incorporation or transformation of international obligations into domestic law. A recasting of the convention through legislation into domestic law may be required.
8. The Inter-American Development Bank (IADB) (2003) database allows for an assessment of congruence of national legislation with ILO Convention 169, which takes into account thirty-six key criteria.
9. For a discussion see Assies (1994). "Internal self-determination" is something that stops short of secession but its scope and depth are ill-defined as well as the way it relates to the state and to representation and participation in decision-making processes.

10. This definition slightly adapts an earlier definition by L. A. Rehof, one of the participants in the Nuuk meeting. The difference resides in the addition of "or on inhabitants of a specific and distinct territory."

11. It is important to note that such parliaments arose in the context of rather solid "Welfare States" and that territoriality perhaps is an emerging issue related to a way of life (reindeer herding). In the Latin American context territoriality still is a central rhetoric issue, despite the fact that indigenous people are often highly deterritorialized as a result of temporary labor migration or definitive migration to urban areas where they may claim autonomous neighborhoods. The question of how to deal with such issues is pending in Latin America. Indigenous movement representatives, even if they have lived in urban areas for most of their lives, tend to adopt a romantic view of "rural life" (interview with Nina Pacari, Quito, March 21, 2001). Rethinking such visions may be one of the main challenges for Latin American indigenous movements and political parties in times ahead.

12. This does not mean that I always follow the IADB classification. According to that classification, for example, the Bolivian Constitution declares the country plurilingual but, curiously for a country with a majority indigenous population, it does not say anything about the official use of indigenous languages. Similarly, the IADB index suggests that Mexico grant indigenous peoples legal status (*personalidad jurídica*) and regional autonomy, which is definitely not the case. The Mexican constitution, reformed in 2001, speaks of indigenous communities as "entities of public interest" and can be considered as an example of ambiguity. For Latin American legislation, see also the compilation by González Guerra (1999).

13. The IADB (2003) database provides some insight into the actual impact of constitutional stipulations on primary and secondary legislation and on jurisprudence. The database uses 142 variables to compare national legislation and jurisprudence yielding an indigenous legislation index and a country ranking different from the one presented here. The difference partly reflects the greater sophistication of the IADB index but it also is suggestive of the problems of classification and comparison.

14. For an analysis of the wording used in Latin American constitutions see Méndez (2002). The ambivalence in wording makes it difficult to present a definitive overview of the rights "granted" in the different constitutions.

    Panama's Constitution speaks of "promoting" bilingual alphabetization and Mexico "favors" bilingual and intercultural education. What words mean in practice depends on ongoing struggles over their interpretation.

15. Van Cott (2001) is more optimistic in this respect than Kuppe (2003), who highlights the ambiguities in Venezuela's constitution.

16. The comarca has its antecedents going back to the times before Panama was separated from Colombia in 1903 to create the canal.

17. Kuna governance is based on village meetings of a political-religious character. Each village has its principal *cacique* or *saila*, versed in Kuna lore. At the village meetings he chants from a hammock in a sacral language and is interpreted by the *argar*. They are assisted by *sualibedis*, a sort of police who maintain order during the meetings and call the population to attend them. The General Congress meets at least twice a year and is made up of *sailas* and a variety of other delegates and invitees. Besides the General Congress, which is the highest political-administrative organism, there is a General Congress of Kuna Culture, which is of a more religious nature and which elects the three principal *caciques* (Saila Dummagan) who then are ratified by the General Congress and represent the Kuna in relation to the Panamanian state.

18. Only in 1998, after long-standing pressure from the Kuna, was the name changed to comarca Kuna Yala. Out of a total of fifty-eight thousand Kuna in Panama some thirty-two thousand live in Kuna Yala (Howe 2002).

19. After attempts by the executive to introduce a reform of the constitution had failed the student movement started a campaign in favor of a Constituent Assembly and a plebiscite was held alongside the 1990 presidential elections. The movement in favor of a reform was partly triggered by drug-trade related violence.
20. Between 1910 and 1918, resistance in the Cauca region was organized by the Quitín Lame movement, called after its leader, who between 1914 and 1916 led the movement in an armed rebellion.
21. In 1970, a government-sponsored *Asociación Nacional de Usuarios Campesinos* (ANUC) was formed, from which an independent shadow-ANUC soon split off and began land invasions. A year later indigenous people in turn split off from this organization and formed the *Consejo Regional Indígena del Cauca* (CRIC) from which a nationwide organization *Organización Nacional Indígena de Colombia* (ONIC) emerged in 1980. At the same time another movement emerged that became known as the *Movimiento de Autoridades Indíge-nas de Colombia* (MAIC), which criticized the CRIC leadership for its conceptualizations of territory and indigenous identity (Findji 1992).
22. This is important to note since it also suggests that the creation of *resguardos* has not re-solved problems of land concentration in other regions, particularly in the Andes region (Arango and Sánchez 2002). The creation of *resguardos* largely relied on the transfer of state lands and much less on redistribution.
23. This stipulation was eliminated in 2001.
24. An arrangement only matched by Venezuela's 1999 Constitution. For a discussion of politi-cal participation of indigenous people through party structures, whether linked to the indig-enous movement or not, see Arango and Sánchez (2002). The success of such participation depends to a large measure on the support of nonindigenous voters in the large cities.
25. Law 60 from 1993, which regulated the transfer of funds to the *resguardos*, was replaced by a new Law 715 in 2001. Both laws expressly stipulate the areas in which transfer funds should be invested (Arango and Sánchez 2002).
26. By 2001 the government had dropped an earlier proposal (DNP-UDT 1999) according to which all *resguardos* would be given a status equal to municipalities and receive funding on that basis.
27. CONAIE was formed out of the *Confederación de Nacionalidades Indígenas de la Ama-zonía Ecuatoriana* (CONFENIAE) and the *Andean Ecuador Runacunapac Riccharimui* (ECUARUNARI) and in 1997 was joined by the *Coordinadora de Organizaciones Indí-genas de la Costa Ecuatoriana* (COINCE). Besides CONAIE exist two rival organizations, the *Federación Ecuatoriana de Indígenas Evangélicos* (FEINE) and the *Federación Nacional de Organizaciones Campesinos, Indígenas y Negros* (FENOCIN). Ecuador counts twelve in-digenous "nationalities" and one of them, the Quichua, who are the most numerous, is in turn subdivided in a dozen "peoples." Since each of these peoples is represented in the CONAIE, and in relations with government agencies in this manner the Quichua balance their numerical majority against the other smaller nationalities.
28. "Sectional governments" are the 22 provinces and the 215 cantons (municipalities). Within the municipalities there are *parroquias* (parishes). According to the constitution the prov-inces and cantons enjoy full autonomy.
29. Interview with Antonio Vargas, CONAIE President, Quito, March 21, 2001.
30. Such rivalries are also related to competition over power shares in the *Consejo de Desarrollo de las Nacionalidades y Pueblos del Ecuador* (CODENPE), a semi-government agency re-sponsible for a broad range of policies concerning indigenous peoples that was established in 1998, replacing earlier agencies (Van Cott 2002).
31. Interview with Miguel Lluco, General Coordinator of the Movimiento Pachakutik, Quito, March 20, 2001. In this interview Lluco clearly expresses his doubts about the territorial

circumscriptions and asserts that they might be a mechanism of self-isolation. On the other hand he stresses participation in elections and points out that the new constitution introduced the elections for *juntas parroquiales*, which were first held in 2000.

32. Interview with Nina Pacari, national deputy for the Pachaktik movement, Quito, March 21, 2001. In this interview Pacari furthermore argues that the theme of territorial circumscriptions still requires debate and points to the issue of the rights of nonindigenous minorities within such circumscriptions. Whereas she argues that in the Amazonian context larger regions might be feasible in the Andes context, the *juntas parroquiales* might want to denominate themselves *circumscripciones territoriales indígenas*. She attributes the lack of progress in the discussion over the circumscriptions to the priority accorded to the confection of a Law on the Indigenous Nationalities and Peoples, which basically would regulate their relations to state agencies with CONAIE as an intermediary instance. Where territories are concerned it should be noted that some territories have been granted in the 1990s in the Amazon region but that this has occurred in an ad hoc manner and without an adequate legal or institutional framework. In the Andes individual titling took place in the context of the agrarian reform legislation of the 1960s and 1970s (Plant and Hvalkof 2002).

33. On the other hand, the movement of Afro-Ecuadorians has developed a proposal for territorial circumscriptions according to which regional territorial councils (of the *palenque*) should be created, which unite various local communities.

34. *Yapti Tasba Masraka nanih asla taranka* (Unity of Children of the Land, YATAMA) emerged in 1987 as an umbrella organization bringing together three existing organizations. For an account of the complexities of local politics and of factionalisms and realignments see Scherrer (1994).

35. In 1995 the constitution was modified. Although initially an attempt was made to reverse the autonomy stipulations of the 1987 constitution, this was impeded by a coalition among indigenous peoples and Sandinista representatives (Díaz-Polanco 1999).

36. At the time ILO Convention 169 was not yet available as a frame of reference and, significantly, the post-Sandinista governments have not been inclined to ratify it (MIN/CALPI 2000). In the negotiations over the autonomy statute the Sandinista leadership rejected the ethnic autonomy proposals forwarded by the Miskito leadership and proposed to create multiethnic regions with limited and vaguely defined competencies. For an account of the episode see Hale (1996).

37. To the forty-five members of the council the national deputies chosen in the region are added. Thus the RAAN council effectively counts forty-eight members and the RAAS council forty-seven.

38. In 1995, the population of the RAAN is estimated at 186,354 inhabitants; 42 percent mestizos, 40 percent Miskitos, 10 percent Creoles, and 8 percent (Mayagnas) Sumos. The RAAS population would be 123,930; 54.8 percent mestizos, 29 percent Creoles, 12.1 percent Miskitos, 1.7 percent Garífunas, 0.7 percent Ramas, and 0.2 percent (Mayagnas) Sumos (Acosta 1996: 11).

39. For an overview of relevant legislation see MIN/CALPI (2000).

40. In their pacification efforts the Sandinistas had given up part of their centralist orientation, which was mostly about nationalism and access to the resources of the Atlantic region. Authority over resources is the main issue at stake for the neoliberal administrations, although they should be ideologically inclined to enhance decentralization and local management.

41. In 1998 the government presented a project for the regulation of indigenous community property in the region, which was related to a project for a biodiversity reserve (BOSAWAS) to be financed by the World Bank. The local population had not been consulted at all and rejected the plans and began to draw up its own law for demarcation of community lands (MIN/CALPI 2000).

42. Ramírez mentions "guaranteed employment, construction of schools, and financing training workshops that were not in accordance with the agenda of the national indigenous movement" (centered, on land) and some pages later mentions the sum of US$25,000 (Ramírez 2002: 150, 156).
43. For an incisive intervention in the debate see Zúñiga (2000). Without denying that there are important questions involved I suspect that the recent buzz over "strategic essentializing" and "performance" is very much part of a backlash discourse that relies on disqualifying the "other" by strategically calling his or her "authenticity" into question by reducing it to some sort of opportunistic rational choice strategizing while denying that they may be capable of reflecting upon themselves, their aims and cultural values. To put things in their proper perspective we rather need to study "reflexive identity politics" (Eriksen 2001).
44. See, for example, Bastos and Camus (2003) and Warren (1998).

References

Acosta, María Luisa. 1996. *Los derechos de las comunidades y pueblos indígenas de la Costa Atlántica en la constitución política de Nicaragua y la implementación de autonomía en las regiones Autónomas de la Costa Atlántica de Nicaragua.* Nicaragua: Agencia Canadiense para el Desarrollo Internacional.

———. 2000. "The State and Indigenous Lands in the Autonomous Regions of Nicaragua: The Case of the Mayagna Community of Awas Tingni." In *The Challenge of Diversity: Indigenous Peoples and Reform of the State in Latin America,* ed. W. Assies, G. van der Haar, and A. Hoekema. Amsterdam: Thela Thesis.

Albó, Xavier. 2002. "Bolivia: From Indian and Campesino Leaders to Councillors and Parliamentary Deputies." In *Multiculturalism in Latin America: Indigenous Rights, Diversity and Democracy,* ed. R. Sieder. Basingstoke: Palgrave Macmillan.

América Indígena. 1995. 55, no. 4: Special Issue on Panama.

Arango, Raúl, and Enrique Sánchez. 2002. *Los pueblos indígenas en el umbral del nuevo milenio,* http://www.dnp.gov. co/01_CONT/DES_TERR/DIV_ET.HTM#8. Bogotá: Departamento Nacional de Planeación.

Arias, Enrique and Mac Chapin. 1998. "Panamá: El proyecto de estudio para el manejo de las áreas silvestres de Kuna Yala (PEMASKY)." In *Derechos Indígenas y conservación de la naturaleza; Asuntos relativos a la gestión,* IWGIA. Copenhagen: IWGIA (Document no. 23).

Assies, Willem. 1994. "Self-Determination and the 'New Partnership'; The Politics of Indigenous Peoples and States." In *Indigenous Peoples' Experiences with Self-Government,* ed. W. Assies and A. J. Hoekema. Copenhagen and Amsterdam: IWGIA and University of Amsterdam (IWGIA Document no. 76).

Assies, Willem, Gemma van der Haar, and André Hoekema, eds. 2000. *The Challenge of Diversity: Indigenous Peoples and Reform of the State in Latin America.* Amsterdam: Thela Thesis.

Barth, Frederik., ed. 1969. *Ethnic Groups and Boundaries: The Social Organization of Cultural Difference.* Oslo and London: The University Press, George Allen and Unwin.

Bastos, Santiago, and Manuela Camus. 2003. *Entre el mecapal y el cielo: Desarrollo del movimiento maya en Guatemala.* Guatemala: FLACSO.

Bengoa, José. 2000. *La emergencia indígena en América Latina.* Mexico City and Santiago: Fondo de Cultura Económica.

Bennagen, Ponciano L. 1992. "Fiscal and Administrative Relations between Indigenous Governments and States." Paper presented at the Meeting of Experts, Nuuk, Greenland, September 24–28.

Bonfil Batalla, Guillermo. 1981. "Lo propio y lo ajeno: una aproximación al problema de control cultural." *Revista Mexicana de Ciencias Politicas y Sociales* 103: 183–191.

Brackelaire, Vicente. 2002. *Balance y perspectivas de la cooperación con los pueblos indígenas en América Latina.* La Paz: Fondo Indígena, Praia.

Calla, Ricardo. 2000. "Indigenous Peoples, the Law of Popular Participation and Changes in Government: Bolivia, 1994–1998." In *The Challenge of Diversity: Indigenous Peoples and Reform of the State in Latin America,* ed. W. Assies, G. van der Haar, and A. Hoekema. Amsterdam: Thela Thesis.

Cepeda Espinosa, Manuel José. 2001. "El Estado multicultural en Colombia; potencialidades y limitaciones de la transformación constitucional." In *Multiethnic Nations in Developing Countries,* ed. M. J. Cepeda Espinosa and T. Fleiner. Basel, Geneva, Munich: Helbing & Lichtenhahn (Institut de Fédéralisme Fribourg Suisse).

Colombia. 1995. "Programa de apoyo y fortalecimento étnico de los pueblos indígenas de Colombia, 1995–1998." *Anuario Indigenista* 34: 155–182.

CONAIE. 1994. "Proyecto político." *Anuario Indigenista,* 33: 203–244.

———. 1998. *Proyecto de constitución del estado plurinacional del Ecuador.* Quito: CONAIE.

Cunningham, Mirna. 1998. "La autonomía regional multiétnica en la Costa Atlántica de Nicaragua." In *Autonomías étnicas y Estados nacionales,* coord. M. A. Bartolomé and A. M. Barabas. Mexico City: CONACULTA, INAH.

Díaz-Polanco, Héctor. 1997. *La rebelión zapatista y la autonomía.* Mexico City: Siglo XXI.

———. 1999. "Los desafíos de la autonomía en Nicaragua (entrevista con Myrna Cunningham)." *Desacatos* 1: 37–55.

DNP-UDT. 1999. *El desarrollo constitucional del proyecto de Ley Orgánica de Ordenamiento Territorial y su articulación con el Plan Nacional de Desarrollo "Cambio para construir la paz."* Bogotá: Departamento Nacional de Planeación.

Eriksen, Thomas Hylland. 2001. "Ethnic Identity, National Identity, and Intergroup Conflict." In *Social Identity, Intergroup Conflict, and Conflict Reduction,* ed. R. D. Ashmore, L. Jussim, and D. Wilder. Oxford, U.K., and New York: Oxford University Press.

Espinosa, María Fernanda. 2000. "Ethnic Politics and State Reform in Ecuador." In *The Challenge of Diversity: Indigenous Peoples and Reform of the State in Latin America,* ed. W. Assies, G. van der Haar, and A. Hoekema. Amsterdam: Thela Thesis.

Findji, María Teresa. 1992. "From Resistance to Social Movement: The Indigenous Authorities Movement in Colombia." In *The Making of Social Movements in Latin America: Identity, Strategy, and Democracy,* ed. A. Escobar and S. E. Alvarez. Boulder, San Francisco, and Oxford, U.K.: Westview Press.

González Guerra, Gisela. 1999. *Derechos de los pueblos indígenas; legislación en América Latina.* Mexico City: Comisión Nacional de Derechos Humanos.

Gustafson, Bret. 2002. "Paradoxes of Liberal Indigenism: Indigenous Movements, State Processes, and Intercultural Reform in Bolivia." In *The Politics of Ethnicity: Indigenous Peoples in Latin American States,* ed. D. Maybury-Lewis. Cambridge, MA, and London: Harvard University Press.

Hale, Charles. 1996. "Entre la militancia indígena y la conciencia multiétnica: Los desafíos de la Autonomía en la Costa Atlántica de Nicaragua." In *Pueblos indios soberanía y globalismo,* coord. S. Varese. Quito: Abya-Yala.

———. 2002. "Does Multiculturalism Menace? Governance, Cultural Rights and the Politics of Identity in Guatemala." *Journal of Latin American Studies* 34: 485–524.

Hoekema, André. J. 1996. "Autonomy and Self-Government, a Fundamental Debate." Internal memo, Project Images of Self Rule, Amsterdam: University of Amsterdam, Department of Sociology and Anthropology of Law.

Hopenhayn, Martín, and Alvaro. Bello 2001. *Discriminación étnico-racial y xenofobia en América Latina y el Caribe*. Santiago: CEPAL (Serie: Políticas Sociales 47).

Howe, James. 1998. *A People Who Would Not Kneel: Panama, the United States, and the San Blas Kuna*. Washington D.C. and London: Smithsonian Institution Press.

———. 2002. "The Kuna of Panama: Continuing Threats to Land and Autonomy." In *The Politics of Ethnicity: Indigenous Peoples in Latin American States*, D. Maybury-Lewis. Cambridge, MA, and London: Harvard University Press.

IADB 2003. "Índice de legislación indígena," http://www.iadb.org/sds/ind/site_3152_e.htm. Accessed August 2, 2003.

Iturralde Guerrero, Diego. A. 1997. "Demandas indígenas y reforma legal: retos y paradojas." *Alteridades 7*, no. 14: 81–98.

Jackson, Jean. 2002. "Caught in the Crossfire: Colombia's Indigenous Peoples during the 1990s." In *The Politics of Ethnicity: Indigenous Peoples in Latin American States*, ed. D. Maybury-Lewis. Cambridge, MA, and London: Harvard University Press.

Kuppe, René. 2003. "Reflections on the Rights of Indigenous Peoples in the New Venezuelan Constitution and the Establishment of a Participatory, Pluricultural and Multiethnic Society." *Law and Anthropology* 12: 52–75.

León Trujillo, Jorge. 1998. "Una descentralización a contracorriente, el caso del Ecuador." In *Alcances y limitaciones de la reforma política en el Ecuador*, ed. G. Chiriboga Zambrano and R. Quintero López. Quito: Friedrich Ebert Stiftung, ILDIS, Proyecto Latinoamericano para Medios de Comunicación, Escuela de Sociología y Ciencias Políticas de la Universidad Central del Ecuador, AAJ.

Levi, Jerome M. 2002. "A New Dawn or a Cycle Restored? Regional Dynamics and Cultural Politics in Indigenous Mexico, 1978–2001." In *The Politics of Ethnicity: Indigenous Peoples in Latin American States*, ed. D. Maybury-Lewis. Cambridge, MA, and London: Harvard University Press.

López y Rivas, Gilberto. 1995. *Nación y pueblos indios en el neoliberalismo*. Mexico City: Plaza y Valdés, UIA.

Macdonald, Theodore, Jr., 2002. "Ecuador's Indian Movement: Pawn in a Short Game or Agent in State Configuration?" In *The Politics of Ethnicity: Indigenous Peoples in Latin American States*, ed. D. Maybury-Lewis. Cambridge, MA and London: Harvard University Press, 169–198.

Marshall, Monty G., and Ted Gurr. 2003. *Peace and Conflict 2003: A Global Survey of Armed Conflicts, Self-Determination Movements, and Democracy*. College Park: University of Maryland, CIDCM.

Martínez Cobo, José R. 1987. "Study of the Problem of Discrimination against Indigenous Populations, Volume V, Conclusions, Proposals and Recommendations." New York: United Nations.

Mattiace, Shannan L., Rosalva A. Hernández, and Jan Rus, eds. 2002. *Tierra, libertad y autonomía: impactos regionales del zapatismo en Chiapas*. Mexico and Copenhagen: CIESAS, IWGIA.

Méndez, Alonso I. 2002. "Los derechos de las naciones indígenas en las constituciones de los países latinoamericanos." Paper presented at *Tercer Congreso Europeo de Latinoamericanistas en Europa*, Amsterdam, July 2–6.

Mendoza, Carlos. n.d. "Indigenous Struggles for Political Recognition and Participation in Guatemala: Long Walk to Democratic Consolidation." Unpublished research paper.

MIN/CALPI. 2000. *Diagnóstico de la legislación nacional sobre los pueblos indígenas deNicaragua y exposición de motivos de la presentación de Convenio 169 como anteproyecto de ley ante la Asamblea Nacional de la República de Nicaragua*. Nicaragua: Movimiento Indígena de Nicaragua (MIN) and Centro de Asistencia Legal a Pueblos Indígenas (CALPI).

Nagel, Joane., and C. Matthew Snipp. 1993. "Ethnic Reorganization: American Indian Social, Economic, Political, and Cultural Strategies for Survival." *Ethnic and Racial Studies* 16, no. 2: 203–235.

Ortega Hegg, Manuel. 1996. "Autonomía regional y neoliberalismo en Nicaragua." In *Democracia y Estado multiétnico en América Latina*, coord. P. González Casanova and M. Roitman Rosemann. Mexico City: CIICH/UNAM, La Jornada.

Padilla, Guillermo. 1995. "What Encompasses Goodness, the Law and the Indigenous People of Colombia." In *Ethnic Conflict and Governance in Comparative Perspective*, Latin American Program Working Paper Series, no. 215. Washington D.C.: The Woodrow Wilson Center.

———. 1996. "Derecho mayor indígena y derecho constitucional; comentarios en torno a sus confluencias y conflictos." In *Pueblos indios, soberanía y globalismo*, coord. S. Varese. Quito: Abya-Yala.

Pérez Archibold, Juan. 1998. "Autonomía kuna y estado panameño." In *Autonomías étnicas y estados nacionales*, coord. M. A. Bartolomé and A. M. Barabas. Mexico City: CONACULTA, INAH.

Pineda, Roberto. 2001. "Colombia y el reto de la construcción de la multiculturalidad en un escenario de conflicto." In *Multiethnic Nations in Developing Countries*, ed. M. J. Cepeda Espinosa and T. Fleiner. Basel, Geneva, and Munich: Helbing and Lichtenhahn, Institut de Fédéralisme Fribourg Suisse.

Plant, Roger. 2000. "Indigenous Rights and Latin American Multiculturalism: Lessons from the Guatemalan Peace Process." In *The Challenge of Diversity: Indigenous Peoples and Reform of the State in Latin America*, ed. W. Assies, G. van der Haar, and A. Hoekema. Amsterdam: Thela Thesis.

Plant, Roger, and Soren Hvalkov. 2002. *Titulación de tierras y pueblos indígenas.* Washington: Banco Interamericano de Desarrollo.

Psacharopoulos, George, and Harry Anthony Patrinos, eds. 1994. *Indigenous People and Poverty in Latin America: An Empirical Analysis.* Washington D.C.: The World Bank.

Ramírez, María Clemencia. 2002. "The Politics of Identity and Cultural Difference in the Colombia Amazon: Claiming Indigenous Rights in the Putumayo Region." In *The Politics of Ethnicity: Indigenous Peoples in Latin American States*, ed. D. Maybury-Lewis. Cambridge, MA, and London: Harvard University Press.

Scherrer, Christian. P. 1994. "Regional Autonomy in Eastern Nicaragua; Four Years of Self-Government Experience in Yapti Tasba." In *Indigenous Peoples' Experiences with Self-Government*, ed. W. Assies and A. J. Hoekema. Copenhagen and Amsterdam: IWGIA and University of Amsterdam (IWGIA Document no. 76).

Sieder, Rachel., ed. 2002. *Multiculturalism in Latin America: Indigenous Rights, Diversity and Democracy.* Basingstoke: Palgrave Macmillan.

Stavenhagen, Rodolfo. 2002. "Indigenous Peoples and the State in Latin America: An Ongoing Debate." In *Multiculturalism in Latin America: Indigenous Rights, Diversity and Democracy*, ed. R. Sieder. Basingstoke: Palgrave Macmillan.

Trujillo, Julio César. 2000. "Los derechos colectivos de los pueblos indígenas del Ecuador: conceptos generales." In *De la exclusión a la participación:Pueblos indígenas y sus derechos colectivos en el Ecuador*, comp. A. M. Bernal. Quito: Abya Yala.

Turpana, Aristides., 1994. "The Duel Nation of the San Blas Comarca: Between Government and Self-Government." In *Indigenous Peoples' Experiences with Self-Government*, ed. W. Assies and A. J. Hoekema. Copenhagen and Amsterdam: IWGIA and University of Amsterdam (IWGIA Document no. 76).

Van Cott, Donna Lee. 2000. *The Friendly Liquidation of the Past: The Politics of Diversity inLatin America.* Pittsburgh: The University of Pittsburgh Press.

————. 2001. "Explaining Ethnic Autonomy Regimes in Latin America." *Studies in Comparative International Development* 35, no. 4: 30–58.

————. 2002. "Constitutional Reform in the Andes: Redefining Indigenous-State Relations." In *Multiculturalism in Latin America: Indigenous Rights, Diversity and Democracy*, ed. R. Sieder. Basingstoke: Palgrave Macmillan.

Vázquez León, Luis. 1992. *Ser indio otra vez: la purepechización de los tarrascos serranos.* Mexico: CONACULTA.

Warren, Kay B. 1998. *Indigenous Movements and their Critics: Pan-Maya Activism in Guatemala.* Princeton: Princeton University Press.

Wray, Natalia. 2000. *Pueblos indígenas Amazónicos y actividad petrolera en el Ecuador; conflictos, estrategias e impactos.* Quito: IBIS, Oxfam.

Zúñiga, Gerardo. 2000. "La dimensión discursiva de las luchas étnicas, Acerca de un artículo de María Teresa Sierra." *Alteridades* 10, no. 19: 55–67.

Political Developments in Bolivia

Introduction

Ton Salman

Willem Assies began to work on Bolivia systematically in 1994 with a range of publications on, for example, tropical rain forest extraction policies, questions of ethnicity, protest movements, and political developments in general, for which he became a frequently asked specialist. In 2000, he was among the first to publish on the now iconic "Water War" in Cochabamba. The first Spanish version of that article was published in 2001 in the Bolivian journal *T'inkazos*; the revised English version of 2003 is published here along with another article on ethnopolitics in Bolivia that was published in 2006. A selection of two writings out of the great number of articles and book chapters Assies published on Bolivia cannot really be said to be representative, but nevertheless they give a good indication of both the width and depth of his research on that country. The article on the Water War in Cochabamba is both a meticulous reconstruction of the course of events and a fascinating attempt to interpret how the rupture in the protest movement came about in recent, neoliberal history, when social protest and popular organization to promote interests was in decline. Assies was innovative in his attempt to come to grips with the compound political vicissitudes of the country. Up to the Water War, the coalitions fostering neoliberal reforms seemed to be in solid positions, hegemonizing the polity and successful in keeping the frequent protests and the growing frustration at bay. By studying the processes at the societal and associativist level, one could clearly see a slow but sure articulation of discontent. Additionally, ethnicity was becoming increasingly important as a factor and a banner to frame a counterdiscourse, in which socioeconomic and ethnic elements merged. Assies was fascinated by this process, including its setbacks and problems. With the benefit of hindsight, it now seems that the 2000 Water War was a crucial episode, not only because of victory for the ad hoc coalition, but because it became evident that these new and unprecedented coalitions would turn into credible electoral alternatives. Assies ended by stating: "It may be premature to say that a 'new social movement' has emerged in Bolivia, but the Water War does suggest a significant change in the dynamics of social protest."

The second selection in part V on ethnopolitics illustrates precisely how the ethnic profile came to dominate the massive protests against the incumbent neoliberal policies in the country. It was not necessarily because the impacts of such policies exclusively affected the indigenous, but because the ad hoc coalition increasingly turned out a convincing discourse and a promising vehicle to express discontent with corruption, prebendalism, and the "sellout" of the country's natural resources. Nationalism became indigenized because of the legitimacy of multiculturalism. Although the prognosis of Assies proved to be accurate, at the time he remained cautious: "For the time being, the MAS has emerged as the most important party and seeks to project itself as a democratic left-wing alternative. If something like that consolidates we might expect a scenario somewhere between, or combining, populist multiculturalism and radical ethno-nationalist development of multiculturalist policies. The situation is extremely fluid, however, and I would not risk predicting the course of events."

David versus Goliath in Cochabamba
Water Rights, Neoliberalism, and the Revival of Social Protest in Bolivia

Introduction

"Ours is a small country and it hardly owns anything anymore. Our mines were privatized, the electrification company was privatized, and the airlines, the telecommunications, the railways, our oil and gas. The things we still own are the water and the air, and we have struggled to make sure that the water continues to be ours," said Oscar Olivera, a trade-union leader from Cochabamba, Bolivia, addressing one of the assemblies protesting the annual spring meeting of the IMF/World Bank in Washington, DC, in April 2000. Olivera had been freshly flown in from the city that had been the scene of violent protests that forced the transnational consortium *Aguas del Tunari* out of Cochabamba Department and called upon the Bolivian government to modify Law 2029 on Potable Water and Sanitary Drainage, proclaimed only five months earlier. The assembly that protested the power of transnational capitalism and neoliberal policies cheered him as a hero. "David has defeated Goliath," claimed Olivera, and "thus set an example for the rest of the world."

From the early days of April Bolivia had been the scene of a wave of protests such as it had not seen for several decades, prompting the Banzer government, elected in 1997, to declare a state of siege. The day the state of siege was declared, 880 police mutinied to press wage demands and students protested in La Paz, and later coca growers from the *Yunga* region set up roadblocks to protest forced eradication. By the time the state of siege was lifted on April 20, the confrontations had claimed five lives, four of them civilian. The government announced that it would return to its economic reactivation plan and that National Dialogue 2, upon which the multilateral debt relief plan was conditioned, would be put on track again. A cabinet crisis was in the air, and on April 25 a reshuffled cabinet took charge.

An important reason for the state of siege was the Water War in Cochabamba. The events in Cochabamba can be considered significant for various reasons. In the first place, many considered the outcome a victory after fifteen years of structural adjustment policies and the suppression of popular protest movements. Second, it diverged from established patterns of mobilization in Bolivia. The trade-union structures that since the 1952 Revolution had been a major vehicle of protest played only a marginal role, and territorial organizations such as neighborhood associations and potable-water committees emerged as the main carriers of protest activity. The other established organization, the Civic Committee,[1] which claimed to be the legitimate representative of the Cochabamba population, proved to represent only a small sector of the population. A new form of organization, a *Coordinadora*, emerged as a leading force. Although, citing the Bolivian Constitution,[2] the government, along with the Civic Committee, at first denied the legitimacy of the *Coordinadora*, it eventually had to accept it as an interlocutor. This points to a further feature of the dynamics of mobilization and government response in Bolivia. In connection with the mobilizations of coca growers Laserna (1999) has introduced the notion of "forced negotiation" to capture the process of escalation of protests and state violence. Typically, Bolivian governments seek to ignore and trivialize the first signs of popular mobilization and then to repress it through increasingly violent means, which only contributes to an intensification of confrontations and the spread of mobilization to other groups. Finally, the government gives in to social pressure and ends up signing last-minute agreements in which it does not believe and that it will not carry out, and this sets the stage for a new round of protest.

In the first part of this article I will review the debate over legislation on water resources in Bolivia. In the second I will show that it was no coincidence that Cochabamba became the focus of protests against the new legislation and its implementation, which made itself felt most concretely through the actions of the *Aguas del Tunari* Consortium. In September 1999 this transnational consortium had been granted the concession for supplying water to the city of Cochabamba and implementing a US$300 million project that was supposed to solve the water scarcity problem in the Cochabamba region. In the third part I will describe the conflicts over water in the Cochabamba region that arose with the expansion of the city in the 1970s, and in the fourth I will examine the Water War of 1999–2000. Finally, I will discuss some of the outcomes and implications of this conflict

Commodification versus Communitarianism: Proposals for a General Water Law

Since the early 1970s the Bolivian state has been working on a new legal framework regarding water resources. The more recent proposals for a general law have been largely inspired by the recommendations of multilateral development agencies and Chile's 1981 water legislation. At the same time they are aligned with the institutional setup introduced under the Sanchez de Lozada administration (1993–1997), a "second generation" of reforms aimed at complementing the structural adjustment policies initiated in 1985 with the implementation, at dramatic social cost, of a New Economic Policy. What the multilateral agencies have proposed is the development of a general law that would provide the framework for secondary legislation with regard to integral resource management and citizen participation either through users' organizations or through the private sector. Such a law would limit the role of the state to supervision, regulation, and planning. It would take into account the economic value of water resources and allow the resources or concessions for exploitation to be freely sold, mortgaged, rented, and so forth, so as to promote market-driven resource distribution. Finally, it would include environmental protection measures.

While incorporating these guidelines, the Bolivian proposals are aligned with the local outcomes of state reform policies and particularly with the *Sistema de Regulación Sectorial* (System for Sectoral Regulation-SIRESE), created in 1994. The SIRESE law introduced a system of superintendencies to regulate sectors likely to constitute natural monopolies. It transferred existing economic functions of the state to the private sector and its regulative role to autarkic superintendencies. To ensure their independence the superintendents are appointed by the president on the basis of a short list proposed by the senate and serve for fixed periods that do not coincide with the president's term of office; they can be removed only through legal process. The economic independence of the superintendencies is ensured through the payment of permit fees by the enterprises subjected to their regulation.

When the executive submitted its draft law on water resources in August 1998, the organizations of peasants, indigenous peoples, and colonists, with the support of nongovernmental organizations (NGOs), were quick to react. They came together as a national technical water board to develop a counterproposal inspired by ILO Convention 169 and Article 171 of the Bolivian constitution, which recognize the social, economic, and cultural rights of indigenous peoples. It rejects the mercantilist- and privatization-oriented conceptions of the governmental project and defines water as a "social and ecological good that guarantees the well-being of the family and the collectivity and (their) social and economic development." It also stresses that the cultural and ritual value of water for indigenous communities must be respected and that water cannot be the object of private appropriation or commercial disposal.

A key aspect of the counterproposal is its defense of communitarian water rights, which are to be exempted from the payment of permit fees. Where mining, oil, and industry are concerned it rejects the system of fifty-year concessions and proposes nontransferable twenty-year authorizations conditioned on a management plan and an agreement with the communities that might be affected. It utterly rejects the idea of a superintendency and contemplates the formation of a national water council composed of representatives of the state and of water users.

While the debate over the general water law was in progress, in November 1999 the government piloted a secondary law on potable water and sanitary sewerage through parliament, and this law in fact legalized the contract with *Aguas del Tunari* that had been signed two months earlier.

Law 2029 on Potable Water and Sewerage

A basic feature of Law 2029 was the introduction of a regime of concessions and licenses for the supply of potable water, with the concessions to apply to centers of population with more than ten thousand inhabitants in which the provision of services is "financially self-sustaining" and the licenses elsewhere. Concessions were for a period of forty years and licenses for five. Concessions and licenses could be granted to any institution with legal status—a municipal public enterprise, a private enterprise, a corporation, a cooperative, a civil organization such as an NGO, or a peasant or indigenous community. However, the conditions for granting concessions clearly favored the formation of large enterprises that functioned according to market criteria. It was expected that water supply in forty-one cities would be rapidly be brought under the concession regime. The law further stipulated that concessionaires would have exclusive rights over the concession area, which meant that existing local organizations such as cooperatives or neighborhood associations would be forced to enter into contracts with the concessionaires. These features of Law 2029 did not fail to be perceived as a menace to the arrangements for water supply that, in the absence of public services, had been created by the population in the form of cooperatives and other local associations classified as *usos y costumbres* (uses and customs).

For the concession areas Law 2029 established a rate structure based on criteria of neutrality, solidarity, redistributions, implicity, transparency, economic efficiency, and financial sufficiency. However, in cases of conflict among these principles the criteria of efficiency and financial sufficiency were to be given priority, and in the event of a contradiction between these last two principles the latter was to prevail. The criterion of economic efficiency was to communicate the scarcity of the resource to its users whereas the criterion of financial sufficiency was to guarantee the recovery of costs and operating expenses and the "remuneration of action holders' patrimony in the same way as any efficient enterprise in a sector of comparable risk [would remunerate them]." As we shall see, these criteria were used to support a rate hike that would help "capitalize" *Aguas del Tunari* to carry out its project, and this was one of the direct causes of the revolt.

Finally, the new law established that concessions and authorizations for the use and exploitation of water resources and their revocation would be granted by the competent superintendency and that until this superintendency was created the Superintendency for Basic Sanitation would perform these functions. As the concessionaires and licensees would be directly contracted by the superintendency, local governments and users would have little recourse against this closed system. With its reference to a superintendency, Law 2029 "smuggled in" the creation of an agency that was strongly contested by the peasant and indigenous organizations, which advocated the creation of a national water council. One outcome of the Water War in Cochabamba and the countrywide peasant protests would be the substantial modification of this law.

Cochabamba, the Thirsty City

Cochabamba was, as it were, overdetermined to become the scene of the Water War. Over the past few decades the city and its surroundings, constituting what is known as the Central V alley,[3] have experienced a process of socioeconomic transformation and rapid population growth. Once agrarian, the region's economy is now dominated by commerce, services, and small-scale industry. This urban transformation has been partly due to an influx of migrants. The closing of the tin mines in 1985 triggered a flow of migrants toward the Cochabamba Department and its capital and transformed the traditional outlets for agrarian produce from the Central Valley. Environmental factors such as the degradation of agricultural lands and the droughts that plagued the region during the 1980s were another element in the process of change and rural-urban migration that produced the chaotic expansion of urban areas. Between 1976 and 1992 the population of the city of Cochabamba grew from 205,000 to 414,000 without corresponding expansion of urban services. Potable-water coverage was reported to be 57 percent and sewerage 48 percent in 1999. The remainder of the population gets its water from tanker trucks, privately constructed wells, or self-help organizations such as cooperatives, associations, and water committees. Estimates of the number of small wells in the Central Valley range from five thousand to seven thousand. In many cases such wells have been drilled with financial support from state agencies, NGOs, or the church.

Meanwhile the rural areas have also undergone important changes. Recent decades have seen the growth of fruit, milk, poultry, and, recently, flower production. This development has been accompanied by an increase in entrepreneurial farming in a region that was once characterized by small family farms and peasant enterprises. It is a region of intensive farming, highly dependent on irrigation. About 70 percent of agricultural land is permanently or temporarily irrigated.

The rapid expansion of the urban population in a context of relative scarcity of water in the Central Valley set the stage for conflicts and for promises of a solution to the problem that have paid off handsomely in political terms. A case in point is the MISICUNI Project. First conceived some fifty years ago and initiated during the Barrientos government (1966–1969), the project would bring in water from the MISICUNI catchment area, some 40 km from the city, through a system of tunnels and aqueducts. As a "multipurpose project" it would supply the city with water and the agricultural areas with irrigation and, in passing, provide hydroelectric energy. It has therefore been regarded as a regional development project and over time has acquired a magical aura in the minds of most Cochabambinos. Institutionalized as a state enterprise in 1987, it produced many a costly feasibility study in subsequent years.

Meanwhile, the water problems of the city of Cochabamba have been handled with stopgap measures implemented by the *Servicio Municipal de Agua Potable y Alcanterillado* (Municipal Potable Water and Sewerage Service— SEMAPA). The easiest short-term fix was drilling wells in the neighboring province of Quillacollo, and this set the stage for rural-urban conflicts.

Cochabamba versus Quillacollo: The Wars of the Wells

While some efforts had been made in the 1960s, it was in 1976–1977, under the de facto government of Colonel Hugo Banzer, that SEMAPA 20 LATIN AMERICAN PERSPECTIVES drilled a battery of ten 120-meter wells in the Vinto District of the Quillacollo Province. Drought had exacerbated Cochabamba's water problems, and although the well-drilling project had given rise to some questioning by the local population it went ahead after SEMAPA guaranteed that the wells would in no way affect water levels in the region or the existing wells constructed by the local population. When Banzer inaugurated the Vinto project in early December 1977, SEMAPA's promises had already turned out to be a hoax. On November 22 the Pro Vinto Committee had protested that drilling had already "resulted in the complete drying up of the wells that supply the population with water," threatening the loss of the country's most important food-producing region. The committee adopted the slogan "Water Is the Patrimony of the Locality," and SEMAPA renewed its commitments for the moment.

The 1977 experience had not been forgotten when in 1994, again in a context of acute water shortage, SEMAPA proposed the drilling of deep wells as a short-term solution. The local authorities declared that they were weary of sacrificing their interests for the benefit of Cochabamba and called for the implementation of the MISICUNI Project. In September 1994 various local organizations formed a defense committee, and on October 7 a March for Life and Water united some ten thousand people from different communities in the Lower Central Valley. Nonetheless, in April 1995 SEMAPA started drilling a 600-meter well on army land in the locality of El Paso under the protection of the police. In 1997–1998 Cochabamba once again faced an acute water shortage, and SEMAPA came up with the usual solution, announcing that it would drill ten wells in Vinto and El Paso. Despite protests, drilling started on army land in early 1998. By mid-1998 the population of the Ironcollo community had forced the SEMAPA engineers and their accompanying military police contingent to withdraw.

In early July SEMAPA manager Arturo Coca announced that by August the Cochabamba population would have run out of potable water and the company declared a 20 percent price hike. The municipal council of the Cercado demanded that the progress of the drilling be guaranteed, local deputies called for criminal prosecution of those opposed to the drilling, and a public assembly organized by the Civic Committee called for the drilling of wells "by force if need be." That same month the newly elected President Hugo Banzer and Defense Minister Fernando Kieffer promised military protection for the drilling of wells (Crespo Flores 1999; PEIRAV 1998).

This series of conflicts prompted two important developments. In the first place, in the mid-1990s a *Federación Departamental Cochabambina de Organizaciones de Regantes* (Cochabamba Department Federation of Irrigators' Organizations—FEDECOR) independent of the established trade-union structure emerged to replace the earlier community-based defense committees. Meanwhile, the original defense of resource ownership had taken on new dimensions. The early experience with well drilling had brought broader issues, among them the ecological aspect and the inequitable distribution of resources resulting from market forces and urban interests, into the picture. The defense of resource ownership evolved into an autonomous popular ecological movement in defense of communitarian access and of a way of life

(Crespo Flores 1999: 72). By the late 1990s FEDECOR had become the main vehicle of protest in the rural area and involved itself in the efforts of the national technical water board to develop alternatives to the official proposals for a general water law. Through meetings and workshops the local bases of FEDECOR became familiar with the debate over water legislation.

Second, by the end of the 1990s the Cochabamba chapter of the *Sociedad de Ingenieros Bolivianos* (Society of Bolivian Engineers—SIB), until then supportive of well drilling, had begun to change its mind. It seriously questioned the productivity of the existing deep wells, which had cost millions of dollars. Moreover, it pointed to the risk of desertification and joined the Association of Municipal Governments of the Lower and Central Valley and FEDECOR in suggesting alternative solutions such as the capture of surface waters and the eternally postponed MISICUNI Project. While most urban-based organizations militantly defended well drilling, the engineers were starting to express doubts.

Aguas del Tunari and the Water War

While conflict raged in the late 1990s, the MISICUNI Project and some alternative projects had remained on the agenda.[4] At the end of the Sanchez de Lozada administration it was announced that the MISICUNI Project would be put out to bid together with SEMAPA, since a package deal like this would ensure profitability. Various interested parties presented themselves when the bidding process was initiated but after studying the terms came up with a series of concerns with regard to feasibility and profitability. In February 1999 the government made the conditions more "flexible," and at this point the only enterprise that showed interest was *Aguas del Tunari*.[5] Instead of opening a new round of bidding, the government authorized further negotiations with *Aguas del Tunari*. The consortium was therefore in a position to impose conditions on a government anxious to proceed. A decree in June 1999 authorized the signing of the contract.

The contract was immediately opposed by local organizations such as the FEDECOR and the Cochabamba College of Engineers. FEDECOR President Omar Fernández asserted that the price for irrigation water would rise to US$0.08 per m3 and that this would drive between fifteen thousand and twenty thousand farmers into bankruptcy. Edgar Montaño, head of the Civic Committee, replied that the price had not yet been fixed. The Ministry for Foreign Trade and Investment and the World Bank (1999) eventually established a price that confirmed Fernandez's statement. The College of Engineers compared the Tunari contract with the original MISICUNI Project and concluded that to guarantee profitability it had been reduced to a "bonsai" version. The quantities of potable water, irrigation water, and electricity to be provided had been halved and the initially projected second and third phases had been practically eliminated. As for the rates for potable water, the College of Engineers compared the SEMAPA rates with the rates anticipated by *Aguas del Tunari* and concluded that the elimination of social criteria would result in price hikes of up to 180 percent for the poorer sectors of the population. Finally, it questioned the way in which the contract had been granted (30 *Dias de Noticias* [CEDIB], June 1999).

From the Defense Committee to the *Coordinadora*

Soon a Committee for the Defense of Water and the Popular Economy emerged, with the engineers Osvaldo Pareja, Gonzalo Maldonado,[6] and Jorge Alvarado among its driving forces. It organized a forum on July 20 in which criticism of the Tunari contract was expressed and its defenders were conspicuous by their absence. Gonzalo Rico, head of the MISICUNI Project, argued that the committee's predictions about future water prices were grossly exaggerated. Prices would rise, he said, but only by 40 percent. Civic Committee president Edgar Montaño declined to recognize the Defense Committee, and Vice Minister of Investment Miguel López did not attend the forum. A week later the committee organized a street protest symbolically carrying the MISICUNI Project to its grave. Urban protests, however, remained a matter of certain professional organizations and certain environmentalists without a broad social base.

At the same time, with the December 1999 municipal elections coming up, Mayor Manfred Reyes Villa and the Civic Committee had their hearts set on signing the MISICUNI contract. On September 3 the contract was signed in the presence of President Banzer, ministers of state, and a range of local authorities. Reyes Villa and Montaño were among the signers. On November 1, without ceremony, *Aguas del Tunari* took over the SEMAPA offices and, through its manager Geoffrey Thorpe, announced that it would immediately set to work to improve the water supply in Cochabamba and implement the MISICUNI Project. Rate increases, covering the month of December and to be paid in January 2000, would, he said, be on the order of 35 percent.

Meanwhile, as noted, Law 2029 on Potable Water and Sewerage was approved, and on November 29 President Banzer proclaimed the new law in the locality of Cliza, Cochabamba, amidst peasant protests. The concession system it introduced would allow *Aguas del Tunari* to control all the wells drilled privately in the Cochabamba Valley and install water meters on these wells at the cost of the user. With the December 5 municipal elections nearing, Basic Sanitation Superintendent Luis Uzín suggested that the rate hike might be reduced. Most of the parties participating in the local elections agreed not to politicize the water issue. Once the elections were over, however, Uzín declared that he had been misinterpreted and that the rate hike would be implemented as foreseen. It should be regarded, he argued, as a "solidarity increase" that would allow expansion of the water supply to the marginal areas. It contributed to the profitability of *Aguas del Tunari*, which contractually was guaranteed a return on equity of 15 percent.

Angry reactions to Uzín's deception quickly followed. The Committee for the Defense of Water and the Household Economy, as it now called itself, restated its opposition to the rate increase, the sell-off of SEMAPA, and the MISICUNI bonsai and insisted that rates would rise much more than 35 percent. At the same time, sectors that had staunchly supported and in some cases cosigned the *Aguas del Tunari* contract began to voice doubts. The new president of the Civic Committee, Mauricio Barrientos,[7] expressed objections to the rate increase and doubts about the contract, and German Mercado, president of the *Federación de Juntas Vecinales* (Federation of Neighborhood Associations—FEJUVE), stated that the citizenry was not disposed to pay high rates for a service that it had yet to receive. Interim Mayor Nestor Villazón said the same, and Mayor-elect Reyes Villa joined in.

Meanwhile, however, the initial opposition had taken on a new dynamic as contacts had been established between FEDECOR and the urban *Federación Departamental de Trabajadores Fabriles de Cochabamba* (Departmental Federation of Factory Workers of Cochabamba-FDTFC), notable for its search for a creative response to the crisis that hit the Bolivian trade-union sector after 1985. Massive layoffs, industrial restructuring and flexibilization, and the informalization of labor relations have resulted in a virtual disarticulation of the once powerful *Central Obrera Boliviana* (Bolivian Workers' Central COB) and, in many cases, the decline of local unions. The FDTFC has maintained a presence in the local media to inform the population about labor conditions and sought to organize unions in the small factories and sweatshops that make up the restructured industrial sector even though the General Labor Law prohibits unionization in establishments with fewer than twenty workers. It has also initiated an "open-door" policy, meaning that it receives all sorts of demands and complaints from the popular sectors and pursues solutions. These creative responses to the crisis of the labor sector have given it significant moral weight in the city (Kruse 2002).

With the adherence of the factory workers' union the Defense Committee was transformed into the *Coordinadora por la Defensa del Agua y la Vida* (Coordination for the Defense of Water and Life). It was led by Oscar Olivera, a shoe-factory worker and president of the FDTFC, and its vice presidency came to be occupied by FEDECOR's president, Omar Fernández; Gabriel Herbas, until then president of the Defense Committee, became the general secretary. Gonzalo Maldonado decided to take a back seat. This new configuration introduced a rural-urban dimension and brought a significant broadening and radicalization to the committee, which had mainly appealed to professional sectors and some environmentalist groups. The FDTFC, strategically located on a comer of the Plaza 14 de Septiembre and easily accessible to the public, became the *Coordinadora* headquarters. On December 28, 1999, the *Coordinadora* organized its first march to the Plaza 14 de Septiembre.

The First Battle for Water, January 2000

In early January 2000, water bills started to reach *Cochabambinos* connected to the municipal water supply system and confirmed what the *Coordinadora* had been predicting: stiff raises, in some cases up to 150 percent. The population was outraged. Hundreds of persons came to the FDTFC offices to complain about their bills. This allowed the *Coordinadora* to gain ample media coverage, providing them with dramatic case histories. The *Coordinadora* called for a refusal to pay the bills. In response *Aguas del Tunari* manager Geoffrey Thorpe categorically stated that in the event of nonpayment the water supply would be cut off.

The *Coordinadora* called a meeting for January 10. The Civic Committee declared a twenty-four-hour civic strike for January 11, and Mayor Reyes Villa instigated FEJUVE to organize a protcst march. The *Coordinadora* meeting, attended by angry citizens, professionals denouncing the deficiencies of the *Aguas del Tunari* contract, trade unionists, and members of irrigators' associations and potable-water committees, resulted in a call for an indefinite shutdown of the city to start on January 11. The city was duly immobilized on that day, but this was not so much the work of organizations such as the Civic Committee or of the trade unions as of the irrigators' associations, which effectively closed the strategic roads, and the potable-water committees and other neighborhood associations of the periphery, which set up a multitude of twenty-five small barricades. The mobilizations in the urban periphery were in many ways spontaneous and loosely coordinated, following what Kowarick (1985) has called the pathways of encounter that make for the gradual articulation of seemingly scattered day-to-day struggles in the workplace and in the neighborhoods.

The next day, although the twenty-four-hour strike of the Civic Committee had ended, the rural roadblocks and those in the city's periphery persisted. Five hundred workers from the Manaco shoe factory mounted their bicycles and rode the 15 km from the factory to the city center to protest the layoff of sixty workers and to call for continued action on the water issue. The *Coordinadora* called for a march and an open town council meeting on January 13. At that stage the transportation workers, divided between the urban transport workers allied with the Civic Committee and the heavy transport workers sympathizing with the *Coordinadora,* organized a meeting between the two groups in which they agreed not to negotiate separately. Thus the Civic Committee sought to save face by relinquishing its claim to a representative monopoly and the *Coordinadora* secured a place at the negotiating table. A ministerial delegation was on its way.

The delegation found itself in a city in convulsions. A massive march and town meeting in the Plaza 14 de Septiembre had ratified the rejection of the *Aguas del Tunari* contract and of Law 2029. It had denounced Mayor Reyes Villa, former Civic Committee President Montaño, MISICUNI President Gonzalo Rico, ex-prefect Guido Camaco, Basic Sanitation Superintendent Luis Uzín, and the former SEMAPA manager Oscar Coca as "traitors" for their role in producing the *Aguas del Tunari* contract. During the march the Civic Committee offices were attacked with stones and their windows broken. Some shops that were still open and public buildings also received their share of stones.

While tear gas clouded the city center, a delegation of four ministers entered into negotiations with representatives of the Civic Committee and the *Coordinadora.* The final outcome was an agreement signed by the governmental representatives, the Civic Committee, a representative of the Cochabamba parliamentary brigade, and a representative of the motor transport federation but not by the representatives of the *Coordinadora,* who argued that they had to consult the people. The agreement included the creation of a commission to study water rates. The *Aguas del Tunari* contract was to be revised to ensure the implementation of the MISICUNI Project, to eliminate clauses that went "against the interest of the state," and to revise water rates. The proposals for a general water law were to be discussed with society at large in an effort to reach consensus, and Law 2029 was to be modified within forty-five days. Finally, it was decided that privately owned water systems in the concession area would not become part of the water sources of the concessionaire (30 *Dias de Noticias* [CEDIB], January 2000). The *Coordinadora* regarded this last point as an important victory. On the whole, however, the first battle over water ended in a truce that was to allow for further study and negotiation. Within a month hostilities would resume.

The Second Battle, February 2000

Negotiations proceeded sluggishly. The government, above all concerned with the investment climate, showed little willingness to review the *Aguas del Tunari* contract or the rates and basically sought to strike a deal with the Civic Committee so as to marginalize the *Coordinadora*. It considered the original MISICUNI Project bound to be unprofitable and therefore infeasible. For its part, the *Coordinadora* denounced the contract as irregular, demanded its rescission, and proposed that SEMAPA be capitalized and converted into a sort of cooperative. At the end of January it organized a burning of water bills.

Meanwhile, tension rose in the national government coalition. The NFR, led by Reyes Villa, opposed the authorization of the rate hike and expressed its discomfort with the irresponsible and unilateral attitudes of the government and Superintendent Uzín. On February 2 the crisis broke, and the representatives of the NFR—twelve deputies and one senator—left (or were expelled from) the coalition.

When on February 4 the government offered its "final proposal" of a 20 percent rate increase,[8] there were massive street protests, and these were met by heavy-handed repression coordinated by Vice Minister of Internal and Police Affairs José Orías. Special Security Group detachments known as "the dalmatians" for their battledress were brought in from La Paz and Oruro. After two days of heavy street fighting, Orías declared that police and military violence had been unavoidable to protect the doors and windows of the Cochabamba Prefecture. Doors and windows remained unbroken, noted the national daily *Presencia* (February 2, 2000), but 70 civilians and 51 policemen were wounded and 172 arrests were made.

Confrontations came to an end in the course of Saturday, February 5, when, after the mediation of Cochabamba's Archbishop Tito Solari and the national ombudsman, Jose Luis Baptista, an agreement was signed by Orías, Mauricio Barrientos of the Civic Committee, Nestor Guzman of the Cochabamba Parliamentary Brigade, and Gonzalo Maldonado of the *Coordinadora*. Prefect Hugo Galindo was absent from the signing, reportedly hospitalized. The main points were that the MISICUNI Project would be implemented and that rates would be reviewed and for the time being frozen at their October 1999 level. Proposals for modification of Law 2029 were to be worked out among the various parties and presented within the forty-five-day period agreed upon in January. A commission with representatives of the various groups was to revise the technical, financial, and legal aspects of the *Aguas del Tunari* contract. After this, peace lasted until April 4.

The Third Battle and the State of Siege, April 2000

By the end of February negotiations were approaching a deadlock. Government and Civic Committee delegates accused the *Coordinadora* of having radicalized its demands beyond the rate issue. The *Coordinadora* argued that the Civic Committee was dragging its feet and that the government delegates were offering little opening. The Civic Committee said that it had been unable to study the contract because "by some mistake" it had not been provided a copy. For his part, Superintendent Uzín stated that there was no alternative to the rate increase. Frustrated, the *Coordinadora* decided to withdraw from the technical meetings.

On March 26 it held a referendum on the issue. Relying on the network of local organizations that by then had become involved in its activities, it had some 150 ballot boxes installed and supervised. The population was asked to answer three questions: (1) Do you accept the rate increase? (2) Should the contract with *Aguas del Tunari* be annulled? (3) Do you agree with the privatization of water in Law 2029? Of the total of 48,276 votes (some 10 percent of the population), 99 percent responded negatively to the first question, 96 percent thought that the contract should be annulled, and 97 percent disagreed with the privatization orientation of Law 2029. Although the referendum had been organized on short notice it had achieved a participation equivalent to 31 percent of the vote in the December 1999 municipal elections. The local press spoke of it as a success. Nevertheless, in another effort to trivialize the issue Vice Minister of Investment and Privatization Humberto Böhrt announced that the referendum was illegal and that the government recognized only the Civic Committee as an interlocutor.

Two days before the referendum the Civic Committee had called a public assembly "sponsored by the institutions duly accredited by the Civic Committee," and this assembly had ratified a preliminary agreement with the government. The agreement included (1) modifications of Law 2029 so as to respect the investments made by neighborhood associations, cooperatives, and other organizations in urban and rural areas; (2) renegotiation of the *Aguas del Tunari* contract; (3) a one-year moratorium on the reclassification of water users while a commission composed of the Superintendency and delegates of the Civic Committee worked out a more equitable scheme; (4) a freezing of rates until December 2000, after which they would increase gradually; (5) the establishment by the concessionaire of an office to receive and process consumer complaints; (6) a guarantee by the government of the completion of the MISICUNI tunnel; and (7) an expression of confidence in the leadership of the Civic Committee, a denunciation of the "anarchist and irresponsible attitudes of the *Coordinadora* leadership, "and a rejection of the referendumas illegal and unverifiable. Leaders who opposed "the prestige and the institutional and democratic integrity" of the Civic Committee were to be banned from further participation.

At that point a group of intellectuals assembled by the *Centro de Estudios de la Realidad Economica y Social* (Center for the Study of Social and Economic Reality—CERES) sought to get negotiations going again. In its view the *Coordinadora* had behaved erratically in the negotiations and the Civic Committee and the government had failed to address the question of a full revision of the *Aguas del Tunari* contract (30 *Dias de Noticias* [CEDIB], March 2000). This attempt found little echo, however, in a situation that was already strongly polarized. At the end of March both the *Coordinadora* and the Civic Committee announced mobilizations if the government failed to respond before March 31. No response came, and independently the two organizations called for a general strike on April 4, after which the government sought to patch up its relations with the Civic Committee.

Around the same time the national peasant organization *Confederación Sindical Unica de Trabajadores Campesinos de Bolivia* (Unitary Union Confederation of Bolivian Peasant Workers—CSUTCB) started to block roads throughout the country to press its own list of demands, including withdrawal of the official proposal for a general water law, and in Cochabamba the local peasantry, led by FEDECOR, blocked the main roads to the city. In the city itself the general strike passed quietly. The government and the Civic Committee congratulated themselves on the seeming impotence and isolation of the *Coordinadora,* and Galindo stated that "there is nothing to negotiate." On the next day, April 5, however, thousands of *Cochabambinos,* among them a variety of water committees as well as the heavy transport workers' union and delegations from the rural areas, filled the Plaza 14 de Septiembre. The crowd rejected the *Coordinadora* proposal to give *Aguas del Tunari* twenty-four hours to leave the city and demanded that the enterprise leave immediately. It then marched to the company headquarters, attacking the Civic Committee offices on the way. At *Aguas del Tunari* the company sign was torn down, and the water treatment plant in the Cala Cala district was spray-painted with the slogan "Aguas del Pueblo" (The People's Water). Intervention by the *Coordinadora* leadership prevented damage to the plant.

On April 6 the Plaza was again taken over by a crowd, though a much smaller one than the previous day. Although initially various ministers had said that talking with *Coordinadora* delegates was out of the question, after mediation by the archbishop and the ombudsman the authorities agreed to meet with the *Coordinadora,* which called on its followers to hold a vigil around the Prefecture, where the meeting would take place. At 10:00 p.m. a harassed group of policemen launched a first round of tear gas, and at 10:30

p.m. a police force cleared the Plaza 14 de Septiembre, entered the Prefecture, and arrested the *Coordinadora* delegates. (They would be released by 4:00 a.m. the next day.)

The surprise arrests were strongly denounced by the church and other mediators, and *Coordinadora* sympathizers were confirmed in their mistrust of the government. On April 7 an unprecedented crowd gathered in the plaza to demand a break with *Aguas del Tunari* and revision of Law 2029, and it was decided to continue the blockades until the demands were met. With the violence of February fresh in their minds, people prepared for the arrival of the army, expecting a grim battle when, later in the afternoon, the first rounds of tear gas were fired. But at 5:00 p.m. the news came that Galindo had announced a break with *Aguas del Tunari*. The crowd celebrated until a few hours later government sources denied the news; Galindo said that he had made the announcement only to avoid a "bloodbath." Meanwhile, some *Coordinadora* leaders were being arrested and others going into hiding. Throughout the country other leaders, such as Felipe Quispe of the CSUTCB, were also arrested and deported to San Joaquin, the "Bolivian Siberia" in tropical Beni Department.

A decree declaring a ninety-day state of siege was made public only in the morning of April 8[9] by Information Minister Ronald MacLean. His claim that the unrest in Cochabamba was being financed by drug traffickers added to the protesters' outrage. The state of siege became simply another reason for mobilization in various parts of the country. In Cochabamba the streets and the plaza filled with protesters, who were doused with tear gas. To keep news from spreading, the power supply to the El Temporal area, where various radio and TV stations are located, was cut by the military. In the afternoon protesters attacked local prisons, burned cars, threw a Molotov cocktail into the municipal offices, and managed to reconquer the plaza. Street kids—the most marginal of the marginal—played a prominent role in defending the reconquered plaza and the various barricades. Operating in well-organized gangs of "water warriors," they vehemently asserted their membership in the movement and their loyalty to the city, general patriotism, and "willingness to die for the cause." By the end of the day the attempts to reestablish order—what the national newspaper *La Prensa* (April 9, 2000) dubbed "a surgical operation with a kitchen knife"—had claimed two lives. In Cochabamba, the student Hugo Daza was shot in the face and died instantly. His body was immediately carried to the plaza, and at the place where he died a shrine was constructed that displayed a bullet-perforated piece of sheet iron. Government and military sources denied that any shots had been fired into the crowd.[10]

On Sunday, April 9, it was officially announced that *Aguas del Tunari* would withdraw, but by then such promises were hard to believe, and a crowd occupied the plaza to wait and see. *Coordinadora* members who had eluded arrest appealed to the government to come up with real solutions. On April 10 a new agreement was signed between government representatives and the *Coordinadora*. It established that SEMAPA would again assume responsibility for water supply in the city under a temporary board made up two representatives of the municipality and four "independents" with links to the *Coordinadora*. Roadblocks would be lifted as soon as parliament approved the modifications of Law 2029 and the Superintendency presented proof of the annulment of the *Aguas del Tunari* contract. The wounded were to be cared for at the expense of the government, indemnification was to be paid to the families of the dead, and those detained at San Joaquin were to be released.

When Oscar Olivera informed the crowd in the plaza of the agreement and claimed victory, he received a tepid response. Peasant delegates, who had become ever more suspicious of government promises, demanded that the modifications of Law 2029 be approved at once. Nevertheless, the crowd disbanded. Modifications to the law were approved in parliament that same night and a modified law, No. 2066, was proclaimed by President Banzer on April 11. The reform contained 36 articles. The main points were that (1) the possibility of creating a national water council was left open; (2) instead of five-year licenses peasant and indigenous organizations now had to register only for "the useful life of the service"; (3) in concession areas the concessionaires would not have monopoly rights and water committees, cooperatives, and other *usos y costumbres* would be recognized; and (4) rate structures were to be established in consultation with the municipalities and the local units of Popular Participation.[11]

While calm returned to Cochabamba, protests continued elsewhere. On April 20, on the eve of the Easter weekend, the state of siege was lifted, President Banzer asked pardon for any errors that might have been made, and the country prepared for what would come after the weekend.

Discussion and Conclusions

At the root of the problems in Cochabamba was a rather classic "urban contradiction" (Castells 1977): the precarious and class-biased distribution of a scarce collective consumption good. The attempts to solve the problem by drilling wells added a touch of "urban bias." However, as Kowarick (1986: 16) has put it, "between concrete conditions of existence and social struggles there are many mediations." It has increasingly been recognized that the analysis of forms of collective action cannot take the unity of a movement for granted but must consider it an outcome or a social construct (Melucci 1999). The processual dimension has therefore gained increasing attention, along with identity formation and the movement's cultural and discursive dimensions (Escobar 1992). Resource mobilization theory, which had hitherto focused on cost and benefit aspects of mobilization, was broadened to include the notion of "cultural framing" (McAdam, McCarthy, and Zald 1996). Touraine (1978) has suggested looking for the stakes in a conflict, the adversary, and the process of identity formation of the contesting party in relation to the former two elements.

The "early riser" (Tarrow 1994) in this protest movement was, as we have seen, the Defense Committee, which broke the silence surrounding the contract when the Civic Committee and the majority of the political parties had decided not to. The Civic Committee had cosigned the contract, and most of the parties were involved in Banzer's "mega-coalition" and disinclined to make the contract an issue in the December 1999 municipal elections. By then, however, the FDTFC and FEDECOR had taken up the question and provided a new mobilizing structure and a broadened social base for protest. The FDTFC had gained significant prestige among the population as a result of its creative response to the crisis of traditional trade unionism. FEDECOR had emerged in the context of earlier conflicts over water and, because of the forms of social control that go with rural water management, was a rather disciplined and cohesive organization. While FEDECOR advanced an articulate critique of the proposals for water legislation, the Defense Committee attacked the *Aguas del Tunari* contract. As in other movements, the convergence between the criticism of middle-class professionals and that of popular organizations was an important element in the emergence of the *Coordinadora* and its capacity to mobilize various sectors of the population.[12]

If we look at the stakes in the conflict and the process of framing or identity formation by which a "discursive community" is constructed (Tarrow 1994: 4), it is clear that people from the city's periphery feared being dispossessed of their water sources, and those who happened to be connected to the SEMAPA system saw their water bills increase. This certainly contributed to the credibility of the *Coordinadora*. The far from transparent negotiation of the contract, the feeble guarantees it provided for the realization of the MISICUNI Project, and the extension of coverage of the distribution system as well as the rate question had already been criticized by the Defense Committee, and the question of water legislation was a long-standing concern of FEDECOR. In the *Coordinadora* these elements fused into a discourse that drew on the rhetorical resources of national popular anti-imperialism, combined with new elements of antiglobalism, protest against the societal and development model imposed through the emblematic Decree 21060 of

1985, and criticism of the government's (non-) policies, kleptocratic practices, and nepotism. The immediate targets of anger were also quite clearly defined: *Aguas del Tunari*, the Civic Committee, and the municipal offices, the former for dispossessing the people in favor of foreign capital and the latter two for their connivance.

But more was at stake than just the water issue. The *Coordinadora* came to constitute an important challenge to the instituted system of legally accredited representation, which failed to channel the concerns and interests of large sectors of the population that had never felt represented by the Civic Committee and had come to perceive the FEJUVE as corrupt and coopted by the municipal government. Nevertheless, despite its rhetoric about "national dialogues" the government insisted on dialoguing only with legally accredited organizations. The dynamics that this approach may trigger are well captured in Laserna's (1999) notion of "forced negotiation." In the case of the Cochabamba conflict, government indifference to early signs of protest and the denial of the legitimacy of the *Coordinadora* added the issue of representation and popular organization to the agenda. It was only under the pressure of protests and violent attempts to quell them that *Coordinadora* representatives were admitted to the negotiating table, and even then the government proved unwilling to negotiate anything while the Civic Committee dragged its feet and narrowed the issue to the rate question. The provisional agreement worked out between the Civic Committee and the government in late March was more of a tactical move to calm the protests than a matter of conviction. When negotiations to end the third round of protests began, the *Coordinadora* seemed to be losing its capacity for mobilization, but the illegal arrest of its representatives and the subsequent declaration of a state of siege prompted unprecedented mobilization. After a bout of equally unprecedented violence, the government finally rescinded the contract with *Aguas del Tunari* and modified Law 2029. According to resource mobilization theory the presence of radical fringe actions may strengthen the negotiating position of the leading spokespersons and organizations (McAdam, McCarthy, and Zald 1996: 14). As we have seen, when protests began to expand the Civic Committee somewhat opportunistically sought to present itself as a moderate opponent to the rate hike and a reliable negotiating partner. Paradoxically, its failure to address other aspects of the contract or the water legislation issue and its vacillations only played into the hands of the *Coordinadora* coalition.

The modifications of the law included better protection of existing organizations involved in local water supply and some social control over rate structures, and the elimination of the criterion of "financial sufficiency" opened the way for consideration of social criteria. Finally, any mention of a water superintendency was eliminated. A next step will therefore be the development of a general water law to replace the obsolete 1906 law. Both the government and the peasant and indigenous organizations have produced proposals for new legislation, and one of the outcomes of the April 2000 conflicts is the promise to prepare a new proposal jointly. The government is moving very slowly, however, and the CSUTCB leader Felipe Quispe seems to have embarked on a strategy of confrontation that blocks further negotiations. This stand is strongly criticized by various CSUTCB base organizations and by NGOs, which argue that this plays into the hands of the government and that new legislation should be developed as soon as possible.

The rescission of the *Aguas del Tunari* contract meant that water supply in Cochabamba returned to SEMAPA, now with some representatives of the *Coordinadora* on its board. Meanwhile, various semipublic enterprises are claiming debts contracted by the old SEMAPA, and the legality of the present SEMAPA management, which took charge as an outcome of the agreement of April 10, is being called into question. It seems, however, that SEMAPA is doing reasonably well and enjoys the sympathy of much of the population. The new management claims that it has succeeded in making SEMAPA a profitable enterprise.

At the same time, the long-term alternatives being discussed envisioned rejecting both a public enterprise plagued by bureaucracy and corruption like the old SEMAPA and privatization that would prioritize profitability over the needs of the population in favor of a cooperative or social and self-managed entity under permanent popular control. In the end it was decided that the enterprise would remain a municipal public one but incorporate new features such as the representation of SEMAPA workers on the management board. At another level, discussions revolved around questions such as the development of a new socially acceptable rate structure and ways of rewarding cooperatives and other self-help initiatives for their incorporation into the SEMAPA system so as to achieve sustainable resource use in the long run and improve the quality of the water supplied. After the Water War, for example, the newly installed SEMAPA management and *Coordinadora* representatives initiated a round of visits to the urban periphery to inquire into the local situation and resolve some of the most pressing problems. Some have argued that, though the battle may have been won, the cause has been lost. This depends on how one evaluates the likelihood that eventually a new socially acceptable and waterproof contract could have been negotiated with *Aguas del Tunari*.

The *Coordinadora* emerged at a specific juncture as a loosely organized single-issue movement that from late 1999 on deployed a variety of initiatives and managed to gain broad sympathy among the population. The town meetings and the referendum were innovations in the action repertoire to promote debate and involvement and serve as instruments of direct democracy. The significance of the movement may therefore extend beyond the Water War itself. One of its demands became the direct election of the Civic Committee and a democratization of the neighborhood organizations, which are often involved in clientelistic relations with the municipality. Another question is the classical issue of the future of the movement or the transition "from revolt to organization" (Melucci 1996: 313). By deciding not to become a formal organization and seek official recognition, the *Coordinadora* has remained more of a network-like structure that links together different types of organization—the FEDECOR, the FDTFC, and the urban territorial organizations such as the water committees. It calls occasional open meetings to discuss issues and decide what to do. Among the issues that have been taken up are the revision of electricity rates and the recovery of the privatized state enterprises, and an initiative was taken to organize an international conference to protest globalization. Besides the classical trade-union demands, consumer issues have taken a more central place, and in the context of the fragmentation of trade-union structures a territorial mode of organization has gained importance. In other parts of the country initiatives have sprung up to create similar network-like and little-formalized coordinating structures. It may be premature to say that a "new social movement" has emerged in Bolivia, but the Water War does suggest a significant change in the dynamics of social protest.

Notes

This is a reprint of the 2003 publication "David versus Goliath in Cochabamba: Water Rights, Neoliberalism and the Revival of Social Protest in Bolivia," in *Latin American Perspectives* 130, 30, no. 3, 14–36. We thank SAGE Publications for its kind permission to republish this text.

1. Civic committees, often departmental, first arose in Bolivia's major cities in the course of the 1970s. They expressed regionalist demands confronting the country's centralism and were a vehicle of opposition to the authoritarian regimes. Though formally broad-based and including a range of organizations, they were largely controlled by the local business sector.

2. Article 4 states that the people govern through their representatives and legally established authorities and that any armed force or assembly of people that attributes popular sovereignty to itself is guilty of sedition. Article 223 defines the legitimate channels of participation as political parties and civic groups that possess legal recognition (*personería jurídica*).

3. Including the Cercado Province, in which the departmental capital Cochabamba is located, and the Quillacollo Province, which in turn is divided into five municipalities.

4. The Corani Reservoir Project is the principal alternative proposed. Favored by the Sanchez de Lozada government, it met with local opposition articulated by the municipal administration of Reyes Villa and the Civic Committee, which were committed to the MISICUNI

Project. The World Bank (1999) considered the MISICUNI Project a white elephant and argued that no public subsidies should be given to ameliorate the increase in water rates in Cochabamba.

5. The consortium was created a few weeks before signing the contract. Shareholders were Bechtel and Abengoa and some national enterprises—50 percent British, 25 percent Spanish, and 25 percent Bolivian.
6. Maldonado was at the time deputy for Cochabamba of the *Nueva Fuerza Republicana* (New Republican Force-NFR), a party created in 1996 as a vehicle for Cochabamba's Mayor Manfred Reyes Villa, nicknamed Bombón (Sweetie). Maldonado would be expelled from the NFR for revealing the implications of the *Aguas del Tunari* contract and thus damaging Bombón.
7. Edgar Montaño had left his post as president of the Civic Committee to join the NFR for the municipal elections.
8. In fact, the proposal was that the fixed charge for the first 12 m3 would increase by 20 percent while additional water would be charged according to the rate structure of the *Aguas del Tunari* contract.
9. The decree is dated April 7. It refers to social unrest, particularly in Cochabamba, and invokes the constitutional stipulations regarding the exercise of popular sovereignty. Given that the decree was made public only on April 8, the preceding nationwide arrests were unlawful.
10. A few days later PAT-TV made public a video film showing a sniper in civilian clothes, later identified as Captain Iriarte, kneeling behind a line of soldiers, who clearly offered him cover, and then taking aim and firing into the crowd. Though what happened was clear for all to see, government officials invented lie after lie to deny any government or army responsibility. Human rights groups in Cochabamba registered fifty-nine wounded, twenty-four of whom had bullet wounds.
11. The 1994 Law on Popular Participation recognizes "territorial base organizations" such as neighborhood associations, rural unions, and indigenous communities, which elect representatives to a vigilance committee charged with monitoring municipal investment plans.
12. For a discussion of similar dynamics in a different context, see Assies (1999).

References

Assies, Willem. 1999. "Theory, Practice, and 'External Actors' in the Making of Urban Social Movements in Brazil." *Bulletin of Latin American Research* 18, no. 2: 211–226.

Castells, Manuel. 1977. *The Urban Question*. London: Edward Arnold Publishers.

Crespo Flores, Carlos. 1999. "Gestión ambiental: el conflicto por la perforación de pozos profundos en Vinto-Sipe Sipe." In *Conflictos ambientales, dos casos: Aguay territorio*, ed. C. Crespo Flores and R. Orellana Halkyer. Cochabamba: CERES.

Escobar, Arturo. 1992. "Culture, Practice, and Politics: Anthropology and the Study of Social Movements." *Critique of Anthropology* 12, no. 4: 355–394.

Kowarick, Lucio. 1985. "Pathways to Encounter." In *New Social Movements and the State in Latin America*, ed. D. Slater. Amsterdam: CEDLA.

———. 1986. "Urban Movements in Contemporary Brazil: An Analysis of the Literature." Paper presented at the 11th World Congress of Sociology in New Delhi, August 18–23.

Kruse, Tom. 2002. "Transición política y recomposición sindical: reflexiones desde Bolivia." In *Ciudadania, cultura política y reforma del Estado en América Latina*, ed. W. Assies, M. Calderón, and T. Salman. Zamora: El Colegio de Michoacan/Instituto Federal Electoral, Michoacan.

Laserna, Roberto. 1999. "Prólogo." In *Empujando la concertación: marchas campesinas, opinión pública y coca*, ed. R. Laserna, N. Camacho, and E. Córdova. La Paz: CERES/PIEB.

McAdam, Doug, John. D. McCarthy, and Mayer N. Zald, eds. 1996. *Comparative Perspectives on Social Movements: Political Opportunities, Mobilizing Structures, and Cultural Framings*. Cambridge, U.K.: Cambridge University Press.

Melucci, Alberto. 1996. *Challenging Codes: Collective Action in the Information Age*. Cambridge: Cambridge University Press.

———. 1999. *Acción colectiva, vida cotidiana y democracia*. Mexico City: El Colegio de Mexico.

PEIRAV (Programa de Enseñanza e Investigación en Riego Andino y de los Valles). 1998. *La guerra del agua: Conflicto y negociación entre organizaciones campesinas y SEMAPA en el Valle de Cochabamba, 1977–1998*. Cochabamba: PEIRAV/UMSS-UAW.

Tarrow, Sidney. 1994. *Power in Movement: Social Movements, Collective Action, and Politics*. Cambridge, U.K.: Cambridge University Press.

Touraine, Alain. 1978. *La voix et le regard*. Paris: Editions du Seuil.

World Bank. 1999. *Bolivia: Public Expenditure Review*. Washington D.C.: World Bank (Report No. 19232-BO).

10 Neoliberalism and the Reemergence of Ethnopolitics in Bolivia

Introduction

Bolivia, although a much poorer country than most of its neighbors, was not a stranger to welfare policies. During the middle decades of the twentieth century, it had taken steps toward the development of programs dedicated to economic and social security. Although the system was limited in many ways, it did provide elements of protection to at least some parts of the population. In the 1980s and 1990s, however, two major trends transformed the Bolivian political landscape. One was neoliberalism, which exposed the population to significant economic hardship and reduced the limited social programs that had been inherited from the past; the second was the political mobilization of indigenous people and the adoption of multiculturalism policies. Given the debates addressed in this book, the key issue is the relation between multiculturalism and neoliberalism. Did multiculturalism in Bolivia contribute to the advance of the neoliberal agenda or not?

To address this issue, in the first place we have to distinguish clearly between identity politics "from below" and recognition policies "from above" or to put it crudely, between "demand" and "supply." What are indigenous movements demanding and what is a neoliberal state willing to concede? Framing the question this way also leads us to explore the relationship between policies of recognition and redistributive policies. In his article on what he calls "neoliberal multiculturalism" Hale (2002) has argued that neoliberal states may be willing to proactively recognize a minimal package of cultural rights, while equally vigorously rejecting the rest of indigenous demands. He proposes that the acceptance of certain cultural demands may lure indigenous movements into a limited form of identity politics that forsakes redistributive issues and thus in the end contributes to neoliberal governmentality. He furthermore suggests that the relationship between "cultural" and "redistributive" issues may be more complex than an either-or question. The emergence of identity politics poses the challenge of rethinking the relation between redistribution and recognition as two, not mutually exclusive, forms of achieving social justice (Fraser 2003) and, in the case at hand, invites an exploration of the complex relations between ethnicity and class (status and class) in a post-colonial society.

This chapter argues that Bolivia provides no significant evidence of a "crowding out" effect in the sense that culturalist demands took precedence over a more general redistributive agenda. Neoliberalism was well established before the effective mobilization of indigenous peoples and the strength of the neoliberal position was not significantly enhanced by the emergence of indigenous movements and parties involved in identity politics. Instead, the dominant pattern seems to be that: (a) neoliberalism was generated by other forces such as the multilateral agencies; but that (b) neoliberal restructuring in turn helped trigger indigenous mobilization and ethnically charged politics. If neoliberal politicians came to adopt multiculturalism policies, this was basically what Van Cott calls a reactive and opportunistic response.

The question of the "corroding" effect is difficult to answer for the Bolivian case if it is framed in terms of indigenous mobilization weakening relations with other groups that would otherwise have coalesced to resist neoliberalism and support wider popular coalitions. In fact, it was neoliberal restructuring that obliterated the existing trade union structures and ethnically charged politics blossomed in the vacuum thus created. A mayor characteristic of contemporary popular protest in Bolivia is that it is highly fragmented. Typically, protest peaks, or what Bolivians call "social convulsions," emerge out of a temporary fusion of disperse mobilizations that coalesce around some issue that emerges as overarching and representative of neoliberal economic policies and the system of governance that allows such policies to be implemented. This, however, at best gives rise to tactical alliances among more or less "radical" groups or leaders, be they indigenous or not.

Do indigenous peoples in Bolivia "misdiagnose" their situation and do they pursue cultural policies that cannot really solve their deep-seated socio-economic problems? It is difficult to speak of misdiagnosis in this sense in the Bolivian case because there are no indigenous movements that are limited to "cultural" issues. If Bolivia can be characterized as a post-colonial society, is it a case of misdiagnosis if indigenous peoples consider themselves as both culturally oppressed and economically exploited and dispossessed of the resources for cultural and economic reproduction?

To develop the argument, the chapter traces the historical development of these issues through several critical cycles. After a brief introduction to the history of Bolivia, the first major section examines the National Revolutionary Cycle, which began in 1952 and established certain welfare policies. The second section examines the development of neoliberal policies and the political constellation that allowed this development. It then traces the emergence of ethnically charged opposition to these policies and the adoption of multiculturalism as an aspect of a second generation of neoliberal reforms in the mid-1990s. It finally shows how these multiculturalism policies failed to enhance support for the neoliberal project as became increasingly clear by the end of the 1990s when indigenous peoples came to play an important role in the resistance against neoliberalism, leading to the Bolivian crisis of 2003. Indigenous movements often played a key role in the opposition to neoliberalism. The final section briefly sums up the argument and considers possible future scenarios.

A Post-Colonial Society with an Indigenous Majority

Although data on numbers of indigenous people are notoriously controversial and difficult to interpret (Gonzalez 1994) it is commonly assumed that indigenous people constitute the majority of the Bolivian population. According to Bolivia's 2001 census, the country counted nearly 8.3 million inhabitants of which 62 percent[1] declared themselves to belong to some indigenous people, principally the Quechuas (31 percent) and the Aymaras (25 percent) of the Andean highlands and the colonization areas in the eastern lowlands, while the remaining 6 percent accounts for some thirty different indigenous peoples in the eastern Amazonian lowlands (Bolivia 2003). According to estimates up to 45 percent of the indigenous population lives in urban areas. Thus, while equating the indigenous population with the rural population—about 38 percent of the total population—is erroneous, it is commonly agreed that 90 percent of the rural population is indigenous (Calla Ortega 2003a: 198; MACPIO 2001). While about 54 percent of the urban population is poor and 26 percent extremely poor, in the rural areas 81 percent is poor and 55 percent extremely poor (UDAPE 2003: 51). Being indigenous and being poor are clearly correlated (PNUD 2004: 108).

Bolivia is a post-colonial society that still has to come to terms with its colonial legacy. It is beyond the scope of this article to thoroughly discuss Bolivian history, but it should be pointed out that after the arrival of the Spaniards a highly stratified society was constructed in the Andes region, inhabited by Aymara and Quechua. It was centered on the silver mining economy that emerged in the Potosí region and later, from the late nineteenth century onward, on tin mining a bit further north. The tropical *Oriente*, inhabited by indigenous peoples practicing swidden agriculture in combination with hunting and gathering, remained largely peripheral until the quinoa and rubber booms of the nineteenth century triggered new incorporation efforts. Present day Bolivia is characterized by a pattern of regional differentiation inherited from the mining economy with its satellite economies that supplied it with agricultural produce through the hacienda system, and a remote eastern periphery. Its historical development influenced the forms in which the indigenous population was incorporated into the dominant economy and the degrees to which it was able to preserve its own forms of organization (Ticona, Rojas, and Albó 1995; Rivera Cusicanqui 2003).

The Chaco war (1932–1935) had profound consequences for the Bolivian polity and paved the way for the Bolivian Revolution of 1952. This disastrous adventure fuelled a change in the national political debate as the so-called "Chaco generation" began to raise the Indian question, the land question, labor issues, and the dependency on the private mines owned by a few tin barons. The war was followed by a period of political instability during which representatives of the "liberal" mining and landholding oligarchy alternated with governments headed by ex-combatants. During such governments Standard Oil of New Jersey, held responsible for the Chaco war, was nationalized and a state enterprise *Yacimientos Petrolíferos Fiscales Bolivianos* (YPFB) was created to manage the nationalized enterprise. The first labor laws saw the light and in the wake of a *Primer Congreso Indigenal*, which took place in 1945, decrees were issued that prohibited serfdom and sought to promote rural education, though with little concrete effect. Meanwhile, new political parties, most importantly the *Movimiento Nacionalista Revolucionaria* (MNR) arose as well as labor unions among which the *Federación Sindical de Trabajadores Mineros de Bolivia* (FSTMB) came to play a vanguard role. Peasant unions began to emerge demanding the establishment of rural schools and contesting the hacienda system. After the MNR gained the 1951 elections it was kept from assuming power by an army intervention that eventually was defeated by the popular insurrection of April 1952. In the view of the revolutionaries the "nation"—middle class, workers, and peasants—had defeated the "anti-nation" represented by the feudal and mining oligarchy and their imperialist allies.

The National Revolutionary Cycle

The coming to power of the MNR initiated the "national-revolutionary cycle" and a state capitalist development model that basically was kept in place until 1985. The 1942 MNR revolutionary program clearly included welfare ideals in its final paragraph on the economic liberation and sovereignty of the Bolivian people. It called for:

- A law that regulates peasant labor, taking regional peculiarities and the customs imposed by geographic circumstances into account, but guaranteeing the health and the satisfaction of the needs of the worker;

- Colonization projects that aim to turn every Bolivian, men or women, into owners of the land;
- The regulation of labor conditions of the organized workers and employees in international enterprises, creating a mechanism whereby salaries and wages are adjusted and to avoid social *malestar* (unwell-being);
- Obligatory social security and the elimination of the mechanisms that hinder the putting into effect of social laws and their benefits for the Bolivians;
- A statute of civil service that protects, assures and regulates the functions of public servants, men and women;
- The death penalty for speculators, usurers, smugglers, falsifiers, those who bribe public servants and traders in vice; and
- The identification of all Bolivians with the aspirations and needs of the peasantry, and we proclaim that social justice is inseparable from the redemption of the Indian for the *economic liberation and sovereignty of the Bolivian people.*[2]

This constitutes a wish list that—except for the death penalty—quite befits a welfare state.

The 1952 Revolution brought four basic transformations:

1. The universal franchise for all Bolivians, male and female, older than twenty-one if unmarried or older than eighteen when married, independent of their income, occupation or degree of education.
2. The nationalization of the holdings of the three tin barons. These mines were brought under the administration of the *Corporación Minera de Bolivia* (COMIBOL) in which, during a first few years, the FSTMB played a key role. The FSTMB had also taken the initiative to create a trade-union umbrella organization, the *Central Obrera Boliviana* (COB), which became a key player in Bolivian politics and forced the MNR to accept "co-government" during the first four years after the Revolution.
3. In 1953 an agrarian reform was decreed under the pressure of peasant unrest and unionization from which the *Confederación Nacional de Trabajadores Campesinos de Bolivia* (CNTCB), initially linked to the COB, emerged. The agrarian reform made an end to the hacienda system that had dominated the Andes region, but failed to improve productivity. A lack of appropriate technical and financial support and the subdivision of holdings upon inheritance led to increasing fragmentation into *minifundia* and resource degradation. On the other hand, development policies adopted in the course of the 1950s would favor large-scale agriculture and extensive cattle breeding in the eastern lowlands, which effectively underwent a socially regressive land reform. By the 1980s the national agrarian structure had become extremely polarized again,

    with an impoverished indigenous peasantry in the Andes region and a lowland region dominated by huge enterprises crowding out the local indigenous population, which would start organizing politically in the 1980s.

4. An education reform was initiated in 1955 and introduced free, obligatory, and universal education. The reform aimed at cultural homogenization and imposed Spanish as the sole teaching language, which probably is one of the reasons for the relatively meager results.

During the years leading up to the 1952 revolution and thereafter a Bolivian version of the welfare state emerged, inspired by the ideology of national developmentism and as part of a nation-building effort. As was the case in other Latin American states (Dos Santos 1987; Oxhorn 2003) this welfare system remained precarious and patchy. Although it espoused a universalist ideology in fact it relied on a selective incorporation of specific groups or sectors of the population according to political convenience. What emerged in Bolivia in the wake of the 1952 Revolution has been described as a pre-bendalist, patrimonialist, or cartorial state; a state and a political regime that rely on doling out jobs in the state bureaucracy to the clientele of the governing sectors (Gamarra and Malloy 1995; Gamarra 2003; PNUD 2002; Tapia Mealla and Toranzo Roca 2000; World Bank 2000). During the first few years of "co-government" between the MNR and the COB, the COMIBOL became an important employment-generating machine with a huge bureaucracy and well-subsidized company stores in the mining centers. As the MNR gradually moved to the right, however, the co-government arrangement broke down by 1956 and since then the relationship between governments and miners were tense if not of open confrontation. On the other hand, the peasantry was placated by the land reform and remained a loyal ally of the MNR governments as well as of the military governments that ruled the country after 1964. This alliance was formalized in a *pacto militar campesino* that lasted until the mid-1970s when the Banzer dictatorship killed between eighty and two hundred peasants protesting its economic policies. The unraveling of the *pacto*, as we shall see, brought a reconciliation between workers and (indigenous) peasants, now united in the struggle against military dictatorships.

The outcome of the national-revolutionary model was that by the mid-1970s the state sector accounted for some 70 percent of the national product with enterprises in the mining and oil and gas sector playing key roles. The state was the main employer and provider of goods and services. Salaries paid to the bureaucracy absorbed about 10 percent of the national product. The number of state employees rose from forty thousand in 1951 to ninety thousand in 1964 and about 170,000 in the late 1970s, about one-third of the economically active population; fifty-five thousand were public employees (of which thirty thousand teachers), thirty thousand worked in the nationalized enterprises, and twenty-two thousand were on the payroll of the armed forces (Berthín Siles 1999: 367–369; World Bank 2000: 1).

In 1956 a unified social security system was created, which was to cover maternity, illness, professional risks, disability, old age, and burial, sort of "from the cradle to the grave." Since the state was the principal employer it contributed most of the funding in its quality of employer, but failed to contribute the share it should fund as state. In the early 1970s the Banzer government sought to rationalize the system. A national fund was to be administered by a *Caja Nacional de Seguro Social*, while alongside, for different affiliated sectors, so-called complementary funds existed. Thus the customs service, the public service, the railways, teachers, the judicial branch, the police, the army, miners, universities, industrial workers, and other sectors had their specific funds to complement the meager national fund disbursals. The result was a hodgepodge of mostly highly bureaucratized small social security funds that unevenly covered a minimal part of the population (Mercado Lora 1998), not to speak of the peasantry.

After twelve years of MNR rule and eighteen years of military governments the social achievements of the revolution were rather modest. Life expectancy and literacy had improved, but per capita GDP may have declined in real terms (Morales 2003: 221; Klein 2003). The land reform had brought redistribution in the Andes region, but thirty years later landholding was highly fragmented and little productive and most of the indigenous peasantry desperately poor. In the *Oriente* a highly polarized rural structure had emerged, dominated by huge estates (Demeure 1999: 269–290). The nationalized mines were often exhausted and mismanaged while little had been invested (Jordán 1999: 219–239). No dynamic "national bourgeoisie" had come into being. The *Oriente* agriculturalists and some medium sized mining enterprises had emerged relying on extremely generous state subsidies (Rodríguez Ostria 1999: 291–304). Cocaine had become one of the major export products. The military regimes bequeathed the country a huge foreign debt.

In sum, the 1952–1982 period was characterized by a politics structured largely around the axes of class and economic interest. In the context of a nation-building effort and state centered national-developmentist economic policies a number of progressive economic and social policies were put into place. On the cultural dimension, the era was characterized by a denial of multiculturalism. The 1952 Revolution expressly abolished the term *indio*, which was regarded as demeaning, and interpellated the rural population as "peasantry." Although the land reform recognized communal holding it basically sought to create individual family farms while other important programs, such as education, were clearly assimilationist.

Democracy, Free Markets and Multiculturalism

After the turbulent 1978–1982 period Bolivia finally returned to civilian government under a left of center coalition, the *Unidad Democrática y Popular* (UDP).[3] Its attempt to revamp the national revolutionary model ended in dismal failure. The COB pressed for pent-up popular demands in the most "maximalist" style while the opposition in parliament—the MNR faction of Victor Paz Estenssoro and the *Acción Democrática Nacionalista* (ADN) of ex-dictator General Banzer—gave the UDP government preciously little room for maneuver. Inflation turned to hyperinflation while chaos was on the rise. In 1985, President Siles Zuazo decided to step down a year before ending his constitutional mandate.

The debacle set the stage for a turn to orthodox neoliberal adjustment policies. In this section I will first discuss Bolivian structural adjustment policies and the system of governance that allowed them to be carried through. In 1985 a "first generation" of adjustment policies was introduced following the Washington Consensus recipe.[4] This shock therapy broke the backbone of the COB, which until then had been the mayor vehicle of popular protest. In political terms, the introduction of neoliberal adjustment policies basically relied on what has become known as "pacted democracy," that is "gentlemen's agreements" among the leaders of the principal parties concerning the division of the spoils. Although formally a representative democracy, this meant that the party system suffered a huge "representation deficit." By the late 1980s some new "neo-populist" parties emerged, which appealed to the indigenous population and criticized the established party system as well as the neoliberal economic model. When between 1993 and 1997 a "second generation" of reforms was introduced multiculturalism would be an important ingredient, partly in response to the neo-populist parties, which were soon coopted into the pacted democracy system. As the neoliberal agenda pursued its course new forms of opposition in which indigenous movements played a prominent role emerged. Faced with this opposition the state increasingly turned to repressive measures, creating the conditions of emergence of the "Bolivian crisis" that culminated in the ouster of President Sánchez de Lozada in October 2003.

Structural Adjustment and Governance

The 1985 elections resulted in a coalition between the MNR and ADN that elected Paz Estenssoro president.[5] A few weeks later he introduced a New Economic Policy, which achieved economic stabilization at tremendous social costs. The package included a reform of the monetary system, rationalization of the bureaucracy through mass dismissal, market liberalization, export promotion, and reform of the tax system. The tin market crash later that year accelerated the overhaul of COMIBOL and twenty-three thousand miners were "relocated," that is dismissed. Due to trade liberalization the market was swamped with cheap imports and many factories closed or downsized. Urban unemployment jumped from 6 percent to 12 percent. The dismissal of the miners and the restructuring of other sectors emasculated the COB.

As elsewhere, the turn to neoliberalism was accompanied by a shift in the social policy paradigm, which now favors targeted assistance, presumably to increase efficiency by limiting the amount of leakage to middle and upper class groups. Under the pressure of multilateral agencies general subsidies and overly bureaucratic welfare policies are replaced by strictly needs-based direct assistance (Abel and Lewis 2002; Oxhorn 2003; Pérez Baltodano 1997; Sottoli 2000). To attenuate the worst effects of the adjustment measures, in 1986 Bolivia created a Social Emergency Fund (FSE)[6] to provide temporary employment in works of "social impact." Originally viewed as a temporary measure, in 1991 the FSE was transformed into a more permanent Social Investment Fund (FIS) to finance health and education infrastructure, as human capital building became a catchword in the new social policy paradigm of "struggle against (extreme) poverty." FIS fund targeting, however, became largely oriented by patronage criteria (Aguirre, Arze, and Montaño 1992; Prisma 2000; World Bank 2000: 53).

The turn to neoliberalism was sustained by what has become known as "pacted democracy." From 1985 onward a series of gentlemen's agreements were concluded among the main party leaders. Whitehead (2001a) has suggested that this system of inter-party bargaining and division of the spoils may present an alternative to what O'Donnell has called "delegative democracy," which "rests on the premise that whoever wins elections is thereby entitled to act as he or she sees fit, constrained only by the hard facts of existing power relations and by a constitutionally limited term of office." Such weakly institutionalized democracies, characterized by a lack of accountability, have carried through the harsh adjustment "packages" of the 1980s (O'Donnell 1999). While Whitehead (2001a) argues that Bolivia's democratic institutions appear to function more effectively than those of various adjoining neo-democracies and that "the broadly neoliberal framework of policy pursued since 1985 seems reasonably compatible with the persistence and even entrenchment of at least a 'low intensity' form of market democracy" (Whitehead 2001b: 39), Bolivia's troubled recent past suggests otherwise. As I have argued elsewhere, rather than being superior to delegative democracy Bolivia's pacted democracy can be viewed as a functional equivalent that shares the features of weak institutionalization and lack of accountability as well as the inability to channel popular discontent with neoliberal policies, which was met with repression. Bolivian democracy became ever more of a *democradura* or what Seoane (2003) has called "armed neoliberalism." It was in this context that ethnically charged politics came to play an increasingly prominent role.

Neoliberalism and the Politization of Ethnicity

As noted, in the wake of the Bolivian Revolution the term *indio* had officially been banned and a class perspective predominated, downplaying cultural or ethnic differences. In the context of the agrarian reform the organization of rural trade unions was strongly promoted. The local *sindicatos* became the basis of the pyramidal structure of the *Confederación Nacional de Trabajadores Campesinos de Bolivia* (CNTCB), strongly linked to the MNR governments and subsequently to the military governments under the formal *pacto military y campesino*.[7] The unraveling of this alliance in the mid-1970s was accompanied by a resurgence of "ethnic conscience." *Katarista* movements, named after the leaders of the late-eighteenth century indigenous revolt, gained increasing influence within the CNTCB. In 1973 the famous *Manifiesto de Tiawanacu* had been launched which, among other things, stated that "We feel economically exploited and culturally and politically oppressed. In Bolivia there has not been an integration of cultures but superposition and domination, and we have been relegated to the lowest and most exploited rungs of this pyramid."[8] Seeking a middle ground between radical indianism and its glorification of an idealized past and the emphasis on class struggle of the left, Katarismo underlined the necessity to look at Bolivia with "two eyes." It stressed the struggle of the Indian population against "internal colonialism" but also viewed the *sindicato* (union) as the principal vehicle of struggle of the exploited *campesino*. It thus sought to synthesize the struggles of "nation and class." In 1979, a congress of "peasant unification" sponsored by the COB resulted in the renaming of the CNTCB as *Confederación Sindical Única de Trabajadores Campesinos de Bolivia* (CSUTCB). Workers and peasants, who had become increasingly divided since 1952, now closed ranks in opposition to the military regimes. However, although Katarismo was important in the formation of the CSUTCB, its role in the political arena remained negligible. Some Katarist and Indianist parties emerged in the late 1970s but they never attracted more than 2 percent of the vote. By the early 1980s Katarism was splintered by factional disputes, but it had prepared the ground for a greater acceptance of the "pluri-multi."

This development received further impetus when the indigenous peoples of the tropical lowlands arrived upon the scene. Since the late 1970s anthropologists and NGOs had promoted "encounters" among the indigenous peoples of the region, leading in 1982 to the formation of the *Confederación Indígena del Oriente Boliviano* (CIDOB). Increasing pressure on local resources in the context of neoliberal policies as well as the continent-wide preparations for the commemoration of the "encounter of cultures" provided the motives and the opportunity for the undertaking of a broadly publicized thirty-five-day March for Territory and Dignity to protest timber exploitation in what where considered indigenous territories. Then president Jaime Paz Zamora (1989–1993) personally went to meet the marchers and subsequently signed a series of decrees recognizing indigenous territories in the eastern lowlands. In 1991 Bolivia ratified ILO Convention 169 on indigenous and tribal peoples in independent states.

By that time ethnicity also had come to play a role in the party system. The system of pacted democracy that had emerged in 1985 relied on three "traditional" parties; the MNR, which by then had adopted the neoliberal creed, the nominally social-democratic MIR, and ex-dictator Banzer's ADN. By the late 1980s, however, two new "neo-populist" parties emerged which in different ways appealed to the indigenous and *cholo*[9] electorate. *Conciencia de Patria* (CONDEPA) was led by the popular radio and TV host Carlos Palenque and had its main base in the La Paz highland region. *Unidad Cívica Solidaridad* (UCS) became the political vehicle of beer magnate Max Fernández and was less regionally confined. What the two parties had in common was that they attracted the protest vote of an impoverished electorate and that ethnic empathy played some role in appealing to this electorate.

Max Fernández's story is one of a "darkish" shoeshine-boy who became a millionaire.[10] He accumulated a fortune, speculating and using credits in the times of hyperinflation to buy up shares in Bolivia's main beer brewery, the *Cervecería Boliviana Nacional.* Always emphasizing that he had known poverty he used part of his fortune to assist the poor in times when social policies were rolled back. Financing schools and clinics in medium-sized towns, where this had a relatively great impact for the less advantaged, and oiling his electoral campaigns with plenty of beer and invectives against the established parties his party garnered up to 16 percent of the vote in the 1997 elections.

This, however, was a condolence vote; in 1995 Max Fernández had died in a plane crash and his party, with little ideological content from the outset, would thenceforward join any government coalition to ward off the payment of a huge tax debt. Nonetheless, Fernández can be considered a precursor of the "anti-systemics" for his "moral" critique of the established parties and his assistentialism in times of neoliberal austerity. And he was "darkish."

While Mayorga (2002) classifies Max Fernández as the more "godfather-like" (*padriño*) type of politician, he classifies Carlos Palenque as the "best-man" (*compadre*) type. While Fernández had a more disperse appeal as a result of philanthropy, beer, and "darkishness," Palenque's appeal was more restricted in regional terms and it built much more on ethnicity—only implied by Fernández's "darkishness"—a rejection of neoliberalism and anti-systemic rhetoric. The "best-man" style, at least discursively, implies a more horizontal relation. Palenque particularly appealed to the Aymara of the La Paz urban and rural highlands; a ground prepared by Katarism. His political career started when he interviewed a drug lord and his radio and TV station was closed in 1988, which caused intense protests. He had become enormously popular, particularly among Aymara women, with a talk show where people exposed their daily and domestic conflicts and problems, were listened to and were helped in some way by Palenque and his team. In those talk shows he was seconded by Remedios Loza, dressing *chola* style—Bowler hat and all—and fluent in Spanish, Aymara and Quechua, while his wife, Mónica Medina, took charge of the "social branch," distributing coffins for the dead, eyeglasses to the sightless, and wheelchairs to the cripple. On that basis, CONDEPA was founded in 1988 to give voice to the oppressed and defenseless through a discourse that stressed Andean values and the antagonism between *cholos* and *q'aras* (white, rich, dominant), denouncing neoliberalism and propagating a model of "endogenous development." In 1997, Palenque died of a heart attack. That year CONDEPA achieved about 17 percent of the vote and entered Hugo Banzer's government coalition from which it soon was expelled as the party was falling apart due to factional struggles over Palenque's legacy.

In a context where miner's and urban trade unionism was shattered as a result of economic restructuring and growing informal (self-) employment these parties appealed to those excluded from the pacted democracy model. However, as Mayorga (2002: 86) argues, although these parties posed a challenge to the established party system they ended up contributing to its consolidation and the hegemony of democratic neoliberalism. They had the capacity to symbolically represent and incorporate new social identities into the democratic dynamic but Mayorga also cautiously points out that this capacity for symbolic incorporation contrasts with a weakness of institutional representation and efficacy in channeling social demands and transforming them into public policy proposals.

In sum, neoliberal adjustment policies, inspired by multilateral agencies and unrelated to multiculturalism policies, transformed the economic and social model of Bolivia and this particularly affected the sectors of the population subject to economic subordination and ethnic discrimination. At the same time, by eroding the bases for trade unionism adjustment policies undermined the conditions for class-based mobilization whereas the pacted democracy model restricted representation of the subordinated. This provided the conditions of emergence for neo-populist parties, which in different ways tapped ethnic empathies but in the end failed to provide a genuine alternative and soon joined the spoils system of pacted democracy. Their appeal to ethnicity, however, paved the way for a reactive and opportunistic turn to multiculturalism among the traditional parties.

Recognition Policies and Second-Generation Reforms

By the early 1990s recognition of the multicultural and pluriethnic composition of the population had become fashionable in Bolivia, as elsewhere in Latin America. The Katarism of the rural trade unions, the new visibility of the indigenous peoples of the *Oriente* and the emergence of two neo-populist parties that somehow tapped identity resources suggested that adopting a multiculturalist ploy might be electorally rewarding. In a reactive response, for instance, by the early 1990s the MNR embraced multiculturalism. Its new leader, Gonzalo Sánchez de Lozada, who had been the architect of the 1985 economic shock therapy, would sit down among indigenous peasants and state how much he liked their typical dishes, though his interlocutors would be a little uneasy about his heavy gringo accent,[11] stating things like "I do not understand a word of what he says." Taking into account a political marketing study Sánchez de Lozada invited one of the moderate and more intellectualist Katarista leaders, Víctor Hugo Cárdenas, to join him in the 1993 presidential race. Although initially this "surprising and bold alliance between Aymaras and neoliberals" (Albó 1994) generated high expectations, the shine soon wore off. Upon assuming the vice presidency Cárdenas had said that the principles of *ama quella, ama llulla, ama sua, ama llunku* (do not be lazy, do not lie, do not steal, do not be servile) would guide him but this was soon held against him as he was accused of being servile to the neoliberal model.[12]

Multiculturalism, however, was to be one of the outstanding features of the package of "second-generation" reforms carried through by the Sánchez de Lozada government (1993–1997).[13] The most outstanding second-generation reforms were:

- Capitalization; a Bolivian variant of privatization whereby half of the shares in the most important national enterprises (electricity, telecommunications, airlines, railways, oil and gas exploitation and transport, and a tin foundry) was handed over to mostly transnational enterprises in return for an equivalent investment in the sector. This reform was related to a reform of the pension system. The other half of the shares of the state enterprises was retained for the Bolivian's and was to be managed by private Pension Fund Administrators that were to assure that every Bolivian reaching the age of sixty-five would receive a minimum pension, the BONOSOL (Mercado Lora 1998). While the privatization of the state enterprises turned out to be fraught with shady deals and often was regarded as a garage sale of the national patrimony, the allegedly low profitability of the privatized enterprises undermined the BONO-SOL. With great difficulty a pension of about US$250 was paid out during the 1997 electoral campaign, but in 1998 the Banzer government scrapped the scheme and later substituted it with the BOLIVIDA of some US$60 per year.[14]
- The law of Popular Participation, which decentralized government and contained elements of multiculturalism. The, until then insignificant, sections of provinces were converted into municipalities. While municipal governments had been effective in at best some twenty larger cities, the country now counts over three hundred municipalities that receive an important share of the national tax revenue. At the same time, Territorial Base Organizations, among them those of indigenous peoples, were recognized and given legal personality.[15] They were to play a role in overseeing municipal governments. Though initially this reform met with resistance of the CSUTCB, but not of the CIDOB, it soon was appropriated by local organizations to make inroads into local government, though not without difficulty or ambiguities (Assies 2003a; Grindle 2000). The coca growers of the Chapare region in Cochabamba are an outstanding example of such appropriation, which provided them with a springboard that allowed for the shakeup of the party system in the 2002 presidential elections.
- Reforms in the agrarian and forestry legislation initially were market oriented in intention but were partly amended as a result of peasant and indigenous protests. As a result, the new legislation was a hybrid. On the one hand it introduced market elements applying to the private sector, while on the other hand peasant smallholdings and community lands continued to be protected. The new legislation also came to include the recognition of Originary Communitarian Lands (TCOs), thus including the territories that had been granted in the lowlands after the

1990 March. It was thought that the TCO concept would only apply to the tropical lowlands, but after a few years it was adopted by highland peoples to stake their territorial claims on the argument that the "law applies to all."[16] Although the reform has brought some tenuous benefits for the lowland peoples it hardly has benefited the highland population, which continues to suffer minifundization, resource degradation and neglect (*Artículo Primero* 2003).

- An educational reform introduced bilingual education and thus abandoned the revolutionary policy of nation building through forcible hispanization.

The flurry of reforms was accompanied by a reform of the constitution that recognized the multiethnic and pluricultural composition of the Bolivian population. It also paved the way for a reform of the electoral system, meant to strengthen the hold of the established parties at the local level or to make them more responsive to local needs. The reform created sixty-eight single-seat districts for the election of part of the 130-seat Chamber of Deputies; a reform that opened the way for the political upheaval of the 2002 presidential elections (Albó 2002; Van Cott 2003).

By the end of the Sánchez de Lozada administration the multilateral agencies regarded Bolivia as an outstanding pupil. The role of the state in the economy had been rolled back and the most important second-generation reforms were more or less in place. The economy was growing, though not spectacularly and with ups and downs, the incidence of poverty and extreme poverty was back to the 1986 level after having peaked around 1990, the human development index (HDI) showed signs of improving due to improvement in health and education standards, and democracy had been in place for some fifteen years in a notoriously unstable country. Such an assessment, however, happily overlooked that Bolivia was one of those cases where the macro-indicators look good, but the population does not fare well. Fanfani's (2001) "felicitous" dictum that "the rich got richer and the poor more numerous" also applies to Bolivia and the 2002 PNUD report characterizes Bolivian performance as a vicious circle of feeble economic growth, worsening income distribution, and increasing poverty for important sectors of the population. Employment in the state sector dropped, and this was not compensated by private sector performance. Growth of some nontraditional exports had its counterpart in the transnationalization of the internal market, crowding out the smaller local industries. Thus unemployment and informal self-employment increased while labor conditions in the more formal sector deteriorated as a result of flexibilization. State capitalism had successfully been dismantled, but it had been replaced by a rather savage brand of crony capitalism. The regulatory system that was to oversee the privatization process and regulate sectors likely to constitute natural monopolies was often inept and open to influence peddling (Grebe López 2001: 176), and it was more concerned with the investment climate and profitability than with consumer concerns. The "representation deficit" of pacted democracy became increasingly notorious. A World Bank report euphemistically states that ever since 1985 states of siege have been declared to "facilitate economic governance" (World Bank 2000: 51).

Thus, in response to the growing presence of indigenous movements and the emergence of ethnically charged politics, multiculturalism became an important feature of the second-generation reforms for pragmatic electoral reasons rather than out of conviction. It was a limited response. Whereas the educational reform introduced bilingual education, the Law of Popular Participation aimed for administrative decentralization in the first place while the recognition of indigenous authorities played a secondary and subordinated role (Calla Ortega 2000). In the cases of new agrarian and forestry legislation indigenous peoples concerns were only taken into account due to mobilizations and pressure of the indigenous peasantry and effective implementation of such legislation where indigenous rights are concerned turned out to be extremely patchy and exceedingly slow as it often collided with the interests of business sectors (agriculture and mining) with strong links to the governing parties and committed to the Bolivian brand of neoliberalism. State sponsored multiculturalism may have generated some expectations but soon it became clear that it fell short where a redistribution of power and resources is concerned.

From Discontent to Social Convulsions

Things became worse under the disastrous Banzer government (1997–2002). Corruption never had been absent in the country but it became rampant and the Banzer clan and its cronies were shamelessly involved.[17] Banzer relied on a "megacoalition" of which the partners were endlessly involved in squabbles over the spoils, and although Banzer had criticized Sánchez de Lozada's neoliberal policies and his sellout of the national patrimony, economic and social policies did not change but rather deteriorated (Assies and Salman 2003). After a brief "honeymoon" with the coca growers relations imploded to "ground zero" due to the militarization of eradication policies on behest of the American Embassy, while the simulated empathy with the plight of indigenous peoples of the Sánchez de Lozada government gave way to a manifest empathy with the large landholders of the *Oriente* and little concern for the highland peasantry (Assies 2002).

Meanwhile, the economy dipped in the wake of the Asian, Brazilian, and Argentine crises, and unemployment reached two-digit levels. The year 2000 started with the protests against the opaque privatization of the water supply system in the Cochabamba region and the consequent price hike. The Water War ended with the ouster of Aguas del Tunari, a company set up by the Bechtel concern and some partners, and a hurried modification of legislation on water rights that had been adopted some months earlier. Locally this was regarded as a first victory after fifteen years of defeats in the face of neoliberalism (Assies 2003b). At the same time peasant protests erupted in the highlands, starting a cycle of protests with increasingly ethnic overtones to demand land, tractors, credit and a series of other things. These protests were led by Felipe Quispe, *el Mallku*,[18] who had become General Secretary of the CSUTCB in 1998. In November 2000 Quispe created his own "political instrument," the Movimiento Indigenista Pachacuti (MIP), to participate in the 2002 presidential elections.[19] Violence also was on the rise in the Chapare region, where the Banzer government stubbornly carried out the "war on drugs" to comply with the fundamentalism of the US Embassy. Although talk about the "sacred leaf" is not absent from the coca growers discourse, it is far less ethnicized than Quispe's strident Indianism. Coca grower's leader Evo Morales would be another presidential candidate in the 2002 elections, borrowing the Movimiento al Socialismo (MAS) label. To everyone's surprise, Morales ended second in these elections with nearly 21 percent of the vote, which made him a potential presidential candidate, while Quispe garnered about 6 percent of the vote, more than any Katarist or Indianist party had ever achieved. Congress was flooded with indigenous Deputies and Senators, turning what had been the perk of "professional" politicians donning suits and ties into a rather colorful tower of Babel. As it turned out, Sánchez de Lozada, who ended first in the elections, only slightly ahead of Morales, managed to broker a pact among the established parties, which brought him to the presidency for the second time. It would not be for long. In February 2003, the introduction of a new income tax, as advised by the multilateral agencies, caused a revolt during which about thirty people were killed and in October Sánchez de Lozada fled the country in the midst of a wave of protests against the intended sale of gas to the US, by way of Chile; an intention that compounded the sell-out of national resources with anti-US and anti-Chile sentiments. By then the attempts to repress these protests had cost over sixty lives.

It is not the place here to discuss these protests and the political turmoil in Bolivia at length, which we have done elsewhere (Assies and Salman 2003; Assies 2004), but rather to point out that indigenous people played a prominent role in this process. I do not share Patzi Paco's (2003) rather exalted view that the conflicts were basically about colonialism and racial oppression or, as some press comments suggested that they essentially were about Aymara nationalism. They rather were popular revolts against an economic model and a type of democracy that exclude a rather significant part of the population, the indigenous among them (Calla Ortega 2003b).[20] On the other hand, the dynamics of ethnic polarization that can be observed in Bolivia seems to corroborate Chua's (2004) thesis that exporting "raw" free market democracy to ethnically divided societies can breed ethnic hatred. She argues that while free-marketeering disempowers the poor and economically empowers an ethnically visible minority, democracy politically empowers the impoverished majority and that may unleash ethnic demagoguery, or worse.[21]

By Way of Conclusion

In this chapter I have sought to show that welfare-state thinking has not been absent from Latin America and not even from Bolivia although, at best, it yielded a stunted and miserly version of a welfare state, wrecked by patronage, clientelism, and corporatism. In 1985 the national revolutionary development model was replaced by neoliberal structural adjustment policies that were implemented under a system of governance known as pacted democracy, inherently suffering from a representation deficit. In a country with a majority indigenous population, adjustment policies brought hardship for these majorities and exacerbated polarization between a rich minority and the rest. At the same time such policies corroded much of the trade union structures that earlier had been a vehicle of popular protest. The rise of neo-populist parties, particularly CONDEPA, was an indication of the discontent with the economic model and the limits of the prevailing mode of governance. Although this prompted an embrace of multiculturalism among the established parties, it did not bring about a change in overall economic policies. This multiculturalism was limited and superficial anyway and did hardly involve a redistribution of resources in favor of indigenous peoples. Instead, in a context of increasingly blatant corruption in government circles, the economic model was upheld through increasingly violent repression of popular protests, culminating in the October 2003 events. Although ethnic factors and Aymara nationalist rhetoric became ever more prominent these protests were essentially popular revolts against an economic model and a mode of governance. The pattern of protest is typically one of fusion and fission from which no enduring coalitions have (yet?) emerged.

In her contribution to this volume, Donna Lee Van Cott sketches five basic scenarios for the future of ethnopolitics and multiculturalism politics in Latin America. What can we say about future scenarios in Bolivia? First of all, I should point out that various pending issues have not been discussed in this chapter and that the "Bolivian condition" is extremely complex and regionally differentiated. The October 2003 "Gas War" and earlier conflicts have clearly called the neoliberal model into question and will certainly lead to modifications, like an enhanced role of the state and a turn to more humane policies. If not, a scenario of "protracted conflict" and popular protest with ethnic overtones, as unfolded during the Banzer and second Sánchez de Lozada governments is likely.

The October events, however, also opened the way for other scenarios. A reform of the Bolivian constitution is on the books, and this reform will have to deal with the extremely tricky and explosive issue of regional autonomy demands. In the foregoing we have touched upon the issue of Aymara nationalism but for reasons of space I have not discussed the elite-driven demands for regional autonomy of the Santa Cruz and Tarija departments, where most of the economic growth occurs and where the most important gas reserves are located. Santa Cruz regionalism, in particular, has in recent years become propped up by a virulently right-wing ethnicized ideology that emphasizes the mestizo character of its population and contrasts it with the highland population, accused of preying upon lowlands. A Constituent Assembly will certainly have to deal with such autonomy claims but given the configuration of power relations in much of the lowlands, with large landholders and cattle raisers playing a key role, greater autonomy for these regions may well result in an exacerbation of land conflicts and increased oppression of local indigenous peoples. Such autonomy claims, therefore, might result in a "multinational state" but not a democratic utopia as envisioned by Van Cott.

Finally, the Bolivian party system is in tatters. For the time being, the MAS has emerged as the most important party and seeks to project itself as a democratic left-wing alternative. If something like that consolidates we might expect a scenario somewhere between, or combining, populist multiculturalism and radical ethnonationalist development of multiculturalist policies. The situation is extremely fluid, however, and I would not risk predicting the course of events.

Notes

First published in 2006 as "Neoliberalism and the Re-Emergence of Ethnopolitics in Bolivia," in *Multiculturalism and the Welfare State: Recognition and Redistribution in Contemporary Democracies*, ed. K. Banting and W. Kymlicka, Oxford, U.K., and New York: Oxford University Press. We kindly thank the editors and Oxford University Press for permission to include this text in our compilation.

1. Of those over fifteen years.

2. The full text is reproduced in Arze Cuadros (2002: 605–643).
3. The coalition was made up from a faction of the MNR joined by the *Movimiento de Izquierda Revolucionaria* (MIR), a left-wing party that had emerged in 1971, and the Bolivian Communist Party (PCB).
4. It should be noted, though, that privatization of state enterprises did not figure prominently among the first generation reforms in Bolivia, basically as a result of the lingering influence of revolutionary nationalism. A Bolivian variant of privatization would be introduced after 1993, as part of the second-generation reforms.
5. If none of the candidates wins a straight majority, the Bolivian Congress elects the president.
6. Bolivia was a pioneer in this field.
7. The CNTCB was formally part of the COB, but as the revolutionary governments veered to the right the COB became increasingly strongly opposed to these governments while the peasantry remained loyal.
8. The full text can be found in Bonfil Batalla (1981: 216–223).
9. Mestizo and/or urbanized indigenous people in the highlands.
10. What follows is largely based on the studies by Mayorga (2002), which provides biographies of Max Fernández and Carlos Palenque, and those contained in Mansilla and Zegada (1996). Romero Ballivián (2003) provides a summary of their careers in the latest edition of his studies on electoral processes and the electoral geography of Bolivia.
11. Sánchez de Lozada was brought up and studied in the United States and never lost his accent.
12. In his speech Cárdenas also stated that "Indigenous development is national development. Each time the criticism that the indigenous not only want to establish states of their own and dismember the country and moreover, seek a 'separate development,' certainly utopian and regressive, is becoming more marginalized. We should recognize that, apart from some radicalized discourses, the indigenous peoples understand their own development as a component of national development, linked to the great objectives of our countries, incorporated in the dynamics of the market and, above all, based in the will to rely on their own effort to achieve that" (cited in Ibarra n.d.). The latter remarks clearly indicate a drift away from his earlier Katarista discourse and its emphasis on looking at reality through the lenses of class and nation.
13. For a detailed and valuable analysis of Bolivian multiculturalism under Sánchez de Lozada see Van Cott (2000). Subsequent events, however, have called into question the optimistic tone of this account and pointed to the limitations of "liberal indigenism" (Gustafson 2002) or what Hale (2002) has dubbed "neoliberal multiculturalism." Recently, Albó (2004) has also emphasized the superficiality of Sánchez de Lozada's conversion to multiculturalism.
14. The subsequent, short-lived, second Sánchez de Lozada government reinstated the BONOSOL.
15. This "territorialization" was also intended to further sideline the already weakened "corporatist" trade union structure.
16. It should be noted that indigenous communities have adopted a double-edged strategy in the face of the new legal framework. On the one hand they seek the recognition of their property as TCO under the agrarian legislation, while on the other hand they seek recognition of their authority structures under the Popular Participation Law and to make this recognition coincide with the recognition of TCOs. In this way they seek to reconstitute territories, not only as property, but rather as areas in which their authorities hold political sway and jurisdiction.
17. Curiously, after recounting the "politicization" of the Customs, which became a domain of Banzer cronies (cf. Sivak 2001), and of the National Service for the Administration of Personnel in the "last 18 months," a starry-eyed or simply cynical World Bank report (2000:

14) states that the "current Government is strongly committed to succeeding with state reform where others have failed."

18. "The Condor," an Andean honorific title. Biographic profiles of Felipe Quispe and Evo Morales can be found in Albó (2003).

19. If we look at Bolivia's electoral geography the coincidence between the old heartland of Katarism, the CONDEPA outreach, and later support for Felipe Quispe's MIP is striking. Romero Ballivián (2003: 311) suggests that this continuity is rooted in the protest against the behavior of governing parties, against inconclusive modernization and frustration with the lack of opportunities among a relatively well-educated population. Since the late 1980s the vote for these parties has been positively correlated with school attendance and ethnic identification, particularly Aymara identification in the case of Katarism and the MIP. While Palenque played out the cholo-q'ara dichotomy, with a discourse of strident Aymara nationalism, for example stating that once he will be president he will create a Ministry for White Affairs, Quispe attracted support from the rural Aymara population of La Paz as well as the urban Aymara of La Paz and El Alto, where he won 17 percent of the vote in 2002.

20. The most recent Human Development Report on Bolivia (PNUD 2004) dedicates a full chapter to the much needed interculturalism for Bolivia. The report distinguishes six codes of self-understanding of identity: (1) a code of polarized opposition, which clearly corresponds to the Palenque and Quispe type of anti-q'ara discourse; (2) a code of multiple defense, which shows similarities with the polarization code, but is mainly found among entrepreneurs, executives of transnational enterprises, and the like; 3) flexible adaptation is a strategy more typical of lowland indigenous people who adapt to circumstances and interlocutors; (4) a missionary code is found among religious groups; (5) a regionalist code reflects center-periphery frictions; and (6) assistentalist corporatism can be wielded against transnational enterprises to force them to become "socially sustainable." Of course none of these codes is the patrimony of a specific segment of society or exists in a chemically pure form. It is an interesting and suggestive classification, however.

21. In a somewhat similar way Schierup (1997: 121) has argued that the contemporary American dilemma "is the incompatibility of elitist appeals for social cohesion and universalist allegiances with all of the powerful political and economic interests that both require and create growing segments of the population as ethnicized, enclavized and bereft of the rights of citizenship."

References

Abel, Christoffer, and Colin M. Lewis, eds. 2002. *Exclusion & Engagement: Social Policy in Latin America*. London: ILAS.

Aguirre, Álvaro, Carlos Arze, and Gary Montaño. 1992. "Análisis integral del programa de ajuste estructural." In *La intencionalidad del ajuste en Bolivia*, ed. Á. Aguirre, C. Arze, H. Larrazábal, G. Montaño, and R. Moscoso. La Paz: CEDLA.

Albó, Xavier. 1994. "And from Kataristas to MNRistas? The Surprising and Bold Alliance between Aymaras and Neoliberals in Bolivia." In *Indigenous Peoples and Democracy in Latin America*, ed. D. L. Van Cott. New York: St. Martin's Press.

———. 2002. "Bolivia: From Indian and Campesino Leaders to Councillors and Parliamentary Deputies." In *Multiculturalism in Latin America: Indigenous Rights, Diversity and Democracy*, ed. R. Sieder. Houndmills, Basingstoke, Hampshire, New York: Palgrave Macmillan.

———. 2003. "Andean Ethnicity Today: Four *Aymara* Narratives from Bolivia." In *Imaging the Andes: Shifting Margins of a Marginal World*, ed. T. Salman and A. Zoomers. Amsterdam: Aksant.

———. 2004. "222 años después: la convulsionada Bolivia multiétnica." *Artículo Primero* 8, no. 16 (October): 39–67.

Artículo Primero. 2003. "Reforma agraria 50 años: TCO y tierras campesinas." *Artículo Primero* 7, no. 14.

Arze Cuadros, Eduardo. 2002. *Bolivia, el programa del MNR y la Revolución Nacional: del movimiento de Reformas Universitaria al ocaso del modelo neoliberal.* La Paz: Plural Publishers.

Assies, Willem. 2002. "From Rubber Estate to Simple Commodity Production: Agrarian Struggles in the Northern Bolivian Amazon." *Journal of Peasant Studies* 29, no. 3–4 (Special Issue on Latin American Peasants, edited by Tom Brass): 83–130.

———. 2003a. "La descentralización a la boliviana y la 'economía política' del reformismo." In *Gobiernos locales y reforma del Estado en América Latina,* ed. W. Assies. Zamora: El Colegio de Michoacán.

———. 2003b. "David versus Goliath in Cochabamba: Water Rights, Neoliberalism, and the Revival of Social Protest in Bolivia." *Latin American Perspectives* 130–30, no. 3: 14–36.

———. 2004. "Bolivia: A Gasified Democracy." *European Review of Latin American and Caribbean Studies* 76: 25–45.

Assies, Willem, and Ton Salman. 2003. *Crisis in Bolivia: The Elections of 2002 and their Aftermath.* London: University of London, Institute of Latin American Studies (Research Paper 56).

Berthin Siles, Gerardo. 1999. "Evolución de las instituciones estatales." In *Bolivia en el siglo XX: La formación de la Bolivia contemporánea,* ed. P. Campero. La Paz: Harvard Club de Bolivia.

Bolivia. 2003. *Bolivia: Características sociodemográficas de la población indígena.* La Paz: República de Bolivia, Ministerio de Hacienda, Instituto Nacional de Estadística.

Bonfil Batalla, Guillermo, comp. 1981. *Utopía y Revolución: El pensamiento político contemporáneo de los indios en América Latina.* Mexico: Editorial Nueva Imagen.

Calla Ortega, Ricardo. 2000. "Indigenous Peoples, the Law of Popular Participation and Changes in Government: Bolivia 1994–1998." In *The Challenge of Diversity: Indigenous Peoples and Reform of the State in Latin America,* ed. W. Assies, G. van der Haar, and A. Hoekema. Amsterdam: Thela Publishers.

———. 2003a. "Hallu Hayllista Huti: Identificación étnica y procesos políticos en Bolivia (1973–1991)." In *Indígenas, política y reformas en Bolivia; Hacia una etnología del estado en América Latina,* ed. R. Calla Ortega. Guatemala: Ediciones ICAPI.

———. 2003b. *La caída de Sánchez de Lozada, la cuestión indígena y la historia reciente de Bolivia: Algunos apuntes y temas para el debate.* La Paz: Plural Publishers.

Chua, Amy. 2004. *World on Fire: How Exporting Free Market Democracy Breeds Ethnic Hatred and Global instability.* New York: Anchor Books.

Demeure V. Juan. 1999. "Agricultura; de la subsistencia a la competencia internacional." In *Bolivia en siglo XX: La formación de la Bolivia Contemporánea.,* ed. F. Campero Prudencio. La Paz: Havard Club de Bolivia.

dos Santos, Wanderley G. 1987. *Cidadanía e justiça: A política social na ordem brasileira,* Second edition. Rio de Janeiro: Campus.

Fanfani, Emilio Tenti. 2001. "Metamorfosis del Estado y la política: del poder central al poder local." In IIG *Biblioteca de Ideas,* Colección de papers, Paper no. 10, http:www//iigov.org.

Fraser, Nancy. 2003. "Social Justice in the Age of Identity Politics: Redistribution, Recognition, and Participation." In *Redistribution or Recognition? A Political-Philosophical Exchange,* ed. N. Fraser and A. Honneth. London and New York: Verso Books.

Gamarra, Eduardo A. 2003. "Political Parties since 1964: The Construction of Bolivia's Multiparty System". In *Proclaiming Revolution. Bolivia in Comparative Perspective,* ed M. Grindle and P. Domingo. Cambridge, Los Angeles, London: Institute of Latin American Studies, University of London and David Rockefeller Center for Latin American Studies, Harvard University, 289–317.

Gamarra, Eduardo A., and James M. Malloy. 1995. "The Patrimonial Dynamics of Party Politics in Bolivia." In *Building Democratic Institutions: Party Systems in Latin America*, ed. S. Mainwaring and T. R. Scully. Stanford: Stanford University Press.

Gonzalez, Mary Lisbeth. 1994. "How Many Indigenous People?" In *Indigenous People and Poverty in Latin America: An Empirical Analysis.*, ed. G. Psacharopoulos and H. Anthony Patrinos. Washington DC: World Bank.

Grebe López, Horst. 2001. "The Private Sector and Democratization." In *Towards Democratic Viability: The Bolivian Experience*, ed. J. Crabtree and L. Whitehead. Houndmills, Basingstoke, Hampshire, New York: Palgrave Macmillan.

Grindle, Merilee. S. 2000. *Audacious Reforms: Institutuional Invention and Democracy in Latin America*. Baltimore and London: The Johns Hopkins University Press.

Gustafson, Bret. 2002. "Paradoxes of Liberal Indigenism: Indigenous Movements, State Processes, and Intercultural Reform in Bolivia." In *The Politics of Ethnicity: Indigenous Peoples in Latin American States*, ed. D. Maybury-Lewis. Cambridge, MA, and London: Harvard University Press.

Hale, Charles. 2002. "Does Multiculturalism Menace? Governance, Cultural Rights and the Politics of Identity in Guatemala." *Journal of Latin American Studies* 34: 485–524.

Ibarra, Hernán. n.d. "Tendencias y cambios en las relaciones indígenas estado en los Andes." In *Pueblos indígenas de América Latina: retos para el nuevo milenio*, OXFAM, Ford Foundation (CD-ROM).

Jordán Pozo, Rolando. 1999. "Minería; Siglo XX: la era del estaño." In *Bolivia en siglo XX: La formación de la Bolivia contemporánea*, ed. F. Campero Prudencio. La Paz: Havard Club de Bolivia.

Klein, Herbert S. 2003. "Social Change in Bolivia since 1952." In *Proclaiming Revolution: Bolivia in Comparative Perspective*, ed. M. S. Grindle and P. Domingo. Cambridge, MA, and London: Harvard University Press.

MACPIO. 2001. *Pueblos indígenas y originarias de Bolivia: diagnóstico nacional*. La Paz: Ministerio de Asuntos Campesinos Pueblos Indígenas y Originarias.

Mansilla, Hugo Celso Felipe and María Teresa Zegada. 1996. *Política, cultura y etnicidad en Bolivia*. La Paz, Cochabamba: CEBEM, CESU.

Marshall, Thomas H. 1950. *Citizenship and Social Class, and Other Essays*. Cambridge, U.K.: Cambridge University Press.

Mayorga, Fernando 2002. *Neopopulismo y democracia: Compadres y padrinos en la política boliviana (1988–1999)*. La Paz, Cochabamba: Plural Publishers, CESU-UMSS.

Mercado Lora, Marcelo. 1998. "La reforma del sistema de pensiones de la seguridad social." In *Las reformas estructurales en Bolivia*, coord. J. C. Chávez Corrales. La Paz: Fundación Milenio.

Morales, J. A. 2003. "The National Revolution and its Legacy." In *Proclaiming Revolution: Bolivia in Comparative Perspective*, ed. M. S. Grindle and P. Domingo, Cambridge, MA, and London: Harvard University Press.

O'Donnell, Guillermo. 1999. "Delegative Democracy." In *Counterpoints: Selected Essays on Authoritarianism and Democratization*, ed. G. O'Donnell. Notre Dame: University of Notre Dame Press.

Oxhorn, Philip. 2003. "Social Inequality, Civil Society, and the Limits of Citizenship in Latin America." In *What Justice? Whose Justice? Fighting for Fairness in Latin America*, ed. S. E. Eckstein and T. P. Wickham-Crowley. Berkeley, Los Angeles, London: University of California Press.

Patzi Paco, Felix. 2003. "Rebelión indígena contra la colonidad y la transnacionalización de la economía: Triunfos y vicisitudes del movimiento indígena desde 2000 a 2003." In *Ya es otro tiempo el presente: Cuatro momentos de insurgencia indígena*, ed. F. Hylton, F. Patzi Paco, S. Serulnikov, and S. Thomson. La Paz: Muela del Diablo.

Pérez Baltodano, Andrés., ed. 1997. *Globalización, ciudadanía y política social en América Latina: tensiones y contradicciones.* Caracas: Nueva Sociedad.

PNUD. 2002. *Informe de desarrollo humano en Bolivia, 2002.* La Paz: Programa de las Naciones Unidas para el Desarrollo.

——. 2004. *Interculturalismo y globalización: La Bolivia possible: Informe Nacional de Desarrollo Humano 2004.* La Paz: Programa de las Naciones Unidas Para el Desarrollo.

Prisma. 2000. *Las políticas sobre la pobreza en Bolivia: Dimensión, políticas y resultados (1985–1999).* La Paz: Instituto Prisma, Plural Publishers.

Rivera Cusicanqui, Silvia. 2003 [1984]. *Oprimidos pero no vencidos: Luchas del campesinado aymara y qhechwa 1900–1980.* La Paz: Yachaywasi.

Rodríguez Ostria, Gustavo. 1999. "Industria; producción, mercancías y empresarios." In *Bolivia en siglo XX: La formación de la Bolivia Contemporánea*, ed. F. Campero Prudencio. La Paz: Havard Club de Bolivia.

Romero Ballivián, Salvador. 2003. *Geografía electoral de Bolivia*, 3rd edition. La Paz: Fundemos.

Schierup, Carl-Ulrik. 1997. "Multiculturalism and Universalism in the United States and EU-Europe." In *Rethinking Nationalism & Ethnicity: The Struggle for Meaning and Order in Europe*, ed. H. R. Wicker. Oxford, U.K., and New York: Berg Publishers.

Seoane, José, comp. 2003. *Movimientos sociales y conflicto en América Latina.* Buenos Aires: CLACSO.

Sivak, Martín. 2001. *El dictador elegido: Biografía no autorizada de Hugo Banzer Suárez.* La Paz: Plural Publishers.

Sottoli, Susana. 2000. "La política social en América Latina bajo el signo de la economía de mercado y la democracia." *European Review of Lían American and Caribbean Studies* 68: 3–22.

Tapia Mealla, Luís, and Carlos Toranzo Roca. 2000. *Retos y dilemas de la representación política.* La Paz: PNUD (Cuaderno de Futuro 8).

Ticona Esteban, Gonzalo Rojas, and Xavier Albó. 1995. *Votos y Wiphalas: Campesinos y pueblos originarios en democracia.* La Paz: Fundación Milenio, CIPCA.

UDAPE. 2003. *Bolivia: evaluación de la economía: primer semestre 2003.* La Paz: Unidad de Análisis de Políticas Sociales y Económicas.

Van Cott, Donna Lee. 2000. *The Friendly Liquidation of the Past: The Politics of Diversity in Latin America.* Pittsburgh: University of Pittsburgh Press.

——. 2003. "From Exclusion to Inclusion: Bolivia's 2002 Elections." *Journal of Latin American Studies* 35: 751–775.

Whitehead, Laurence. 2001a. "The Viability of Democracy." In *Towards Democratic Viability: The Bolivian Experience*, ed. J. Crabtree and L. Whitehead. Houndmills and New York: Palgrave Macmillan.

——. 2001b. "The Emergence of Democracy in Bolivia." In *Towards Democratic Viability: The Bolivian Experience*, ed. J. Crabtree and L. Whitehead. Houndmills and New York: Palgrave Macmillan.

World Bank. 2000. *Bolivia: From Patronage to a professional State: Bolivia Institutional and Governance Review (Vol. I, Main Report).* Washington D.C.: World Bank (Report No. 20115-BO).

Contributors

Geert Banck is emeritus professor Utrecht University, Utrecht, and the Centre for Latin American Studies and Documentation (CEDLA), Amsterdam. He supervised Willem Assies's PhD thesis. He published extensively on themes of political anthropology and social movement studies in Brazil.

Cristóbal Kay is emeritus professor in Rural Development and Development Studies at the International Institute of Social Studies in The Hague, the Netherlands. His research interests are in the fields of rural development and development theory, with particular reference to Latin America. His collaboration with Willem Assies was mainly as contributors to, and editorial advisory board members of, *the Journal of Peasant Studies.*

Gemma van der Haar is a development sociologist interested in the ethnography of political practice in conflict and post-conflict situations. Her previous research experience was centered on the Zapatista uprising in Chiapas. Current research interests include local government, parallel governance and contested state formation, post-war reconstruction and the reordering of land tenure, as well methodological issues (the options and dilemmas in collaborative research). Currently, she is assistant professor at the Department of Disaster Studies at Wageningen University.

André Hoekema is professor in Legal Pluralism at the University of Amsterdam, the Netherlands. Together with Willem Assies on various occasions, he researched and published comprehensively on multiethnic states, particularly the legal position of indigenous peoples and minority communities, concentrating on matters such as land and territorial rights, legal reform, and ways to "pluralize" the state and its legal order, mostly in Latin American and some African countries. He also engaged Willem Assies in 1995 to participate as a researcher-interviewer in a project designed together with the anthropologist and filmmaker Peter Oud, to sketch ways in which north and central

American indigenous peoples manage their official autonomy (Documentary: *A Sketch of Freedom*).

Ton Salman studied philosophy and anthropology and did his PhD in 1993 on grassroots organizations in Chile under Pinochet. He specialized on Latin America, and he does research and publishes on social movements, democratization, ethnicity, and citizenship. At present he is associate professor at the Department of Social and Cultural Anthropology at the VU University Amsterdam.

Salvador Martí i Puig studied political science and Latin American history and received his PhD in 1997 on the Nicaraguan revolution and peasant counterrevolution. His research focuses on comparative politics, including processes of democratization, social movements, indigenous peoples, parties, and party systems in Latin America. At present he is a permanent lecturer at the University of Salamanca and member of CIDOB-Barcelona.

Bibliography Willem Assies

Books

With G. Burgwal and T. Salman

1990. *Structures of Power, Movements of Resistance: An Introduction to the Theories of Urban Movements in Latin America*. Amsterdam: CEDLA.

1992. *To Get Out of the Mud: Neighborhood Associativism in Recife, 1964–1988*. Amsterdam: CEDLA.

With A. J. Hoekema, eds.

1994. *Indigenous Peoples' Experiences with Self-Government*. Copenhagen and Amsterdam: IWGIA and University of Amsterdam (IWGIA Document no. 76).

1997. *Going Nuts for the Rainforest*. Amsterdam: Thela Publishers.

With G. van der Haar and A. J. Hoekema, eds.

1999. *El reto de la diversidad: pueblos indígenas y reforma del Estado en América Latina*. Zamora: El Colegio de Michoacán.

2000. *The Challenge of Diversity: Indigenous Peoples and Reform of the State in Latin America*. Amsterdam: Thela Publishers.

With M. Calderón and T. Salman, eds.

2002. *Ciudadanía, cultura política y reforma del estado en América Latina*. Zamora: El Colegio de Michoacán e Instituto Federal Electoral de Michoacán.

Ed.

2003. *Gobiernos locales y reforma del estado en América Latina; innovando la gestión pública*. Zamora: El Colegio de Michoacán.

With T. Salman

2003. *Crisis in Bolivia: The Elections of 2002 and their Aftermath*. London: University of London, Institute of Latin American Studies (Research Paper no. 56).

With M. Calderón and T. Salman, eds.

2005. *Citizenship, Political Culture and State Transformation in Latin America*. Amsterdam and Zamora: Dutch University Press, El Colegio de Michoacán.

With H. Gundermann, eds.

2007. *Movimientos indígenas y gobiernos locales en América Latina*. San Pedro de Atacama: Universidad del Norte, IIAM, Chile, with El Colegio de Michoacán, Zamora, Mexico, and International Work Group for Indigenous Affairs (IWGIA), Copenhagen, Denmark.

With J. M. Ubink and A. J. Hoekema, eds.

2009. *Legalising Land Rights: Local Practices, State Response and Tenure Security in Africa, Asia and Latin America*. Leiden: Leiden University Press.

Chapters in Books

1989. "Organização de moradores e poder municipal na cidade do recife." In *Políticas territoriais e gestão metropolitana no norte e nordeste*, org. J. Bitoun, E. Maranhão Pessoa da Costa, and J. Lemos de Freitas. Recife: UFPE, 106–132.

1990. "Of Structured Moves and Moving Structures: An Overview of Theoretical Perspectives on Social Movements." In *Structures of Power, Movements of Resistance: An Introduction to the Theories of Urban Movements in Latin America*, ed. W. Assies, G. Burgwal, and T. Salman. Amsterdam: CEDLA, 9–98.

1992. "Urban Associativism and 'Democratic Transition' in the Municipality of Recife (Brazil)." In *Urban Restructuring and Deregulation in Latin America*, ed. M. Carmona. Delft: Delft University of Technology, Department of Building Sciences, 171–190.

1994. "Re-constructing the Meaning of Urban Land in Brazil: The Case of Recife (Pernambuco)." In *Methodology for Land and Housing Market Analysis*, ed. G. Jones and P. Ward. London: UCL Press, 102–117.

1994. "Self-Determination and the 'New Partnership'; the Politics of Indigenous Peoples and States." In *Indigenous Peoples' Experiences with Self-Government*, ed. W. J. Assies and A. J. Hoekema. Copenhagen and Amsterdam: IWGIA and University of Amsterdam (IWGIA Document no. 76), 31–71.

1997. "Urban Social Movements, Democratization and Democracy in Brazil." In *The Diversity of Development, Essays in Honour of Jan Kleinpenning*, ed. T. van Naerssen, M. Rutten, and A. Zoomers. Assen: Van Gorcum, 302–313.

1997. "Niet-hout bosprodukten en duurzame ontwikkeling in Amazonia." In *Duurzame landbouw in ontwikkelingslanden tussen theorie en toepassing*, red. M. v. d. Glas. Zeist, Utrecht: ICCO, CERES, 53–66.

1998. "Ruraal-urbane migratie en stedelijke migranten in Brazilië." In *Mensen op Drift; migratie en ontwikkeling*, Themabundel Ontwikkelingsproblematiek nr. 9, red. J. J. F. Heins and H. L. M. Kox. Amsterdam: Interfacultaire Commissie Ontwikkelingsproblematiek, Vrije Universiteit, 46–75.

2000. "Indigenous Peoples and Reform of the State in Latin America." In *The Challenge of Diversity: Indigenous Peoples and Reform of the State in Latin America*, ed. W. Assies, G. van der Haar, and A. J. Hoekema. Amsterdam: Thela Publishers, 3–21.

2000. "Multi-Ethnic Constitutionalism, Territories and Internal Boundaries: The Bolivian Case." In *Fronteras: Towards a Borderless Latin America*, ed. CEDLA. Amsterdam: CEDLA, 319–348.

1997. "Lands, Territories and Indigenous Peoples' Rights." In *Current Land Policy in Latin America Regulating Land Tenure under Neoliberalism*, ed. A. Zoomers and G. van der Haar. Amsterdam: KIT, Vervuert, 93–109.

With A. J. Hoekema

2000. "Managing Resources: between Autonomy and Partnership." In *The Challenge of Diversity: Indigenous Peoples and Reform of the State in Latin America*, ed. W. Assies, G. van der Haar, and A. J. Hoekema. Amsterdam: Thela Publishers., 245–260.

With G. van der Haar and A. J. Hoekema

2000. "Diversity as a Challenge: A Note on the Dilemmas of Diversity." In *The Challenge of Diversity: Indigenous Peoples and Reform of the State in Latin America*, ed. W. Assies, G. van der Haar, and A. J. Hoekema. Amsterdam: Thela Publishers, 295–315.

With M. A. Calderón and T. Salman

2002. "Ciudadanía, cultura política y reforma del estado en América Latina." In *Ciudadanía, cultura política y reforma del estado en América Latina*, ed. M. Calderón, W. Assies, and T. Salman. Zamora: El Colegio de Michoacán and Instituto Federal Electoral, 17–51.

2002. "Apuntes Sobre la Ciudadanía, la Sociedad Civil y Los Movimientos Sociales." In *Ciudadanía, Cultura Política y Reforma del Estado en América Latina*, ed. M. Calderón, W. Assies, and T. Salman. Zamora: El Colegio de Michoacán and Instituto Federal Electoral, 45–170.

2003. "From Rubber Estate to Simple Commodity Production: Agrarian Struggles in the Northern Bolivian Amazon." In *Latin American Peasants*, ed. T. Brass. London and Portland, OR: Frank Cass Publishers, 83–130.

2003. "Indian Justice in the Andes: Re-rooting or Re-routing?" In *Imaging the Andes: Shifting Margins of a Marginal World*, ed. T. Salman and A. Zoomers. Amsterdam: Aksant, 167–186.

2003. "El derecho indígena en el marco de los Estados contemporáneos: Tensiones y desafíos." In *Resolución de conflictos en el derecho mapuche: Un estudio desde la perspectiva del pluralismo*, coord. R. Lillo. Temuco: Universidad Católica de Temuco, 31–80.

2003. "La descentralización en perspectiva." In *Gobiernos locales y reforma del estado en América Latina; innovando la gestión pública*, ed. W. Assies. Zamora: El Colegio de Michoacán, 13–34.

2003. "La descentralización à la boliviana y la 'economía política' del reformismo." In *Gobiernos locales y reforma del Estado en América Latina; innovando la gestión pública*, ed. W. Assies. Zamora: El Colegio de Michoacán, 135–160.

2004. "Diversidad, Estado y democracia: unos apuntes." In *La democracia en América Latina; hacia una democracia de ciudadanas y ciudadanos, contribuciones para el debate*, ed. PNUD. Buenos Aires: Aguilar, Altea, Alfaguara, 229–243.

2005. "Two Steps Forward, One Step Back: Indigenous Peoples and Autonomies in Latin America." In *Autonomy, Self-Governance and Conflict Resolution: Innovative Approaches to Institutional Design in Divided Societies*, ed. S. Wolff and M. Weller. London and New York: Routledge, 180–212.

2005. "El constitucionalismo multiétnico en América Latina: El caso de Bolivia." In *Los derechos de los pueblos indios y la cuestión agraria*, ed. C. H. Durand Alcántara. Mexico: Librería Porrúa, 107–128.

2005. "Recursos naturales, pueblos indígenas y negros. Derechos y desafíos." In *Gente de campo: patrimónios y dinámicas rurales en México*, Vol. II, ed. E. Barragán López. Zamora: El Colegio de Michoacán, 297–318.

2006. "Reforma estatal y multiculturalismo latinoamericano al inicio del siglo XXI." In *Agua y derecho: políticass hídricas, derechos consuetudinarios e identidades locales*, ed. R. Boelens, D. Getches, and A. Guevara Gil. Lima: IEP, WALIR, 59–81.

2006. "Neoliberalism and the Re-Emergence of Ethnopolitics in Bolivia." In *Multiculturalism and the Welfare State: Recognition and Redistribution in Contemporary Democracies*, ed. K. Banting and W. Kymlicka. Oxford, U.K., and New York: Oxford University Press, 297–319.

2007. "Prólogo." In *El Gobierno de Lagos, los pueblos indígenas y el 'nuevo trato': las paradojas de la democracia chilena*, ed. N. Yáñez and J. Aylwin. Santiago: LOM Ediciones/Observatorio Derechos de los Pueblos Indígenas, 9–17.

2007. "Land Tenure Legalization, Pluriculturaluism and Multiethnicity in Bolivia." In *Bolivia en movimiento, acción colectiva y poder politico*, coord. J. Espasandín López and P. Iglesias Turrión. Barcelona: Ediciones de Intervención Cultural/El Viejo Topo (on DVD included in the book).

With H. Gundermann

2007. "Introducción." In *Movimientos indígenas y gobiernos locales en América Latina*, ed. W. Assies and H. Gundermann. San Pedro de Atacama: Universidad del Norte, IIAM, Chile, with El Colegio de Michoacán, Zamora, Mexico, and International Work Group for Indigenous Affairs (IWGIA), Copenhagen, Denmark, 11–25.

2007. "Los pueblos indígenas, la tierra, el territorio y la autonomía en tiempos de globalización." In *Pueblos indígenas y política en América Latina; El reconocimiento de sus derechos y el impacto de sus demandas a inicios del siglo XXI*, ed. S. Martí i Puig. Barcelona: Fundació CIDOB, 227–245.

With T. Salman

2007. "Anthropology and the Study of Social Movements." In *Handbook of Social Movements across Disciplines*, ed. B. Klandermans and C. Roggeband. New York: Springer Science + Business Media, 205–265.

2009. "Land Tenure in Bolivia: From Colonial Times to Post-Neoliberalism." In *Legalising Land Rights: Local Practices, State Response and Tenure Security in Africa, Asia and Latin America*, ed. J. M. Ubink, A. J. Hoekema, and W. J. Assies. Leiden: Leiden University Press, 293–323.

With E. Duhau

2009. "Land Tenure and Tenure Regimes in Mexico: An Overview." In *Legalising Land Rights: Local Practices, State Response and Tenure Security in Africa, Asia and Latin America*, ed. J. M. Ubink, A. J. Hoekema, and W. J. Assies. Leiden: Leiden University Press, 355–385.

2010. "The Limits of State Reform and Multiculturalism in Latin America: Contemporary Illustrations." In *Out of the Mainstream: Water Rights, Politics and Identity*, ed. R. Boelens, D. Getches, and A. Guevara-Gil. London and Washington D.C.: Earthscan, 57–73.

2010. "Terres, territories, multiculturalisme et pluriethnicité en Bolivie." In *Politique de la terre et de l'appartenance; droits fonciers et citoyenneté locale dans les sociétés de Sud*, Paris: Karthala, 351–373.

Articles in International (Refereed) Journals

1987. "The Agrarian Question in Peru: Some Observations on the Roads of Capital." *Journal of Peasant Studies* 14, no. 4: 500–532.

1993. "Urban Social Movements and Local Democracy in Brazil." *European Review of Latin American and Caribbean Studies* no. 55: 39–58.

1994. "Urban Social Movements in Brazil: A Debate and its Dynamics." *Latin American Perspectives* 81, 21, no. 2 (Spring 1994): 81–105.

1997. "The Extraction of Non-Timber Forest Products as a Conservation Strategy in Amazonia." *European Review of Latin American and Caribbean Studies* no. 62: 33–53.

1997. "Muchas cáscaras y pocas nueces; Extracción y desarrollo sustentable en la Amazonía." *Debate Agrario* no. 26: 41–57.

1997. "Extractivisme et développement durable en Amazonie: l'état d'Acre (Brésil) et le nord Bolivien." *Problèmes d'Amérique Latine* no. 26: 83–100.

1999. "Theory Practice and 'External Actors' in the Making of New Urban Social Movements in Brazil." *Bulletin of Latin American Research* 18, no. 2: 211–226.

2002. "From Rubber Estate to Simple Commodity Production: Agrarian Struggles in the Northern Bolivian Amazon." *Journal of Peasant Studies* 29, no. 3–4: 83–130.

With M. A. Calderón and T. Salman

2002. "Ciudadanía, cultura política y reforma del Estado en América Latina." *América Latina Hoy* 32: 55–90.

2003. "David versus Goliath in Cochabamba: Water Rights, Neoliberalism and the Revival of Social Protest in Bolivia." *Latin American Perspectives* 30, no. 3: 14–36.

With T. Salman

2003. "Bolivian Democracy: Consolidating or Disintegrating?" *Focaal, European Journal of Anthropology* no. 42: 141–160.

2003. "La descentralización en perspectiva." TOP, Tecnología para la Organización Pública: Publicaciones, publicaciones académicas, biblioteca virtual sobre gestión pública, www.top.org.ar/publicac.htm

2004. "Bolivia: A Gasified Democracy." *European Review of Latin American and Caribbean Studies* no. 76: 25–45.

2005. "The Challenge of Diversity in Rural Latin America: A Rejoinder to Jean-Pierre Reed (and Others)." *Journal of Peasant Studies* 32, no. 2: 361–371.

With T. Salman

2005. "Ethnicity and Politics in Bolivia." *Journal of Ethnopolitics* 4, no. 3: 269–297.

2005. "Territorialidad, indianidad y desarrollo: las cuentas pendientes." *Labour Again Publications, Rural and Indigenous Mobilisation in Latin America* (www.iisg.nl/labouragain/ruralmobilisation.php).

With L. Ramírez Sevilla and M. del C. Ventura Patiño

2006. "Autonomy Rights and the Politics of Constitutional Reform in Mexico." *Latin American and Caribbean Ethnic Studies* 1, no. 1: 37–62.

2006. "La 'Media Luna' sobre Bolivia: nación, región, etnia y clase social." *América Latina Hoy* 43 (August): 87–105.

With L. Ramírez Sevilla and M. del C. Ventura Patiño

2006. "Derechos de autonomía y la política de reforma constitucional en México, con un enfoque en la reforma fallida en Micoacán." *Boletín de Antropología Americana* no. 42: 133–170.

2006. "Land Tenure Legislation in a Pluri-cultural and Multi-ethnic Society: The Case of Bolivia." *Journal of Peasant Studies* 33, no. 4: 569–611.
2008. "Land Tenure and Tenure Regimes in Mexico: An Overview." *Journal of Agrarian Change* 8, no. 1: 33–63.
2009. "Land Tenure, Land Law and Development: Some Thoughts on Recent Debates." *Journal of Peasant Studies* 36, no. 3: 573–589.
2009. "Legal Empowerment of the Poor: With a Little help from their Friends?" *Journal of Peasant Studies* 36, no. 4: 923–938.

Articles in National (Refereed) Journals

1994. "Democratisering en stedelijke sociale bewegingen in Brazilië." *Derde Wereld* 12, nr. 3: 59–81.
1997. "Noten, rubber en duurzame ontwikkeling in Amazonia." *Derde Wereld* 15, nr. 3/4: 309–327.
1999. "Inheemse volken in Latijns Amerika: enige kanttekeningen t.b.v. beleidsvorming." *Recht der Werkelijkheid* 20, no. 1: 33–58.
1999. "Muitas cascas e poucas nozes. Extrativismo e desenvolvimento sustentável na Amazônia." *Mosaico, Revista de Ciências Sociais* 1, no. 1: 61–81.
2001. "David vs. Goliat en Cochabamba: los derechos del agua, el neoliberalismo y la renovación de la protesta social en Bolivia." *T'inkazos*: 106–131.
2001. "La oficialización de lo no oficial; ¿Re-encuentro de dos mundos?" *Alteridades* 11, no. 21: 83–96.

With G. van der Haar and A. J. Hoekema

2002. "Los pueblos indígenas y la reforma del estado en América Latina." *Papeles de Población Nueva Época* año 8, no. 31: 95–115.

2003. "David Fights Goliath in Cochabamba: Water Rights, Neoliberalism and the Renovation of Social Protest in Bolivia." *T'inkazos* (February): 179–205.
2003. "Transiciones, transacciones y unos interrogantes." *Trayectorias, Revista de Ciencias Sociales* 5, no. 11: 26–43.

With T. Salman

2004. "La democracia boliviana entre la consolidación, la profundización y la incertidumbre." *T'inkazos* no. 16: 67–98.

2005. "Reforma indígena en Michoacán y pluralismo jurídico." *Revista de Interculturalidad* 1, no. 1: 135–157.

2009. "Pueblos indígenas y sus demandas en los sistemas politicos." *Revista CIDOB d'Afers Internacionals* no. 85–86: 89–107.

Review Essays

1988. "Agrarian Policies and Debate in Peru." *Boletín de Estudios Latinoamericanos y del Caribe* no. 44: 67–75.

1997. "Mouvements sociaux, démocratie et culture politique au Brésil." *Cahiers du Brésil Contemporain* no. 31: 177–189.

1997. "Social Movements, Democracy and Political Culture in Brazil." *European Review of Latin American and Caribbean Studies* no. 63: 111–119.

1998. "Movimentos sociais, democracia e cultura política no Brasil." *Comunicação e Política* 5, no. 1 (nova série): 215–225.

1999. "Multi-ethnicity, the State and the Law." *Journal of Legal Pluralism* no. 43: 145–158.

With T. Salman

1997. "Políticas y culturas: la visión del post-progresismo." *T'inkazos* no. 6: 161–178.

2000. "Revisioning Cultures of Politics." *Critique of Anthropology* 20, no. 3: 289–307.

2003. "Globalism, Localism and Neo-Zapatism." *European Review of Latin American and Caribbean Studies* no. 74: 101–105.

Book Reviews

1990. Review of "Movimentos Sociais e Políticas Públicas," by Pedro Jacobi. *European Review of Latin American and Caribbean Studies* no. 48.

1993. Review of "Guerrillas and Revolution in Latin America, a Comparative Study of Insurgents and Regimes Since 1956," by T. P. Wickham-Crowley. *European Review of Latin American and Caribbean Studies* no. 54.

With T. Salman

1993. Review of "The Making of Social Movements in Latin America: Identity, Strategy and Democracy," ed. A. Escobar and S. E. Alvarez. *European Review of Latin American and Caribbean Studies* no. 55.

1993. Review of "Latin American Land Reforms in Theory and Practice; a Retrospective Analysis," by P. Dorner. *European Review of Latin American and Caribbean Studies* no. 55.

1994. Review of "Brazil, the Challenges of the 1990s," ed. Maria D'Alva G. Kinzo. *European Review of Latin American and Caribbean Studies* no. 56.

1994. Review of "Orpheus and Power, The *Movimento Negro* of Rio de Janeiro and São Paulo, Brazil, 1945–1988," by M. G. Hanchard. *European Review of Latin American and Caribbean Studies* no. 57.

1995. Review of "Social Struggles and the City: The Case of São Paulo," ed. Lúcio Kowarick. *European Review of Latin American and Caribbean Studies* no. 58.

1996. Review of "Theorizing Social Movements," by J. Foweraker. *European Review of Latin American and Caribbean Studies* no. 60.

1998. Review of "Dimensionen der demokratisierung; öffentlichkeit, zivilgesellschaft und lokale partizipation in brasilien," by Sérgio Costa. *Bulletin of Latin American Research* 17, no. 1.

1998. Review of "Forests in International Environmental Politics; International Organisations, NGOs and the Brazilian Amazon," by Ans Kolk. *Development and Change* 29, no. 3.

1998. Review of "Return of the Indian, Conquest and Revival in the Americas," by Phillip Wearne. *European Review of Latin American and Caribbean Studies* no. 64.

1999. Review of "The Friendly Liquidation of the Past: The Politics of Diversity in Latin America," by Donna Lee Van Cott. *European Review of Latin American and Caribbean Studies* no. 67.

2000. Review "La Liquidación amigable del pasado" ("The Friendly Liquidation of the Past: The Politics of Diversity in Latin America"), by Donna Lee Van Cott. *T'inkazos* no. 6.

2000. Review of *Endangered Mexico: An Environment on the Edge*, by J. Simon, London: LAB, and *Mexico and the NAFTA Environment Debate*, by B. Hogenboom, 1998, Utrecht: International Books. *European Review of Latin American and Caribbean Studies* no. 68.

2001. Review of *Peripherer Marxismus; kritische theorie in Mexico*, by Stefan Gandler, Hamburg: Argument Sonderband Neue Folge 270, Argument Verlag, 1999. *European Review of Latin American and Caribbean Studies* no. 70.

2001. Review of *Popular Movements and State Formation in Revolutionary Mexico: The Agraristas and Cristeros of Michoacán*, by Jennie Purnell, Durham and London: Duke University Press, 1999. *European Review of Latin American and Caribbean Studies* no. 71.

2001. Review of *Escritos Urbanos*, by Lúcio Kowarick, São Paulo: Editora 34, 2000. *European Review of Latin American and Caribbean Studies* no. 71.

2002. Review of *Peripherer Marxismus; kritische theorie in Mexico*, by Stefan Gandler, Hamburg: Argument Sonderband Neue Folge 270, Argument Verlag, 1999. *Thesis 11* no. 71.

2003. Review of *Multiculturalism in Latin America: Indigenous Rights, Diversity and Democracy*, ed. Rachel Sieder, Basingstoke: Palgrave Macmillan, 2002. *Journal of Latin American Studies* no. 35.

2003. Review of *Contemporary Indigenous Movements in Latin America*, ed. Erick D. Langer with Elena Muñoz, Wilmington, DE: Jaguar Books on Latin America, 2003. *European Review of Latin American and Caribbean Studies* no. 75.

2003. Review of *The Quiet Revolution: Decentralization and the Rise of Political Participation in Latin American Cities*, by Tim Campbell, Pittsburgh: The University of Pittsburgh Press, 2003. *Development and Change* 34, no. 5.

2004. Review of *Justice beyond our Borders: Judicial Reforms for Latin America and the Caribbean*, ed. Christina Biebesheimer and Francisco Mejía, Baltimore, MA: Inter-American Development Bank, 2000, and *Rule of Law in Latin America: The International Promotion of Judicial Reform*, ed. Pilar Domingo and Rachel Sieder, London: University of London, Institute of Latin American Studies, 2001. *European Review of Latin American and Caribbean Studies* no. 76.

2004. Review of *Indians, Oil and Politics: A Recent History of Ecuador*, by Allen Gerlach, Wilmington and Delaware: Scholarly Resources Inc., Imprint, 2002. *European Review of Latin American and Caribbean Studies* no. 77.

2004. Review of *Water Rights and Empowerment*, ed. Rutgerd Boelens and Paul Hoogendam. Assen: Van Gorcum, 2002. *Journal of Latin American Studies* 36, part 3.

2006. Review of *Pueblos indígenas y derechos constitucionales en América Latina: un panorama*, by Cletus Gregor Barié. Mexico and Quito: Comisión Nacional para el Desarrollo de los Pueblos Indígenas, Banco Mundial Fideicomiso Noruego, Abya Yala, 2003. *Journal of Latin American Studies* no. 38.

2006. Review of *The Judicialization of Politics in Latin America*, ed. Rachel Sieder, Line Schjolden, and Alan Angel. Houndmills and Basingstoke: Palgrave Macmillan, 2005. *European Review of Latin American and Caribbean Studies* no. 81.

2007. Review of *The Chiapas Revolt and What it Means for Radical Politics*, by Mihalis Mentinis, London and Ann Arbor, MI: Pluto Press, 2006. *European Review of Latin American and Caribbean Studies* no. 82.

2008. Review of *Highland Indians and the State in Modern Ecuador*, ed. A. Kim Clark and Marc Becker, Pittsburgh: University of Pittsburgh Press, 2007. *European Review of Latin American and Caribbean Studies* no. 85.

2008. "Inheemse rechten en zelfbeschikking in Colombia." In *Behind the Mask of Recognition: Defending Autonomy and Communal Resource Management in Indigenous Resguardos, Colombia* (proefschrift, Universiteit van Amsterdam), ed. J. J. van de Sandt. *Recht der Werkelijkheid*, 29ᵉ jaargang, 2008/2.

Other

With C. de Groot and T. Kee
1978. *De demokratisering van de vervoersfederatie.* Groningen: Projektgroep Vakbeweging, Sociologisch Instituut, R. U. Groningen.

1987. *Een land zonder Mensen? Inheemse volken en de kolonisatie van het Peruaanse Amazonegebied.* Amsterdam: Werkgroep Inheemse Volken/Peru Komitee Nederland.

With A. J. Hoekema
1994. *Memorandum on Systems of Self-Government for Indigenous Peoples and Netherlands' Foreign Policy.* Amsterdam: University of Amsterdam, Faculty of Law, Department of Sociology and Anthropology of Law (Memorandum prepared for the Netherlands Ministry of Foreign Affairs).

1996. "Research Project: Brazil Nut Exploitation in the Amazonian Region." *ETFRN News* no. 19.

1997. "Local Struggles and Global Problems, the Rubber Tappers' Movement in Acre against the Greenhouse Effect." Paper presented at the Brazilian Studies Association Third Conference, King's College, Cambridge, U.K., September 7–10. In *Third BRASA Conference Proceedings.* Albuquerque, NM: BRASA.

1997. "Brazil Nut Extraction and Sustainable Development in Amazonia." *Tropenbos Newsletter* no. 14–15.

With M. A. F. Ros-Tonen, T. van Andel, J. F. W. van Dijk, J. F. Duivenvoorden, M. C. van der Hammen, W. de Jong, M. Reinders, C. A. Rodríguez Fernández, and J. L. C. H. van Valkenburg

1998. *Methods for Non-Timber Forest Products Research: The Tropenbos Experience.* Wageningen: The Tropenbos Foundation (Tropenbos Document 14).

With W. Dijkman, D. Stoian, A. B. Henkemans, and R. G. A. Boot

1998. "Temporal and Spatial Dynamics in the Extraction of Non-Timber Forest Products in the Northern Bolivian Amazon." In *Tropenbos Seminar Proceedings Research in Tropical Rain Forests: Its Challenges for the Future (25–26 November 1997).* Wageningen: The Tropenbos Foundation.

1998. "La reforma del estado Boliviano y los pueblos indígenas." In *Memoria, revista mensual de política y cultura* no. 118.

1999. "Amazon Nuts, Forests and Sustainability in Bolivia and Brazil." In *NTFP Research in the Tropenbos Programme: Results and Perspectives*, ed. M. A. F. Ros-Tonen. Wageningen: The Tropenbos Foundation.

1999. *Nederlands Beleid en Inheemse Volken in Latijns Amerika: Enige Kanttekeningen.* Amsterdam: CEDLA (Memorandum prepared for the Netherlands Ministry of Foreign Affairs).

2000. "El constitucionalismo multietnico en América Latina: El caso de Bolivia." In Actas XII Congreso Internacional Derecho Consuetudinario y Pluralismo Legal: Desafíos del Tercer Milenio, March 13–17, 2000, Arica, coord. M. Castro Lucic and X, Albó, University of Chile, University of Tarapacá.

2000. *La situación de los derechos humános de los pueblos indígenas en el contexto latinoamericano.* Paper prepared for Unidos en la Diversidad por Nuestro Derecho al Territorio, organizado por el Programa de Pueblos Indígenas dependiente del Ministerio de Justicia y Derechos Humanos, July, Santa Cruz, Bolivia.

With G. van der Haar and A. Hoekema

2001. "Los Pueblos indígenas y la reforma del estado en América Latina" in *Biblioteca de ideas,* Instituto Internacional de Gobernabilidad (http://www.iigov.org/iigov/pnud/bibliote/documentos/docu0016.htm).

With G. van der Haar and A. Hoekema

2001. "Claroscuros del estado multiétnico." *Cuarto Intermedio* no. 58 (February): 68–94.

With M. A. Calderón and T. Salman

2002. "Ciudadanía, cultura política y reforma del estado en América Latina." *Ziranda* no. 2, Michoacán: Instituto Federal Electoral.

2003. "Transiciones, transacciones y unos interrogantes." *Cuaderno de trabajo número 3: Los electores en la consolidación democrática.* Mexico: Instituto Federal Electoral (annexed in CD-ROM). A modified versión was published in *Ziranda: Ediciones de cultura política y educación cívica del IFE en Michoacán* (no. 5, 2004; Special issue on abstensionism).

2005. "Pluralismo, autodeterminación y desarrollo." *Artículo Primero, Revista de Debate Social y Jurídico* 9, no. 17.

2005. "La territorialidad, indianidad y desarrollo." *Artículo Primero, Revista de Debate Social y Jurídico* 9, no. 17.

2005. "Rapa Nui: Indigenous Struggles at the Navel of the World." IWGIA notice board(www. iwgia.org).

2005. "El multiculturalismo latinoamericano al inicio del siglo XXI." Paper presented at the Jornadas Pueblos Indígenas de América Latina, Barcelona: Obra Social Fundación la Caixa, April, 27–28 (http://portal1.lacaixa.es/Channel/Ch_redirect_Tx?dest=1–95–10–01000).

2007. *Legalizing Land Tenure for Development? A Bibliography*, compiled by W. Assies (with CD-ROM containing printable versions of articles and policy documents). Leiden: Van Vollenhoven Institute for Law, Governance and Development.

Index